MEMORIALS OF ALFRED MARSHALL

Alfred Marshall

1921

MEMORIALS OF
ALFRED MARSHALL

EDITED BY

A. C. PIGOU, M.A.

PROFESSOR OF POLITICAL ECONOMY
IN THE UNIVERSITY OF CAMBRIDGE

Ecco di qua chi ne darà consiglio,
Se tu da te medesmo aver nol puoi.

REPRINTS OF ECONOMIC CLASSICS

AUGUSTUS M. KELLEY · PUBLISHERS
NEW YORK · 1966

FIRST EDITION 1925

(London: Macmillan & Co., Ltd., 1925)

LIBRARY OF CONGRESS CATALOGUE CARD NUMBER

66-24415

PRINTED IN THE UNITED STATES OF AMERICA
by SENTRY PRESS, NEW YORK, N. Y. 10019

EDITOR'S PREFACE

IN the will of the late Alfred Marshall there is a clause in which he requests his successor in the Chair of Political Economy at Cambridge to edit, from his manuscripts, "such material as he considers to be of value, aiming at brevity, suppressing controversial matter, and also deciding in the negative when he has any doubt at all whether any matter should be published." In the volume that follows I have endeavoured to carry out the trust with which Dr Marshall honoured me, and have ventured so far to depart from his directions as to include, along with selections from his writings, the memorial notices which form the first Part of this book, and a number of letters which form the third Part. In some of the papers I have incorporated alterations that Marshall had made in the margin of his private copies. Of the Memoranda and evidence which he contributed in connection with various official enquiries nothing is printed here. A project for publishing, under the auspices of the Royal Economic Society, some of the more important of these is being considered by the Council of that body. Mrs Marshall (to whom the index is due) has given me continuous and invaluable help. Mr Keynes, besides contributing the Memoir and bibliography, which begin and end the book, has also, along with Mr Guillebaud, shared with me in the more general work of making ready this tribute to our Master. My thanks are also due to Professor Edgeworth, Professor Fay and Mr Benians for their reminiscences.

A. C. P.

April, 1925

CONTENTS

PART I

IN MEMORIAM

PART II

SELECTIONS FROM ALFRED MARSHALL'S WRITINGS

PART III
LETTERS

CONTENTS

PORTRAITS

PART I

IN MEMORIAM

ALFRED MARSHALL, 1842–1924[1]

by J. M. KEYNES

I

ALFRED MARSHALL was born at Clapham on July 26, 1842, the son of William Marshall, a cashier in the Bank of England, by his marriage with Rebeccah Oliver. The Marshalls were a clerical family of the West of England, sprung from William Marshall, incumbent of Saltash, Cornwall, at the end of the seventeenth century. Alfred was the great-great-grandson of the Reverend William Marshall[2], the herculean parson of Devonshire, who, by twisting horseshoes with his hands, frightened local blacksmiths into fearing that they blew their bellows for the devil[3]. His great-grandfather was the Reverend John Marshall, Headmaster of Exeter Grammar School, who married Mary Hawtrey, daughter of the Reverend Charles Hawtrey, Sub-Dean and Canon of Exeter, and aunt of the Provost of Eton[4].

His father, the cashier in the Bank of England, was a tough old character, of great resolution and perception, cast in the mould of the strictest Evangelicals, bony neck, bristly projecting chin, author of an Evangelical epic in a sort of Anglo-Saxon language of his own invention which found some favour in its appropriate circles, surviving despotically-minded into his ninety-second year. The nearest objects of his masterful

---

[1] In the preparation of this Memoir, which was first published in the *Economic Journal* (September 1924), I have had great assistance from Mrs Marshall. I have to thank her for placing at my disposal a number of papers and for writing out some personal notes from which I have quoted freely. Alfred Marshall himself left in writing several autobiographical scraps, of which I have made the best use I could.

[2] By his third wife, Mary Kitson, the first child he christened in his parish, of whom he said in joke that she should be his little wife, as she duly was twenty years later.

[3] This is one of many stories of his prodigious strength which A. M. was fond of telling—how, for example, driving a pony trap in a narrow Devonshire lane and meeting another vehicle, he took the pony out and lifted the trap clean over the hedge. But we come to something more prognostical of Alfred in a little device of William Marshall's latter days. Being in old age heavy and unwieldy, yet so affected with gout as to be unable to walk up and down stairs, he had a hole made in the ceiling of the room in which he usually sat, through which he was drawn in his chair by pulleys to and from his bedroom above.

[4] Thus Alfred Marshall was third cousin once removed to Ralph Hawtrey, author of *Currency and Credit*—so there is not much in the true theory of Money which does not flow from that single stem. A. M. drew more from the subtle Hawtreys than from the Reverend Hercules.

instincts were his family, and their easiest victim his wife; but
their empire extended in theory over the whole of womankind,
the old gentleman writing a tract entitled *Man's Rights and
Woman's Duties*. Alfred Marshall did not escape the influence
of this parental mould. An inborn masterfulness towards womankind warred in him with the deep affection and admiration which
he bore to his own wife, and with an environment which threw
him in closest touch with the education and liberation of women.

II

At nine years of age Alfred was sent to Merchant Taylors'
School, for which his father, perceiving the child's ability, had
begged a nomination from a Director of the Bank. "Do you
know that you are asking me for £200?" said the Director;
but he gave it. In mingled affection and severity his father
recalls James Mill. He used to make the boy work with him
for school, often at Hebrew, until eleven at night. Indeed Alfred
was so much overworked by his father that, he used to say, his
life was saved by his Aunt Louisa, with whom he spent long
summer holidays near Dawlish. She gave him a boat and a gun
and a pony, and by the end of the summer he would return
home, brown and well. At school he was small and pale, badly
dressed, looked overworked and was called "tallow candles" by
his fellows. He cared little for games, and did not readily make
friends. His chief school intimates were H. D. Traill, later
Fellow of St John's College, Oxford, and Sidney Hall, afterwards
an artist. Traill's brother gave him a copy of Mill's *Logic*,
which Traill and he read with enthusiasm and discussed at meals
at the Monitors' table. "As a boy," Mrs Marshall writes,
"Alfred suffered severely from headache, for which the only cure
was to play chess. His father therefore allowed chess for this purpose; but later on he made Alfred promise never to play chess.
This promise was kept all through his life, though he could
never see a chess problem in the newspapers without getting
excited. But he said that his father was right to exact this
promise, for otherwise he would have been tempted to spend all
his time on it." Marshall himself once wrote: "We are not at
liberty to play chess games, or exercise ourselves upon subtleties
that lead nowhere. It is well for the young to enjoy the mere

WILLIAM MARSHALL

pleasure of action, physical or intellectual. But the time presses; the responsibility on us is heavy."

Rising to be Third Monitor, he became entitled in 1861 to a scholarship at St John's College, Oxford, under old Statutes, in the last year that one was offered, which would have led in three years to a Fellowship, and would have furnished him with the same permanence of security as belonged in those days to Eton Scholars at King's or Winchester Scholars at New College. It was the first step towards ordination in the Evangelical ministry for which his father designed him. But this was not the main point for Alfred—it meant a continued servitude to the Classics[1]. He had painful recollections in later days of his tyrant father keeping him awake into the night for the better study of Hebrew, whilst at the same time forbidding him the fascinating paths of mathematics. His father hated the sight of a mathematical book, but Alfred would conceal Potts' Euclid in his pocket as he walked to and from school. He read a proposition and then worked it out in his mind as he walked along, standing still at intervals, with his toes turned in. The fact that the curriculum of the Sixth Form at Merchant Taylors' reached so far as the Differential Calculus, had excited native proclivities. Airey, the mathematical master, said that "he had a genius for mathematics." Mathematics represented for Alfred emancipation, and he used to rejoice greatly that his father could not understand them. No! he would not take the scholarship and be buried at Oxford under dead languages; he would run away—to be a cabin-boy at Cambridge and climb the rigging of geometry and spy out the heavens.

At this point there came to his assistance a well-disposed uncle, willing to lend him a little money (for his father was too poor to help further, when the Oxford Scholarship was abandoned)—

[1] Near the end of his life A. M. wrote the following characteristic sentences about his classical studies: "When at school I was told to take no account of accents in pronouncing Greek words. I concluded that to burden my memory with accents would take up time and energy that might be turned to account; so I did not look out my accents in the dictionary; and received the only very heavy punishment of my life. This suggested to me that classical studies do not induce an appreciation of the value of time; and I turned away from them as far as I could towards mathematics. In later years I have observed that fine students of science are greedy of time: but many classical men seem to value it lightly. I will add that my headmaster was a broad-minded man; and succeeded in making his head form write Latin Essays, thought out in Latin: not thought out in English and translated into Latin. I am more grateful for that than for anything else he did for me."

repaid by Alfred soon after taking his degree from what he
earned by teaching—which, with a Parkin's Exhibition[1] of £40
a year from St John's College, Cambridge[2], opened to him the
doors of Mathematics and of Cambridge. Since it was a legacy
of £250 from this same uncle which enabled him, fourteen years
later, to pay his visit to the United States, the story of this
uncle's wealth, which Alfred often told, deserves a record here.
Having sought his fortunes in Australia and being established
there at the date of the gold discoveries, he indulged a certain
strain of eccentricity by seeking an advantage indirectly. He
remained a pastoralist, but, to the mirth of his neighbours,
refused to employ anyone about his place who did not suffer
from some physical defect, staffing himself entirely with the halt,
the blind, and the maimed. When the gold boom reached its
height, his reward came. All the able-bodied labourers migrated
to the gold-fields and Charles Marshall was the only man in the
place able to carry on. A few years later he returned to England
with a fortune, prepared to take an interest in a clever, rebel-
lious nephew.

In 1917 Marshall put into writing the following account of his
methods of work at this time and later: "An epoch in my life
occurred when I was, I think, about seventeen years old. I was
in Regent Street, and saw a workman standing idle before a
shop-window: but his face indicated alert energy, so I stood
still and watched. He was preparing to sketch on the window
of a shop guiding lines for a short statement of the business
concerned, which was to be shown by white letters fixed to the
glass. Each stroke of arm and hand needed to be made with a
single free sweep, so as to give a graceful result; it occupied perhaps two seconds of keen excitement. He stayed still for a few
minutes after each stroke, so that his pulse might grow quiet.
If he had saved the minutes thus lost, his employers would
have been injured by more than the value of his wages for a
whole day. That set up a train of thought which led me to the

---

[1] He was promoted to a Scholarship in the same year.

[2] There is a letter from Dr Bateson, Master of St John's, to Dr Hessey, Headmaster
of Merchant Taylors', dated June 15, 1861, announcing this Exhibition, and giving early
evidence of the interest which Dr Bateson—like Dr Jowett in later days—always
maintained in Alfred Marshall. When A. M. applied for the Bristol appointment in
1877, Dr Bateson wrote: "I have a great admiration for his character, which is remarkable for its great simplicity, earnestness, and self-sacrificing conscientiousness."

REBECCAH MARSHALL

resolve never to use my mind when it was not fresh; and to regard the intervals between successive strains as sacred to absolute repose. When I went to Cambridge and became full master of myself, I resolved never to read a mathematical book for more than a quarter of an hour at a time, without a break. I had some light literature always by my side, and in the breaks I read through more than once nearly the whole of Shakespeare, Boswell's *Life of Johnson*, the *Agamemnon* of Æschylus (the only Greek play which I could read without effort), a great part of Lucretius and so on. Of course I often got excited by my mathematics, and read for half an hour or more without stopping: but that meant that my mind was intense, and no harm was done." A power of intense concentration for brief periods, with but little power of continuous concentration, was characteristic of him all his life. He was seldom able to execute at white heat any considerable piece of work. He was also bothered by the lack of a retentive memory: even as an undergraduate his mathematical book-work troubled him as much as the problems did. As a boy he had a strong arithmetical faculty, which he afterwards lost.

Meanwhile at St John's College, Cambridge, Alfred Marshall fulfilled his ambitions. In 1865 he was Second Wrangler[1], the year when Lord Rayleigh was Senior, and he was immediately elected to a Fellowship. He proposed to devote himself to the study of molecular physics. Meanwhile he earned his living (and repaid Uncle Charles) by becoming for a brief period a mathematical master at Clifton, under Percival, for whom he had a great veneration. A little later he returned to Cambridge and took up coaching for the Mathematical Tripos for a short time. In this way "Mathematics," he said, "had paid my arrears. I was free for my own inclinations."

The main importance of Marshall's time at Clifton was that he made friends with H. G. Dakyns, who had gone there as an assistant master on the foundation of Clifton College in 1862, and, through him, with J. R. Mozley. These friendships opened to him the door into the intellectual circle of which Henry Sidgwick was the centre. Up to this time there is no evidence of

[1] One of the famous band of Second Wranglers, which includes Whewell, Cler Maxwell, Kelvin, and W. K. Clifford, and also Airey, Marshall's own teacher at Merchant Taylors'.

Marshall's having been in touch with the more eminent of his contemporaries, but soon after his return to Cambridge he became a member of the small, informal Discussion Society known as the "Grote Club."

The Grote Club came into existence with discussions after dinner in the Trumpington Vicarage of the Reverend John Grote, who was Knightbridge Professor of Moral Philosophy from 1855 till his death in 1866. The original members, besides Grote, were Henry Sidgwick, Aldis Wright, J. B. Mayor, and John Venn[1]. J. R. Mozley of King's and J. B. Pearson of St John's joined a little later. Marshall wrote[2] the following account of his own connection with the Society:

When I was admitted in 1867, the active members were Professor F. D. Maurice (Grote's successor), Sidgwick, Venn, J. R. Mozley and J. B. Pearson....After 1867 or 1868 the club languished a little; but new vigour was soon imparted to it by the advent of W. K. Clifford and J. F. Moulton. For a year or two Sidgwick, Mozley, Clifford, Moulton, and myself were the active members; and we all attended regularly. Clifford and Moulton had at that time read but little philosophy; so they kept quiet for the first half-hour of the discussion, and listened eagerly to what others, and especially Sidgwick, said. Then they let their tongues loose, and the pace was tremendous. If I might have verbatim reports of a dozen of the best conversations I have heard, I should choose two or three from among those evenings in which Sidgwick and Clifford were the chief speakers. Another would certainly be a conversation at tea before a Grote Club meeting, of which I have unfortunately no record (I think it was early in 1868), in which practically no one spoke but Maurice and Sidgwick. Sidgwick devoted himself to drawing out Maurice's recollections of English social and political life in the 'thirties, 'forties, and 'fifties. Maurice's face shone out bright, with its singular holy radiance, as he responded to Sidgwick's inquiries and suggestions; and we others said afterwards that we owed all the delight of that evening to him....

It was at this time and under these influences that there came the crisis in his mental development, of which in later years he often spoke. His design to study physics was (in his own words) "cut short by the sudden rise of a deep interest in the philosophical foundation of knowledge, especially in relation to theology."

In Marshall's undergraduate days at Cambridge a preference for Mathematics over Classics had not interfered with the integrity of his early religious beliefs. He still looked forward

---

[1] For Dr Venn's account of early meetings, see *Henry Sidgwick: a Memoir*, p. 134.
[2] Printed in *Henry Sidgwick: a Memoir*, p. 137.

to ordination, and his zeal directed itself at times towards the field of Foreign Missions. A missionary he remained all his life, but after a quick struggle religious beliefs dropped away, and he became, for the rest of his life, what used to be called an agnostic. Of his relationship to Sidgwick at this time, Marshall spoke as follows (at the meeting for a Sidgwick Memorial, Trinity Lodge, Nov. 16, 1900):

> Though not his pupil in name, I was in substance his pupil in Moral Science, and I am the oldest of them in residence. I was fashioned by him. He was, so to speak, my spiritual father and mother: for I went to him for aid when perplexed, and for comfort when troubled; and I never returned empty away. The minutes that I spent with him were not ordinary minutes; they helped me to live. I had to pass through troubles and doubts somewhat similar to those with which he, with broader knowledge and greater strength, had fought his way; and perhaps of all the people who have cause to be grateful to him, none has more than I.

Marshall's Cambridge career came just at the date which will, I think, be regarded by the historians of opinion as the critical moment at which Christian dogma fell away from the serious philosophical world of England, or at any rate of Cambridge. In 1863 Henry Sidgwick, aged twenty-four, had subscribed to the Thirty-Nine Articles as a condition of tenure of his Fellowship[1], and was occupied in reading Deuteronomy in Hebrew and preparing lectures on the Acts of the Apostles. Mill, the greatest intellectual influence on the youth of the age, had written nothing which clearly indicated any divergence from received religious opinions up to his *Examination of Hamilton* in 1865[2]. At about this time Leslie Stephen was an Anglican clergyman, James Ward a Nonconformist minister, Alfred Marshall a candidate for holy orders, W. K. Clifford a High Churchman. In 1869 Sidgwick resigned his Trinity Fellowship, "to free myself from dogmatic obligations." A little later none of these could have been called Christians. Nevertheless Marshall, like Sidgwick[3], was as far as possible from adopting an "anti-religious" attitude. He sympathised with Christian morals and Christian ideals and Christian incentives. There is nothing in his writings

---

[1] He had decided in 1861 not to take orders.

[2] Mill's *Essays on Religion*, which gave his final opinions, were not published until 1874, after his death.

[3] For a most interesting summary of Sidgwick's attitude in later life, see his *Memoir*, p. 508. Or see the last paragraph of W. K. Clifford's "Ethics of Religion" (*Lectures and Essays* II 244) for another characteristic reaction of Marshall's generation.

depreciating religion in any form; few of his pupils could have spoken definitely about his religious opinions. At the end of his life he said, "Religion seems to me an attitude," and that, though he had given up Theology, he believed more and more in Religion.

The great change-over of the later 'sixties was an intellectual change, not the ethical or emotional change which belongs to a later generation, and it was a wholly intellectual debate which brought it about. Marshall was wont to attribute the beginning of his own transition of mind to the controversy arising out of H. L. Mansel's *Bampton Lectures*, which was first put into his hands by J. R. Mozley[1]. Mansel means nothing to the present generation. But, as the protagonist of the last attempt to found Christian dogma on an intellectual basis, he was of the greatest importance in the 'sixties. In 1858 Mansel, an Oxford don and afterwards Dean of St Paul's, "adopted from Hamilton[2] the peculiar theory which was to enlist Kant in the service of the Church of England[3]"—an odd tergiversation of the human mind, the influence of which was great in Oxford for a full fifty years. Mansel's Bampton Lectures of 1858 brought him to the front as an intellectual champion of orthodoxy. In 1865, the year in which Marshall took his degree and had begun to turn his mind to the four quarters of heaven, there appeared Mill's *Examination of Sir William Hamilton's Philosophy*, which included a criticism of Mansel's extension of Hamilton to Christian Theology. Mansel replied. Mansel's defence of orthodoxy "showed me," Marshall said, "how much there was to be defended." The great controversy dominated Marshall's thoughts and drove him for a time to metaphysical studies, and then onwards to the social sciences.

[1] Mr Mozley (having read the above) writes to me: " I remember the account which *The Times* gave of these lectures at the time; how crowded St Mary's at Oxford was with undergraduates to hear them; how metaphysical points, which would generally be unfashionable, became in his hands lively and brilliant; how Kant's Practical Reason was represented by him as a backward step from his Pure Reason, and as standing self-condemned. The unknowableness of God was elevated into a principle of supreme value, and (though I do not precisely remember) I have no doubt all sorts of questionable things were justified by it."

[2] In 1836 Sir William Hamilton, having established his genealogy and made good his claim to a baronetcy, had been appointed to the Chair of Logic and Metaphysics at Edinburgh, and delivered during the next eight years the famous lectures which attempted the dangerous task of superimposing influences drawn from Kant and the German philosophers on the Scottish tradition of common sense.

[3] Stephen, *English Utilitarians*, III. 382.

Meanwhile in 1859, the year following the Bampton Lectures, the *Origin of Species* had appeared, to point away from heaven or the clouds to an open road on earth; and in 1860–62 Herbert Spencer's *First Principles* (unreadable as it now is) took a new direction, dissolved metaphysics in agnosticism, and warned all but ingrained metaphysical minds away from a blind alley. At about the same time, the publication of *Essays and Reviews* and the excommunication of Bishop Colenso were signs of the disruptive forces at work within the Church itself. Within less than twenty years of Sir Charles Lyell's *Principles of Geology*, before which even serious philosophers could take the first chapter of Genesis literally, the beliefs of ages had crumbled away and the whole educated world was acquiring a totally new outlook. A great gulf separated sons from parents. Metaphysical agnosticism, Evolutionary progress, and—the one remnant still left of the intellectual inheritance of the previous generation—Utilitarian ethics, joined to propel the youthful mind in a new direction.

From Metaphysics, therefore, Marshall turned his mind to Ethics. It would be true, I suppose, to say that Marshall never departed explicitly from the Utilitarian ideas which dominated the generation of economists who preceded him. But it is remarkable with what caution—in which respect he goes far beyond Sidgwick and is at the opposite pole from Jevons—he handled all such matters. There is, I think, no passage in his works in which he links economic studies to any ethical doctrine in particular. The solution of economic problems was for Marshall, not an application of the hedonistic calculus, but a prior condition of the exercise of man's higher faculties, irrespective, almost, of what we mean by "higher." The economist can claim, and this claim is sufficient for his purposes, that "the study of the causes of poverty is the study of the causes of the degradation of a large part of mankind[1]." Correspondingly, the possibility of progress "depends in a great measure upon facts and inferences, which are within the province of economics; and this it is which gives to economic studies their chief and their highest interest[2]." This remains true even though the question also "depends partly on the moral and political capabilities of human nature; and on these matters the economist has no special

---

[1] *Principles* (1st ed.), pp. 3, 4.   [2] *Ibid.*

means of information; he must do as others do, and guess as best he can[1]."

This was his final position. Nevertheless it was only through Ethics that he first reached Economics. In a retrospect of his mental history, drawn from him towards the end of his life, he said:

From Metaphysics I went to Ethics, and thought that the justification of the existing condition of society was not easy. A friend, who had read a great deal of what are now called the Moral Sciences, constantly said: "Ah! if you understood Political Economy you would not say that." So I read Mill's *Political Economy* and got much excited about it. I had doubts as to the propriety of inequalities of *opportunity*, rather than of material comfort. Then, in my vacations I visited the poorest quarters of several cities and walked through one street after another, looking at the faces of the poorest people. Next, I resolved to make as thorough a study as I could of Political Economy.

His passage into Economics is also described in his own words in some pages[2], written about 1917 and designed for the Preface to *Money Credit and Commerce*:

About the year 1867 (while mainly occupied with teaching Mathematics at Cambridge), Mansel's *Bampton Lectures* came into my hands and caused me to think that man's own possibilities were the most important subject for his study. So I gave myself for a time to the study of Metaphysics; but soon passed to what seemed to be the more progressive study of Psychology. Its fascinating inquiries into the possibilities of the higher and more rapid development of human faculties brought me into touch with the question: how far do the conditions of life of the British (and other) working classes generally suffice for fullness of life? Older and wiser men told me that the resources of production do not suffice for affording to the great body of the people the leisure and the opportunity for study; and they told me that I needed to study Political Economy. I followed their advice, and regarded myself as a wanderer in the land of dry facts; looking forward to a speedy return to the luxuriance of pure thought. But the more I studied economic science, the smaller appeared the knowledge which I had of it, in proportion to the knowledge that I needed; and now, at the end of nearly half a century of almost exclusive study of it, I am conscious of more ignorance of it than I was at the beginning of the study.

In 1868, when he was still in his metaphysical stage, a desire to read Kant in the original led him to Germany. "Kant my guide," he once said, "the only man I ever worshipped: but I

---

[1] *Principles* (1st ed.), pp. 3, 4.

[2] Rescued by Mrs Marshall from the waste-paper basket, whither too great a proportion of the results of his mental toil found their way;—like his great-great-uncle, the Reverend Richard Marshall, who is said to have been a good poet and was much pressed to publish his compositions, to which, however, he had so great an objection that lest it be done after his death, he burnt all his papers.

could not get further: beyond seemed misty, and social problems came imperceptibly to the front. Are the opportunities of real life to be confined to a few?" He lived at Dresden with a German professor who had previously coached Henry Sidgwick. He was again in Germany, living in Berlin, in the winter of 1870–71, during the Franco-German War. Hegel's *Philosophy of History* greatly influenced him. He also came in contact with the work of the German economists, particularly Roscher. Finally, Dr Bateson, the Master of St John's, was instrumental in giving him a career in life by persuading the College to establish for him a special lectureship in Moral Science[1]. He soon settled down to Economics, though for a time he gave short courses on other branches of Moral Science—on Logic and on Bentham[2].

His dedication to economic study—for so he always considered it, not less ordained in spirit than if he had fulfilled his father's desire—was now effected. His two years of doubt and disturbance of mind left on his imagination a deep impression, to which in later years he would often recur with pupils whom he deemed worthy of the high calling—for so he reckoned it—of studying with scientific disinterestedness the modes and principles of the daily business of life, by which human happiness and the opportunities for good life are, in great measure, determined.

Before we leave the early phase, when he was not yet an economist, we may pause a moment to consider the colour of his outlook on life, as, at that time, it was already fixed in him.

Like his two colleagues, Henry Sidgwick and James Ward, in the Chairs of the Moral Sciences at Cambridge during the last decades of the nineteenth century, Alfred Marshall belonged to the tribe of sages and pastors; yet, like them also, endowed with a double nature, he was a scientist too. As a preacher and

[1] In a conversation I had with him a few weeks before his death he dwelt especially on Hegel's *Philosophy of History* and the friendly action of Dr Bateson as finally determining the course of his life. Since J. B. Mayor, the first "Moral Science lecturer" in Cambridge, had held a similar lectureship at St John's for some time, whilst the Rev. J. B. Pearson was also a Johnian and a moral scientist, the appointment of another lecturer in the subject was a somewhat unusual step. Henry Sidgwick had been appointed to a lectureship in Moral Science at Trinity in the previous year, 1867; and Venn had come back to Cambridge as a Moral Science lecturer at Caius in 1862.

[2] Mrs Marshall remembers how in the early 'seventies at Newnham, Mary Kennedy (Mrs R. T. Wright) and she had to write for him "a dialogue between Bentham and an Ascetic."

pastor of men he was not particularly superior to other similar
natures. As a scientist he was, within his own field, the greatest
in the world for a hundred years. Nevertheless it was to the
first side of his nature that he himself preferred to give the
preeminence. This self should be master, he thought; the second
self, servant. The second self sought knowledge for its own
sake; the first self subordinated abstract aims to the need for
practical advancement. The piercing eyes and ranging wings
of an eagle were often called back to earth to do the bidding of
a moraliser.

This double nature was the clue to Marshall's mingled strength
and weakness; to his own conflicting purposes and waste of
strength; to the two views which could always be taken about
him; to the sympathies and antipathies he inspired.

In another respect the diversity of his nature was pure
advantage. The study of economics does not seem to require
any specialised gifts of an unusually high order. Is it not,
intellectually regarded, a very easy subject compared with the
higher branches of philosophy and pure science? Yet good, or
even competent, economists are the rarest of birds. An easy
subject, at which very few excel! The paradox finds its explanation, perhaps, in that the master-economist must possess a
rare *combination* of gifts. He must reach a high standard in
several different directions and must combine talents not often
found together. He must be mathematician, historian, statesman,
philosopher—in some degree. He must understand symbols and
speak in words. He must contemplate the particular in terms
of the general, and touch abstract and concrete in the same
flight of thought. He must study the present in the light of the
past for the purposes of the future. No part of man's nature or
his institutions must lie entirely outside his regard. He must
be purposeful and disinterested in a simultaneous mood; as
aloof and incorruptible as an artist, yet sometimes as near the
earth as a politician. Much, but not all, of this ideal manysidedness Marshall possessed. But chiefly his mixed training
and divided nature furnished him with the most essential of the
economist's needed gifts—he was conspicuously historian and
mathematician, a dealer in the particular and the general, the
temporal and the eternal, at the same time.

III

The task of expounding the development of Marshall's Economics is rendered difficult by the long intervals of time which generally separated the initial discovery and its oral communication to pupils from its final publication in a book to the world outside. Before attempting this, it will be convenient to trace briefly the outward course of his life from his appointment to a lectureship at St John's College, Cambridge, in 1868 to his succession to the Chair of Political Economy at Cambridge in 1884.

For nine years Marshall remained Fellow and Lecturer of St John's, laying the foundations of his subject but publishing nothing[1]. After his introduction to the Grote Club he became intimate with W. K. Clifford[2] and Fletcher Moulton. Clifford was chief favourite, though "he was too fond of astonishing people." As a member, a little later on, of the "Eranus" Marshall was in touch with Sidgwick, Venn, Fawcett, Henry Jackson and other leaders of that first age of the emancipation of Cambridge. At this time he used to go abroad almost every long vacation. Mrs Marshall writes:

He took with him £60[3] and a knapsack, and spent most of the time walking in the high Alps. This walking, summer after summer, turned him from a weak into a strong man. He left Cambridge early in June jaded and overworked and returned in October brown and strong and upright. Carrying the knapsack pulled him upright, and until he was over eighty he remained so. He even then exerted himself almost painfully to hold himself straight. When walking in the Alps his practice was to get up at six and to be well on his way before eight. He would walk with knapsack on his back for two or three hours. He would then sit down, sometimes on a glacier, and have a long pull at some book—Goethe or Hegel or Kant or Herbert Spencer—and then walk on to his next halting-place for the night. This was in his philosophic stage. Later on he worked out his theories of Domestic and Foreign Trade in these walks. A large box of books, etc., was sent on from one stage to another, but he would go for a week or more just with a knapsack. He would wash his shirt by holding it in a fast-running stream and dry it by carrying it on his alpen-stock over his shoulder. He did most of his hardest thinking in these solitary Alpine walks.

[1] The occasional articles belonging to this period are included in the Bibliography below.

[2] Clifford, who was three years Marshall's junior, came up to Trinity in 1863, was elected to a Fellowship in 1868, and resided in Cambridge, where his rooms were "the meeting point of a numerous body of friends" (*vide* Sir F. Pollock's Memoir), until 1871.

[3] He used to reckon that his necessary expenditure as a bachelor Fellow amounted to £300 a year, including £60 for vacation travel.

These *Wanderjahre* gave him a love for the Alps which he always retained, and even in 1920 (for the last time) we went to the South Tyrol, where he sat and worked in the high air.

Alfred always did his best work in the open air. When he became Fellow of St John's he did his chief thinking between 10 a.m. and 2 p.m. and between 10 p.m. and 2 a.m. He had a monopoly of the Wilderness in the daytime and of the New Court Cloisters at night. At Palermo in the early eighties he worked on the roof of a quiet hotel, using the cover of the bath as an awning. At Oxford he made a 'Den' in the garden in which he wrote. At Cambridge he worked on the balcony, and later in a large revolving shelter, fitted up as a study, called 'The Ark,' and in the Tyrol he arranged a heap of stones, a camp stool and an air cushion into what he called a 'throne,' and in later years we always carried a tent shelter with us, in which he spent the day.

In 1875 Marshall visited the United States for four months. He toured the whole of the East, and travelled as far as San Francisco. At Harvard and Yale he had long talks with the academic economists, and he had many introductions everywhere to leading citizens. But his chief purpose was the "study of the Problem of Protection in a New Country." About this he inquired on all hands, and towards the end of his trip was able to write in a letter home: "In Philadelphia I spent many hours in conversation with the leading protectionists. And now I think, as soon as I have read some books they have recommended me to read, I shall really know the whole of their case; and I do not believe there is or ever has been another Englishman who could say the same."

On his return to England he read a paper to the Cambridge Moral Science Club on American Industry, Nov. 17, 1875, and later on he lectured at Bristol, in 1878, on "The Economic Condition of America." The American trip made on him a great impression, which influenced all his future work. He used to say that it was not so much what he actually learnt, as that he got to know what things he wanted to learn; that he was taught to see things in proportion; and that he was enabled to expect the coming supremacy of the United States, to know its causes and the directions it would take.

Meanwhile he had been helping Fawcett, who was Professor, and Henry Sidgwick, to establish Political Economy as a serious study in the University of Cambridge. Two of his earliest pupils, H. S. Foxwell and, later on, my father, John Neville Keynes,

1855   1869

With MRS MARSHALL, 1877   1892

ALFRED MARSHALL

who took the Moral Sciences Tripos in 1875, joined these three as lecturers on Political Economy in the University.

In 1876 Alfred Marshall became engaged to Miss Mary Paley, a great-granddaughter of the famous Archdeacon. Miss Paley was a former pupil of his and was a lecturer in Economics at Newnham. She had been one of the small band of five pioneers who in 1871, before the foundation of Newnham College, came into residence under Miss Clough at 74 Regent Street, Cambridge, which had been taken and furnished for them by Henry Sidgwick. She and Miss Bulley, who took the Moral Sciences Tripos in 1874, as Students of the "Association for Promoting the Higher Education of Women in Cambridge," were the first of the forerunners of Newnham to take honours at Cambridge.

Marshall's first book, *The Economics of Industry*, published in 1879, was written in collaboration with Mrs Marshall; indeed it had been, at the start, her book and not his, having been undertaken by her at the request of a group of Cambridge University Extension lecturers. They were married in 1877. During forty-seven years of married life his dependence upon her devotion was complete. Her life was given to him and to his work with a degree of unselfishness and understanding that makes it difficult for friends and old pupils to think of them separately or to withhold from her shining gifts of character a big share in what his intellect accomplished.

Marriage, by involving, under the Statutes of that day, the loss of his Fellowship, meant his finding a new means of liveli-hood. For a week or two Marshall entertained the idea of becoming a candidate for the Esquire Bedellship at Cambridge. But "the more I look at the poker," he finally concluded, "the less I like it." He was actually, for a short time, Steward of St John's. But a new opening offered itself, and, as soon as he was married, Marshall went to Bristol as the first Principal of University College, and as Professor of Political Economy. "Just at that time," Marshall has recorded, "Balliol and New Colleges at Oxford were setting up at Bristol the first 'University College': that is, a College designed to bring higher educa-tional opportunities within the reach of the inhabitans of a large city, which had no University of its own. I was elected its first Principal: my wife lectured on Political Economy to a class consisting chiefly of ladies in the morning, and I lectured in the evening to a class composed chiefly of young business men." Apart from his regular classes he gave a number of public evening lectures (references to some of which will be found in the Bibliographical Note below[1]), including a series on Henry George's *Progress and Poverty*. The work of the Marshalls at Bristol was much appreciated there, and the town kept up an interest in his career long after he had left it. But the administrative work, especially the business of begging money, which, in view of the meagre endowments of the college, was one of the main duties of the Principal, proved irksome and uncongenial. Soon after his marriage his health and nerves began to break down, chiefly as a result of stone in the kidney. He was anxious to resign the position of Principal, but there was no convenient opportunity until 1881, when the appointment of Professor Ramsay to the Department of Chemistry provided a suitable successor.

The following sentences are from some notes taken at the farewell address which he delivered on leaving Bristol, Sept. 29, 1881:

It has been said that everyone—everyone of the academic tone that is—must have an attack of philosophy as you have an attack of measles—my attack was a very bad one. Then I thought I should get on better if I read some economics first. I thought I would read Mill and a few other books and then I should do. But I found that would not do...I read the Socialists: and found much with which anyone who has a heart at all must sympathise, and yet I found not one Socialist who had really grasped economic science. There is no principle of progressive improvement in socialism. The problem rose before me: How to get rid of such evils in society as arise from a lack of material wealth?

Religion has this quality: that it belongs to all men alike; and the joys of religion are the highest joys of which men are capable. The poor man who is religious is far happier than the rich man who is not. (I use the word religion in its widest sense, of all that elevates the soul of man towards God.) But there is a kind of poverty that interferes even with religious happiness—a man who is worn out and has no leisure can hardly rise to it.

But setting religion aside, there are few other pleasures that a man can enjoy who is destitute of material wealth. He cannot become the noble being he might be: he cannot be, if we may so say, what God intended him to be. If he is used up in a hand to mouth struggle for existence he cannot develop as he should.

The work I have set before myself is this:—How to get rid of the evils of competition while retaining its advantages.

[1] The lecture on "Water as an Element of National Wealth" is particularly interesting.

Representing the question by a length of a thousand miles, the progress I hope to make towards it may be four or five inches. If I make that progress I shall be well contented with my life—if I make it possible for the next man to start four or five inches nearer the goal than I have....

After leaving Bristol, Marshall and his wife went to Italy for nearly a year. He worked quietly on the roof of a small hotel at Palermo for five months and then moved on to Florence and to Venice. He came back to Bristol, where he was still Professor of Political Economy, in 1882 with his health much restored; but he remained for the rest of his life somewhat hypochondriacal and inclined to consider himself on the verge of invalidism. He proved, in fact, to have considerable constitutional strength underneath apparent weakness, and he remained in harness as a writer up to a very advanced age. But his nervous equilibrium was easily upset by unusual exertion or excitement or by controversy and difference of opinion; his power of continuous concentration on difficult mental work was inferior to his wishes; and he became dependent on a routine of life adapted even to his whims and fancies. In truth he was haunted by a feeling that his physical strength and power of continuous concentration were inferior to the fields of work which he saw stretching ahead, and to the actual constructions he had conceived but not yet given to the world. By 1877, when he was thirty-five years of age, he had worked out within him the foundations of little less than a new science, of great consequence to mankind; and a collapse of health and strength during the five years following, when he should have been giving all this to the world, partly broke his courage, though not his determination.

Amongst the Governors of University College, Bristol, were Dr Jowett, the Master of Balliol, and Professor Henry Smith, and these two were accustomed to stay with the Marshalls on their periodic visits to Bristol. Jowett's interest in Economics was always lively. While Tutor of Balliol he had given courses of set lectures on Political Economy, and he continued to direct individual undergraduates in the subject up to the end of his life[1]. Jowett's interest and belief in Alfred Marshall were

[1] In the charming little obituary of Jowett which Marshall contributed to the *Economic Journal* (vol. III. p. 745), he wrote: "He took part in most of the questions which agitate modern economists; but his own masters were Plato and Ricardo. Everything that they

keenly aroused by the long evening talks which followed the meetings of the Governing Body; and, on the premature death of Arnold Toynbee in 1883, he invited Marshall to take his place as Fellow of Balliol and Lecturer in Political Economy to the selected candidates for the Indian Civil Service.

Marshall's Oxford career was brief but successful. He attracted able pupils, and his public lectures were attended by larger and more enthusiastic classes than at any other period of his life. He encountered with credit, on different occasions, Henry George and Hyndman in public debate, and was taking a prominent position in the University. In November 1884, however, Fawcett died, and in January 1885 Marshall returned to Cambridge as Professor of Political Economy.

IV

Marshall's serious study of Economic Theory began in 1867; his characteristic doctrines were far developed by 1875; and by 1883 they were taking their final form. Nevertheless no part of his work was given to the world at large in adequate shape until 1890 (*Principles of Economics*), and that part of the subject, at which he had worked earliest and which was most complete by 1875, was not treated in a published book until nearly fifty years later, in 1923 (*Money Credit and Commerce*). Meanwhile he had not kept his ideas to himself, but had shared them without reserve in lecture and in talk with friends and pupils. They leaked out to wider circles in a privately printed pamphlet and through the writings of his pupils, and were extracted in cross-examination by Royal Commissions. Inevitably when the books themselves appeared, they lacked the novelty and path-breaking powers which would have been acclaimed in them a generation earlier, and those economists all over the world who know Marshall only by his published work may find it difficult to understand the extraordinary position claimed for him by his

said, and all that rose directly out of what they said, had a special interest for him....In pure economics his favourite subject was the Currency, and he took a keen interest in the recent controversy on it. His views were generally conservative; and he was never converted to bimetallism. But he was ready to follow wherever Ricardo had pointed the way; and in a letter written not long ago he raised the question whether the world would not outgrow the use of gold as its standard of value, and adopt one of those artificial standards which vex the soul of Mr Giffen" (cf. *post*, p. 292). Jowett always remained very fond of Alfred Marshall, and, after the Marshalls left Oxford, it was with them that he generally stayed on his visits to Cambridge.

English contemporaries and successors. It is proper, therefore, that I should make an attempt, necessarily imperfect from lack of full data, to trace the progress of his ideas; and then to set forth the reasons or the excuses for the unhappy delay in their publication.

Marshall's serious study of Economics began in 1867. To fix our ideas of date: Mill's *Political Economy*[1] had appeared in 1848; the seventh edition, in 1871, was the last to receive Mill's own corrections; and Mill died in 1873. *Das Kapital* of Marx appeared in 1868; Jevons' *Theory of Political Economy*[2] in 1871; Menger's *Grundsätze der Volkswirtschaftslehre*, also in 1871; Cairnes' *Leading Principles* in 1874.

Thus when Marshall began, Mill and Ricardo still reigned supreme and unchallenged. The notion of applying mathematical methods was in the air; but it had not yet yielded anything substantial. Cournot's *Principes Mathématiques de la Théorie des Richesses* (1835) is mentioned by Marshall in the Preface to the first edition of the *Principles of Economics* as having particularly influenced him;—this book must have come into his hands sometime between 1867 and 1870[3]. Cournot, and the natural reaction of Ricardo on a Cambridge mathematician of that date, with perhaps some hints of algebraical treatment in the arithmetical examples of Mill's Book III, chapter xviii[4], on "International Values," were all that Marshall had to go upon at the beginning. This was the age of Clerk Maxwell and

[1] What a contrast to Marshall's *Principles* the drafting of this famous book presents! Mill's *Political Economy* was commenced in the autumn of 1845 and was ready for the press before the end of 1847. In this period of little more than two years the work was laid aside for six months while Mill was writing articles in the *Morning Chronicle* (sometimes as many as five a week) on the Irish Peasant problem. At the same time Mill was occupied all day at the India Office. (See Mill's *Autobiography*.)

[2] Jevons' *Serious Fall in the Value of Gold ascertained, and its Social Effects set forth*, had appeared in 1863 and his *Variation of Prices* in 1865, from which two papers the modern method of Index Numbers takes its rise. His main papers on the Periodicity of Commercial Crises were later (1875-1879).

[3] For a complete bibliography of early hints and foreshadowings of mathematical treatment see the appendix to Irving Fisher's edition of Cournot's book. Fleeming Jenkin's brief paper of 1868 was not generally available until 1870 and did not influence Marshall. Jevons' *Brief Account of a General Mathematical Theory of Political Economy* was presented to the Cambridge Meeting of the British Association in 1862 and published in the *Statistical Journal* in 1866; but this paper does not actually contain any mathematical treatment at all. Its purpose is to adumbrate the idea of "the coefficient of utility" (*i.e.* final utility), and to claim that this notion will allow the foundations of economics to be worked out as a mathematical extension of the hedonistic calculus. See also, in this connection, Marshall's letter of March 24, 1908, addressed to Prof. J. B. Clark, which is printed below (p. 416).

[4] Particularly §§ 6-8, which were added by Mill to the third edition (1852).

W. K. Clifford, when the children of the Mathematical Tripos
were busy trying to apply its apparatus to the experimental
sciences. An extension to the moral sciences was becoming
obvious. Boole and Leslie Ellis, a little earlier, were an important influence in the same direction. Alfred Marshall, in
1867, trained as he was, an intimate of W. K. Clifford,
turning his attention to Ricardo, was *bound* to play about
with diagrams and algebra. No other explanations or influences
are needed.

An account of the progress of his thought from 1867 to his
American trip in 1875, which Marshall himself put into writing[1],
is appropriate at this point:—

While still giving private lessons in mathematics[2], he translated as many
as possible of Ricardo's reasonings into mathematics; and he endeavoured
to make them more general. Meanwhile he was attracted towards the new
views of economics taken by Roscher and other German economists; and
by Marx, Lassalle and other Socialists. But it seemed to him that the
analytical methods of the historical economists were not always sufficiently
thorough to justify their confidence that the causes which they assigned
to economic events were the true causes. He thought indeed that the
interpretation of the economic past was almost as difficult as the prediction
of the future. The Socialists also seemed to him to underrate the difficulty
of their problems, and to be too quick to assume that the abolition of
private property would purge away the faults and deficiencies of human
nature....He set himself to get into closer contact with practical business
and with the life of the working classes. On the one side he aimed at learning
the broad features of the technique of every chief industry; and on the other
he sought the society of trade unionists, co-operators and other working-
class leaders. Seeing, however, that direct studies of life and work would
not yield much fruit for many years, he decided to fill the interval by
writing a separate monograph or special treatise on Foreign Trade; for the
chief facts relating to it can be obtained from printed documents. He
proposed that this should be the first of a group of monographs on special
economic problems; and he hoped ultimately to compress these monographs
into a general treatise of a similar scope to Mill's. After writing that
larger treatise, but not before, he thought he might be ready to write a
short popular treatise. He has never changed his opinion that this is the
best order of work; but his plans were overruled, and almost inverted, by
the force of circumstances. He did indeed write the first draft of a monograph on Foreign Trade; and in 1875 he visited the chief seats of industry
in America with the purpose of studying the problem of Protection in a
new country. But this work was suspended by his marriage; and while
engaged, in conjunction with his wife, in writing a short account of the
Economics of Industry, forcibly simplified for working-class readers, he

---

[1] This account was contributed by him to a German compilation of Portraits and
Short Lives of leading Economists.   [2] In 1867.

contracted an illness so serious that for some time he appeared unlikely to be able to do any more hard work. A little later he thought his strength might hold out for recasting his diagrammatic illustrations of economic problems. Though urged by the late Professor Walras about 1873 to publish these, he had declined to do so; because he feared that if separated from all concrete study of actual conditions, they might seem to claim a more direct bearing on real problems than they in fact had. He began, therefore, to supply some of the requisite limitations and conditions, and thus was written the kernel of the fifth book of his *Principles*. From that kernel the present volume was extended gradually backwards and forwards, till it reached the form in which it was published in 1890.

The fateful decision was the abandonment of the project to write "a group of monographs on special economic problems" in favour of a comprehensive treatise which should be born complete and fully-armed from the head of an economic Jove;— particularly when the special problems on which Marshall had worked first, Money and Foreign Trade, were held to occupy, logically, the latest sections of this treatise, with the result that they did not see the light for fifty years.

The evidence as to the order of his studies is as follows: In 1867 he began with the development of diagrammatic methods, with special regard to the problems of foreign trade, mainly under the influence of Ricardo, Cournot and Mill. To this was added the influence of von Thünen, by which he "was led to attach great importance to the fact that our observations of nature, in the moral as in the physical world, relate not so much to aggregate quantities, as to increments of quantities, and that in particular the demand for a thing is a continuous function, of which the 'marginal' increment is, in stable equilibrium, balanced against the corresponding increment of its cost of production. It is not easy to get a clear full view of Continuity in this aspect without the aid either of mathematical symbols or of diagrams[1]."

By 1871 his progress along these lines was considerably advanced. He was expounding the new ideas to pupils and the foundations of his diagrammatic economics had been truly laid. In that year there appeared, as the result of independent work, Jevons' *Theory of Political Economy*. The publication of this book must have been an occasion of some disappointment and annoyance to Marshall. It took the cream of novelty off the

---

[1] Preface to 1st edition of *Principles of Economics*.

new ideas which Marshall was slowly working up, without giving them—in Marshall's judgment—adequate or accurate treatment. Nevertheless it undoubtedly gave Jevons priority of publication as regards the group of ideas connected with "marginal" (or, as Jevons called it, "final") utility. Marshall's references to the question of priority are extremely reserved. He is careful to leave Jevons' claim undisputed, whilst pointing out, indirectly, but quite clearly and definitely, that his own work owed little or nothing to Jevons[1].

In 1872 Marshall reviewed[2] Jevons' *Political Economy* in *The Academy*. This was, so far as I am aware, his first appearance in print (at thirty years of age); yet it foreshadows in many respects his permanent attitude to the subject. The review, whilst not unfavourable, is somewhat cool and it points out several errors. "The main value of the book," it concludes, "does not lie in its more prominent theories, but in its original treatment of a number of minor points, its suggestive remarks and careful analyses. We continually meet with old friends in new dresses....Thus it is a familiar truth that the total utility of any commodity is not proportional to its final degree of utility....But Prof. Jevons has made this the leading idea of the costume in which he has displayed a large number of economic facts." When, however, Marshall came, in later years, to write the *Principles* his desire to be scrupulously fair to Jevons and to avoid the least sign of jealousy is very marked. It is true that in one passage[3] he writes: "It is unfortunate that here as elsewhere Jevons' delight

---

[1] See, particularly, (1) his footnote relating to his use of the term "marginal" (Preface to *Principles*, 1st ed.), where he implies that the word was suggested to him, as a result of reading von Thünen (though von Thünen does not actually use the word), *before* Jevons' book appeared (in his British Association paper of 1862, published in 1866, Jevons uses the term "coefficient of utility"), that, after its appearance, he temporarily deferred to Jevons and adopted his word "final" (*e.g.* in the first *Economics of Industry*), and that later on he reverted to his original phrase as being the better (it is also an almost literal equivalent of Menger's word "Grenznutzen"); and (2) his footnote to Book III, chap. vi, § 3 on Consumers' Rent (or Surplus), where he writes (my italics): "The notion of an exact measurement of Consumers' Rent was published by Dupuit in 1844. But his work was forgotten; and the first to publish a clear analysis of the relation of total to marginal (or final) utility in the English language was Jevons in 1871, when he had not read Dupuit. The notion of Consumers' Rent was suggested *to the present writer* by a study of the mathematical aspects of demand and utility under the influence of Cournot, von Thünen and Bentham."

[2] I believe that Marshall only wrote two reviews in the whole of his life—this review of Jevons in 1872, and a review of Edgeworth's *Mathematical Psychics* in 1881.

[3] p. 166 (3rd ed.).

in stating his case strongly has led him to a conclusion, which
not only is inaccurate, but does mischief...." But he says
elsewhere[1]: "There are few writers of modern times who have
approached as near to the brilliant originality of Ricardo as
Jevons has done," and "There are few thinkers whose claims on
our gratitude are as high and as various as those of Jevons[2]."

In truth, Jevons' *Theory of Political Economy* is a brilliant,
but hasty, inaccurate and incomplete *brochure*, as far removed
as possible from the painstaking, complete, ultra-conscientious,
ultra-unsensational methods of Marshall. It brings out unfor-
gettably the notions of final utility and of the balance between
the disutility of labour and the utility of the product. But it
lives merely in the tenuous world of bright ideas—and how
disappointing are the fruits, now that we have them, of the
bright idea of reducing Economics to a mathematical application
of the hedonistic calculus of Bentham!—when we compare it
with the great working machine evolved by the patient, persistent toil and scientific genius of Marshall. Jevons saw the
kettle boil and cried out with the delighted voice of a child;
Marshall too had seen the kettle boil and sat down silently
to build an engine.

Meanwhile Marshall worked on at the generalised diagrammatic scheme, disclosed in his papers on the Pure Theory of
Foreign Trade and Domestic Values. These must have been
substantially complete about 1873 and were communicated to
his pupils (particularly to Sir H. H. Cunynghame) about that
date. They were drafted as non-consecutive[3] chapters of *The
Theory of Foreign Trade, with some Allied Problems relating to
the Doctrine of Laisser Faire*, which he nearly completed in
1875-7 after his return from America, embodying the results of
his work from 1869 onwards[4]. In 1877 he turned aside to write
the *Economics of Industry*, with Mrs Marshall. In 1879 Henry
Sidgwick, alarmed at the prospect of Marshall's right of priority
being taken from him, printed the two chapters for private circulation and copies were sent to leading economists at home and

[1] In the *Note on Ricardo's Theory of Value*, which is, in the main, a reply to Jevons.
[2] See also Marshall's remarks about his review of Jevons, written many years later, which are published below, pp. 99-100.
[3] The last proposition of *Foreign Trade* (which comes first) is Prop. XIII; the first of *Domestic Values* is Prop. XVII.
[4] "Chiefly between 1869 and 1873"—see *Money Credit and Commerce*, p. 330.

abroad[1]. These chapters, which are now very scarce, have never been published in their entirety to the world at large, but the most significant parts of them were incorporated in Book V, chaps. xi and xii of the *Principles of Economics*, and (fifty years after their origination) in Appendix J of *Money Credit and Commerce*.

Marshall's mathematical and diagrammatic exercises in Economic Theory were of such a character in their grasp, comprehensiveness and scientific accuracy and went so far beyond the "bright ideas" of his predecessors, that we may justly claim him as the founder of modern diagrammatic economics—that elegant apparatus which generally exercises a powerful attraction on clever beginners, which all of us use as an inspirer of, and a check on, our intuitions and as a shorthand record of our results, but which generally falls into the background as we penetrate further into the recesses of the subject. The fact that Marshall's results percolated to the outer world a drop at a time and reached in their complete form only a limited circle, lost him much international fame, which would otherwise have been his, and even, perhaps, retarded the progress of the subject. Nevertheless we can, I think, on reflection understand Marshall's reluctance to open his career with publishing his diagrammatic apparatus by itself.

For, whilst it was a necessary appurtenance of his intellectual approach to the subject, an appearance of emphasising or exalting such methods pointed right away from what he regarded, quite early in his life, as the proper attitude to economic inquiry. Moreover, Marshall, as one who had been Second Wrangler and had nourished ambitions to explore molecular physics, always felt a slight contempt, from the intellectual or æsthetic point of view, for the rather "potty" scraps of elementary algebra, geometry, and differential calculus which make up mathematical economics. Mathematical economics often exercise an excessive fascination and influence over students who approach the subject without much previous training in technical mathematics. They are so easy as to be within the grasp of almost anyone, yet do introduce the student, on a small scale, to the delights of

---

[1] See the Preface to the first edition of the *Principles*. Jevons refers to them in the 2nd edition of his *Theory*, published in 1879; and Pantaleoni reproduced much of them in his *Principii di Economia Pura* (1889).

perceiving constructions of pure form, and place toy bricks in his hands that he can manipulate for himself, which gives a new thrill to those who have had no glimpse of the sky-scraping architecture and minutely embellished monuments of modern mathematics. Nevertheless, unlike physics, for example, such parts of the bare bones of economic theory as are expressible in mathematical form are extremely easy compared with the economic interpretation of the complex and incompletely known facts of experience[1], and lead one but a very little way towards establishing useful results.

Marshall felt all this with a vehemence which not all his pupils have shared. The preliminary mathematics was for him child's-play. He wanted to enter the vast laboratory of the world, to hear its roar and distinguish the several notes, to speak with the tongues of business men, and yet to observe all with the eyes of a highly intelligent angel. So "he set himself," as is recorded in his own words above (p. 20), "to get into closer contact with practical business and with the life of the working classes."

Thus Marshall, having begun by founding modern diagrammatic methods, ended by using much self-obliteration to keep them in their proper place. When the *Principles* appeared, the diagrams were imprisoned in footnotes, or, at their freest, could but exercise themselves as in a yard within the confines of a brief Appendix. As early as 1872, in reviewing Jevons' *Political Economy*, he wrote: "We owe several valuable suggestions to the many investigations in which skilled mathematicians, English and continental, have applied their favourite method to the treatment of economical problems. But all that has been important in their reasonings and results has, with scarcely an exception, been capable of being described in ordinary language. ...The book before us would be improved if the mathematics were omitted, but the diagrams retained." In 1881, reviewing

[1] Professor Planck of Berlin, the famous originator of the Quantum Theory, once remarked to me that in early life he had thought of studying economics, but had found it too difficult! Professor Planck could easily master the whole corpus of mathematical economics in a few days. He did not mean that! But the amalgam of logic and intuition and the wide knowledge of facts, most of which are not precise, which is required for economic interpretation in its highest form, is, quite truly, overwhelmingly difficult for those whose gift mainly consists in the power to imagine and pursue to their furthest points the implications and prior conditions of comparatively simple facts which are known with a high degree of precision.

Edgeworth's *Mathematical Psychics*, after beginning "This book shows clear signs of genius, and is a promise of great things to come," he adds, "It will be interesting, in particular, to see how far he succeeds in preventing his mathematics from running away with him, and carrying him out of sight of the actual facts of economics." And finally, in 1890, in the Preface to the *Principles*, he first emphasises his preference for diagrams over algebra, then allows the former a limited usefulness[1], and reduces the latter to the position of a convenience for private use[2].

In his reaction against excessive addiction to these methods, and also (a less satisfactory motive) from fear of frightening "business men" away from reading his book, Marshall may have gone too far. After all, if "there are many problems of pure theory, which no one who has once learnt to use diagrams will willingly handle in any other way," such diagrams must surely form a part of every advanced course in economics —Marshall himself always used them freely in his lectures— and they should be available for students in the fullest and clearest form possible[3].

Whilst, however, Marshall's reluctance to print the results of his earliest investigations is mainly explained by the profundity of his insight into the true character of his subject in its highest and most useful developments, and by his unwillingness to fall short of his own ideals in what he gave to the world, it was a great pity that *The Theory of Foreign Trade with some Allied Problems relating to the Doctrine of Laisser Faire*, did not see the light in 1877, even in an imperfect form[4]. After all, he had

---

[1] "The argument in the text is never dependent on them; and they may be omitted; but experience seems to show that they give a firmer grasp of many important principles than can be got without their aid; and that there are many problems of pure theory, which no one who has once learnt to use diagrams will willingly handle in any other way."

[2] "The chief use of pure mathematics in economic questions seems to be in helping a person to write down quickly, shortly and exactly, some of his thoughts for his own use....It seems doubtful whether anyone spends his time well in reading lengthy translations of economic doctrines into mathematics, that have not been made by himself."

[3] Two former pupils of Marshall's, Sir Henry Cunynghame and Mr A. W. Flux, have done something to supply the want. But we still, after fifty years, lack the ideal textbook for this purpose. Professor Bowley's lately published *Mathematical Groundwork of Economics* runs somewhat counter to Marshall's precepts by preferring, on the whole, algebraical to diagrammatic methods.

[4] Indeed, it is not very clear why he abandoned the publication of this book. Certainly up to the middle of 1877 he still intended to publish it. My father noted in his diary on Feb. 8, 1877: "Marshall has brought me part of the MS. of a book on foreign trade that he is writing, for me to look over." Both Sidgwick and Jevons had also read it in manuscript, and had formed a high opinion of it, as appears from their testimonials

originally embarked on this particular inquiry because, in this case, "the chief facts relating to it can be obtained from printed documents"; and these facts, supplemented by those which he had obtained first-hand during his visit to the United States about the actual operation of Protection in a new country, might have been deemed sufficient for a monograph. The explanation is partly to be found in the fact that, when his health broke down, he believed that he had only a few years to live and that these must be given to the working out of his fundamental ideas on Value and Distribution.

We must regret still more Marshall's postponement of the publication of his *Theory of Money* until extreme old age, when time had deprived his ideas of freshness and his exposition of sting and strength. There is no part of Economics where Marshall's originality and priority of thought are more marked than here, or where his superiority of insight and knowledge over his contemporaries was greater. There is hardly any leading feature in the modern Theory of Money which was not known to Marshall forty years ago. Here too was a semi-independent section of the subject ideally suited to separate treatment in a monograph. Yet apart from what is embedded in his evidence before Royal Commissions and occasional articles, not one single scrap was given to the world in his own words and his own atmosphere at the right time. Since *Money* was from the early 'seventies onwards one of his favourite topics for lectures, his main ideas became known to pupils in a general way[1], with the result that there grew up at Cambridge an oral tradition, first from Marshall's own lectures and since his retirement from those of Professor Pigou, different from, and (I think it may be claimed) superior to, anything that could be found in printed books until recently[2]. It may be convenient at this point to

written in June, 1877, when Marshall was applying for the Bristol appointment. Sidgwick wrote: "I doubt not that his forthcoming work, of which the greater part is already completed, will give him at once a high position among living English economists." And Jevons: "Your forthcoming work on the theory of Foreign Trade is looked forward to with much interest by those acquainted with its contents, and will place you among the most original writers on the science."

[1] His unsystematic method of lecturing prevented the average, and even the superior, student from getting down in his notes anything very consecutive or complete.

[2] Professor Irving Fisher has been the first, in several instances, to publish in bookform ideas analogous to those which had been worked out by Marshall at much earlier dates.

attempt a brief summary of Marshall's main contributions to Monetary Theory.

Marshall printed nothing whatever on the subject of Money[1] previously to the Bimetallic controversy, and even then he waited a considerable time before he intervened. His first serious contribution to the subject was contained in his answers to a questionnaire printed by the Royal Commission on the Depression of Trade and Industry in 1886. This was followed by his article on "Remedies for Fluctuations of General Prices" in the *Contemporary Review* for March 1887; and a little later by his voluminous evidence before the Gold and Silver Commission in 1887 and 1888. In 1899 came his evidence before the Indian Currency Committee. But his theories were not expounded in a systematic form until the appearance of *Money Credit and Commerce* in 1923. By this date nearly all his main ideas had found expression in the works of others. He had passed his eightieth year; his strength was no longer equal to much more than piecing together earlier fragments; and its jejune treatment, carefully avoiding difficulties and complications, yields the mere shadow of what he had had it in him to bring forth twenty[2] or (better) thirty years earlier. It happens, however, that the earliest extant manuscript of Marshall's, written about 1871, deals with his treatment of the Quantity Theory. It is a remarkable example of the continuity of his thought from its first beginnings between 1867 and 1877, that the whole of the substance of Book I, chapter iv of his *Money Credit and Commerce* is to be found here, worked out with fair completeness and with much greater strength of exposition and illustration than he could manage fifty years later. I have no evidence at what date he had arrived at the leading ideas underlying his *Contemporary Review* article or his evidence before the Gold and Silver Commission[3]. But the passages about Commercial Crises in the *Economics of Industry*, from which he quoted freely in

[1] *The Economics of Industry* (1879) was not intended to cover this part of the subject and contains only a brief reference to it. The references to the Trade Cycle in this book are, however, important.

[2] I can speak on this matter from personal recollection, since it was only a little later than this (in 1906) that I attended his lectures on Money.

[3] In expounding his "Symmetallism" to the Commissioners he said (Q. 9837): "I have a bimetallic hobby of my own....I have had it by me now for more than 10 years"— which brings this particular train of thought back to before 1878.

his reply to the Trade Depression Commissioners, show that he was on the same lines of thought in 1879. The following are the most important and characteristic of Marshall's original contributions to this part of Economics.

(1) *The exposition of the Quantity Theory of Money as a part of the General Theory of Value.* He always taught that the value of money is a function of its supply on the one hand, and the demand for it, on the other, as measured by "the average stock of command over commodities which each person cares to keep in a ready form." He went on to explain how each individual decides, how much to keep in a ready form, as the result of a *balance* of advantage between this and alternative forms of wealth. "The exchange value of the whole amount of coin in the Kingdom," he wrote in the manuscript of 1871 mentioned above, "is just equal to that of the whole amount of the commodities over which the members of the community have decided to keep a command in this ready form. Thus with a silver currency if we know the number of ounces of silver in circulation we can determine what the value of one ounce of silver will be in terms of other commodities by dividing the value of above given amount of commodities by the number of ounces. Suppose that on the average each individual in a community chose to keep command over commodities in a ready form to the extent of one-tenth of his year's income. The money, supposed in this case exclusively silver, in the Kingdom will be equal in value to one-tenth of the annual income of the kingdom. Let their habits alter, each person being willing, for the sake of gain in other ways, to be to a greater extent without the power of having each want satisfied as soon as it arises. Let on the average each person choose to keep command over commodities in a ready form only to the extent of a twentieth part of his income. So much silver as before not being wanted at the old value, it will fall in value. It would accordingly be more used in manufactures, while its production from the mines would be checked....[1]" He points out that the great advantage of this method of approach is that it avoids the awkward conception of "rapidity of circulation" (though he is able to show the exact logical

---

[1] When I attended his lectures in 1906 he used to illustrate this theory with some very elegant diagrams.

relation between the two conceptions): "When, however, we try to establish a connection between 'the rapidity of circulation' and the value of money, it introduces grave complications. Mr Mill is aware of the evil (*Political Economy*, Book III, chap. viii, § 3, latter part), but he has not pointed the remedy[1]." Marshall also expounded long ago the way in which distrust of a currency raises prices by diminishing the willingness of the public to hold stocks of it—a phenomenon to which recent events have now called everyone's attention; and he was aware that the fluctuation in the price level, which is an accompaniment of the trade cycle, corresponds to a fluctuation in the volume of "ready command[2]" which the public desire to hold.

(2) *The distinction between the "real" rate of interest and the "money" rate of interest, and the relevance of this to the credit cycle, when the value of money is fluctuating.* The first clear exposition of this is, I think, that given in the *Principles* (1890), Book VI, chap. vi (concluding note)[3].

(3) *The causal train by which, in modern credit systems, an additional supply of money influences prices, and the part played by the rate of discount.* The *locus classicus* for an account of this, and the only detailed account for many years to which students could be referred, is Marshall's Evidence before the Gold and Silver Commission, 1887 (particularly the earlier part of his evidence), supplemented by his Evidence before the Indian Currency Committee, 1899. It was an odd state of affairs that one of the most fundamental parts of Monetary Theory should, for about a quarter of a century, have been available to students nowhere except embedded in the form of question-and-answer before a Government Commission interested in a transitory practical problem.

(4) *The enunciation of the "Purchasing Power Parity" Theory as determining the rate of exchange between countries with mutually inconvertible currencies.* In substance this theory is due to Ricardo, but Professor Cassel's restatement of it in a form applicable

---

[1] This extract, as well as that given above, is from the manuscript of 1871.

[2] This is Marshall's phrase for what I have called "real balances."

[3] In repeating the substance of this Note to the Indian Currency Committee (1899) he refers in generous terms to the then-recent elaboration of the idea in Professor Irving Fisher's *Appreciation and Interest* (1896). See also for some analogous ideas Marshall's first *Economics of Industry* (1879), Book III, chap. i, §§ 5, 6.

to modern conditions was anticipated by Marshall in the memorandum[1] appended to his Evidence before the Gold and Silver Commission (1888). It also had an important place in the conclusions which he laid before the Indian Currency Committee in 1899. The following, from an abstract of his opinions handed in by Marshall to the Gold and Silver Commission, gives his theory in a nutshell: "Let B have an inconvertible paper-currency (say roubles). In each country prices will be governed by the relation between the volume of the currency and the work it has to do. The gold price of the rouble will be fixed by the course of trade just at the ratio which gold prices in A bear to rouble prices in B (allowing for cost of carriage)."

(5) *The "chain" method of compiling index-numbers.* The first mention of this method is in a footnote to the last section (entitled *How to estimate a Unit of Purchasing Power*) of his "Remedies for Fluctuations of General Prices" (1887).

(6) *The proposal of paper currency for the circulation* (*on the lines of Ricardo's* "Proposals for an Economical and Secure Currency") *based on gold-and-silver symmetallism as the standard.* This suggestion is first found in his reply to the Commissioners on Trade Depression in 1886. He argued that ordinary bi-metallism would always tend to work out as alternative-metallism. "I submit," he went on, "that, if we are to have a great disturbance of our currency for the sake of bi-metallism, we ought to be sure that we get it....My alternative scheme is got from his (Ricardo's) simply by wedding a bar of silver of, say, 2000 grammes to a bar of gold of, say, 100 grammes; the government undertaking to be always ready to buy or sell a wedded pair of bars for a fixed amount of currency....This plan could be started by any nation without waiting for the con-currence of others." He did not urge the immediate adoption of this system, but put it forward as being at least preferable to bi-metallism. The same proposal was repeated in 1887 in his

---

[1] Entitled *Memorandum as to the Effects which Differences between the Currencies of different Nations have on International Trade.* His illustrations are in terms of English gold and Russian paper roubles; and alternatively of English gold and Indian silver. He argues that a prolonged departure from purchasing power parity (he does not use this term) is not likely except when there is "a general distrust of Russia's economic future, which makes investors desire to withdraw their capital from Russia,"—a re-markable prevision of recent events. A portion of this Memorandum was reproduced as the first part of Appendix G of *Money Credit and Commerce.*

article on "Remedies for Fluctuations of General Prices," and in 1888 in his Evidence before the Gold and Silver Commission[1].

(7) *The proposal of an official Tabular Standard for optional use in the case of long contracts.* This proposal first appears in an appendix to a paper on remedies for the discontinuity of employment, which Marshall read at the "Industrial Remuneration Conference" in 1885[2]. He repeated, and added to, what he had said there, in his Reply to the Commissioners on Trade Depression in 1886.

A great cause of the discontinuity of industry (he wrote) is the want of certain knowledge as to what a pound is going to be worth a short time hence....This serious evil can be much diminished by a plan which economists have long advocated. In proposing this remedy I want government to help business, though not to do business. It should publish tables showing as closely as may be the changes in the purchasing power of gold, and should facilitate contracts for payments to be made in terms of units of fixed purchasing power....The unit of constant general purchasing power would be applicable, at the free choice of both parties concerned, for nearly all contracts for the payment of interest, and for the repayment of loans; and for many contracts for rent, and for wages and salaries....I wish to emphasise the fact that this proposal is independent of the form of our currency, and does not ask for any change in it. I admit that the plan would seldom be available for the purposes of international trade. But its importance as a steadying influence to our home trade could be so great, and its introduction would be so easy and so free from the evils which generally surround the interference of Government in business, that I venture to urge strongly its claims on your immediate attention.

This important proposal was further developed in Marshall's remarkable essay on "Remedies for Fluctuations of General Prices," which has been mentioned above. The first three sections of this essay are entitled: I. *The Evils of a Fluctuating Standard of Value;* II. *The Precious Metals cannot afford a good Standard of Value;* III. *A Standard of Value independent of Gold and Silver.* Marshall had a characteristic habit in all his writings of reserving for footnotes what was most novel or important in what he had to say[3]; and the following is an extract from a footnote to this essay:

Every plan for regulating the supply of the currency, so that its value shall be constant, must, I think, be national and not international. I will

---

[1] See also *Money Credit and Commerce*, pp. 64–67.

[2] Entitled: "How far do remediable causes influence prejudicially (a) the continuity of employment, (b) the rates of wages?"

[3] It would almost be better to read the footnotes and appendices of Marshall's big volumes and omit the text, rather than *vice versa.*

indicate briefly two such plans, though I do not advocate either of them. On the first plan the currency would be inconvertible. An automatic Government Department would buy Consols for currency whenever £1 was worth more than a unit, and would sell Consols for currency whenever it was worth less....The other plan is that of a convertible currency, each £1 note giving the right to demand at a Government Office as much gold as at that time had the value of half a unit together with as much silver as had the value of half a unit[1].

The *Economist* mocked at Symmetallism and the optional Tabular Standard; and Marshall, always a little over-afraid of being thought unpractical or above the head of the "business man" (that legendary monster), did not persevere[2].

V

I promised, above, that I would endeavour to set forth the reasons or the excuses for the delay in the publication of Marshall's methods and theories concerning Diagrammatic Methods, the Theory of Foreign Trade, and the Principles of Money and Credit. I think that the reasons, some of which apply to all periods of his life, were partly good and partly bad. Let us take the good ones first.

Marshall, as already pointed out above, arrived very early at the point of view that the bare bones of economic theory are not worth much in themselves and do not carry one far in the direction of useful, practical conclusions. The whole point lies in applying them to the interpretation of current economic life. This requires a profound knowledge of the actual facts of industry and trade. But these and the relation of individual men to them are constantly and rapidly changing. Some extracts from his Inaugural Lecture at Cambridge[3] will indicate his position:

The change that has been made in the point of view of Economics by the present generation is due to the discovery that man himself is in a

---

[1] The last part of this sentence presumes the adoption of Symmetallism. The second plan is akin to Prof. Irving Fisher's "Compensated Dollar."

[2] In December 1923, after I had sent him my *Tract on Monetary Reform* he wrote to me: "As years go on it seems to become ever clearer that there ought to be an international currency; and that the—in itself foolish—superstition that gold is the 'natural' representative of value has done excellent service. I have appointed myself amateur currency-mediciner; but I cannot give myself even a tolerably good testimonial in that capacity. And I am soon to go away; but, if I have opportunity, I shall ask new-comers to the celestial regions whether you have succeeded in finding a remedy for currency-maladies." As regards the choice between the advantages of a national and of an international currency I think that what he wrote in 1887 was the truer word, and that a constant-value currency must be, in the first instance at least, a national currency.

[3] *The Present Position of Economics*, 1885.

great measure a creature of circumstances and changes with them. The chief fault in English economists at the beginning of the century was not that they ignored history and statistics, but that they regarded man as so to speak a constant quantity, and gave themselves little trouble to study his variations. They therefore attributed to the forces of supply and demand a much more mechanical and regular action than they actually have. Their most vital fault was that they did not see how liable to change are the habits and institutions of industry. But the Socialists were men who had felt intensely, and who knew something about the hidden springs of human action of which the economists took no account. Buried among their wild rhapsodies there were shrewd observations and pregnant suggestions from which philosophers and economists had much to learn. Among the bad results of the narrowness of the work of English economists early in the century, perhaps the most unfortunate was the opportunity which it gave to sciolists to quote and misapply economic dogmas. Ricardo and his chief followers did not make clear to others, it was not even quite clear to themselves, that what they were building up was not universal truth, but machinery of universal application in the discovery of a certain class of truths. While attributing high and transcendent universality to the central scheme of economic reasoning, I do not assign any universality to economic dogmas. It is not a body of concrete truth, but an engine for the discovery of concrete truth[1].

Holding these views and living at a time of reaction against economists when the faults of his predecessors, to which he draws attention above, were doing their maximum amount of harm, he was naturally reluctant to publish the isolated apparatus of economics, divorced from its appropriate applications. Diagrams and pure theory by themselves might do more harm than good, by increasing the confusion between the objects and methods of the mathematical sciences and those of the social sciences, and would give what he regarded as just the wrong emphasis. In publishing his intellectual exercises without facing the grind of discovering their points of contact with the real world, he would be following and giving bad example. On the other hand, the relevant facts were extremely hard to come by— much harder than now. The progress of events in the 'seventies and 'eighties, particularly in America, was extraordinarily rapid; and organised sources of information, of which there are now so many, scarcely existed. In the twenty years from 1875 to 1895 he was, in fact, greatly increasing his command over real facts and his power of economic judgment, and the work which he

---

[1] This is a portmanteau quotation,—I have run together non-consecutive passages. Parts of this lecture were transcribed almost verbatim in the *Principles*, Book I, chap. iv.

could have published between 1875 and 1885 would have been much inferior to what he was capable of between 1885 and 1895.

The other valid reason was a personal one. At the critical moment of his life his health was impaired. After health was restored, the preparation of lectures and the time he devoted to his pupils made big interruptions in the writing of books. He was too meticulous in his search for accuracy, and also for conciseness of expression, to be a ready writer. He was particularly unready in the business of fitting pieces into a big whole and of continually re-writing them in the light of their reactions on and from the other pieces. He was always trying to write big books, yet lacked the power of rapid execution and continuous concentration (such as J. S. Mill had) and that of continuous artistic sensibility to the whole (such as Adam Smith had) which are necessary for the complete success of a Treatise.

We are now approaching in our explanations what we must admit as bad reasons. Given his views as to the impossibility of any sort of finality in Economics and as to the rapidity with which events change, given the limitations of his own literary aptitudes and of his leisure for book-making, was it not a fatal decision to abandon his first intention of separate, independent monographs in favour of a great Treatise? I think that it was, and that certain weaknesses contributed to it.

Marshall was conscious of the great superiority of his powers over those of his surviving contemporaries. In his Inaugural Lecture of 1885 he said: "Twelve years ago England possessed perhaps the ablest set of economists that there have ever been in a country at one time. But one after another there have been taken from us Mill, Cairnes, Bagehot, Cliffe Leslie, Jevons, Newmarch and Fawcett." There was no one left who could claim at that date to approach Marshall in stature. To his own pupils, who were to carry on the Economics of the future, Marshall was ready to devote time and strength. But he was too little willing to cast his half-baked bread on the waters, to trust in the efficacy of the co-operation of many minds, and to let the big world draw from him what sustenance it could. Was he not attempting, contrary to his own principles, to achieve an impossible finality? An Economic Treatise may have great educational value. Perhaps we require one treatise, as a *pièce de résistance,* for each generation. But in view of the transitory character of economic facts, and the bareness of economic principles in isolation, does not the progress and the daily usefulness of economic science require that pioneers and innovators should eschew the Treatise and prefer the pamphlet or the monograph? I depreciated Jevons' *Political Economy* above on the ground that it was no more than a brilliant brochure. Yet it was Jevons' willingness to spill his ideas, to flick them at the world, that won him his great personal position and his unrivalled power of stimulating other minds. Every one of Jevons' contributions to Economics was in the nature of a pamphlet. Malthus spoilt the *Essay on Population* when, after the first edition, he converted it into a Treatise. Ricardo's greatest works were written as ephemeral pamphlets. Did not Mill, in achieving by his peculiar gifts a successful Treatise, do more for pedagogics than for science, and end by sitting like an Old Man of the Sea on the voyaging Sinbads of the next generation? Economists must leave to Adam Smith alone the glory of the Quarto, must pluck the day, fling pamphlets into the wind, write always *sub specie temporis*, and achieve immortality by accident, if at all.

Moreover, did not Marshall, by keeping his wisdom at home until he could produce it fully clothed, mistake, perhaps, the true nature of his own special gift? "Economics," he said in the passage quoted above, "is not a body of concrete truth, but an engine for the discovery of concrete truth." This engine, as we employ it to-day, is largely Marshall's creation. He put it in the hands of his pupils long before he offered it to the world. The building of this engine was the essential achievement of Marshall's peculiar genius. Yet he hankered greatly after the "concrete truth" which he had disclaimed and for the discovery of which he was not specially qualified. I have very early memories, almost before I knew what Economics meant, of the sad complaints of my father, who had been able to observe as pupil and as colleague the progress of Marshall's thought almost from the beginning, of Marshall's obstinate refusal to understand where his special strength and weakness really lay, and of how his unrealisable ambitions stood in the way of his giving to the world the true treasures of his mind and genius. Economics all over the world might have progressed much faster and Marshall's authority and influence would have been far greater, if his temperament had been a little different.

Two other characteristics must be mentioned. First, Marshall was too much afraid of being wrong, too thin-skinned towards criticism, too easily upset by controversy even on matters of minor importance. An extreme sensitiveness deprived him of magnanimity towards the critic or the adversary. This fear of being open to correction by speaking too soon aggravated other tendencies. Yet after all there is no harm in being sometimes wrong—especially if one is promptly found out. Nevertheless this quality was but the defect of the high standard he never relaxed—which touched his pupils with awe—of scientific accuracy and truth.

Second, Marshall was too anxious to do good. He had an inclination to undervalue those intellectual parts of the subject which were not *directly* connected with human well-being or the condition of the working classes or the like, although *indirectly* they might be of the utmost importance, and to feel that when he was pursuing them he was not occupying himself with the Highest. It came out of the conflict, already remarked, between an intellect, which was hard, dry, critical, as unsentimental as you could find, with emotions and aspirations, generally unspoken, of quite a different type. When his intellect chased diagrams and Foreign Trade and Money, there was an evangelical moraliser of an imp somewhere inside him, that was so ill-advised as to disapprove. Near the end of his life, when the intellect grew dimmer and the preaching imp could rise nearer to the surface to protest against its lifelong servitude, he once said: "If I had to live my life over again I should have devoted it to psychology. Economics has too little to do with ideals. If I said much about them I should not be read by business men." But these notions had always been with him. He used to tell the following story of his early life:

About the time that I first resolved to make as thorough a study as I could of Political Economy (the word Economics was not then invented) I saw in a shop-window a small oil painting [of a man's face with a strikingly gaunt and wistful expression, as of one 'down and out'] and bought it for a few shillings. I set it up above the chimney-piece in my room in college and thenceforward called it my patron saint, and devoted myself to trying

how to fit men like that for heaven. Meanwhile I got a good deal interested
in the semi-mathematical side of pure Economics, and was afraid of becoming a mere thinker. But a glance at my patron saint seemed to call
me back to the right path. That was particularly useful after I had been
diverted from the study of ultimate aims to the questions about Bimetallism,
etc., which at one time were dominant. I despised them, but the 'instinct
of the chase' tempted me towards them.

This was the defect of that other great quality of his, which
also touched his pupils—his immense disinterestedness and
public spirit.

VI

At any rate, in 1877 Marshall turned aside to help his wife
with the *Economics of Industry* (published in 1879), designed as
a manual for Cambridge University Extension lecturers, which,
as it progressed, became more and more his work. In later years
Marshall grew very unfriendly to the little book. After the
publication of the *Principles* he suppressed it and replaced it in
1892 with an almost wholly different book under the same title,
which was mainly an abridgment of the *Principles* and "an
attempt to adapt it to the needs of junior students." Marshall's
feelings were due, I think, to the fact that his theory of value,
which was here first published to the world, was necessarily
treated in a brief and imperfect manner, yet remained for eleven
years all that the outside world had to judge from. His controversies in the *Quarterly Journal of Economics* in 1887 and
1888[1] with American economists who had read the little book
accentuated this feeling. He also revolted later on from the
thought of Economics as a subject capable of being treated
in a light and simple manner for elementary students by half-
instructed Extension lecturers[2] aided by half-serious books.
"This volume," he wrote in 1910 to a Japanese translator of the
1879 book, "was begun in the hope that it might be possible to
combine simplicity with scientific accuracy. But though a simple
book can be written on selected topics, the central doctrines of
Economics are not simple and cannot be made so."

Yet these sentiments do an injustice to the book. It won
high praise from competent judges and was, during the whole of

---

[1] See the Bibliographical Note.

[2] So far, however, from being out of sympathy with the ideals underlying the Extension
Movement (or its modern variant the W.E.A.), Marshall had been connected with it
from the beginning, and had himself given Extension Courses at Bristol for five years.

its life, much the best little text-book available[1]. If we are to
have an elementary text-book at all, this one was probably, in
relation to its contemporaries and predecessors, the best thing
of the kind ever done—much better than the primers of Mrs
Fawcett or Jevons or any of its many successors. Moreover, the
latter part of Book III, on Trade Combinations, Trade Unions,
Trade Disputes and Co-operation, was the first satisfactory
treatment on modern lines of these important topics.

After this volume[2] was out of the way, Marshall's health was
at its worst. When in 1881 he went abroad to recuperate, his
mind did not return to Money or to Foreign Trade, but was
concentrated on the central theories which eventually appeared
in the *Principles*[3]. Subject to the successive interruptions of his
Oxford appointment, his removal to Cambridge, the preparation
of his lectures there, his incursion into the Bimetallic controversy
and his Evidence before the Gold and Silver Commission, the
next nine years were spent on the preparation of this book.

Marshall intended at first to cover the whole field of Economics
in a single volume. His theory of Distribution was taking shape
in 1883 and 1884[4]. In the summer of 1885 (in the Lakes), the
first of his Cambridge Long Vacations, the volume began to
assume its final form. "The work done during this year," he
wrote[5], "was not very satisfactory, partly because I was
gradually outgrowing the older and narrower conception of my
book, in which the abstract reasoning which forms the backbone
of the science was to be made prominent, and had not yet
mustered courage to commit myself straight off to a two-volume
book which should be the chief product (as gradually improved)
of my life's work[6]." In 1886, "my chief work was recasting the

---

[1] So much did the public like it, that 15,000 copies had been sold before it was
suppressed.

[2] Its preface mentioned a forthcoming companion volume on the "Economics of
Trade and Finance," which was never written.

[3] Mrs Marshall writes: "Book III on Demand was largely thought out and written
on the roof at Palermo, Nov. 1881–Feb. 1882."

[4] It appears in outline in an article written in about two days in the summer of 1884,
when he was staying at Rocquaine Bay, Guernsey. This was published in the *Co-operative
Annual* for 1885 under the title "Theories and Facts about Wages," and was reprinted in
the same year as an appendix to his paper read before the Industrial Remuneration
Conference.

[5] The following extracts are from some notes he put together summarising his work
from 1885 to 1889.

[6] Also, "Work during the summer a good deal interrupted by making plans for my
new house in Madingley Road."

plan of my book. This came to a head during my stay at Sheringham near Cromer in the summer. I then put the contents of my book into something like their final form, at least so far as the first volume is concerned. And thenceforward for the first time I began to try to put individual chapters into a form in which I expected them to be printed." In 1887 (at Guernsey), "I did a great deal of writing at my book; and having arranged with Macmillan for its publication, I began just at the end of this academic year to send proofs to the printers: all of it except about half of Book VI being typewritten in a form not ready for publication, but ready to be put into a form for publication— I mean the matter was nearly all there and the arrangement practically settled." In 1888, "by the end of the Long Vacation I had got Book V at the printers, Book IV being almost out of my hands. Later on I decided to bring before the Book on Normal Value or Distribution and Exchange a new Book on Cost of Production further considered[1], putting into it (somewhat amplified) discussions which I had intended to keep for the later part of the Book on Normal Value. That Book now became Book VII. This decision was slowly reached, and not much further progress was made during this Calendar year." "During the first four months of 1889 I worked at Book VI, finishing the first draft of the first four chapters of it, and working off Book V. Meanwhile I had paid a good deal of attention to the Mathematical Appendix and got a good part of that into print. The Long Vacation, of which eight weeks were spent at Bordeaux Harbour, was occupied chiefly with Book VI, chaps. v and vi, and Book VII, chaps. i–v." The work was now pushed rapidly to a conclusion and was published in July 1890.

By 1890 Marshall's fame stood high[2], and the *Principles of Economics*[3], *Vol. I*[4], was delivered into an expectant world. Its success was immediate and complete. The book was the subject

---

[1] After the first edition, this Book was incorporated in Book V; so that *Value* again became Book VI.

[2] "Rarely in modern times," said the *Scotsman*, "has a man achieved such a high reputation as an authority on such a slender basis of published work."

[3] This was the first book in England to be published at a *net* price, which gives it an important place in the history of the publishing trade. (See Sir F. Macmillan's *The Net Book Agreement*, 1899, pp. 14–16.) The dates of the successive editions are given in the Bibliographical Note. 37,000 copies have been sold up to the present time.

[4] The suffix vol. I was not dropped until the sixth edition in 1910.

of leading articles and full-dress reviews throughout the Press. The journalists could not distinguish the precise contributions and innovations which it contributed to science; but they discerned with remarkable quickness that it ushered in a new age of economic thought. "It is a great thing," said the *Pall Mall Gazette*, "to have a Professor at one of our old Universities devoting the work of his life to recasting the science of Political Economy as the Science of Social Perfectibility." The New Political Economy had arrived, and the Old Political Economy, the dismal science, "which treated the individual man as a purely selfish and acquisitive animal, and the State as a mere conglomeration of such animals," had passed away; not that the Old Political Economy was really thus, but this was the journalists' way of expressing the effect which Marshall's outlook made on them. "It will serve," said the *Daily Chronicle*, "to restore the shaken credit of political economy, and will probably become for the present generation what Mill's *Principles* was for the last." "It has made almost all other accounts of the science antiquated or obsolete," said the *Manchester Guardian*, "It is not premature to predict that Professor Marshall's treatise will form a landmark in the development of political economy, and that its influence on the direction and temper of economic inquiries will be wholly good." These are samples from a general chorus.

It is difficult for those of us who have been brought up entirely under the influence of Marshall and his book to appreciate the position of the science in the long interregnum between Mill's *Principles of Political Economy* and Marshall's *Principles of Economics*, or to define just what difference was made by the publication of the latter. The following is an attempt, with help from notes supplied by Professor Edgeworth, to indicate some of its more striking contributions to knowledge[1].

(1) The unnecessary controversy, caused by the obscurity of Ricardo and the rebound of Jevons, about the respective parts played by Demand and by Cost of Production in the determina-

---

[1] Including hints and anticipations in earlier writings; as Professor Edgeworth wrote, reviewing the first edition of the *Principles* (*The Academy*, Aug. 30, 1890): "Some of Professor Marshall's leading ideas have been more or less fully expressed in his earlier book (the little *Economics of Industry*), and in certain papers which, though unpublished, have not been unknown. The light of dawn was diffused before the orb of day appeared above the horizon."

tion of Value was finally cleared up. After Marshall's analysis
there was nothing more to be said.

The new light thrown on Cost of Production (Prof. Edgeworth writes)
enabled one more clearly to discern the great part which it plays in the
determination of value; that the classical authors had been rightly guided
by their intuitions, as Marshall has somewhere said, when they emphasised
the forces of Supply above those of Demand. The rehabilitation of the older
writers—much depreciated by Jevons, Böhm-Bawerk and others in the
'seventies and 'eighties of last century—produced on the reviewer of the
first edition an impression which is thus expressed: "The mists of ephemeral
criticism are dispelled. The eternal mountains reappear in their natural
sublimity, contemplated from a kindred height."

(2) The general idea, underlying the proposition that Value
is determined at the equilibrium point of Demand and Supply,
was extended so as to discover a whole Copernican system, by
which all the elements of the economic universe are kept in their
places by mutual counterpoise and interaction[1]. The general
theory of economic equilibrium was strengthened and made
effective as an organon of thought by two powerful subsidiary
conceptions—*the Margin* and *Substitution*. The notion of the
Margin was extended beyond Utility to describe the equilibrium
point in given conditions of any economic factor which can be
regarded as capable of small variations about a given value,
or in its functional relation to a given value. The notion of
Substitution was introduced to describe the process by which
Equilibrium is restored or brought about. In particular the
idea of *Substitution at the Margin*, not only between alternative
objects of consumption, but also between the factors of production, was extraordinarily fruitful in results. Further, there
is "the double relation in which the various agents of production
stand to one another. On the one hand they are often rivals for
employment; any one that is more efficient than another in
proportion to its cost tending to be substituted for it, and thus
limiting the demand price for the other. And on the other hand,
they all constitute the field of employment for each other; there
is no field of employment for any one, except in so far as it is
provided by the others: the national dividend which is the joint

---

[1] Already in 1872, in his review of Jevons, Marshall was in possession of the idea of
the mutually dependent positions of the economic factors. "Just as the motion of every
body in the solar system," he there wrote, "affects and is affected by the motion of every
other, so it is with the elements of the problem of political economy."

product of them all, and which increases with the supply of each of them, is also the sole source of demand for each of them[1]."

This method allowed the subsumption of wages and profits under the general laws of value, supply and demand,—just as previously the theory of money had been so subsumed. At the same time the peculiarities in the action of demand and supply which determine the wages of the labourer or the profits of the employer were fully analysed.

(3) The explicit introduction of the element of Time as a factor in economic analysis is mainly due to Marshall. The conceptions of the "long" and the "short" period are his, and one of his objects was to trace "a continuous thread running through and connecting the applications of the general theory of equilibrium of demand and supply to different periods of time[2]." Connected with these there are further distinctions, which we now reckon essential to clear thinking, which are first explicit in Marshall—particularly those between "external" and "internal" economies[3] and between "prime" and "supplementary" cost. Of these pairs the first was, I think, a complete novelty when the *Principles* appeared; the latter, however, already existed in the vocabulary of manufacture, if not in that of economic analysis.

By means of the distinction between the long and the short period, the meaning of "normal" value was made precise; and with the aid of two further characteristically Marshallian conceptions—Quasi-Rent and the Representative Firm—the doctrine of Normal Profit was evolved.

All these are path-breaking ideas which no one who wants to think clearly can do without. Nevertheless this is the quarter in which, in my opinion, the Marshall analysis is least complete and satisfactory, and where there remains most to do. As he says himself in the Preface to the first edition of the *Principles*, the element of time "is the centre of the chief difficulty of almost every economic problem."

(4) The special conception of Consumers' Rent or Surplus, which was a natural development of Jevonian ideas, has perhaps proved less fruitful of practical results than seemed likely at

---

[1] *Principles*, Book VI, chap. xi, § 5.   [2] *Ibid*. Book VI, chap. xi, § 1.
[3] The vital importance of this distinction to a correct theory of Equilibrium under conditions of increasing return is, of course, now obvious. But it was not so before the *Principles*.

first[1]. But one could not do without it as part of the apparatus of thought, and it is particularly important in the *Principles* because of the use of it (in Prof. Edgeworth's words) "to show that *laissez-faire*, the maximum of advantage attained by unrestricted competition, is not necessarily the greatest possible advantage attainable." Marshall's proof that *laissez-faire* breaks down in certain conditions *theoretically*, and not merely practically, regarded as a principle of maximum social advantage, was of great philosophical importance. But Marshall does not carry this particular argument very far[2], and the further exploration of that field has been left to Marshall's favourite pupil and successor, Professor Pigou, who has shown in it what a powerful engine for cutting a way in tangled and difficult country the Marshall analysis affords in the hands of one who has been brought up to understand it well.

(5) Marshall's analysis of Monopoly should also be mentioned in this place; and perhaps his analysis of increasing return, especially where external economies exist, belongs better here than where I have mentioned it above.

Marshall's theoretical conclusions in this field and his strong sympathy with socialistic ideas were compatible, however, with an old-fashioned belief in the strength of the forces of competition. Professor Edgeworth writes:

I may record the strong impression produced on me the first time I met Marshall—far back in the 'eighties, I think—by his strong expression of the conviction that Competition would for many a long day rule the roast as a main determinant of value. Those were not his words, but they were of a piece with the dictum in his article on *The Old Generation of Economists and the New*[3]: "When one person is willing to sell a thing at a price which another is willing to pay for it, the two manage to come together in spite of prohibitions of King or Parliament or of the officials of a Trust or Trade-Union."

[1] Nevertheless, Professor Edgeworth points out, even "before the publication of the *Principles* Marshall quite understood—what the critics of the doctrine in question have not generally understood, and even some of the defenders have not adequately emphasised—that the said measurement applies accurately only to transactions which are on such a scale as not to disturb the marginal value of money."

[2] *Industry and Trade*, however, is partly devoted to illustrating it. "The present volume," he says in the Preface to that book, "is in the main occupied with the influences which still make for sectional and class selfishness: with the limited tendencies of self-interest to direct each individual's action on those lines, in which it will be most beneficial to others; and with the still surviving tendencies of associated action by capitalists and other business men, as well as by employees, to regulate output, and action generally, by a desire for sectional rather than national advantage."

[3] *Quarterly Journal of Economics*, 1897, vol. xi, p. 129.

(6) In the provision of terminology and apparatus to aid thought I do not think that Marshall did economists any greater service than by the explicit introduction of the idea of "elasticity." Book III, chap. iii, of the first edition of the *Principles*, which introduces the definition of "Elasticity of Demand[1]," is virtually the earliest treatment[2] of a conception without the aid of which the advanced theory of Value and Distribution can scarcely make progress. The notion that demand may respond to a change of price to an extent that may be either more or less than in proportion had been, of course, familiar since the discussions at the beginning of the nineteenth century about the relation between the supply and the price of wheat[3]. Indeed it is rather remarkable that the notion was not more clearly disentangled either by Mill or by Jevons[4]. But it was so. And the concept $e = \dfrac{dx}{x} \div -\dfrac{dy}{y}$ is wholly Marshall's.

The way in which Marshall introduces Elasticity, without any suggestion that the idea is novel, is remarkable and characteristic. The field of investigation opened up by this instrument of thought is again one where the full fruits have been reaped by Professor Pigou rather than by Marshall himself.

(7) The historical introduction to the *Principles* deserves some comment. In the first edition Book I includes two chapters entitled "The Growth of Free Industry and Enterprise." In the latest editions most of what has been retained out of these chapters has been relegated to an Appendix. Marshall was

---

[1] Supplemented by the mathematical note in the Appendix.

[2] Strictly, the earliest reference to "elasticity" is to be found in Marshall's contribution "On the Graphic Method of Statistics" to the Jubilee Volume of the *Royal Statistical Society* (1885), p. 260. But it is introduced there only in a brief concluding note, and mainly with the object of showing that a simple diagrammatic measure of elasticity is furnished by the ratio between the two sections into which that part of the tangent to the demand curve which lies between the axes is divided by the point of contact. Mrs Marshall tells me that he hit on the notion of elasticity, as he sat on the roof at Palermo shaded by the bath-cover in 1881, and was highly delighted with it.

[3] Mill quotes Tooke's *History of Prices* in this connection.

[4] Professor Edgeworth in his article on "Elasticity" in Palgrave's *Dictionary* refers particularly to Mill's *Political Economy*, Book III, chap. ii, § 4, and chap. viii, § 2, as representative of the pre-Marshall treatment of the matter. The first of these passages points out the varying proportions in which demand may respond to variations of price; the second treats (in effect) of the unitary elasticity of the demand for money. Professor Edgeworth now adds a reference to Book III, chap. xviii, § 5, where Mill deals in substance with the effect of elasticity on the Equation of International Demand. Elsewhere in this chapter Mill speaks of a demand being "more extensible by cheapness" (§ 4) and of the "extensibility of their [foreign countries'] demand for its [the home country's commodities" (§ 8).

always in two minds about this. On the one hand his view about the perpetually changing character of the subject-matter of Economics led him to attach great importance to the historical background as a corrective to the idea that the axioms of to-day are permanent. He was also dissatisfied with the learned but half-muddled work of the German historical school. On the other hand he was afraid of spending too much time on these matters (at one period he had embarked on historical inquiries on a scale which, he said, would have occupied six volumes), and of overloading with them the essential matter of his book. At the time when he was occupied with economic history, there was very little ready-made material to go upon, and he probably wasted much strength straying unnecessarily along historical by-ways and vacillating as to the importance to be given in his own book to the historical background. The resulting compromise, as realised in the *Principles*, was not very satisfactory. Everything is boiled down into wide generalisations, the evidence for which he has not space to display [1]. Marshall's best historical work is to be found, perhaps, in *Industry and Trade*, published in 1919, many years after most of the work had been done. The historical passages of the *Principles* were brusquely assailed by Dr William Cunningham in an address before the Royal Historical Society, printed in the *Economic Journal*, vol. II (1892); and Marshall, breaking his general rule of not replying to criticism, came successfully out of the controversy in a reply printed in the same issue of the *Journal* [2].

The way in which Marshall's *Principles of Economics* is written, is more unusual than the casual reader will notice. It is elaborately unsensational and under-emphatic. Its rhetoric is of

---

[1] Marshall himself wrote (in his reply to Dr Cunningham, *Economic Journal*, vol. II, p. 507): "I once proposed to write a treatise on economic history, and for many years I collected materials for it. Afterwards I selected such part of these as helped to explain why many of the present conditions and problems of industry are only of recent date, and worked it into the chapters in question. But they took up much more space than could be spared for them. So I recast and compressed them; and in the process they lost, no doubt, some sharpness of outline and particularity of statement."

[2] Dr Clapham writes: "In reading the Appendices to *Industry and Trade* I was very much impressed with Marshall's knowledge of economic history since the seventeenth century, as it was known thirty years ago, *i.e.* at the time of the controversy. I feel sure that at that time he understood the seventeenth to nineteenth centuries better than Cunningham, and he had—naturally—a feeling for their quantitative treatment to which Cunningham never attained."

the simplest, most unadorned order. It flows in a steady, lucid stream, with few passages which stop or perplex the intelligent reader, even though he know but little economics. Claims to novelty or to originality on the part of the author himself are altogether absent[1]. Passages imputing error to others are rare; and it is explained that earlier writers of repute must be held to have *meant* what is right and reasonable, whatever they may have said[2]. The connexity and continuity of the economic elements, as signified in Marshall's two mottoes, "Natura non facit saltum" and "The many in the one, the one in the many," are the chief grounds of difficulty. But, subject to this, the chief impression which the book makes on the minds of uninitiated readers—particularly on those who do not get beyond Book IV— is apt to be, that they are perusing a clear, apt and humane exposition of fairly obvious matters.

By this stylistic achievement Marshall attained some of his objects. The book reached the general public. It increased the public esteem of Economics. The minimum of controversy was provoked. The average reviewer liked the author's attitude to his subject-matter, to his predecessors, and to his readers, and delighted Marshall by calling attention to the proper stress laid by him on the ethical element and to the much required humanising which the dismal science received at his hands[3]; and, at the same time, could remain happily insensible to the book's intellectual stature. As time has gone on, moreover, the in-

[1] As one intelligent reviewer remarked (*The Guardian*, Oct. 15, 1890): "This book has two aspects. On the one hand, it is an honest and obstinate endeavour to find out the truth; on the other hand, it is an ingenious attempt to disclaim any credit for discovering it, on the ground that it was all implicitly contained in the works of earlier writers, especially Ricardo." But most of them were taken in. The following is typical (*Daily Chronicle*, July 24, 1890): "Mr Marshall makes no affectation of new discoveries or new departures; he professes merely to give a modern version of the old doctrines adjusted to the results of more recent investigation."

[2] Marshall carried this rather too far. But it was an essential truth to which he held firmly, that those individuals who are endowed with a special genius for the subject and have a powerful economic intuition will often be more right in their conclusions and implicit presumptions than in their explanations and explicit statements. That is to say, their intuitions will be in advance of their analysis and their terminology. Great respect, therefore, is due to their general scheme of thought, and it is a poor thing to pester their memories with criticism which is really verbal. Marshall's own economic intuition was extraordinary, and lenience towards the apparent errors of great predecessors is treatment to which in future times he will himself have an exceptional claim.

[3] Fashions change! When, nearly thirty years later, *Industry and Trade* appeared, one reviewer wrote (*Athenæum*, Oct. 31, 1919): "Perhaps its least satisfactory feature is its moral tone. Not because that tone is low—quite the contrary; but because, in a scientific treatise, a moral tone, however elevated, seems altogether out of place."

tellectual qualities of the book have permeated English economic thought, without noise or disturbance, to an extent which can easily be overlooked.

The method has, on the other hand, serious disadvantages. The lack of emphasis and of strong light and shade, the sedulous rubbing away of rough edges and salients and projections, until what is most novel can appear as trite, allows the reader to pass too easily through. Like a duck leaving water, he can escape from this douche of ideas with scarce a wetting. The difficulties are concealed; the most ticklish problems are solved in foot-notes; a pregnant and original judgment is dressed up as a platitude. The author furnishes his ideas with no labels of salesmanship and few hooks for them to hang by in the wardrobe of the mind. A student can read the *Principles*, be fascinated by its pervading charm, think that he comprehends it, and, yet, a week later, know but little about it. How often has it not happened even to those who have been brought up on the *Principles*, lighting upon what seems a new problem or a new solution, to go back to it and to find, after all, that the problem and a better solution have been always there, yet quite escaping notice! It needs much study and independent thought on the reader's own part, before he can know the half of what is contained in the concealed crevices of that rounded globe of knowledge, which is Marshall's *Principles of Economics*.

VII

The Marshalls returned in 1885 to the Cambridge of the early years after the reforms, which finally removed restrictions upon the marriage of Fellows. They built for themselves a small house, called Balliol Croft, on St John's College land in the Madingley Road, close to the Backs, yet just on the outskirts of the town, so that on one side open country stretched towards Madingley Hill. Here Alfred Marshall lived for nearly forty years. The house, built in a sufficient garden, on an unconventional plan so as to get as much light as possible, just accommodated the two of them and a faithful maid. His study, lined with books, and filled transversally with shelves, had space by the fire for two chairs. Here were held his innumerable *tête-à-têtes* with pupils, who would be furnished as the afternoon wore on with a cup of tea and a slice of cake on an adjacent stool or shelf. Larger gatherings took place downstairs, where the dining-room and Mrs Marshall's sitting-room could be thrown into one on the occasion of entertainments. The unvarying character of the surroundings—upstairs the books and nests of drawers containing manuscript, downstairs the Michaelangelo figures from the Sistine Chapel let into the furniture, and at the door the face of Sarah the maid[1]—had a charm and fascination for those who paid visits to their Master year after year, like the Cell or Oratory of a Sage.

In that first age of married society in Cambridge, when the narrow circle of the spouses-regnant of the Heads of Colleges and of a few wives of Professors was first extended, several of the most notable Dons, particularly in the School of Moral Science, married students of Newnham. The double link between husbands and between wives bound together a small cultured society of great simplicity and distinction. This circle was at its full strength in my boyhood, and, when I was first old enough to be asked out to luncheon or to dinner, it was to these houses that I went. I remember a homely, intellectual atmosphere which it is harder to find in the swollen, heterogeneous Cambridge of to-day. The entertainments at the Marshall's were generally occasioned, in later days, by the visit of some fellow-economist, often an eminent foreigner, and the small luncheon party would usually include a couple of undergraduates and a student or young lecturer from Newnham. I particularly remember meeting in this way Adolf Wagner and N. G. Pierson, representatives of a generation of economists which is now almost passed. Marshall did not much care about going to other people's houses, and was at his best fitting his guests comfortably into a narrow space, calling out staff directions to his wife, in unembarrassed, half-embarrassed mood, with laughing, high-pitched voice and habitual jokes and phrases. He had great conversational powers on all manner of matters; his cheerfulness and gaiety were unbroken; and, in the presence of his bright

---

[1] She lived with them for more than forty years on terms almost of intimacy. Marshall would often extol her judgment and wisdom. He himself designed the small kitchen, like a ship's cabin, in which she dwelt at Balliol Croft. Marshall was always much loved by his servants and College gyps. He treated them as human beings and talked to them about the things which he was interested in himself.

eyes and smiling talk and unaffected absurdity, no one could feel dull.

In earlier days, particularly between 1885 and 1900, he was fond of asking working-men leaders to spend a week-end with him,—for example, Thomas Burt, Ben Tillett, Tom Mann and many others. Sometimes these visits would be fitted in with meetings of an undergraduate Discussion Society, which the visitor would address. In this way he came to know most of the leading co-operators and Trade Unionists of the past generation. In truth he sympathised with the Labour Movement and with Socialism (just as J. S. Mill had) in every way, except intellectually[1].

Marshall was now settled in an environment and in habits which were not to be changed, and we must record in rapid survey the outward events of his life from 1885 to the resignation of his professorship in 1908.

From 1885 to 1890 he was mainly occupied, as we have seen, with the *Principles*. But the bibliographical note, below, records other activities, particularly his paper before the Industrial Remuneration Conference in 1885, his evidence before the Gold and Silver Commission in 1887–8, and his Presidential Address before the Co-operative Congress in 1889. In the summer of 1890 he delivered his interesting Presidential Address on "Some Aspects of Competition" to the Economic Section of the British Association at Leeds. He was also much occupied with his lectures, and these five years were the most active and productive of his life.

He gave two lectures a week in a general course, and one

---

[1] In the Preface to *Industry and Trade* he wrote:—"For more than a decade, I remained under the conviction that the suggestions, which are associated with the word 'socialism,' were the most important subject of study, if not in the world, yet at all events for me. But the writings of socialists generally repelled me, almost as much as they attracted me; because they seemed far out of touch with realities: and, partly for that reason, I decided to say little on the matter, till I had thought much longer. Now, when old age indicates that my time for thought and speech is nearly ended, I see on all sides marvellous developments of working-class faculty: and, partly in consequence, a broader and firmer foundation for socialistic schemes than when Mill wrote. But no socialistic scheme, yet advanced, seems to make adequate provision for the maintenance of high enterprise and individual strength of character; nor to promise a sufficiently rapid increase in the business plant and other material implements of production....It has seemed to me that those have made most real progress towards the distant goal of ideally perfect social organisation, who have concentrated their energies on some particular difficulties in the way, and not spent strength on endeavouring to rush past them."

lecture a week on special theoretical difficulties; but he lectured, as a rule, in only two terms out of three, making about forty-five lectures in the year. Two afternoons a week, from four to seven, Professor Marshall, it was announced, "will be at home to give advice and assistance to any members of the University who may call on him, whether they are attending his lectures or not." In the late 'eighties the attendance at his general courses would vary between forty and seventy, and at his special courses half that number. But his methods choked off—more or less deliberately—the less serious students, and as the academic year progressed the attendance would fall to the lower figure.

It was not Marshall's practice to write out his lectures.

He rarely used notes (Mrs Marshall writes), except for lectures on Economic History. He sometimes made a few notes before he went to lecture, and thought over them on his way to the class. He said that the reason why he had so many pupils who thought for themselves was that he never cared to present the subject in an orderly and systematic form or to give information. What he cared to do in lectures was to make the students *think with him*. He gave questions once a week on a part of the subject which he had not lectured over, and then answered the questions in class. He took immense pains in looking over the answers, and used red ink on them freely[1].

I think that the informality of his lectures may have increased as time went on. Certainly in 1906, when I attended them, it was impossible to bring away coherent notes. But the above was always his general method. His lectures were not, like Sidgwick's, books in the making. This practice may have contributed, incidentally, to the retardation of his published work. But the sharp distinction which he favoured between written instruction by book and oral instruction by lecture was, as he developed it, extraordinarily stimulating for the better men and where the class was not too large. It is a difficult method to employ where the class exceeds forty at the most (my memory of the size of his class when I attended it is of nearer twenty than forty), and it is not suited to students who have no real aptitude or inclination for economics (in whose interest the curricula of the vast Economic Schools of to-day are mainly designed). The following

[1] I have papers which I wrote for him on which his red-ink comments and criticisms occupy almost as much space as my answers.

titles of successive courses, soon after he arrived in Cambridge, indicate the ground which he purported to cover:

    1885–6. October Term: Foreign Trade and Money.

            Easter   ,,   : Speculation, Taxation, etc. (Mill, IV and V).

    1886–7. October ,, : Production and Value.

            Lent   ,,   : Distribution.

After the publication of the *Principles* in 1890, his first task was to prepare the abridgment, entitled *Economics of Industry*[1], which appeared early in 1892[2]. He also spent much time on the successive revisions of the *Principles*, the most important changes being introduced in the third edition, published in 1895, and the fifth edition in 1907. It is doubtful whether the degree of improvement effected corresponded to the labour involved. These revisions were a great obstacle to his getting on with what was originally intended to be vol. II of the *Principles*.

The main interruption, however, came from his membership of the Royal Commission on Labour, 1891–1894. He welcomed greatly this opportunity of getting into close touch with the raw material of his subject, and he played a big part in the drafting of the Final Report. The parts dealing with Trade Unions, Minimum Wage, and Irregularity of Employment were especially his work.

Meanwhile he was at work on the continuation of the *Principles*. "But he wasted a great deal of time," Mrs Marshall writes, "because he changed his method of treatment so often. In 1894 he began a historical treatment, which he called later on a White Elephant, because it was on such a large scale that it would have taken many volumes to complete. Later on he used fragments of the White Elephant in the descriptive parts of *Industry and Trade*."

Marshall's work on the Labour Commission was only one of a series of services to Governmental inquiries. In 1893 he gave evidence before the Royal Commission on the Aged Poor, in which he proposed to associate Charity Organisation Committees

---

[1] This book was frequently reprinted, and revised editions were prepared in 1896 and 1899; 81,000 copies of it have been sold up to date.

[2] The concluding chapter on "Trade Unions" goes outside the field of the *Principles* and incorporates some material from the earlier *Economics of Industry*.

with the administration of the Poor Law. Early in 1899 he gave carefully prepared evidence before the Indian Currency Committee. His evidence on monetary theory was in part a repetition of what he had said to the Gold and Silver Commission eleven years earlier, but he himself considered that the new version was an improvement and constituted his best account of the theory of money. The parts dealing with specifically Indian problems were supported by many statistical diagrams. His interest in the economic and currency problems of India had been first aroused during the time at Oxford when it was his duty to lecture to Indian Civil Service Probationers. He was pleased with his detailed realistic inquiries into Indian problems[1], and the great rolls of Indian charts, not all of which were published, were always at hand as part of the furniture of his study.

Later in the same year, 1899, he prepared Memoranda on the Classification and Incidence of Imperial and Local Taxes for the Royal Commission on Local Taxation. In 1903, at the height of the Tariff Reform controversy, he wrote, at the request of the Treasury, his admirable Memorandum on "The Fiscal Policy of International Trade." This was printed in 1908 as a Parliamentary paper, at the instance of Mr Lloyd George, then Chancellor of the Exchequer, "substantially as it was written originally." The delay of a critical five years in the date of publication was characteristically explained by Marshall as follows:

Some large corrections of, and additions to, this Memorandum were lost in the post abroad[2] in August 1903; and when I re-read the uncorrected proofs of it in the autumn, I was so dissatisfied with it that I did not avail myself of the permission kindly given to me to publish it independently. The haste with which it was written and its brevity are partly responsible for its lack of arrangement, and for its frequent expression almost dogmatically of private opinion, where careful argument would be more in place. It offends against my rule to avoid controversial matters; and, instead of endeavouring to probe to the causes of causes, as a student's work should, it is concerned mainly with proximate causes and their effects. I elected, therefore, to remain silent on the fiscal issue until I could incorporate what I had to say about it in a more careful and fuller discussion; and I am now engaged on that task. But it proceeds slowly; and time flies.

Marshall's growing inhibitions are exposed in these sentences.

[1] He had many devoted Indian (and also Japanese) pupils.
[2] They were stolen by a local post-mistress in the Tyrol for the sake of the stamps on the envelope.

The difficulties of bringing him to the point of delivering up his mind's possessions were getting almost insuperable. In 1908 he resigned his Professorship, in the hope that release from the heavy duties of lecturing and teaching might expedite matters.

VIII

During his twenty-three years as Professor, Marshall took part in three important movements, which deserve separate mention —the foundation of the British Economic Association (now the Royal Economic Society), the Women's Degrees Controversy at Cambridge, and the establishment of the Cambridge Economics Tripos.

(1) The circular letter entitled "Proposal to Form an English Economic Association," which was the first public step towards the establishment of the Royal Economic Society, was issued on Oct. 24, 1890, over the sole signature of Alfred Marshall, though, of course, with the co-operation of others[1]. It invited all lecturers on Economics in any University or public College in the United Kingdom, the members of the Councils of the London, Dublin and Manchester Statistical Societies, and the members of the London Political Economy Club, together with a few other persons, including members of the Committee of Section F of the British Association, to attend a private meeting at University College, London, on Nov. 20, 1890, under the Chairmanship of Lord Goschen, the Chancellor of the Exchequer, "to discuss proposals for the foundation of an Economic Society or Association, and, in conjunction therewith, of an Economic journal." This initial circular letter lays down the general lines which the Society has actually pursued during the thirty-four years of its existence[2].

[1] Marshall signed, I think, primarily in his capacity as President of the Economics Section of the British Association for 1890, at that year's meeting of which the need for the establishment of an Economic journal had been strongly urged.

[2] The chief difference of opinion, discovered at the outset, regarding the Society's scope, was indicated as follows: "Almost the only question on which a difference of opinion has so far shown itself is whether or not the Association should be open to all those who are sufficiently interested in Economics to be willing to subscribe to its funds.... There are some who think that the general lines to be followed should be those of an English 'learned Society,' while others would prefer those of the American Economic Association, which holds meetings only at rare intervals, and the membership of which does not profess to confer any sort of diploma." At the meeting a resolution was carried

(2) The controversy about admitting women to degrees, which tore Cambridge in two in 1896, found Marshall in the camp which was opposed to the women's claims. He had been in closest touch with Newnham since its foundation, through his wife and through the Sidgwicks. When he went to Bristol, he had been, in his own words, "attracted thither chiefly by the fact that it was the first College in England to open its doors freely to women." A considerable proportion of his pupils had been women. In his first printed essay (on "The Future of the Working Classes," in 1873), the opening passage is an eloquent claim, in sympathy with Mill, for the emancipation of women. All Mill's instances "tend to show," he says in that paper, "how our progress could be accelerated if we would unwrap the swaddling-clothes in which artificial customs have enfolded woman's mind and would give her free scope womanfully to discharge her duties to the world." Marshall's attitude, therefore, was a sad blow to his own little circle, and, being exploited by the other side, it played some part in the overwhelming defeat which the reformers eventually suffered. For his taking this course Marshall's intellect could find excellent reasons. Indeed the lengthy fly-sheet, which he circulated to members of the Senate, presents, in temperate and courteous terms, a brilliant and perhaps convincing case against the complete assimilation of women's education to that of men. Nevertheless, a congenital bias, which by a man's fifty-fourth year of life has gathered secret strength, may have played a bigger part in the conclusion than the obedient intellect.

(3) Lastly there are Marshall's services in the foundation of the Cambridge School of Economics.

When Marshall came back to Cambridge in 1885, papers on Political Economy were included both in the Moral Sciences Tripos and in the History Tripos[1]. The separate foundation of these two schools some twenty years earlier had worked a great

---

unanimously, proposed by Mr Courtney and supported by Professor Sidgwick and Professor Edgeworth, "that any person who desires to further the aims of the Association, and is approved by the Council, be admitted to membership." The wording of our constitution shows some traces of compromise between the two ideas, but in practice the precedent of the American Economic Association has always been followed.

[1] At Marshall's lectures in the later 'eighties, apart from students from other departments and B.A.'s who might be attracted out of curiosity about the subject, there would be a dozen or less Moral Science students and two dozen or less History students.

revolution in liberalising the studies of the University[1]. But, almost as soon as he was Professor, Marshall felt strongly that the time had come for a further step forward; and he particularly disliked the implication of the existing curriculum, that Economics was the sort of subject which could be satisfactorily undertaken as a subsidiary study. Immediately that he was back in Cambridge in 1885 he was in rebellion against the idea that his lectures must be adapted to the requirements of an examination of which Economics formed but a part[2]. His Inaugural Lecture constituted, in effect, a demand that Economics should have a new status; and it was so interpreted by Sidgwick. The following declaration from that lecture is of some historical importance as almost the first blow in the struggle for the independent status which Economics has now won almost everywhere:

There is wanted wider and more scientific knowledge of facts: an organon stronger and more complete, more able to analyse and help in the solution of the economic problems of the age. To develop and apply the organon rightly is our most urgent need; and this requires all the faculties of a trained scientific mind. Eloquence and erudition have been lavishly spent in the service of Economics. They are good in their way; but what is most wanted now is the power of keeping the head cool and clear in tracing and analysing the combined action of many combined causes. Exceptional genius being left out of account, this power is rarely found save amongst those who have gone through a severe course of work in the more advanced sciences. Cambridge has more such men than any other University in the world. But, alas! few of them turn to the task. Partly this is because the only curriculum in which Economics has a very important part to play is that of the Moral Sciences Tripos. And many of those who are fitted for the highest and hardest economic work are not attracted by the metaphysical studies that lie at the threshold of that Tripos.

This claim of Marshall's corresponded to the conception of the subject which dominated his own work. Marshall was the first great economist *pur sang* that there ever was; the first who

---

[1] Marshall summarised the history of the matter as follows in his *Plea for the Creation of a Curriculum in Economics* (1902):—"In foreign countries economics has always been closely associated with history or law, or political science, or some combination of these studies. The first (Cambridge) Moral Sciences Examination (1851–1860) included ethics, law, history, and economics; but not mental science or logic. In 1860, however, philosophy and logic were introduced and associated with ethics; while history and political philosophy, jurisprudence and political economy formed an alternative group. In 1867 provision was made elsewhere for law and history; and mental science and logic have since then struck the keynote of the Moral Sciences Tripos."

[2] For his contentions with Sidgwick about this (and for a characteristic specimen of Sidgwick's delightful and half-humorous reaction to criticism) see *Henry Sidgwick: a Memoir*, p. 394.

devoted his life to building up the subject as a separate science, standing on its own foundations, with as high standards of scientific accuracy as the physical or the biological sciences. It was Marshall who finally saw to it that "never again will a Mrs Trimmer, a Mrs Marcet, or a Miss Martineau earn a goodly reputation by throwing economic principles into the form of a catechism or of simple tales, by aid of which any intelligent governess might make clear to the children nestling around her where lies economic truth[1]." But—much more than this—after his time Economics could never be again one of a number of subjects which a Moral Philosopher would take in his stride, one Moral Science out of several, as Mill, Jevons, and Sidgwick took it. He was the first to take up this professional, scientific attitude to the subject, as something above and outside current controversy, as far from politics as physiology from the general practitioner.

As time went on, Political Economy came to occupy, in Part II of the Moral Sciences Tripos, a position nearer to Marshall's ideal. But he was not satisfied until, in 1903, his victory was complete by the establishment of a separate School and Tripos in Economics and associated branches of Political Science[2].

Thus in a formal sense Marshall was Founder of the Cambridge School of Economics. Far more so was he its Founder in those informal relations with many generations of pupils, which played so great a part in his life's work and in determining the course of their lives' work.

To his colleagues Marshall might sometimes seem tiresome and obstinate; to the outside world he might appear pontifical or unpractical; but to his pupils he was, and remained, a true sage and master, outside criticism, one who was their father in the spirit and who gave them such inspiration and comfort as they drew from no other source. Those eccentricities and individual ways, which might stand between him and the world, became, for them, part of what they loved. They built up sagas round him (of which Professor Fay is, perhaps, the chief reposi-

---

[1] From his article "The Old Generation of Economists and the New," *Quarterly Journal of Economics*, Jan. 1897.

[2] Sidgwick had been finally converted to the idea in 1900, shortly before his death. Marshall's ideals of economic education are set forth in his "Plea for the Creation of a Curriculum in Economics" and his "Introduction to the Tripos in Economics...."

tory), and were not content unless he were, without concession, his own unique self. The youth are not satisfied, unless their Socrates is a little odd.

It is difficult to describe on paper the effect he produced or his way of doing it. The pupil would come away with an extra-ordinary feeling that he was embarked on the most interesting and important voyage in the world. He would walk back along the Madingley Road, labouring under more books, which had been taken from the shelves for him as the interview went on, than he could well carry, convinced that here was a subject worthy of his life's study. Marshall's double nature, coming out informally and spontaneously, filled the pupil seated by him with a double illumination. The young man was presented with a standard of intellectual integrity, and with it a disinterestedness of purpose, which satisfied him intellectually and morally at the same time. The subject itself had seemed to grow under the hands of master and pupil, as they had talked. There were endless possibilities, not out of reach. "Everything was friendly and informal," Mr Sanger has written of these occasions (*Nation*, July 19, 1924),

there was no pretence that economic science was a settled affair—like grammar or algebra—which had to be learnt, not criticised; it was treated as a subject in the course of development. When once Alfred Marshall gave a copy of his famous book to a pupil, inscribed "To ——, in the hope that in due course he will render this treatise obsolete," this was not a piece of mock modesty, but an insistence on his belief that economics was a growing science, that as yet nothing was to be considered as final.

It must not be supposed that Marshall was undiscriminating towards his pupils. He was highly critical and even sharp-tongued. He managed to be encouraging, whilst at the same time very much the reverse of flattering. Pupils, in after life, would send him their books with much trepidation as to what he would say or think. The following anecdote of his insight and quick observation when lecturing is told by Dr Clapham: "You have two very interesting men from your College at my lectures," he said to a College Tutor. "When I come to a very stiff bit, A. B. says to himself, 'This is too hard for me: I won't try to grasp it.' C. D. tries to grasp it but fails,"—Marshall's voice running off on to a high note and his face breaking up into

IN THE TYROL, 1909

1913

his smile. It was an exact estimate of the two men's intelligences and tempers.

It is through his pupils, even more than his writings, that Marshall is the father of Economic Science as it exists in England to-day. So long ago as 1888, Professor Foxwell was able to write: "Half the economic chairs in the United Kingdom are occupied by his pupils, and the share taken by them in general economic instruction in England is even larger than this[1]." To-day through pupils and the pupils of pupils his dominion is almost complete. More than most men he could, when the time came for him to go away, repeat his *Nunc Dimittis*, on a comparison of his achievement with the aim he had set himself in the concluding sentence of his Inaugural Lecture in 1885:

> It will be my most cherished ambition, my highest endeavour, to do what with my poor ability and my limited strength I may, to increase the numbers of those whom Cambridge, the great mother of strong men, sends out into the world with cool heads but warm hearts, willing to give some at least of their best powers to grappling with the social suffering around them; resolved not to rest content till they have done what in them lies to discover how far it is possible to open up to all the material means of a refined and noble life.

IX

Marshall retired from the Chair of Political Economy at Cambridge in 1908, aged sixty-six. He belonged to the period of small salaries and no pensions. Nevertheless he had managed out of his professorial stipend (of £700, including his fellowship), which he never augmented either by examining or by journalism, whilst all his many services to the State were, of course, entirely unpaid, to maintain at his own expense a small lending library for undergraduates, to found a triennial Essay Prize of the value of £60[2] for the encouragement of original research, and privately to pay stipends of £100 a year to two, or sometimes three, young lecturers for whom the University made no provision and who could not have remained otherwise on the teaching staff of the School of Economics. At the same time, with the aid of receipts from the

---

[1] "The Economic Movement in England," *Quarterly Journal of Economics*, vol. II, p. 92.

[2] In 1913 he transferred to the University a sufficient capital sum to provide an equivalent income in perpetuity.

sales of his books[1], he had saved just sufficient to make retirement financially possible. As it turned out, the receipts from his books became, after the publication of *Industry and Trade*, so considerable that, at the end of his life, he was better off than he had ever been; and he used to say, when Macmillan's annual cheque arrived, that he hardly knew what to do with the money. He has left his Economic library to the University of Cambridge, and most of his estate and any future receipts from his copyrights are also to fall ultimately to the University for the encouragement of the study of Economics.

Freed from the labour of lecturing and from the responsibility for pupils[2], he was now able to spend what time and strength were left him in a final effort to gather in the harvest of his prime. Eighteen years had passed since the publication of the *Principles*, and masses of material had accumulated for consolidation and compression into books. He had frequently changed his plans about the scope and content of his later volumes, and the amount of material to be handled exceeded his powers of co-ordination. In the preface to the fifth edition of the *Principles* (1907) he explains that in 1895 he had decided to arrange his material in three volumes: I. *Modern Conditions of Industry and Trade*; II. *Credit and Employment*; III. *The Economic Functions of Government*. By 1907 four volumes were becoming necessary. So he decided to concentrate upon two of them, namely: I. *National Industry and Trade;* and II. *Money Credit and Employment*. This was the final plan, except that, as time went on, *Employment* was squeezed out of the second of these volumes in favour of International Trade or *Commerce*. Even so, twelve more years passed by, before, in his seventy-seventh year, *Industry and Trade* was published.

During this period the interruptions to the main matter in hand were inconsiderable. He wrote occasional letters to *The Times*—on Mr Lloyd George's Budget (1909), in controversy with Professor Karl Pearson on "Alcoholism and Efficiency"

---

[1] He always insisted on charging a lower price for his books than was usual for works of a similar size and character. He was a reckless proof-corrector, and he kept matter in type for years before publication. Some portions of *Industry and Trade*, which he had by him in proof for fifteen years before publication, are said to constitute a "record." He never regarded books as income-producing objects, except by accident.

[2] He still continued, up to the time of the war, to see students in the afternoons— though perhaps former pupils (by that time young dons) more than new-comers.

(1910), on "A Fight to a Finish" and "Civilians in Warfare" on the outbreak of war (1914), and on Premium Bonds (1919). He wrote to *The Economist* in 1916 urging increased taxation to defray the expenses of the war; and in 1917 he contributed a chapter on "National Taxation after the War" to *After-War Problems*, a volume edited by Mr W. H. Dawson.

Marshall's letters to *The Times* on the outbreak of war are of some interest. When he was asked, before war was actually declared, to sign a statement that we ought not to go to war because we had no interest in the coming struggle, he replied: "I think the question of peace or war must turn on national duty as much as on our interest. I hold that we ought to mobilise instantly, and announce that we shall declare war if the Germans invade Belgium; and everybody knows they will." For many years he had taken seriously Pan-Germanic ambitions; and he headed his letter "A Fight to a Finish." Thus he took up a definitely anti-pacifist attitude, and did not fluctuate from this as time went on. But he was much opposed to the inflaming of national passions. He remembered that he had "known and loved Germany," and that they were "a people exceptionally conscientious and upright[1]." He held, therefore, that "it is our interest as well as our duty to respect them and make clear that we desire their friendship, but yet to fight them with all our might." And he expressed "an anxiety lest popular lectures should inflame passions which will do little or nothing towards securing victory, but may very greatly increase the slaughter on both sides, which must be paid as the price of resisting Germany's aggressive tendencies." These sentiments brought down on him the wrath of the more savage patriots.

At last, in 1919, *Industry and Trade* appeared, a great effort of will and determination on the part of one who had long passed the age when most men rest from their labours.

It is altogether a different sort of book from the *Principles*. The most part of it is descriptive. A full third is historical and summarises the results of his long labours in that field. The

---

[1] "Those," he wrote to *The Times* on August 20, 1914, "who know and love Germany, even while revolted at the hectoring militarism which is more common than here, should insist that we have no cause to scorn them, though we have good cause to fight them....As a people I believe them to be exceptionally conscientious and upright, sensitive to the calls of duty, tender in their family affections, true and trusty in friendship. Therefore they are strong and to be feared, but not to be vilified."

co-ordination of the parts into a single volume is rather artificial. The difficulties of such co-ordination, which had beset him for so many years, are not really overcome. The book is not so much a structural unity, as an opportunity for bringing together a number of partly related matters about which Marshall had something of value to say to the world. This is particularly the case with its sixteen Appendices, which are his device for bringing to birth a number of individual monographs or articles. Several of these had been written a great number of years before the book was issued. They were quite well suited to separate publication, and it must be judged a fault in him that they were hoarded as they were.

The three books into which the volume is divided would, like the Appendices, have suffered very little if they had been published separately. Book I, entitled *Some Origins of Present Problems of Industry and Trade*, is a history of the claims to industrial leadership of England, France, Germany and the United States mainly during the second half of the nineteenth century. Book II, on *Dominant Tendencies of Business Organisation*, whilst not definitely historical, is also in the main an account of the evolution of the forms of Business Organisation during the second half of the nineteenth century. Book I is an account of the economic evolution of that period considered nationally; Book II is an account of it considered technically. Book III, on *Monopolistic Tendencies: their Relations to Public Well-being*, deals in more detail with the special problems which arose in regard to Transport and to Trusts, Cartels and Combinations during the same period.

Thus such unity as the book possesses derives from its being an account of the forms of individualistic capitalism as this had established itself in Western Europe at about the year 1900, of how they came to pass, and of how far they served the public interest. The volume as a whole also illustrates what Marshall was always concerned to emphasise, namely the transitory and changing character of the forms of business organisation and of the shapes in which economic activities embody themselves. He calls particular attention to the precarious and impermanent nature of the foundations on which England's industrial leadership had been built up.

The chief value of the book lies, however, in something less definite and more diffused than its central themes. It represents the fruits of Marshall's learning and ripe wisdom on a host of different matters. The book is a mine rather than a railway—like the *Principles*, a thing to quarry in and search for buried treasure. Like the *Principles*, again, it appears to be an easy book; yet it is more likely, I believe, to be useful to one who knows something already than to a beginner. It contains the suggestions, the starting points for many investigations. There is no better book for suggesting lines of original inquiry to a reader so disposed. But for the ignorant the broad generalisations of the book are too quiet, smooth, urbane, undogmatic, to catch him.

Industry and Trade was a remarkable success with the public. A second edition was called for immediately, and, by the end of 1923, 11,000 copies had been printed. The fact that it was reaching wide circles of readers and met with no damaging criticisms was a cause of great encouragement and consolation to the aged author, who could feel that, after all, he had not been prevented by time, the enemy, from delivering his words to the world.

But, all the same, time's wingèd chariot was hurrying near. "Old age," as he wrote in the Preface to *Industry and Trade*, "indicates that my time for thought and speech is nearly ended." The composition of great Treatises is not, like that of great pictures, a work which can be continued into extreme old age. Much of his complete scheme of ordered knowledge would never be delivered. Yet his determination and his courage proved just equal to the publication of one more volume.

His powers of concentration and of memory were now beginning to fail somewhat rapidly. More and more he had to live for the book alone and to save for that every scrap of his strength. Talk with visitors tired him too much and interfered too seriously with his power of work. More and more Mrs Marshall had to keep them away from him, and he lived alone with her, struggling with Time. He would rest much, listening to his favourite melodies on the auto-piano, which was a great solace to him during the last ten years of his life, or hearing Mrs Marshall read over again a familiar novel. Each night he walked alone in the dark along the Madingley Road. On his seventy-eighth birthday he said that he did not much want a future life. When Mrs Marshall asked him whether he would not like to return to this world at intervals of (say) a hundred years, to see what was happening, he replied that he should like it from pure curiosity. "My own thoughts," he went on, "turn more and more on the millions of worlds which may have reached a high state of morality before ours became habitable, and the other millions of worlds that may have a similar development after our sun has become cool and our world uninhabitable[1]." His greatest difficulty, he said, about believing in a future life was that he did not know at what stage of existence it could begin. One could hardly believe that apes had a future life or even the early stages of tree-dwelling human beings. Then at what stage could such an immense change as a future life begin?

Weaknesses of digestion, which had troubled him all his life, increased in later years. In September 1921, in his eightieth year, he made the following notes:

Tendency of work to bring on feeling of pressure in the head, accompanied by weariness, is increasing; and it troubles me. I must work on, so far as strength permits, for about two full years (or say four years of half-time) if that is allowed to me: after that, I can say 'Nunc dimittis.' I care little for length of life for its own sake. I want only so to arrange my work as to increase my chance of saying those things which I think of chief importance.

In August 1922, soon after his eightieth birthday, *Money Credit and Commerce* was finished, and it was published in the following year, 1923. The scope of the volume differed from his design, in that it did not include "a study of the influences on the conditions of man's life and work which are exerted by the resources available for employment." But he managed to bring within the covers of a book his chief contributions to the theories of Money and of Foreign Trade. The book is mainly pieced together from earlier fragments, some of them written fifty years before, as has been recorded above, where also the nature of his main contributions to these subjects have been summarised. It shows the marks of old age in a way which *Industry and Trade* did not. But it contains a quantity of materials and ideas, and

---

[1] *Cf.* the remarkable footnote to p. 101 of *Money Credit and Commerce*.

Alfred Marshall
1920

collects together passages which are otherwise inaccessible to the student or difficult of access. "If much of it might have been written in the 'eighties of last century," Professor Edgeworth wrote of it in the *Economic Journal*, "much of it will be read in the 'eighties of this century."

"Although old age presses on me," he wrote in the Preface to *Money Credit and Commerce*, "I am not without hopes that some of the notions which I have formed as to the possibilities of social advance may yet be published." Up to his last illness, in spite of loss of memory and great feebleness of body, he struggled to piece together one more volume. It was to have been called *Progress: its Economic Conditions*. But the task was too great. In a way his faculties were still strong. In writing a short letter he was still himself. One day in his eighty-second year he said that he was going to look at Plato's *Republic*, for he would like to try and write about the kind of Republic that Plato would wish for, had he lived now. But though, as of old, he would sit and write, no advance was possible.

In these last days, with deep-set and shining eyes, wisps of white hair, and black cap on his head, he bore, more than ever, the aspect of a Sage or Prophet. At length his strength ebbed from him. But he would wake each morning, forgetful of his condition and thinking to begin his day's work as usual. On July 13, 1924, a fortnight before his eighty-second birthday, he passed away into rest.

REMINISCENCES

by PROFESSOR F. Y. EDGEWORTH

ALFRED MARSHALL first became for me a notable name when Jevons, conversing about mathematical economics, recommended as the latest contribution to that subject the now celebrated Papers on the *Pure Theory of Foreign Trade and Domestic Values*. At the same time Jevons highly praised the then recently published *Economics of Industry*. Eagerly studying these writings I discerned a new power of mathematical reasoning not only in the Papers bristling with curves and symbols, but also in certain portions of the seemingly simple textbook. With reference to such passages, writing in the year 1881, I characterized the author by a phrase which he himself afterwards acknowledged to be appropriate, "bearing under the garb of literature the armour of mathematics." The phrase might be applied to many passages in the text of the *Principles of Economics*.

Excelling in the concurrent use of pure reasoning and concrete knowledge, Marshall was very sensible of the dangers attending the use of the first factor by itself. In many a letter he has warned me against this danger. Burke could hardly have denounced more insistently the abuse of abstract theory applied to human affairs. Marshall would, no doubt, have subscribed to Burke's dictum: "The excellence of mathematics and metaphysics is to have but one thing before you; but he forms the best judgment in all moral disquisitions who has the greatest number and variety of considerations in one view." But Marshall was also actuated by a less intrinsic reason, the fear of offending the weak brother. The application of mathematics to Political Economy appeared less respectable in the 'eighties and early 'nineties than it has since become, mainly through the example of Marshall. Jowett, for instance, as I can testify, much as he liked Marshall, disliked his mathematical apparatus. The authority of Jowett on the question of method was indeed not particularly great, for he had not realized that the use of curves and symbols does not imply the use of exact numerical calculation. But Jowett was representative of cultivated opinion. Naturally Marshall, who desired above all things to be useful, deferred to the prejudices of those whom he wished to persuade.

These characteristics—supreme skill and extreme caution in the application of abstract reasoning—may be traced in most of Marshall's writings. I refer to some of them in no methodical order, but as they recur to me associated with reminiscences of the writer. It is difficult to abstract the work of Marshall from himself.

The publication of the Paper on Foreign Trade was put off because, as Marshall himself explains, he feared that, if separated from all concrete study of actual conditions, it might seem to claim a more direct bearing on real problems than it in fact had. How exhaustive was his interim study of actual conditions was manifested to me when, *apropos* of differential tariffs in favour of the Dominions, he wrote long letters setting forth the conditions under which different kinds of grain are produced in the United States. (See below, p. 439.)

When the investigation of particular conditions has been pushed as far as possible, we may have to fall back on general presumptions afforded by common experience. That was the lesson which I gathered from a letter in which Marshall took me to task for having argued about a peculiar case of international trade put by Sidgwick after Torrens without pointing out the peculiarity of the data, and as if the conclusion had some bearing on practice. Elsewhere Marshall has written: "It is not by trained economists...that the defence of free trade is based on absolute *a priori* reasoning. On the contrary it is based on a study of details" (*Economic Journal*, Vol. XI. (1901), p. 266). I gathered, however, from the letter referred to that the argument may require common sense presumptions which, as contrasted with the study of details, might be called "a priori."

The fall of prices and the consequent agitation in favour of Bimetallism form another subject in connection with which I was brought into contact with Marshall. He was a member of the Committee appointed by the British Association in 1887 to consider measurement of changes in the value of money; on which subject it devolved on me as Secretary of the Committee to draw up certain memoranda. In criticising the draft of these documents Marshall showed his characteristic concern for the "general reader." He would prune whatever was ambitious in mathematical expression or mechanical analogy. He would have approved, I think, of Dean Swift's advice to a young preacher, to omit philosophical terms and "notions of the metaphysical or abstracted kind."

One somewhat abstract notion was suggested to me by Marshall: the definition of a stable money as one of which the unit is procured by a certain amount of effort and sacrifice. The conception was introduced by Marshall at the opening of his evidence before the Gold and Silver Commission. I recollect the sensation which his employment of this standard excited in a debating society where many Bimetallists were present. "Gold," he said, in that high-pitched voice with peculiar intonation which gave emphasis to a startling statement, "Gold has behaved very well" [in keeping level with labour, rather than commodities; money wages remaining nearly constant while prices fell]. I do not know whether he continued to attach importance to the conception. It does not recur, I think, in his latest writing about Money. If it was only an *obiter dictum*, it was one of a kind which only men like him can let drop, suggestive of deep questions. For before applying Index-numbers to secure stability in the value of money must we not know what constitutes stability? How can we aim with precision at an object the position of which within wide limits we do not discern clearly?

In 1890 appeared the *Principles of Economics*, and my letters swelled the torrent of criticisms which, as he has told us (*Economic Journal*, Vol. III. (1893)), poured in upon the author. In particular, I found difficulties in the description of Rent as "not entering into the cost of production." From a purely mathematical point of view it might seem sufficient to impose the condition that land is limited in quantity and with this reservation to put it on a par with other factors of which the amount may be increased by human action at a cost which is not infinite. But Marshall, seeking fruit as much as light, and intent on the social consequences of the nation's land being limited, and impressed with the importance of those consequences being generally recognised, stood out for the older phraseology. He made it clear, however, as he has done in the later editions of the *Principles*, that from the standpoint of the individual entrepreneur land enters into the calculation of maximum profit *pari passu* with the other factors of production. Belief in the Copernican theory is quite consistent with the retention in ordinary parlance and for practical purposes of expressions, such as "sundown," savouring of the Ptolemaic system.

I much regret not having kept the letters which I received from Marshall on this topic, as they would not only have been of scientific interest, but also would have preserved touches of his peculiar humour. There would also have been shown his great good-nature. For, sensitive as he was under adverse criticism, the controversy must have caused him much pain.

His kindness was further shown in another series of letters relating to the management of the *Economic Journal*, of which I was appointed Editor in the Autumn of 1890. New to that sort of work I wrote to Marshall asking for advice on every small difficulty which arose, until he protested that, if the correspondence was to go on at that rate, he would have to use envelopes with my address printed on them.

The second edition of the *Principles* contains additions on a topic about which I had pressed Marshall to express himself more fully, the "discounting of future pleasures." I questioned whether the formula given in the first Note of the Appendix to the first edition had any other basis than the practice of the loan market, the objective fact of interest. Marshall relegated the treatment of this topic to his notes and appendix, explaining to me that it was a question of "hedonics," not interesting to business men. He was intent on more purely economic aspects of the relation between time and value—the distinction between "long and short periods," the conception of "quasi-rent," and other principles which will be for ever associated with the name of Marshall.

Time, argued Marshall, works both for and against the manual workers in their dealing with the capitalist-employing class. On the one hand, a rise in present wages may be attended with a check to the growth of capital such that in the course of time the state of Labour may be worse than if there had not occurred the rise of wages. On the other hand, better wages tend to an improvement in the morale and physique, and therewith the efficiency, at least of the coming, if not the present, generation.

These cumulative effects of time, together with other incidents peculiar to the labour-market, when first exhibited by Marshall, seemed almost a revelation. Economists who have grown up in an intellectual atmosphere charged with ideas which he introduced can hardly appreciate the originality of Marshall's chapters on the Earnings of Labour. The impression which they produced at the time of publication is recorded in a review which I contributed to the *Academy* (July, 1890). After referring approvingly to the author's analysis of the "peculiarities" in the action of supply and demand which constitutes the labour-market, the review continues: "We recommend the economist who wishes to test this judgment to write out, before reading the last part of the *Principles of Economics*, what he himself has to say in answer to questions like the following: 'What are the peculiarities in that action of demand and supply which determines the wages of the labourer or the profits of the employer?' Then let him compare the suggestions of his own memory and meditation with our author's original and exhaustive treatment of the subject. He must be a very great, or a very small, man who in making this comparison does not recognise his superior."

Marshall's success in handling the theory of wages was largely due to his sympathy with the wage-earners. To use one of his own metaphors, his study of industrial life was not like "the exercises of a chess-player without a sigh for the knights or pawns which may be sacrificed" (Preface to L. L. Price's *Industrial Peace*). His enquiries were stimulated by an ardent desire to improve the condition of the great mass of workers (*Principles*, I. iv. 4). He could truly say, so far back as 1893, in evidence before the Royal Commission on the Aged Poor: "I have devoted myself for the last twenty-five years to the problem of poverty; and very little of my work has been devoted to any enquiry which does not bear upon that." He enjoyed an advantage which does not fall to the lot of many academic economists, that of acquaintance and friendship with leading men among the ranks of Labour. I had an opportunity of observing how much he was appreciated by and how well he "got on with" members of that class when I stayed in the same hotel as the Marshalls at Ipswich on the occasion of that Co-operative Congress (1889) at which as President he delivered a memorable address full of hope for the future of co-operative Labour. I can well believe what I have heard from the Principal of Ruskin College that work-people studying the *Principles of Economics* recognized in the author a sympathetic friend. The only other economist about whom they had the same feeling was Mill.

Marshall is indeed comparable with Mill in ardour of public spirit, and capacity of sympathizing with all classes. But there is a difference which it may be worth noticing, considering the interest which attaches to the working of great minds. The aspiration towards the removal of extreme poverty and degrading toil was no doubt felt by Mill as well as by Marshall. But Marshall did not think, as Mill seems to have thought, that the term "pleasure" was suited to represent the incentive to such aspirations (*Economic Journal*, Vol. III. p. 389). Marshall observed, what according to Tacitus is most difficult, moderation in philosophy. He had not Bentham's rabid antipathy to other people's formulae. He had a good word for T. H. Green. But his conduct, I think, was not affected by that metaphysician's dictum that the "greatest possible sum of pleasure" is "intrinsically unmeaning"..."a phrase to which no idea really corresponds." Rather, in the vein of Bentham, Marshall aimed at increasing the "sum-total of happiness" (*Lectures on Progress and Poverty*, 1883); he held that the "hurt" caused by raising £1000 by levies of £20 from each of fifty incomes of £200 is "unquestionably greater" than that caused by taking it from a single income of £10,000 (*National Taxation after the War*, 1917).

Utilitarians seeking the happiness of great numbers are apt to miss their mark by aiming at too low an average of welfare: consulting the tastes of the many as they are, not as they may become—*panem et Circenses*, comfort and cinemas, rather than more liberal pleasures. But Marshall valued improvement in physical surroundings chiefly as rendering it possible for the many to lead a noble life. In the good time to which he looked forward manual labourers would enjoy the status of the liberal professions, respected and self-respecting though performing unpleasant tasks, as now officers and surgeons have to do. "Is it necessary that large numbers of people should be exclusively occupied with work that has no elevating character?" is one of the questions which, he tells us, the economist should have in view. He himself would no doubt answer the question in the negative.

In Marshall's ideal State family life would play a leading part. The central figure would be the wife and mother practising pristine domestic virtues. But her interests were not to be confined to the family circle. At the opening of his remarkable discourse on the future of the working classes 1873—comparable with Mill's chapter on that subject—Marshall asks "Whether the quick insight of woman may not be trained so as to give material assistance to man in ordering public as well as private affairs." Nothing that I have heard him say or have read in his writings leads me to believe that he answered this question in the negative. He had in his own home a proof that all the virtues and graces of domestic life could be combined with ability to assist in the preparation of the greatest modern treatise on the economic interests of men.

Concern for the practice of family duties was the ground of Marshall's opposition to the granting of degrees to women (1896). Without offering an opinion on this issue, I may point out that his arguments were deduced from principles which with general approbation he applied to another issue, that which is raised by Socialism. Again and again he has expressed sympathy with the generous aspirations of the Socialists, while declining to follow them far on untried abrupt paths. In a similar spirit he urges the Cambridge Senate to begin with half measures, to wait for experience before taking a step of doubtful policy but great magnitude.

It was not only in the matter of education that Marshall deprecated the identical treatment of men and women. In the most intimate of the talks which I have had with him he expressed himself as opposed to current ideas which made for shaping the lives of men and women on the same model. In this connection he expressed strong dissent from some of Mill's utterances. The tenor of his objections was similar to Leslie Stephen's criticisms of Mill's view on the "rights of women," Mill's treatment of sex as an "accident" (*English Utilitarians*, Vol. III.). Some loss of individual liberty, Marshall thought, should be risked for the sake of preserving the family. He regarded the family as a cathedral, something more sacred than the component

parts. If I might complete the metaphor in my own words so
as to convey the impression which I received: whereas the
structure as it stands is not perfectly symmetrical, the attempt
to make it so might result in pulling it down.

But I hesitate to report Marshall's opinions in words other
than his own. Everyone who has studied his writings, and
especially those rare passages in which, referring to criticisms,
he has explained his meaning, must be aware how exactly his
words were fitted to his thoughts, how unwilling he was that
other words should be substituted. Just as a misquotation of
good poetry is always less elegant than the original, so a variation
of Marshall's diction will generally incur some loss of accuracy.
So I abandon the attempt to reproduce his sayings. I can only
describe them in words which Sidgwick used about a lost friend:
"I never knew any one more free from what Goethe calls 'was
uns alle bändigt das Gemeine.' After conversing with him I
always felt that the great realities of Life...the true concerns of
the human spirit, became more real and fresh and vivid to me."

REMINISCENCES

by PROFESSOR C. R. FAY

ON the day of the Freshmen's Sports (1902) I was asked to lunch with Professor Marshall. We had chicken and bacon, fancy pudding and ginger. There were present two Indians, one large-boned lady, one ferrety-eyed undergraduate and myself. I only remember that everything I said (which was little) meant several other things, and that Marshall sat on a little stool by the fire-side. I was too late for the 100 yards, the only race for which I had any chance.

I went to one or two of his lectures in my 2nd year—as a result of the first I bought a large fiscal blue book. At the second Marshall arrived with his umbrella, the fiscal blue book and a copy of *The Times*, the two last in a bag which he kept by the side of the desk. "I make it a rule never to talk politics," he began, "but this last speech of Mr Joseph Chamberlain is... really..." and for the rest of the hour we listened to an apology for Free Trade.

It was only after I took my degree that I got to know him. Pigou told me I ought to go and see him about a subject for a Fellowship Dissertation. So one October afternoon towards twilight I went to Balliol Croft. "Come in—come in" he said, running in from a little passage: and I went with him upstairs. "Have you any idea what to do?" he asked me. I said "No." "Well then, listen," he said, producing a small black book. He proceeded to read out a list of subjects, having previously ordered me to hold up my hand when he came to one that I liked. In my nervousness I tried to close with the first subject, but Marshall took no notice and read on. About half-way through the second page he arrived at "The recent German Financial Crisis." Having been to Greifswald for a summer I signalled acquiescence. "It wouldn't suit you at all," he said. I kept quiet for another five minutes, and, catching the word "Argentine," made another noise, which stopped him. My only reason was that two of my uncles had been in business there. "Have you ever been there yourself?" he asked. "No" I replied, and he went on. A few moments later he stopped and said, "Have you found a subject you like?" "I don't know," I began. "No one ever does," he said, "but that's my method. Now, what would you like to do?" I gasped out "a comparison of German and English labour." Upon which (for it was now quite dark) he produced a little lantern with an electric button and began prowling around the shelves, handing out books English and German—von Nostitz, Kuhlmann, about thirty in all. "Now," he said, "I'll leave you to smell; when you've finished, blow down the tube and Sarah will bring you some tea." In response to a blow, the tea came in on a low trolley and I ate and drank alone. I went away too late for Hall, staggering under an armload of books, and next day came back with a bag for the balance. I had them nearly three years.

Gradually I arrived at my subject—Co-operation. I was under a bond with him to write down on a separate page in my note book the proposed title, altering it each week till it fitted my ambition. At last it became "Co-operation at Home and Abroad, an analysis and description." It was while I was doing my thesis that he asked me to lecture on Economic History for the new Economics Tripos. At a time when there were no College or University posts in Economics, he paid three of us £100 a year out of his own pocket. It was the first money I ever earned. He prepaid me with a note saying, "Please do not acknowledge receipt." He supplied all the books, which I was to take away in a cab. He telephoned for a four-wheeler, ran out down his drive when it appeared, and escorted me on my several journeys from the door step to the road, dancing his little lamp into the shadows. As I left, Mrs Marshall returned on her bicycle and he cried, "Mr Fay is going away in a cab." The Jehu started up and I saw out of the window the little lantern shining perilously near the back wheel. "Goodbye—goodbye."

I was a B.A. when I attended his last course of lectures. He pretended that he was nervous of so learned a man as myself!! The lectures were on "Trade and Industry." I remember most distinctly one on Venetian glass, after which we had a correspondence on the demerits of modern glass by comparison with the exhibits of old work at Murano. After one of these lectures I put my foot in it. He had been explaining the constructive services rendered to the Cartels by Austrian Jews. Filing past his desk at 1.10 p.m. I said "I think you were very lenient to the Jews." For I was just returned from Neuwied on the Rhine, the headquarters of the Raiffeisen village banks, which had rescued the peasants from usury, and I began to talk about the Jewish cattle traders. "Hush" he said and walked out of the Literary Lecture Rooms with me. I reached for my bicycle inside the chains and began again. "Not a word" said he, "come with me." So leaving my bicycle against the Porter's Lodge I walked through St John's over the Bridge of Sighs and into the Wilderness. "Now we can talk," he said; "there was a Jewess in the front row; you might have ruined the Tripos!"

In the May term of that year I went to tea several times. Once I arrived when he and Mrs Marshall were playing Italian Bowls, which consisted in striking a croquet ball across the uneven lawn at a white jack. He attacked his task on the principle of a curve, steering his ball gently up the hill, so that it should trickle down again into position. I aimed straight and forcefully across the lawn, with the result that I hit the jack and drove it into the bank. This impressed him very much, for, as we adjourned to the summer house, he said "Do you know, my Tutor one term thought I would not get my first." "Were you ill?" I asked. "No" he said. "But why did he think you wouldn't?" I asked in surprise. "Sport" he replied. "But I did not know you were an athlete like Maitland," I said, "what sport was it?" and in reply, in a thin delighted voice, came the single word "Bowls."

I used to have tea with him once or twice every year, until the War. It was to me a holy pilgrimage. I am not by nature a person with any reverence for my seniors: but in his presence I was just a worshipper, and I invariably came away with that strange internal commotion which in a boy accompanies exceptional athletic success.

In 1918, when the Germans had broken our Fifth Army, I was sent home to lecture to the Staff School at Caius. I was then at the G.H.Q. Machine Gun School and we were trying to get more machine guns out of the War Office. At the instigation of my Colonel I drafted an unofficial and unlawful memorandum to present to General Smuts, an honorary Fellow of my College. I sent a

draft of it to Marshall. About 10 minutes after I arrived home
the telephone bell rang and I heard Marshall's voice saying "Have
you got a pencil? It will probably take about ten minutes."
"But can't I come round?" I said, "I can't hear very well."
"All right—all right, come at 10.30, but you must not stay long."
When I arrived he greeted me with, "I am not prepared to argue,
just write"; and he dictated a new draft of my memorandum,
which was obviously an immense improvement. "You might
have ruined your whole career by putting it that way," he said,
"what you are really trying to say is in your appendix." Incidentally he displayed a perfect mechanical knowledge of the
differences between a Vickers and a Lewis gun, on which my
tactical argument was based. "Now go," he said, "and I will
let Black Bird talk." Black Bird was a mechanical piano. So
saying he stretched himself on the floor on some cushions, and,
after pressing the button, folded his arms and rested. I gradually
withdrew.

Last year, before I came out again to Canada, my wife and
I had tea with him for the last time. He told us of the small
legacy which he devoted to his tour of America fifty years ago.
I made one short remark about the monotony of modern
industrialism, whereupon he jumped up and began to picture
the romance of modern steel. But I had broken my promise to
Mrs Marshall, for I had been with him two minutes over the
allotted ten. So I rose to go, but he anticipated us and slipped
out into the garden.

I tell these stories because those who know him only by his
books will find it hard to understand his intense humanity and
the affection he gave and inspired. I am a fool at mathematics;
and on the one occasion when we talked about it, he, the great
mathematical economist, declared with impatience that this part
of economics was now-a-days much overdone. The tonic has
lasted me from that day to this.

REMINISCENCES

by E. A. BENIANS

I ATTENDED Marshall's lectures in the academical year 1900–1901. He used to lecture a great deal at that time—an elementary course twice a week for three terms and an advanced course three times a week for one term. In later years he lectured substantially less. The fame of Marshall drew a large throng, which was evidently not what he desired. Amongst the first sentences in his opening lecture I remember: "If you have come to me for the knowledge with which to pass the Tripos, you will certainly fail. I know more than you and I shall defeat you. You had better go elsewhere." This won all hearts. But the first lectures were a sifting process, and we soon settled down to the term's work with about half the original number. Marshall's style was not popular and he was at his best with a small class. He did not impart information, but sought to awaken understanding. One gave up note-taking in despair. From seventy lectures or more I brought away about as many pages of notes as one might gather from half-a-dozen of a more ordinary type. I doubt if the originality of Marshall's ideas could ever be vindicated, as that of Adam Smith's has been, from a student's notes. The connection of Marshall's thought was hard to follow. There was something elusive and baffling, though always stimulating, in his style, which stirred the mind, but, except for a telling phrase or unexpected illustration, left little in the memory. His manner was easy, as of a person talking, and he seemed supremely happy in the lecture-room. Memory still recaptures the man coming into his room in the Divinity School, his head bent forward as if in thought, mounting his platform with a little fluster of manner, leaning on his desk, his hands clasped in front of him, his blue eyes lit up, now talking easily, now chuckling over some story, now questioning his class, now pausing impressively, with rapt expression, his eyes in a far corner of the room, now speaking in solemn prophetic tones of some problem of the future—the feeding of India, the prospect of England maintaining her greatness, the banishment of poverty from the world.

He had a singular power of illustration. His mind was stored with facts, though they never came out except in their subsidiary place. He dived into the remote past, or drew on recent statistics, on letters in the papers, on some play then being performed, on his own observation. He was never out of touch with life. His range of information and his habit of simple, concrete and apt illustration recalled the *Wealth of Nations*. Who would forget the malignant form of competition illustrated from the old Mathematical Tripos, or the lady who put aside her dresses till the fashions came round again, or the widow buying the name-plate, "John Smith, Dentist," at an auction, on the ground that you never knew what might happen? Humour played an important part in his lectures. He had good stories, and no one enjoyed their fun more than himself. He sometimes brought notes, though I doubt if he ever followed them; and even when he announced beforehand the topics of a lecture, he would often depart altogether from them, pursuing some new train of thought that had suddenly suggested itself to him. Occasionally he invited questions or remarks, but few people were ever bold enough to speak under Marshall's intent and expectant gaze. He was not always particular about time when the subject interested him, especially with his advanced class, and lectures which began at twelve often went on long after one, and on one occasion till after two, though it is only fair to add that on that occasion he stopped to warn us that he should need another hour. Of history, especially recent economic history, he made extensive use, though with historians he often dealt very faithfully. They repeated one another's errors from generation to generation. "When causes and events make melodramatic combinations, historians connect them—suspect the connection." He loved to contrast the supposed and the real causes of events, to lay stress on the significance of concealed or ignored facts—this unsuspected cause, this minute circumstance, this neglected coincidence, changed the course of history. Though he did not, I think, show much love of history for its own sake, his generalisations and interpretations of history were of great originality and interest, and I have since learned that he had thought at one time of writing an extensive treatise on Economic History. He generally set questions with his lectures. The answers of the elementary class he farmed out in my day, but those of the advanced class he read himself and with considerable care. The papers were returned with much writing in red ink upon them—humorous criticism, generous praise, sweeping censure. It was part of Marshall's impulsive nature that whatever came, came with a good deal of force.

He was certainly a unique teacher. He seemed to grip the mind of his hearer and force it through unaccustomed exercises, with many a violent jolt and breathless chase. He loved to puzzle and perplex you and then suddenly to dazzle you with unexpected light. "Ages of darkness and moments of vision," was one description of his lectures, I remember. But the vision was worth it, and was not to be appreciated without the preliminary bewilderment. Always to look beneath the surface was the burden of his teaching, and many arresting sentences and terse injunctions emphasised his meaning. He was particularly fond of the phrase "the one in the many, the many in the one," applied to the unity of economic phenomena. "Disregard what men deny, listen to what they affirm," he said; and, speaking of the functions of Government, "Do you mean Government all wise, all just, all powerful, or Government as it now is?" Sometimes the personal note was sounded: "I should be a Socialist if I had nothing better to do"; or things were thrown out in a challenging way: "I don't matter at all, you don't matter much, the only people who matter are those under three." Often he spoke with a laugh and a choking exuberance of utterance ending in falsetto. These mannerisms were gratifying and memorable to the undergraduate. What we brought away from Marshall's lectures was certainly not any ordered knowledge of economics, not enough, as he had predicted, for passing an examination, but perhaps an awakened interest, a little more insight, the memory of some moment of illumination and a sense of the importance of economics. Economics, we had learnt, was a difficult science, unsuited for the schoolroom; useful, but with very definite limitations to its powers; and yet with a high purpose for the furtherance of human welfare which made it worthy of a man's pursuit.

IN MEMORIAM: ALFRED MARSHALL[1]

by PROFESSOR A. C. PIGOU

To those who are, or have been, students of economics at Cambridge it will, I think, seem fitting that some public word should be said here in remembrance of Alfred Marshall. As I occupy the Chair which he made distinguished, it falls to me—little fitted as I am—to try to say that word. We have all been pupils of Marshall through his writings; some of us also—those of us who are older—through his personal teaching and inspiration. The voice is silent: the work done. In reverence and gratitude we take our leave of him.

This is not the place, nor is it yet the time, for any attempt to estimate with accuracy or fullness what Marshall accomplished for the advancement of economic science. But something in rough outline I should like to say of the way in which he approached his subject and of the general tendencies of his thought.

To anyone reading for the first time some of the more rigorous parts of his work, his papers on the pure theory of foreign and domestic trade, for example, or his evidence before the Gold and Silver Commission, it might well appear that in him we had to do with one whose approach was primarily an intellectual approach; whose interest was logical and abstract; who stood away, as it were, from the human side of social life. And, as we came to realise more and more the immense power of the intellectual apparatus that he wielded, that impression would be deepened. There was a tradition when I was an undergraduate—I do not know what foundation of truth it had—that, when a difficult mathematical treatise came his way, Marshall's method was to read the first chapter and the last chapter, and then to stand in front of the fire and evolve for himself the middle. But, though his intellectual power was very great and though it was lavished without stint in the service of economics, it was not in its aspect as an intellectual problem that economics primarily attracted him. He told me once—I cannot remember whether it was privately or in a lecture to a class—that for some

---

[1] A lecture delivered in Cambridge on Oct. 24, 1924.

two years after taking his degree his interest was centred in philosophy. He used to wander about Switzerland, carrying on his back, not, as some of us do, apparatus and food to enable us to climb high mountains, but Kant's *Critique of Pure Reason*: and, when he reached a suitable spot, he used to sit down under a rock and study that work. Concluding, as I understand, that, on the deeper metaphysical problems, mankind could never hope to know more than a very little, he turned more and more to ethics: and it was through ethics that he came to economics: because, when you have decided what things, or, if you will, what states of consciousness, are ultimately good, it becomes your duty to try and bring about these things, and, in order to bring them about, you need, above all, ability to trace the interworking of causes and effects in the economic sphere. So economics for him was a handmaid to ethics, not an end in itself, but a means to a further end: an instrument, by the perfecting of which it might be possible to better the conditions of human life. Things, organisation, technique were incidents: what mattered was the quality of man. Listen to a passage from a public lecture that he delivered so long ago as 1877:

Of course mechanical work—the work of artisans—is paid for. And there is in what is called the society of culture a habit of talking of such work as though there were necessarily something mean and sordid about it. Of course some machines are made merely for the sake of being sold: but so are a great many pictures and poems. It is better to make a wheelbarrow for the sake of money, and only for the sake of money, than it is to write a partisan poem merely to please a patron, as many poets did in earlier times: for they deliberately coined into money the best things that they possessed: while the wheelbarrow maker need not allow his inner life to be much disturbed by his making of wheelbarrows. But, if a poet or a painter or a wheelbarrow maker thinks first of doing his work well and only secondly of the money he will get for it, neither he nor his work is in any way lowered or debased by his being paid for it. If you convince a man that his work is sordid when it is not sordid, you do him a deadly injury. The belief that it is sordid will cramp him and go a long way towards making him sordid. But, if there is in his business room for vigorous and creative intellect adapting means to ends, and devising new means and new ends, and you can convince him of this, you will do him a service. All the force and the energy that is within him will be drawn out towards his work; and he will become strong by doing hard things. If there is room in his business for imagination and delicacy and grace, and you can convince him of this, you will do him a great service. If he is the right man for the work, all that is best within him will go forth towards that which is best in his trade. He will aim at excellence for the sake of excellence, he will take an artistic pride in the things that he makes and sells. I do not suppose, I do not hope, that we shall ever cease to be a nation of manufacturers and merchants, of artisans and shopkeepers: but I do hope and think that we may become a nation of artists, of men who glory in their work, because it is the best work that their heads and hands can do; because they have tried to make it satisfy their notions of fitness and adaptation to its purpose, of grace and beauty better than anything of its kind that has gone before.

In this passage you have the spirit behind his thought: and from it you can readily see what the impulse was that drove him to economics. "The study of the causes of poverty," he wrote, "is the study of the causes of the degradation of a large part of mankind." Again in a lecture given in 1883 he said:

As invention after invention has been made, hope after hope has been formed that poverty and extreme hard work would pass away—but hope after hope has been disappointed. The yarn that in old times it would have taken a man 10 years to spin is now spun in a day by the machines which one man can manage, and yet there are people who have no clothing but rags. Each pound of coal that goes into the furnace of a steam engine does as much work as the weary muscles of a man in a day; and yet even in England and in other Western countries there are workers whose physical toil is so hard that they have no strength left for the higher life of man. This state of things must appal every person who thinks; and from time immemorial protests have been raised against a state of society in which such things can be. There are two great questions which we cannot think too much about. The first is, Is it necessary that, while there is so much wealth, there should be so much want? The second is, Is there not a great fund of conscientiousness and unselfishness latent in the breasts of men, both rich and poor, which could be called out if the problems of life were set before them in the right way, and which would cause misery and poverty rapidly to diminish?

There you have again the feeling that moved his life: a vivid sense of the paradox of poverty: a strong stream of human sympathy. Behind the mass of his intellectual work, at the back of it, as the source of it was simply this.

But there is another side. Though, as he held, the end and the warrant of economic study is to help forward social improvement, eagerness for that end must not lead us to scamp the necessary means, or to advance to the attack without an adequate preparation. "Enthusiasm," another great Cambridge thinker, Henry Sidgwick, once wrote, "is often a turbid issue of smoke and sparks. Culture must refine this to a steady glow." In a like spirit Marshall himself wrote:

Enthusiasm for the ideal in faith, in hope, and in charity is the best of human possessions; and the world owes very much to those who have been thrown off their balance by it. But, on the other hand, a responsible student of social problems must accept mankind as he finds them; and must base his estimates on that which is practicable. He must nourish the ideal in his heart: but his actions, his conversation, and even his thought must be occupied mainly with the actual: he must resist every temptation to make a short cut to the ideal. For indeed a traveller in a difficult country, who makes for his ultimate goal by a straight course, is likely to waste his time and strength and perhaps to meet disaster.

So, though, for the economist, the goal of social betterment must be held ever in sight, his own especial task is not to stand in the forefront of attack, but patiently behind the lines to prepare the armament of knowledge. His contribution is not with his own hand to devise detailed practical expedients, but to provide an organisation of thought and of method that will enable practical expedients to be devised successfully: that will prevent slow-working and hidden reactions, often more important than those which are immediate and obvious, from being left out of account; that, beneath the sign, will show the thing signified; that will furnish for those whom pity drives to action the lamp of assured knowledge and the sharp sword of right analysis. And for this labour is needed: the stress of long-continued thought: the accumulation of great masses of facts. Challenged once, when he was pleading for the establishment of what is now the Economic Tripos, whether economics really afforded enough material for a course of three years, he exclaimed: "For three years; there is enough for 3000 years!"

Starting out then with the firm view that economic science is chiefly valuable, neither as an intellectual gymnastic nor even as a means of winning truth for its own sake, but as a handmaid of ethics and a servant of practice, Marshall resolutely set himself to mould his work along lines conforming to that ideal. Though a skilled mathematician, he used mathematics sparingly. He saw that excessive reliance on this instrument might lead us astray in pursuit of intellectual toys, imaginary problems not conforming to the conditions of real life: and, further, might distort our sense of proportion by causing us to neglect factors that could not easily be worked up in the mathematical machine. He emphasised the need, for example, of accompanying sets of statistical curves with written notes of non-statistical events, lest we should fall tacitly into the fallacy of regarding what is tractable to our intellectual machinery as equivalent to what is important. In the same spirit, though his main strength was undoubtedly on the analytical side, he was a tireless collector of realistic detail. He told me once that, in his early days, he had set himself to master the broad principles of all the mechanical operations performed in factories: that, after a time, when he visited a factory, he was able to guess correctly the wages that different workmen would be getting by watching them for a few moments, and that, when his guess was significantly wrong, there was always some special explanation. In the same spirit he eagerly welcomed the opportunity of serving on the Royal Commission on Labour, on which he came into close personal touch with many representative workpeople and employers of labour. What he aimed at in all this was to get, as it were, the *direct feel* of the economic world, something more intimate than can be obtained from merely reading descriptions, something that should enable one, with sure instinct, to set things in their true scale of importance, and not to put in the forefront something that is really secondary merely because it presents a curious problem for analysis. Germans, he said once, when they write, try to say everything that is true: Englishmen everything that is true *and* important. In this he was typically an Englishman. In this, perhaps I may add, he was also particularly exasperating to certain of his students. I remember, not once but many times, getting hold of some problem, and, after labouring over it with toil and pain, imagining proudly that I had made an original contribution to economic thought. I then turned to Marshall's *Principles*, and almost invariably in some obscure footnote there was half a clause, inside a parenthesis perhaps, which made it obvious that Marshall had solved this problem long ago but had not thought it worth while to write the answer down.

His conviction that the chief value of economics was as a handmaid to practice had another important effect upon Marshall's method. He endeavoured always to write in a way intelligible to men of affairs as well as to professed students of economics. To the fact that he succeeded in doing this the width, as distinct from the depth, of his influence is, no doubt, partly due. But, as I am probably addressing some who are beginning economic study, I may perhaps add here a warning from my own experience. The method of writing to which this aim of Marshall's led is apt at first to mislead. Somebody once said that his book was written as though it were one enormous platitude. I confess that, when I read it first many years ago, I thought it was just that: I thought how very much better I could have written it myself! The first time one reads the *Principles* one is very apt to think that it is all perfectly obvious. The second time one has glimpses of the fact that one does not understand it at all. If then one reads some other book on the same subject and comes back to it, one discovers at the third or fourth reading that in these platitudinous sentences difficulties are faced and solved that elsewhere are not perceived at all or are slurred over. One discovers behind the smooth sentences, which hide it like a façade, an engine of polished steel. Read, for instance, the chapter on Trade Unions at the end of the small version of the *Principles, The Economics of Industry*. A smooth platitudinous argument it seems at first: later on one discovers with a shock that the central part of it is a translation into ordinary language of a close mathematical argument, not perhaps to be grasped completely until it has been translated back again into the symbolic form in which it must first have been built up. I say this to you as a warning. When one discovers that one did not really know beforehand everything that Marshall has to say, one has taken the first step towards becoming an economist!

What I have said of Marshall's eager search for facts must not be taken to suggest that he regarded economics as a mere descriptive catalogue of the present and the past. Facts for their own sake are not the goal. "Facts," he wrote, "are the bricks on which reason builds the edifice of knowledge." Without facts we can do nothing: but with facts, until they have been passed through the mill of thought and their lessons educed from them by reason, we can still do nothing. Speaking of economic doctrine in its most fundamental aspect he wrote: "It is not a body of concrete truths, but an engine for the discovery of concrete truths." It is, if I may paraphrase his words, a machinery that we build up in our minds, a method, an organon of enquiry that can be turned on to particular problems as they arise; that in different conditions will yield different answers to similar questions; but it does not in itself consist of any body of answers or any scheme of dogma. The dominant contribution which Marshall made to science was not in the work that he himself accomplished with this instrument of thought, great and important though that was, but in what he did to build up and strengthen and enormously improve the instrument itself. In accounts of the development of the theory of value it is common to speak of Marshall as synthesising and fashioning into a coherent whole the complementary but one-sided contributions of Ricardo and Mill on the one side and of Jevons on the other. This he certainly did. But he did much more than this. He saw, among other things, as nobody had seen before him, the enormous difficulties that had to be overcome in developing an analysis of value that should take proper account of the element of time. With the conceptions associated with the words quasi-rent, representative firm, external and internal economies, consumers' surplus, elasticity of demand, he has built a structure as different from anything known before as a modern locomotive is different from Stephenson's 'Rocket.' It is in this kind of building, whether in the analysis of value generally, or of money or of foreign trade, that he is supreme. Skilled and tireless user of tools as he was, it is as a maker of tools that he, alone among English economists, stands the companion and the equal of Adam Smith and of Ricardo.

But it is not matters of this kind that concern us most to-day. Marshall's position in economic thought was unique: he was our leader, acknowledged, undisputed. But he was much more than a great thinker. He was, for all of us who knew him, a shining example of single-eyed devotion to an unselfish aim. A student in whom he saw promise would show him up some half-digested answer to a question. Marshall's comment in red ink would be as long as the student's answer. A crank would write to him describing some crack-brained panacea for all the ills of society. Marshall would spend hours of careful thought in composing an appropriate reply. You would go to him on one of his afternoons at home with some difficulty that was puzzling you. It was an instructive experience. That anything so simple as your real difficulty could possibly puzzle anybody would never occur to

him. Immediately he would perceive rank upon rank of complicated problems that had never so much as entered your head,
and pour out by the hour, enthusiastically, unrestrainedly, a
wealth of knowledge that bewildered and overwhelmed you.
You went away with your difficulty probably not even touched
upon: but with a very healthy sense of your own incompetence:
with the conviction that here was an astonishing personality:
that this man at least believed whole-heartedly that economics
was worth while: that he even believed that you, with all your
weakness and immaturity, might, if you really tried, some day
do something of service to your fellow-men. I cannot properly
make for you a picture of one of those interviews: but there
were many of them, and in many lives they stand out, I am sure,
not merely a vivid memory, but a lasting and indelible influence.

Marshall's view was that economics is a field needing the
co-operative work of many men with many different bents of
mind. He would have nothing to do with controversies between
deductive schools, inductive schools, historical schools and so on.
There was work for all, and he welcomed all. Constructive work
was what he wanted. He did not care for mere negative criticism.
Nearly everything, he said once, of a positive sort that the
great classical economists wrote, is, when properly interpreted,
right: but much of what they have written in criticism of one
another is wrong. He was generous, some would say unduly
generous, in his interpretations of earlier writers. But, whatever
we may think of that, the spirit that inspired his generosity no
one can do other than admire. All economists for him were
fellow-workers. It was not in the least amusing to discover a
blunder that somebody else had made, and to distinguish oneself
in exposing it. The truth which other people had found was the
thing that mattered, not their mistakes. Co-operation, not
rivalry, was the way to advance science. And so he endeavoured
to lead more and more men and women to the study of economics,
looking to their joint labours to forward the science and to
supersede, so soon as might be, the work alike of his contemporaries and of himself. As one means to this, he set himself to
developing economic studies at Cambridge. At first he worked
in connection with the History Tripos and the Moral Sciences
Tripos, but in 1903 he succeeded in securing the establishment

of the Economics Tripos. To the organisation of this he devoted an immense amount of thought and time, and, after he had retired from the professorship, he continued to the last to watch with anxious interest the progress of the Economics Department and the growth in the number of its students: this, not at all because the Tripos was a child of his own effort, but because he saw in the development of organised economic study a means to the advancement of economic science, which itself was a means to the betterment of social life. Joint work towards a common goal, motived by human sympathy, that was his conception of the task before those he trained to become economists, and to the forwarding of which he looked to Cambridge. When he came back here as Professor in 1885, he concluded his Inaugural Lecture with these words:

It will be my most cherished ambition, my highest endeavour, to do what with my poor ability and my limited strength I may to increase the numbers of those whom Cambridge, the great mother of strong men, sends out into the world with cool heads but warm hearts, willing to give some at least of their best powers to grappling with the social suffering around them; resolved not to rest content till they have done what in them lies to discover how far it is possible to open up to all the material means of a refined and noble life.

To his vision, the task to which he called us has in it nothing small or petty. On us tyros, who, entering into a new field, might think it easy, he, the master, imposed his own sense of its great difficulty and of the great mass of work still remaining to be done. For him the economist's calling was a high and responsible one, worthy to fill a man's life. Here is a passage that I have found among the manuscripts in which he defines the student's duty to the State.

Students of social science must fear popular approval: evil is with them when all men speak well of them. If there is any set of opinions by the advocacy of which a newspaper can increase its sale, then the student, who wishes to leave the world in general and his country in particular better than it would be if he had not been born, is bound to dwell on the limitations and defects and errors, if any, in that set of opinions: and never to advocate them unconditionally even in an *ad hoc* discussion. It is almost impossible for a student to be a true patriot and to have the reputation of being one in his own time.

That was the austere ideal in the light of which he himself worked. A student must own no allegiance to any party: he must never acquiesce in a bad argument, even though it be used in support of an end in which he believes. He is a servant of society: his service is to follow with constant mind the flying feet of truth.

I come then to my concluding word. The Master whom we all revere is dead: full of honour, full of years, his life-work done: and you to whom I speak, many of you, have less than a quarter of his age. If it were possible I should wish to stand as an interpreter of his spirit to you in your youth and to hand on some message, not unworthy of his thought and of his life. We are set together in the world for a little time. Of what lies behind and beyond we may frame guesses, we may, if we can, cherish hopes, but we *know* nothing. One thing, however, is certain for us: the lives here—the brief lives—of multitudes of our fellow-men are shadowed with sorrow and strained with want. It is open to us, if we will, to stand aside, or to hinder or to help. If we would help, there are many ways. One way is the way of thought and study and the building up of knowledge. That was the way he took. It is the way for some, but not for all, of you, and the message of his life is not only for those who follow that way. Whatever way you choose, choose it with your whole heart. Follow the star that leads you: follow without turning, whatever the toil, whatever the pain. Do not hoard your life: spend it; spend it on an aim outside yourselves, the worth of which you feel. It may be that that way you will save your life, it may be you will lose it. But, save it or lose it, you will have saved or lost it well:

> Oh young mariner, you that are watching
> The grey magician with eyes of wonder,
> This is Merlin, and he is dying,
> This is Merlin who followed the gleam.
>
> *			*			*			*			*
>
> After it: follow it: follow the gleam.

PART II

SELECTIONS FROM
ALFRED MARSHALL'S WRITINGS

I

MR JEVONS' THEORY OF POLITICAL ECONOMY[1] (1872)

THIS book claims to "call in question not a few of the favourite doctrines of economists." Its main purpose is to substitute for Mill's Theory of Value the doctrine that "value depends entirely upon utility." The rate of exchange of two commodities will, when the equilibrium has been attained, be such that the utility to each individual of the last portion of the commodity which he obtains is only just equal to that of the last portion of the other commodity which at this rate he gives in exchange for it. The utility of a commodity is in part "prospective," that is, dependent on the benefit which will at a future time accrue from its possession: and this depends partly upon the difficulty that there might be in obtaining something before that time to supply its place. Though "labour is often found to determine value," it yet does so "only in an indirect manner by varying the degree of the utility of the commodity through an increase in the supply." Bearing in mind what has been said about prospective utility, it is almost startling to find that the author regards the Ricardian theory as maintaining labour to be the origin of value in a sense inconsistent with this last position. But the language of Ricardo on this point was loose with system: and that of many of his more prominent followers differs from his only in that its looseness is not systematic. By a natural reaction, attempts have been made by a series of able men to found the theory of value exclusively upon the neglected truth.

Although the difference between the two sets of theories is of great importance, it is mainly a difference in form. We may, for instance, read far into the present book without finding any important proposition which is new in substance. But at length he definitely commits himself: at the end of his Theory of Exchange we read—

Labour affects supply, and supply affects the degree of utility which governs value, or the ratio of exchange. But it is easy to go too far in considering labour as the regulator of value; it is equally to be remembered that labour is itself of unequal value....I hold labour to be essentially

---

[1] *Academy*, April 1, 1872.

variable, so that its value must be determined by the value of the produce, not the value of the produce by that of the labour.

The confusion here implied is not merely one of words. He returns again in his concluding remarks to his attack upon the ordinary theory of the variation of wages in different employments, and says "the wages of a working man are ultimately coincident with what he produces after the deduction of rent, taxes, and the interest on capital." He does not see that, since rent, taxes, etc. are not paid in kind, we must have before us a complete theory of value in order that we may perform this subtraction. He does not speak of the amount of the wages, and the exchange value of the products as varying elements, the variations of each of which affect those of the other. He considers that value is determined absolutely and independently, and that wages are determined afterwards. He goes on:

I think that in the equation,

$$\text{Produce} = \text{profit} + \text{wages},$$

the quantity of produce is essentially variable, and that profit is the part to be first determined. If we resolve profit into wages of superintendence, insurance against risk, and interest, the first part is really wages itself; the second equalises the result in different employments; and the interest is, I believe, determined as stated in the last chapter.

The attempt, here referred to, to give an account of interest independent of any theory of wages or value, is bold and subtle. The reasoning is mathematical; but the argument may be expressed by the following example. Suppose that A and B employ the same capital in producing hats by different processes. If A's process occupies a week longer than B's, the number of hats he obtains in excess of the number obtained by B must be the interest for a week on the latter number. Thus the rate of interest is expressed as the ratio of two numbers without the aid of any theory of value—expressed, but not determined—yet in the passage quoted it is spoken of as determined. The relative productiveness of slow and rapid processes of manufacture is but one of the determining causes of the rate of interest: if any other cause made this fall, B's process would be abandoned. The rate of interest affects the duration of the remunerative processes of manufacture no less than it is affected by it. Just as the motion of every body in the solar system affects and is affected by the motion of every other, so it is with the elements of the problem of political economy. It is right and necessary to break up the problem; to neglect for the time the influence of some elements; to investigate the variations of any one element which must, *caeteris paribus*, accompany certain assumed variations in one or more others. Such investigations give results which, even as they stand, are roughly applicable to certain special cases. But this does not justify us in speaking, in general, of one element as determined by another; as, for instance, of value as determined by cost of production, or of wages as determined by value. It is difficult to remember a prominent Ricardian writer who has not attained brevity at the expense of accuracy by employing the former of these expressions. Professor Jevons' use of the latter of them will have done good service if it calls attention to the danger of such parsimony.

The main value of the book, however, does not lie in its more prominent theories, but in its original treatment of a number of minor points, its suggestive remarks and careful analyses. We continually meet with old friends in new dresses; the treatment is occasionally cumbrous, but the style is always vigorous, and there are few books on the subject which are less open to the charge of being tedious. Thus it is a familiar truth that the total utility of any commodity is not proportional to "its final degree of utility," *i.e.* the utility of that portion of it which we are only just induced to part with, or to put ourselves to the trouble of procuring, as the case may be. But Professor Jevons has made this the leading idea of the costume in which he has displayed a large number of economic facts. In estimating, for instance, the benefit of foreign trade, we must pay attention to the total utility of what we obtain by it, as much as to its final utility, which alone is indicated by the rate of exchange. His attack on Mill on this point is worth reading, though it is in parts open to criticism; and though, while Mill pleads the difficulty of the subject in excuse of his neglect of the total utility of international trade, Jevons does not overcome the difficulty. Again, the whole advantage of capital to industry— its total utility—cannot be measured by the rate of interest, which corresponds only to its final degree of utility. Again, the final degree of utility to a labourer of his wages diminishes as their amount increases, while the final degree of pain resulting from the labour, at all events after a certain time, increases as the amount becomes greater: consequently, the artisan as soon as his real wages have ceased to be barely sufficient for his support, strikes for shorter times, rather than for the further increase in wages.

Among his more interesting incidental discussions are those on the difficulties Thornton has found in the theory of value, and on the economy of muscular effort. He contributes to the definition of the terms "market," "labour," "capital," "circulating capital," but he does not keep sufficiently distinct the various connections in which each of them is employed. His lucidity serves to render darkness visible; to make us conscious of the absence of a specialised economic vocabulary, perhaps, on the whole, the severest penalty that the science has paid for its popularity. He supplies, indeed, one expression which, with a little more care, might be rendered a useful one. Capital which "consists of a suitable assortment of all kinds of food, clothing, utensils, furniture, and other articles which a community requires for its ordinary sustenance," he calls "free capital," because it "can be indifferently employed in any branch or kind of industry." The term "value," indeed, he considers as hopeless, and he expresses an intention, to which he does not adhere, of avoiding its use.

Value in exchange expresses nothing but a ratio, and the term should not be used in any other sense. To speak simply of the value of an ounce of gold is as absurd as to speak of the ratio of the number seventeen.

There does not seem to be any greater absurdity in speaking of the value of an ounce of gold, or of a cubic inch of gold, than there is in speaking of the weight of a cubic inch of gold. In each case reference is made to some unit conventionally adopted at some particular place and time. He complains that "persons are led to speak of such a nonentity as intrinsic value": but the examiner, who has asked for a definition of specific gravity, is fortunate if he has not heard of "intrinsic weight." The abuse of a term is not a sufficient cause for its rejection. We cannot afford to dispense with the phrase "the rate of wages," though Ricardo has employed it in a forced sense, which Professor Jevons himself has failed to catch.

He has done good service, moreover, in protesting against

Mill's saying:—"Happily there is nothing in the laws of value which remains for the present or any future writer to clear up; the theory of the subject is complete." It is probable that Mill intended this to be interpreted in a very narrow sense; but anyhow, it is unfortunate. As Jevons says, it would be rash to make such a statement about any science. It would be very rash to make it about the law of gravitation. Mill would probably have been more correct if he had stated that, taking into account only questions which have already occurred, there is no one side of the theory of value which does not require for its completion a greater amount of scientific investigation than has, up to the present time, been applied to the whole of political economy—that there is scarcely any question which can be asked with regard to value to which a complete answer is forthcoming. Take, for instance, a question which Professor Jevons has made prominent—What is the influence which a rise in price of hats, owing to an increased demand, has on the wages of hat-makers? Of course one element to be considered is the facilities which exist for introducing new workmen into the trade. How far, then, is this dependent on the number of parents occupied in this and other employments who have been able to give their sons an education sufficiently good to fit them to become hat-makers, but not a much better one. What is the relation between the cost of production of an average skilled labourer and his remuneration? This is but one question out of many. We know, perhaps, in what direction to look for the answers: but the point is that they are not yet formulated. And who can tell what difficulties will have to be overcome before they are formulated?

Professor Jevons has expressed almost all of his reasonings in the English language, but he has also expressed almost all of them in the mathematical. He argues at great length and with much force the applicability of mathematical method to political economy:

If there be any science which determines merely whether a thing be, or be not—whether an event will happen, or will not happen—it must be a purely logical science; but if the thing may be greater or less, or the event may happen sooner or later, nearer or farther, then quantitative motions enter, and the science must be mathematical in nature, by whatever name we call it.

He insists that mathematics have been successfully employed in physical sciences of which the data are very inexact; and that innumerable possibilities of economical statistics exist already half tabulated in the books of mercantile houses great and small. His remarks on these and some similar points are singularly good. In general, indeed, he makes but little use of mathematical methods of reasoning. And he has not even fully availed himself of the accuracy which he might have derived from the use of the language. He does not always point out what are the variables as a function of which his quantities are expressed. It is often necessary to understand independently the whole of his reasoning, in order to know whether he means his differential co-efficients to be total or partial; and in several cases he seems almost to have himself forgotten that they are total. He has expressed the fact that "the last increments in an act of exchange must be exchanged in the same ratio as the whole quantities exchanged" by the equation

$$\frac{dy}{dx} = \frac{y}{x}.$$

He does not indicate the existence of any relation between the Δy and Δx, of which he considers dy and dx to be the limits, which can constitute $\frac{dy}{dx}$ a differential co-efficient: the mathematical phrase merely confuses. Some amusement has been derived from the absurd result which is obtained by integrating the equation. But this implies a misapprehension. A point on a locus may be determined by an equation with a differential co-efficient in it. If we integrate the equation, we get, not this locus, but some other intersecting it at the point to be determined. An instance of a different kind of inaccuracy, for which his making use of mathematical language leaves him without excuse, occurs in his investigation of the influence on the rate of international exchange exerted by a tax on imports. He tacitly assumes that the government levies the tax in kind, and destroys it, or, at all events, consumes it in such a way as not to interfere with the demand there would otherwise have been in the country for it.

We owe several valuable suggestions to the many investigations in which skilled mathematicians, English and continental, have applied their favourite method to the treatment of economical problems. But all that has been important in their reasonings and results has, with scarcely an exception, been capable of being described in ordinary language: while the language of diagrams, or, as Professor Fleeming Jenkin calls it, of graphic representation, could have expressed them as tersely and as clearly as that of the mathematics. The latter method, moreover, is not well adapted for registering statistics until the laws of which they are instances have been at least approximately determined: and it is not intelligible to all readers. The book before us would be improved if the mathematics were omitted, but the diagrams retained.

COMMENT ON THE ABOVE REVIEW IN AN UNDATED MS. FOUND AMONG DR MARSHALL'S PAPERS

I looked with great excitement for Jevons' *Theory*: but he gave me no help in my difficulties and I was vexed. I have since learnt to estimate him better. His manysidedness, his power of combining statistical with analytical investigations, his ever fresh honest sparkling individuality and suggestiveness impressed me gradually; and I reverence him now as among the very greatest of economists. But even now I think that the central argument of his *Theory* stands on a lower plane than the work of Cournot and von Thünen. They handled their mathematics gracefully: he seemed like David in Saul's armour. They held a mirror up to the manifold interactions of nature's forces: and, though none could do that better than Jevons when writing on money or statistics or on practical issues, he was so encumbered by his mathematics in his central argument, that he tried to draw nature's actions out into a long queue. This was partly because the one weakness of his otherwise loyal and generous character showed itself here: he was impressed by the mischief which the almost pontifical authority of Mill exercised on young students; and he seemed perversely to twist his own doctrines so as to make them appear more inconsistent with Mill's and Ricardo's than they really were. But the genius which enabled Ricardo—it was not so with Mill—to tread his way safely through the most slippery paths of mathematical reasoning, though he had no aid from mathematical training, had made him one of my heroes; and my youthful loyalty to him boiled over when I read Jevons' *Theory*. The editor of the *Academy*, having heard that I had been working on the same lines, asked me to review the book: and, though a quarter of a century has passed, I have a vivid memory of the angry phrases which would force themselves into my draft, only to be cut out and then reappear in another form a little later on, and then to be cut out again. That article is the first of the kind I ever wrote, and is particularly crude in form. But it contains the kernel of the theory of distribution which I hold to-day: it is based in the first instance on Adam Smith, Malthus and Ricardo, and in the second on von Thünen as regards substance, and Cournot as regards the form of the thought. On many aspects of economics I have learnt more from Jevons than from any one else. But the obligations which I had to acknowledge in the Preface to my *Principles* were to Cournot and von Thünen and not to Jevons.

II

THE FUTURE OF THE WORKING CLASSES (1873)[1]

Mr Mill has given in his *Autobiography* a more detailed account than we had hitherto possessed of that aid that he derived from his wife in most of the best work he has done. This information has great value at a time at which, partly by the voice of Mr Mill himself, we are being awakened to the importance of the question whether the quick insight of woman may not be trained so as to give material assistance to man in ordering public as well as private affairs. He says—"In all that concerns the application of philosophy to the exigencies of human society I was her pupil, alike in boldness of speculation and cautiousness of practical judgment." All the instances that he gives of this tend to show how our progress would be accelerated if we would unwrap the swaddling clothes in which artificial customs have enfolded woman's mind and would give her free scope womanfully to discharge her duties to the world. But one instance strikingly illustrates that intimate connection, to which all history testifies, between the free play of the full and strong pulse of woman's thoughts and the amelioration of the working classes.

The chapter of the *Political Economy* (he says) which has had a greater influence on opinion than all the rest, that on the "Probable Future of the Labouring Classes," is entirely due to her: in the first draft of the book that chapter did not exist. She pointed out the need of such a chapter and the extreme imperfection of the book without it: she was the cause of my writing it; and the more general part of the chapter—the statement and discussion of the two opposite theories respecting the proper condition of the labouring classes—was wholly an exposition of her thoughts, often in words taken from her own lips.

Other women may have spoken much as she spoke; but, for one reason or another, their words have been almost as though they had not been. Let us be grateful that on this topic one woman has spoken not in vain.

The course of inquiry which I propose for to-night will never

[1] A Paper read at a Conversazione of the Cambridge "Reform Club," Nov. 25, 1873, and printed shortly afterwards for private circulation. It is here reproduced without amendment or alteration of any kind; though it bears marks of the over-sanguine temperament of youth. A few passages in it have been included in more recent writings, which are still in print. (Manuscript footnote about 1923.)

lie far apart from that pursued by Mr and Mrs Mill, but will seldom exactly coincide with it. I propose to sketch in rough outline a portion of the ground that must be worked over if we would rightly examine whether the amelioration of the working classes has limits beyond which it cannot pass; whether it be true that the resources of the world will not suffice for giving to more than a small portion of its inhabitants an education in youth and an occupation in after-life, similar to those which we are now wont to consider proper to gentlemen.

There are large numbers of unselfish men and women who are eager to hope, but who find themselves impelled to doubt. From time to time there reaches them some startling but well-authenticated account of working men, who have misspent their increased wages, who have shown little concern for anything higher than the pleasures of eating and drinking, or possibly those amusements which constitute the miserable creature who is called the sporting man. From time to time they meet with some instance in which servants have made use of such improvements as have already taken place in their position only to adopt a tone of captious frivolity and of almost ostentatious indifference to the interests of those whom they have undertaken to serve. Thus minds unwilling to doubt are harassed by doubts such as these: whether a large amount of hard, nay, of coarse manual work will not always have to be done much as it is done now; whether a very high degree of cultivation would not render those who have to perform this work unfit for it, and, since they cannot escape from it, unhappy in performing it; whether an attempt to extend beyond certain boundaries the mental cultivation of such workers must not be almost certain to fail, and would not, if successful, be almost a calamity; whether what we see and hear is not an indication that these dread boundaries are narrow and not far off.

The question for us to-night is, Can this doubt be resolved? The question is not whether all men will ultimately be equal— that they certainly will not—but whether progress may not go on steadily if slowly, till the official distinction between working man and gentleman has passed away; till, by occupation at least, every man is a gentleman. I hold that it may, and that it will.

Let us first make clear to ourselves what it is that is really implied by the distinction established in usage between the occupation of a gentleman and that of a working man. This usage cannot be defended etymologically, but words better for the purpose are not forthcoming. The distinction is well established, but singularly difficult of definition; and some of those accounts of it which may most readily suggest themselves must be, in explicit terms, set aside if we would free from confusion the inquiry what are the special circumstances of the working classes on the removal of which their progress depends.

Who are the working classes? Of course they are not all who work; for every man, however wealthy he may be, if he be in health and a true man, does work, and work hard. They are not all who live by selling the work of their hands, for our noblest sculptors do that. They are not all who for payment serve and obey, for officers in the army serve for payment, and most implicitly obey. They are not all who for payment perform disagreeable duties, for the surgeon is paid to perform duties most disagreeable. They are not even all those who work hard for low pay, for hard is the work and low is the pay of the highly cultured governess. Who then are they?

Is it not true that when we say a man belongs to the working classes we are thinking of the effect that his work produces on him rather than of the effect that he produces on his work? If a man's daily task tends to give culture and refinement to his character, do we not, however coarse the individual man may happen to be, say that his occupation is that of a gentleman? If a man's daily task tends to keep his character rude and coarse, do we not, however truly refined the individual man may happen to be, say that he belongs to the working classes?

It is needful to examine more closely the characteristics of those occupations which directly promote culture and refinement of character. They demand powers and activities of mind of various kinds. They demand the faculty of maintaining social intercourse with a large number of persons; they demand, in appearance at least, the kindly habit of promptly anticipating the feelings of others on minor points, of ready watchfulness to avoid each trivial word or deed that may pain or annoy. These qualities are required for success, and they are therefore prepared in youth by a careful and a long continued education. Throughout life they are fostered and improved by exercise and by contact with persons who have similar qualities and require them of their associates. A man's sympathies thus become broad because he knows much of life, and is adapted for taking interest in what he knows. He has a wide range of pleasures; each intellectual energy, each artistic perception, each fellow-feeling with men far off and near, gives him a new capacity of enjoyment, removes from him more and more the desire for coarse delights. Wealth is not indispensable; but it frequently gives its aid. It has been said that there is in the breast of every man some portion of the spirit of a flunkey. Possibly: but we do not respect a man half as much as we are wont to suppose we do, simply on account of what he *has*. We are thinking of what he *is* far more than we are aware. The qualities which win entrance into a lucrative career or success in any career are in general, to some extent, admirable. Wealth, in general, implies a liberal education in youth, and throughout life broad interests and refined associations; and it is to these effects on character that the chief attractiveness of wealth is due. Were it true that the homage paid to a wealthy man is in general direct worship of wealth, the prospects of the world would be darker than they are, and the topic to be discussed to-night would require a different treatment.

It is not, however, sufficient to remark that the occupations which we are wont to call the occupations of gentlemen elevate the character and educate the faculties, directly and indirectly, by training and by association, in hours of business and in hours of leisure. We must also remark that such occupations exclude almost entirely those lowering influences which will force themselves upon our notice when we come to examine the lot of the working classes.

We must pause to notice the intermediate class—a class whose occupations bring with them some influences that do elevate and refine, and some influences that do not. The sculptor, the products of whose chisel add to his country's fame, who lives amid material and intellectual luxuries, is distinctly a gentleman by profession. Proceeding downwards along the scale of art, we come to the highly skilled, highly paid artisan, who adorns our public buildings with their exquisite carvings; but there is another long space to be traversed before we arrive at the ordinary mason, who, with much exertion of muscle, and with but little energy of thought, rounds off a block, or makes it square, in obedience to explicit directions. At what point, then, in the scale do we first meet the working man? It is an important and a hopeful fact that we cannot say where—that the chain is absolutely continuous and unbroken. There is a tendency to regard somewhat slightingly the distinction between skilled and unskilled labour. But the fact remains that artisans whose manual labour is not heavy, who are paid chiefly for their skill and the work of their brains, are as conscious of the superiority of their lot over that of their poorer brethren as is the highest nobleman of the land. And they are right; for their lot does just offer them the opportunity of being gentlemen in spirit and in truth; and, to the great honour of the age be it said, many of them are steadily becoming gentlemen. They are steadily striving upwards; steadily aiming at a higher and more liberal preparation in youth; steadily learning to value time and leisure for themselves, learning to care more for this than for mere increase of wages and material comforts; steadily developing independence and a manly respect for themselves, and, therefore, a courteous respect for others; they are steadily accepting the private and public duties of a citizen; steadily increasing their grasp of the truth that they are men, and not producing machines. They are steadily becoming gentlemen. Steadily: we hope to be able ere long to say "steadily and rapidly"; but even now the picture is not altogether a gloomy one.

But let us turn our eyes on that darker scene which the lot of unskilled labour presents. Let us look at those vast masses of men who, after long hours of hard and unintellectual toil, are wont to return to their narrow homes with bodies exhausted and with minds dull and sluggish. That men do habitually sustain hard corporeal work for eight, ten or twelve hours a day, is a fact so familiar to us that we scarcely realize the extent to which it governs the moral and mental history of the world; we scarcely realize how subtle, all-pervading and powerful may be the effect of the work of man's body in dwarfing the growth of the man.

Some of us, perhaps, scarcely know what is meant by violent and sustained physical exertion. Others have perhaps had occasional experience of it on walking tours. We are then enlivened by fresh air and by novelty of scene, and a light book or newspaper is never more grateful to us than then. But have we ever, when thoroughly fatigued, attempted really hard study? I remember once in the Alps, after three days of exceptionally severe climbing, resolving to take a day's rest and to read a book on Philosophy. I was in good training. I was not conscious of any but physical weariness; but when the first occasion for hard thought arrived, my mind absolutely refused to move. I was immensely angry with it, but my anger was in vain. A horse when harnessed to a load too great for his strength will some-times plant his feet firmly in the ground, and back. That is just what my mind did, and I was defeated. I have found that in like cases others are in like manner defeated, though their minds be well broken in to study, even though they be students by profession. And physiologists tell us that it must be so; that by severe bodily exertion the blood is for a time impoverished; that so the brain is not nourished, and that when the brain is not vigorous the mind cannot think.

Is it, then, a wonderful thing that the leisure hours of a wearied labourer are not always seized eagerly for self-improvement? It is often a toil to him to read; how, then, can he be incited by the pleasures of study to contend against fatigue? The man born deaf knows not the pleasure of music, but he lives among those who know it, and he believes in it. But the poor labourer may live and die without ever realizing what a joy there is in knowledge, or what delight in art; he may never have conceived how glorious a thing it is to be able to think and to feel about things and with many men. Still he may not be wholly unblessed. He may pass a tranquil and restful evening in a healthy and a happy home, and so may win some of the best happiness that is granted to man. He may, but alas! if he be uneducated, he is not likely to have a very healthy home.

There is another terrible fact about exhausting work. It is that physical fatigue in its extremest forms causes physical

unrest and physical cravings that hound a man on to his un-
doing. There is overwhelming evidence that in all those occupations in which men are tempted to consume in a day's work
almost more strength than the vital forces of the body suffice
to repair, and in which work is therefore systematically irregular,
the pleasures of home cannot compete with the coarse pleasures
of the public-house. A man may seek in the public-house, as
in a club, the pleasures of social intercourse, which will well
supplement the pleasures of home, and will raise, not lower him.
He may: but if his toil has been fierce, and so his brain is
dulled, he is apt to seek there only the coarser pleasures—drink,
ignoble jests, and noise. We have all heard what rude manners
have been formed by the rough work of the miners; but even
among them the rougher the work of the body, the lower the
condition of the mind. Iron miners, for instance, are a superior
race to colliers. And if it be true that men such as these do
value high wages mainly as affording them an opportunity of
using their bodies as furnaces for the conversion of alcohol into
fumes, is it not a somewhat pitiful amusement merely to abuse
them? is it not more profitable to raise the inquiry—must these
things be?

There are some things which we have decided must *not* be.
A Parliamentary Commission reports in 1866 of the training
which the world had given to men such as these, and by which
it had formed them. It tells us how lads and maidens, not eight
years old, toiled in the brickfields under monstrous loads from
five o'clock in the morning till eight o'clock at night; their faces
haggard, their limbs misshaped by their work, their bodies
clothed with mud, and their minds saturated with filth. Yes;
but there is a thing worse than even such filth: that is despair.
We are told that "the worst feature of all is that the brickmakers
despair of themselves"; and the words of one of them are
quoted—"You might as well try to raise and improve the devil
as a brickie, sir." These things are not to be; but things nearly
as bad are now (1873); and these things have formed the men
whose words and deeds are quoted, when it is argued that the
working classes cannot rise.

Thus awful, then, is the picture of unduly sustained work
that is heavy. But can light work, however long sustained,

bring no curse? Let us look at one more picture—our sad old picture of the needle-woman:

> Work, work, work,
>   From weary chime to chime;
> Work, work, work,
>   As prisoners work for crime.
> Band and gusset and seam,
>   Seam and gusset and band,
> Till the heart is sick and the brain benumbed
>   As well as the weary hand.
>
> Work, work, work,
>   In the dull December light,
> And work, work, work
>   When the weather is warm and bright;
> While underneath the eaves
>   The brooding swallows cling,
> As if to show me their sunny backs,
>   And twit me with the spring.
>
> Oh! but to breathe the breath
>   Of the cowslip and primrose sweet—
> With the sky above my head,
>   And the grass beneath my feet!
> For only one short hour
>   To feel as I used to feel
> Before I knew the woes of want
>   And the walk that costs a meal!
>
> Oh! but for one short hour,
>   A respite, however brief!
> No blessed leisure for love or hope,
>   But only time for grief!
> A little weeping would ease my heart,
>   But in their briny bed
> My tears must stop, for every drop
>   Hinders needle and thread.

"The heart is sick and the brain benumbed. No blessed leisure for love or hope, but only time for grief." Surely we see here how work may depress, and keep low "the working classes." Man ought to work in order to live: his life, physical, moral, and mental, should be strengthened and made full by his work. But what if his inner life be almost crushed by his work? Is there not then suggested a terrible truth by the term working man, when applied to the unskilled labourer—a man whose occupation tends in a greater or less degree to make him live for little save for that work that is a burden to bear?

The ancients argued that Nature had ordained slavery: that without slaves the world could not progress; no one would have time for culture; no one could discharge the duties of a citizen. We have outgrown this belief; we have got to see how slavery dries up the sap of moral life in every state, at whose roots it is laid. But our thoughts are from youth upwards dominated by a Pagan belief not very different from the old one—the belief that it is an ordinance of Nature that multitudes of men must toil a weary toil, which may give to others the means of refinement and luxury, but which can afford to themselves scarce any opportunity of mental growth. May not the world outgrow this belief, as it has outgrown the other? It may, and it will.

We shall find it easier to see how exaggerated have been the difficulties which lie in the way of the removal of those circumstances which are distinctive of the lot of the working classes in the narrower sense of the term, if we allow ourselves a little license. Let us venture to picture to ourselves the state of a country from which such circumstances have been excluded. We shall have made much progress on our way, when we have seen that such a country would contain within it no seeds of the ruin of its material or moral prosperity; that it would be vigorous and full of healthy life.

The picture to be drawn will resemble in many respects those which have been shown to us by some socialists, who attributed to every man an unlimited capacity for those self-forgetting virtues that they found in their own breasts; who recklessly suggested means which were always insufficient and not seldom pernicious—recklessly, because their minds were untrained, and their souls absorbed in the consciousness of the grandeur of their ends. Their memories are therefore scorned by all but a very few men: but among those very few is included perhaps every single man who has ever studied patiently the wild deep poetry of their faiths. The schemes of the socialists involved a subversion of existing arrangements, according to which the work of every man is chosen by himself and the remuneration he obtains for it is decided by free competition; and their schemes have failed.

But such a subversion is not required for the country which we are to picture to ourselves. All that is required is that no one in it should have any occupation which tends to make him anything else than a gentleman.

We have seen that manual and disagreeable work is now performed for payment at competition prices by gentlemen. It is true that their work involves mental training, and that the associations by which they are surrounded are refined; but, since the brain cannot always be in full action, it is clear that, provided these associations be retained, we need not exclude from our new society even manual and disagreeable work that does not give direct training to the mental faculties. A moderate amount of such work is not inconsistent with refinement. Such work has to be done by every lady who takes part in the duties of a hospital. She sees that it is necessary, and she does not shrink from it; for, if she did, she would not be a lady. It is true that such work is not now willingly undertaken for payment by an educated man, because in general he can obtain higher pay for doing work in which the training of his mental faculties can be turned to account; and because, as his associates would be uneducated, he would incur incidental discomforts and would lose social position. But, by the very definition of the circumstances of our supposed country, such deterrent motives would not exist in it. An educated man, who took a share of such little unskilled labour as required to be done in such a country, would find that such labour was highly paid, because without high pay no one would undertake it: and as his associates would be as refined as himself and in the same position, he would have no social discomforts to undergo. We all require for the purposes of health an hour or two daily of bodily exercise, during which the mind is at rest, and, in general, a few hours more of such work would not interfere materially with our true life.

We know then pretty clearly what are the conditions under which our fancied country is to start; and we may formulate them as follows. It is to have a fair share of wealth, and not an abnormally large population. Everyone is to have in youth an education which is thorough while it lasts, and which lasts long. No one is to do in the day so much manual work as will leave him little time or little aptitude for intellectual and artistic enjoyment in the evening. Since there will be nothing tending to render the individual coarse and unrefined, there will be nothing tending to render society coarse and unrefined. Exceptional morbid growths must exist in every society; but otherwise every man will be surrounded from birth upwards by almost all the influences which we have seen to be at present characteristic of the occupations of gentlemen; everyone who is not a gentleman will have himself alone to blame for it. This, then, is the condition in which our fancied country is to be when we first consider it. We have to inquire whether this condition can be maintained. Let us examine such obstacles to its maintenance as may be supposed to exist.

First, it may be argued that a great diminution of the hours of manual labour below their present amount would prevent the industry of the country from meeting its requirements, so that the wealth of the country could not be sustained. This objection is an instance of the difficulty with which we perceive things that are familiar. We all know that the progress of science and invention has multiplied enormously the efficiency of labour within the last century. We all know that even in agriculture the returns to labour have much increased; and most of us have heard that, if farmers had that little knowledge which is even now obtainable, the whole of the produce consumed in a country as thickly populated as England is, might be grown in it with less proportionate expenditure of labour than that now required. In most other branches of production the increase in the efficiency of labour has been almost past computation. Take a cotton factory for example. We must allow for the expense of making and driving the machinery; but when this is provided, a man working it will spin more than three thousand times as rapidly as he could by hand. With numbers such as this before us, can we believe that the resources of the world would fail if the hours of our daily labour were halved, and yet believe that our simple ancestors obtained an adequate subsistence? Should we not be driven to the conclusion that the accounts we have received of men who lived and flourished before the invention of the steam engine are myths? But, further, the only labour excluded from our new society is that which is so conducted as to stunt the mental growth, preventing people from rising out of old narrow grooves of thought and feeling, from obtaining increased knowledge, higher tastes, and more comprehensive interests. Now it

is to such stunting almost alone that indolence is due. Remove
it, and work rightly applied, the vigorous exercise of faculties
would be the main aim of every man. The total work done per
head of the population would be greater than now. Less of it
would be devoted directly to the increase of material wealth,
but far more would be indirectly efficient for this end. Knowledge is power; and man would have knowledge. Inventions
would increase, and they would be readily applied. All labour
would be skilled, and there would be no premium on setting
men to tasks that required no skill. The work which man directs
the forces of nature to perform for him, would thus be incomparably greater than now. In the competition for employment
between man's muscles and the forces of nature, victory would
remain with the latter. This competition has been sustained so
long, only because the supply of mere muscular force fit only to
contend against nature has been so plentiful, and the supply of
skill fit to direct nature has been so scarce. Recollect that even
with the imperfect machinery we now have one pound of coal
will raise a hundred pounds twelve thousand feet high; and that
the daily work of a man cannot exceed this even if we work
him into the dust, and obtain, in lieu of a man's life, so much
pulling and pushing and hewing and hammering. Recollect that
with an ordinary tide the water rushing in and out of a reser-
voir of a square mile in area, even if nine-tenths of its force
were wasted through imperfections of machinery, would do as
much work in a day as the muscles of one hundred thousand men.

But, secondly, it might be argued that short hours of work
might ruin the foreign trade of the country. Such a doctrine
might derive support from the language of some of our public
men, even in recent times. But it is a fallacy. It contradicts a
proposition which no one who had thought on the subject would
dream of deliberately denying; one which is as well established
and as rigorously proved as any in Euclid. This proposition is,
that low wages, if common to all occupations, cannot enable
one country to undersell another. A high rate of wages, or short
hours of work, if common to all industries, cannot cause a
country to be undersold: though, if they were confined to some
industries, they might of course cause these particular industries
to be undersold.

A danger, however, might be incurred by high wages or short hours of work. If the rate of profits were reduced thereby, capital would be tempted to migrate. But the country we are picturing to ourselves would be specially defended against such a danger. To begin with, its labourers would be highly skilled. And the history of the progress of manufactures in England and throughout the world proves that, if the number of hours' work per day be given, the capitalist can afford to pay almost any rate of wages in order to secure highly skilled labour. But such labour, partly as a cause and partly as a consequence of its skill, has in general not very many hours in its working-day; and for every hour, during which his untiring machinery is lying idle, the capitalist suffers loss. In our society the hours of labour are to be very short, but it does not follow that the hours of work of the machinery would be short too. The obstacles that now exist to the general adoption of the system of working in "shifts" are due partly to the unenlightened selfishness of workmen, partly to their careless and dishonest maltreatment of machinery, but mainly to the fact that, with the present number of hours' work done by each shift, one shift would have to commence work very early and the other to end work very late. But in our new society none of these obstacles would exist. A man would not in general perform manual work for more than six hours a day. Thus one set would work perhaps from 6 to 9.30 a.m. and from 2 to 4.30 p.m.; the other set from 10 a.m. to 1.30 p.m. and from 5 to 7.30 p.m. In heavy work three sets of men might each work a shift of four hours. For we must not suppose that an educated man would consent for any pay whatever to continue exhausting physical work so far as to cause the stupefaction of his intellect. For his severe work he would be highly paid; and, if necessary, he might add to his income by a few hours of lighter work.

But there is another special reason why capital should not leave our fancied country. All industries might be partly conducted by capitalists with labourers working for hire under them. But in many industries production would be mainly carried on, as Mr and Mrs Mill have prophesied, by "the association of labourers among themselves on terms of equality, collectively owning the capital with which they carry on their operations, and working under managers elected and removable by themselves." It will be said that such associations have been tried, and have seldom succeeded. They have not been tried. What have been tried are associations among, comparatively speaking, uneducated men, men who are unable to follow even the financial calculations that are required for an extensive and complicated business. What have to be tried are associations among men as highly educated as are manufacturers now. Such associations could not but succeed; and the capital that belonged to them would run no risk of being separated from them.

Again, it might be objected that it would be impossible to maintain that high standard of education which we have throughout assumed. Some parents, it might be said, would neglect their duty to their children. A class of unskilled labourers might again grow up, competing for hard toil, ready to sacrifice the means of their own culture to increased wages and physical indulgences. This class would marry improvidently: an increased population would press on the means of subsistence, the difficulty of imparting a high education would increase, and society would retrograde until it had arrived at a position similar to that which it now occupies—a position in which man, to a great extent, ignores his duty of anticipating, before he marries, the requirements of the bodily and mental nurture of his children; and thereby compels Nature, with her sorrowful but stern hands, to thin out the young lives before they grow up to misery. This is the danger most to be dreaded. But even this danger is not so great as it appears. An educated man would not only have a high conception of his duty to his children; he would be deeply sensitive to the social degradation which he and they would incur if he failed in it. Society would be keenly alive to the peril to itself of such failure, and would punish it as a form of treason against the State. Education would be unfailingly maintained. Every man, before he married, would prepare for the expense of properly educating his family; since he could not, even if he would, shirk this expense. The population would, therefore, be retained within due limits. Thus every single condition would be fulfilled which was requisite for the continued and progressive prosperity of the country which we have pictured. It would grow in wealth—material and mental.

Vigorous mental faculties imply continual activity. Work, in its best sense, the healthy energetic exercise of faculties, is the aim of life, is life itself; and in this sense every one would be a worker more completely than now. But men would have ceased to carry on mere physical work to such an extent as to dull their higher energies. In the bad sense, in which work crushes a man's life, it would be regarded as a wrong. The active vigour of the people would continually increase; and in each successive generation it would be more completely true that every man was by occupation a gentleman.

Such a state of society in a country would then, if once attained, be ever maintained. Such a country would have in it the conditions of vitality more fully satisfied than any other country would. Is it not, then, a reasonable thing to believe that every movement towards the attainment of such conditions has vitality also? And, if we look around us, do we not find that we are steadily, if slowly, moving towards that attainment? All ranks of society are rising; on the whole they are better and more cultivated than their forefathers were; they are no less eager to do, and they are much more powerful greatly to bear, and greatly to forbear. Read of the ignorant crime that accompanied popular outbreaks even a generation ago, and then look at the orderly meetings by which the people now expresses its will. In the broad backbone of moral strength our people have never been wanting; but now, by the aid of education, their moral strength is gaining new life. Look at the grand conduct of the Lancashire artisans during the cotton famine. In old times of ignorance they would have struggled violently against the inevitable; but now their knowledge restrained them, and they suffered with quiet constancy. Nay, more; the Northern army was destroying the cotton on which their bread depended; yet, firm in their allegiance to the struggle against slavery, they never faltered. Listen to the reply that President Lincoln gave to the address of sympathy that they sent him: "Under the circumstances, I cannot but regard your decisive utterances upon the question as an instance of sublime Christian heroism which has not been surpassed in any age or country."

And thus it is. In every age of the world people have delighted in piquant stories, which tell of some local or partial retro-gression; but, if we look at the broad facts of history, we find progress. Of the progress of the artisans we have spoken; how all are rising; how some are, in the true sense of the word, becoming gentlemen. Some few of them may, indeed, interpret this to mean little more than becoming, at times, dandyfied perambulating machines, for the display of the cheaper triumphs of the haberdasher and the tailor. But many artisans are becoming artists, who take a proud interest in the glories of their art, are truly citizens, are courteous, gentle, thoughtful, able, and independent men. Even if we take the ruder labourers, we find something to set off against the accounts of their habits of indulging in drink and rough pastimes. Such habits were but a short time ago common among country squires. But country squires had in them the seeds of better things, and when a new age opened to them broader and higher interests, they threw off the old and narrow ones. And our colliers even are doing the same. A series of reports by well-informed, unprejudiced men proves that, on the whole, their faults have diminished and their virtues increased. And the late Parliamentary Committee has shown how a solid foundation of their further improvement has been laid in the improvement of their houses, how they are now learning to take pride in their homes and to love them.

What limits are there then to the rapidity of our progress? How are we let or hindered? History shows that on a basis of mere energy a marvellous edifice can be speedily erected. Two centuries ago England exported raw in exchange for manu-factured produce; she had no mechanical skill, and imported foreigners one after another to overcome her engineering difficulties. A century ago the agriculture of the Scotch lowlands seemed as hopelessly bad as any in Europe: now it is a model school for the world. It was mainly from the rough uncultured population of the trading cities of Italy and the Netherlands that there arose that bright glory of art which in the middle ages illumined all Europe. Why then should not the energy which our working classes have, when once turned in the right direction, lead to a progress as rapid and as brilliant?

Alas! there is one great hindrance. One of the first uses we are making of our increased knowledge is, as it ought to be, to save from disease and want multitudes who, even a few years ago, would have sunk under their influence. As a result, population is increasing rapidly. The truth that every father owes to his children the duty of providing them with a lot in life, happier and better than his own, has not yet been grasped. Men who have been brought up, to use their own phrase, "anyhow," are contented that their children should be brought up "anyhow." Thus there is kept up a constant supply of unskilled labourers, who have nothing but their hands to offer for hire, and who offer these without stint or reserve. Thus competition for food dogs the heels of progress, and perpetually hinders it. The first most difficult step is to get rid of this competition. It is difficult, but it can be made. We shall in vain tell the working man that he must raise his standard while we do not raise ours: he will laugh at us, or glare on us. But let the same measure be meted out to all. Let this one principle of action be adopted by us all—*just as a man who has borrowed money is bound to pay it back with interest, so a man is bound to give to his children an education better and more thorough than he has himself received.* This he is bound to do. We may hope that many will do more than they are bound to do.

And what is society bound to do? It is bound to see that no child grows up in ignorance, able only to be a producing machine, unable to be a man; himself low and limited in his thoughts, his tastes, his feelings, his interests and his aims, to some extent probably low and limited in his virtues, and in every way lowering and limiting his neighbours. It is bound to compel children, and to help them, to take the first step upwards; and it is bound to help them to make, if they will, many steps upwards. If the growth of a man's mind, if his spiritual cultivation be the end of life; and material wealth, houses and horses, carpets and French cookery merely means; what temporary pecuniary loss can we set against the education of the nation? It is abundantly clear that, unless we can compel children into the schools, we cannot enable multitudes of them to escape from a life of ignorance so complete that they cannot fail to be brutish and degraded. It is not denied that a school-board alone can save from this ruin those children whose parents are averse to education; that at least in our towns there are many whom no voluntary system can reach. And yet throughout the length and breadth of the country we are startled by finding that some of those, who are most anxious that the Bible should be taught, are those who are most unwilling that a State, which has with success invested capital in telegraphs, should now venture to invest capital in men; that they are those who are most ready to urge men "not to rush headlong on" a rate of some pence in the pound. I will only urge that, for consistency, such people should teach an expurgated edition of the Bible. Let every page be cut out in which it is implied that material wealth may be less important than the culture of the man himself, the nurture of his inner life. They will not have heavy work, they will not have many pages left to teach.

But in truth material welfare, as well as spiritual, will be the lot of that country which, by public and private action, devotes its full energies to raising the standard of the culture of the people. The difference between the value of the labour of the educated man and that of the uneducated is, as a rule, many times greater than the difference between the costs of their education. If the difference between the value of the work done by a good breed of horses and a bad one be much greater than the difference between the costs of maintaining them, can there be any doubt that the good breed will drive out the bad one? But no individual reaps the full gains derived from educating a child, from taking a step towards supplanting the race of uneducated labourers by a race of educated labourers. Still, if the State work for this end, the State will gain. If we all work together for this end, we shall all gain together. Then will be removed every let and hindrance to the attainment of that condition which we have pictured—a condition which, if it be hard to be attained, is easy to be maintained—a condition in which every man's energies and activities will be fully developed —a condition in which men will work not less than they do now but more; only, to use a good old phrase, most of their work will be a work of love; it will be a work which, whether conducted for payment or not, will exercise and nurture their faculties. Manual work, carried to such an excess that it leaves little opportunity for the free growth of his higher nature, that alone will be absent; but that *will* be absent. In so far as the working classes are men who have such excessive work to do, in so far will the working classes have been abolished.

III

MR MILL'S THEORY OF VALUE (1876)[1]

IT has often been noted that what a man writes in condemnation
of the opinions of another is open to all the sources of error that
affect his work when he expounds his own opinions, and to
others in addition: for he may have failed rightly to track the
thoughts which he believes himself to be criticising. When a
truth assumes great importance for a man and he sees it clearly,
he will make others see it clearly; he will be trustworthy so long
as he writes of it constructively. But, though he may be wholly
superior to the temptation so to lower the reputation of previous
writers that his own may be the more eminent, his devotion to
the truth which is dominant in his own mind will be apt not
only to render him jealous of the position of complementary
truths, but so far to pre-occupy his thoughts as to hinder him
from perceiving all that these truths have worked in the minds
of others. It is not, therefore, an unhealthy sign of the times
that a series of attacks has been made by various writers on
various sides of the central doctrine of the book by which most
living English economists have been educated; and it is not a
matter of wonder that some of these attacks have been made by
thinkers of great power. It may be possible, without detracting
from the worth of what they have contributed towards the
construction of the Theory of Value, to show that many of their
destructive criticisms are due to their not having perceived the
full power, which is latent, if not patent, in Mill's work. If this
can be effected, some energy which is now consumed in quarrels
in the economists' camp may be turned to use in the common
cause, and do good service against error. The aim of the present
article is to indicate in outline Mill's position, so as to display
its strength. I shall refer in footnotes to some criticisms on Mill
contained in a work by Professor Cairnes[2]. His already well-
earned reputation, the soundness of his judgment, the lucidity
and grace of his style, the tact and skill with which he has
brought out clearly defined results, have combined to render

---

[1] *Fortnightly Review*, April, 1876.
[2] *Some Leading Principles of Political Economy.*

that work extremely popular. Although Cairnes may be regarded as one of Mill's most distinguished disciples, yet a considerable portion of his book is devoted to a new exposition of some principles which he apparently thought had not been adequately appreciated or stated with sufficient accuracy by Mill. These points of difference between the two writers have been seized upon with avidity by an influential set of men, who, by the recent publication of Mill's *Autobiography*, had been put in a mood to regard Mill as a slighter man than they had thought him before. I believe that in most instances in which Mill's doctrines have been criticised by Cairnes, and by other writers, Mill is substantially right. I also think that Cairnes considered that the difference between himself and Mill is greater than it really is. The better class of readers used to puzzle over a difficult passage of Mill's till they got to see, more or less, its whole drift. Now such readers readily adopt Cairnes' authoritative suggestion, that it contains a blunder: they see distinctly that half of the truth which Cairnes has written out for them in a bold, clear hand; they do not trouble themselves to hunt out that more recondite half, to which Mill was, as it seems to me, working his way, but with which Cairnes has not concerned himself. There is no doubt that Cairnes was a genuinely sincere friend of Mill and truth. I am grateful for the services he has rendered to Economics: I cannot express that gratitude better than by unflinchingly pointing out cases in which he seems to me not to have got hold of the whole of Mill's meaning.

A critic of Mill's writings may not ignore the following facts. In the small leisure that was left to him free from official work, Mill wrote on a wide variety of questions which had already been discussed by great thinkers. On almost every one of these questions his thoughts, whatever faults they contained, were in some respect new. Therefore he had not much time for elaborating the explanation of his thoughts. His style was that of a man having great power of exposition; but in one respect this power injured him. For it caused men to assume that whatever error appeared in his writings was due, not to imperfect presentation of clear thought, but to perfect presentation of confused thought. They have overlooked the fact that this power could not avail him for the task of drilling a large body

of thoughts into such order that they should in all their movements present a clear front to the reader. For this task time
alone avails.

In writing his *Political Economy* he laboured under special
disadvantages. He wished to compress into it a vast amount of
matter; but his style is so easeful as to incite his readers to
overmuch rapidity. Hence it occurs that he is frequently charged
not only with omitting truths of which he has taken account,
but even with holding erroneous doctrines which he has in due
place demolished, and thereafter ignored. He did not even
consider himself at liberty to select his terms freely: he feared
to weight the science, which was not then popular, with the
burden of technical terms. Moreover he was finely jealous for
his predecessors: he gave not only to Ricardo, but, in opposition
to the current of the time, to Adam Smith whatever credit he
could. Nearly all of those phrases of his which are unfortunate
are phrases of theirs which he has been unwilling to discard.
Thus he has been induced to retain the use of some expressions
which he has affirmed to be neither sufficiently flexible nor
sufficiently firm for the proper purposes of science.

Those, then, who wish rightly to construe any of Mill's
economic doctrines must learn the special part which he intended
that doctrine to perform, to the end that they may not demand
from it the discharge of functions which he has assigned to some
other portion of his system; and they must remember that he
is not always careful to repeat an indication that he has once
given of the special application which he intends to make of a
word or a phrase in a particular discussion. They must, therefore,
consider each passage in connection with its context; and when
its interpretation cannot by this means be conclusively settled,
they must with generous caution reject any rendering of it
which is inconsistent with the general purport of his writings.
Readers who will observe these rules may find in Mill's economic
doctrines much exposition that requires to be supplemented,
and many abrupt lines of thought which require to be continued.
But they will find that it is true of his thought, as of Adam
Smith's, that much even of the work which most invites the attack
of the destructive critic is, in the main, sound as far as it goes.
This is, as it appears to me, the case with his account of value.

It was known, even before the publication of his *Autobiography*, that Mill regarded, as perhaps the chief of the services which he had rendered to economics, his work in breaking up and rearranging its chief problems; and, though experience may have shown that in some details his arrangement is not wholly successful, we are bound to take account of the important truth which the general plan of his arrangement embodies.

This plan was, in separate books, first to treat of the nature of human efforts, and the laws of the production of wealth generally; secondly, the distribution of wealth; and thirdly, to devote a book exclusively to "the machinery of exchange." His first book is mainly concerned with the causes which affect generally the efficiency of labour in production. The analysis contained here enables him, when he treats of exchange value, to dismiss this aspect of cost of production with a reference to his first book; and the curt statement, "What the production of a thing costs to its producers, or its series of producers, is the labour expended in producing it[1]." In his second book he develops Adam Smith's grand doctrine, which shows how the distribution of wealth would be effected "naturally," *i.e.* as the average result of free competition operating through many generations. This distribution would be such that the wages which a man receives would vary, according to certain laws, with the efforts and sacrifices demanded from him, conjointly with the efforts and sacrifices which his special education demanded from his parents and others; and that thus the remuneration of each task would in a manner measure the efforts it had cost to society as a whole, or rather to those members of society who, directly or indirectly, had contributed to its performance. Mill explains the artificial hindrances to this correspondence between the remuneration of various tasks and their total effort-costs. He shows how these hindrances are due not only to formal trade regulations, but also to the special difficulties against which parents in the various grades of society have to contend, if they desire to secure high wages to their sons in the future at the expense of a present sacrifice to themselves. He points out that, roughly speaking, English labour falls into four "different grades," between which

[1] Book III, chap. iv, § 1. Attention may be directed to the extensions of this analysis in Hearn's *Plutology*, and in Jevons' *Theory of Political Economy*.

"the line of demarcation has hitherto been so strongly marked as to be almost equivalent to a hereditary distinction of caste; each employment being chiefly recruited from the children of those already employed in it, or in employments of the same rank with it in social estimation, or from the children of persons who, if originally of a lower rank, have succeeded in raising themselves by their exertions[1]." These four grades are:—(i) the liberal professions; (ii) the more highly skilled manual employments; (iii) the lower classes of skilled employments; (iv) unskilled labourers. Labourers of the second grade are partly supplied from "the class of tradesmen who rank with them"; so are those of the third. "The wages of each class have been hitherto regulated by the increase of its own population." But "the general relaxation of conventional barriers, and the increased facilities which already are, and will be in a much greater degree, brought within the reach of all, tend to produce, among many excellent effects, one which is the reverse: they tend to bring down the wages of skilled labour." Mill is so far from ignoring "conventional barriers," that he regards it as his special task to insist that the "arrangements" which were due to them should be distinguished from the "natural laws" of political economy; and enforces this distinction by the arrangement of his work. In a similar strain he continues Adam Smith's account of profits[2]. And after indicating how the element of rent may in

[1] Book II, chap. xiv. Cairnes has done good service by insisting on this fact. Mill's account is complete, but too terse. Few persons have any more notion than Cairnes had that his far-famed account of the four grades of labour had been anticipated, not only in outline, but in detail by Mill.

[2] The drift of part of his argument on this point might be made clearer by building in some material from the fourth of his important, but neglected, *Essays on Unsettled Questions of Political Economy*. Though it is a digression, I may venture to remark that his treatment of the influence which the distribution of wealth exerts on the accumulation of capital is one of the weakest portions of his system, even if account be taken of his essay (*Fortnightly Review*, vol. v, N.S. p. 515) to introduce into his old theory of the wages-fund, "the qualifications and limitations necessary to make it admissible." Scant justice has been done to the arguments by which Mill supports the position that, partly on account of its being badly formulated, this doctrine gave countenance to the notion that the distribution of the produce of industry between capitalists and wage-receivers is governed by a "natural" and "immutable law," and is not capable of being modified by a readjustment of "the arrangements of society." He does not argue that any action such as that of trades unions can suddenly cause a *great* change in these arrangements, or the consequent distribution of wealth; he contends merely that the claims of trades unions to make *a* change must be discussed freely; they are not to be ruled out of court without a hearing, as condemned by a "natural law." Much work must be done before we even approach a solution of the difficulties which Mill here indicates. Some of his critics, including Professor Cairnes, ignore these difficulties, and quote against him principles which underlie his reasonings throughout his treatise (see not only Book II,

general be eliminated from the problems of the third book, he concludes the second book with the statement that the discussion of the subject with which it deals will be taken up again in the fourth book, and that he will interpolate "a separate book" devoted to "the instrumentality by which, in a civilised society, the distribution is effected—the machinery of exchange and price." This statement is repeated and dwelt upon in the introduction to his third book, and it appears to me to be sufficiently emphatic; but additional emphasis has recently been given to it, in so far at least as it refers to the special functions of the second book, by the account of the tone of his treatise on political economy, which occurs in his *Autobiography*. He there speaks of—

That general tone by which it is distinguished from all previous expositions of political economy that had any pretension to be scientific, and which made it so useful in conciliating minds which those previous expositions had repelled. This tone consisted chiefly in making the proper distinction between the laws of the production of wealth, which are real laws of nature, dependent on the properties of objects, and the modes of its distribution, which, subject to certain conditions, depend on human will. The common run of political economists confuse these together, under the designation of economic laws, which they deem incapable of being defeated or modified by human effort; ascribing the same necessity to things dependent on the unchangeable conditions of our earthly existence, and to those which, being but the necessary consequences of particular social arrangements, are merely co-extensive with these: given certain institutions and customs, wages, profits, and rent will be determined by certain causes; but this class of political economists drop the indispensable presupposition, and argue that these causes must, by an inherent necessity, against which no human means can avail, determine the shares which fall in the division of the produce to labourers, capitalists, and landlords. The *Principles of Political Economy* yielded to none of its predecessors in aiming at the scientific appreciation of the action of these causes under the conditions which they presuppose; but it set the example of not regarding those conditions as final. The economic generalizations which depend, not on necessities of nature, but on those combined with the existing arrangements of society, it deals with as only provisional, and as liable to be much altered by the progress of social improvement[1].

chap. xi, but also Book I, chaps. v, vi, and xi; Book II, chap. xv; Book IV, chaps. iv, vi). The simple suggestion has been publicly made that in his later years he may have forgotten these elementary principles.

[1] Mill's *Autobiography*, pp. 246–7. Cairnes appears to me not to take sufficient account of the general plan of Mill's work. He takes no account of the vital importance which Mill found in the distinction between the human habits by which freedom of competition between various classes of labours is controlled, and the mechanical agencies by which exchanges are effected. Many of his criticisms almost imply that Mill's third book claims to be a complete treatise on Economics.

Thus (i) natural laws determine the total stock of the material wealth or material sources of enjoyment, which will at any stage of progress be produced at the total cost of given human efforts and sacrifices: (ii) the "human will" and "particular social arrangements[1]" determine the scheme according to which remuneration shall be distributed out of this total sum to each class of efforts and sacrifices: (iii) this distribution is effected by the instrumentality of a "machinery of exchange," the greater part of which would be put in requisition under almost any social arrangements that are likely to exist in the civilised world. The science of this machinery is the proper province of "pure" or "abstract" economic investigations.

If it be given that a bottle of wine and a pound of tea can be disposed of for the same price in the same open market at a given period, the gratifications of the purchasers in this market at this time due to the bottle of wine and the pound of tea, have this price as their common exchange measure; and the machinery of exchange is not concerned with any other of their properties. If it be given that twenty minutes' work by a physician, or two days' work by a watchmaker, or four days' work by a carpenter, or a fortnight's work by an agricultural labourer, can be bought in a given market at the same time for a guinea, and that the sacrifice involved in the loan of twenty guineas for a year can be bought by a guinea, then these several efforts and this abstinence are equivalent to one another for the purposes of the machinery of exchange working in that market at that time. These data being given, the machinery takes no further account of the pleasures or pains concerned. A chemist's balance takes no account of the medical properties of an ounce of arsenic, but the chemist does. Mill in due place takes account of the fatigue due to the work of the watchmaker and the carpenter; but the machinery treated of in his third book does not[2]. Wherever the phrase "a ratio between the costs of production of two commodities" occurs, cost of production cannot mean the aggregate of the diverse efforts and abstinences that have been required

---

[1] This phrase occurs not only in the above passage, but also in the *Political Economy* (Book III, chap. i, § 1).

[2] Professor Cairnes implies (p. 75) that the law of cost of production is subject in this connexion to an important limitation which Mill has overlooked. Here again he seems not to have noticed the relation in which Mill's second book stands to his third.

for the production of the commodity. Mill was aware, though some of his critics forget, that one aggregate of diverse efforts and abstinences does not bear a ratio to another. When we speak of ratio between an effort and an abstinence, or even between two diverse efforts, we assume, *ipso facto*, an artificial mode of measuring them in terms of some common unit, and refer to the ratio between their measures. The pure science of Ethics halts for lack of a system of measurement of efforts, sacrifices, desires, etc., fit for her wide purposes. But the pure science of Political Economy has found a system that will subserve her narrower aims. This discovery, rather than any particular proposition, is the great fact of the pure science.

It has been remarked that, in general, the truths by the discovery of which epochs in history have been made have been simple truths. An epoch has been created not by a new doctrine, but by the acquisition of the point of view from which the doctrine proceeded. A point of view was conquered for us by Adam Smith, from which a commodity is regarded as the embodiment of measurable efforts and sacrifices. Whosoever will put himself at this point of view may, with ease, see through fallacies which clouded the vision of statesmen not only of ancient times, but of an age that had gained the right point of view for the corresponding physical problem of the laws of motion of material masses.

Proceeding from its new point of view, Political Economy has analysed the efforts and sacrifices that are required for the production of a commodity for a given market at a given time; she has found a measure for them in their *cost to the person who will purchase them*, and then enunciated her central truth. This central truth is that producers, each governed under the sway of free competition by calculations of his own interest, will endeavour so to regulate the amount of any commodity which is produced for a given market during a given period, that this amount shall be just capable on the average of finding purchasers during this period at a remunerative price: a remunerative price being defined to be a price which shall be just equal to the sum of the exchange measures of those efforts and sacrifices which are required for the production of the commodity when this particular amount is produced, *i.e.*, to the sum of the expenses which must be incurred by a person who would purchase the performance of these efforts and sacrifices. Mill has retained the usage which applies to this sum the name "cost of production," without further explanation than is supplied by the context. I do not maintain that no advantage would have been gained if Mill had invented some new term for this sum, say "expenses of production," and had used the term "cost of production" only when he was speaking of efforts and sacrifices as they affected those who underwent them. I may concede that recent experience strengthens the arguments in favour of such a change, and I propose to say, in future, that the exchange-values of two commodities tend to bear to one another the same ratio as their *expenses of production*. But I maintain that when a ratio between costs of production is spoken of in the first chapters of Mill's third book, a misinterpretation, by which cost is referred to efforts instead of to measures of effort, is as inexcusable as one by which a traveller in New York or Nova Scotia should assume that allusions to *The Times*, or to *Halifax*, refer to *The Times* of London or the *Halifax* of Yorkshire. For besides guarding against such a misinterpretation implicitly, Mill puts a brief but clear warning against it into the most prominent place he could have chosen—the commencement of his chapter on the Analysis of Cost of Production. There, as I have said, he starts by an allusion to the fact that his treatment of labour *quâ* effort is to be found in his first book, and then says, "What the production of a thing costs to its producer, or its series of producers, is the labour expended in producing it[1]."

The form into which I have thrown Mill's account of the relative values of commodities produced freely in the same country is chosen in order to make manifest the continuity that exists between this and other portions of his theory of value. Some persons fail to see that his "Law of Cost of Production" is regarded by him as operative only as a result of, or corollary from, the law according to which the action of the producers of a commodity is governed by their calculations of the circumstances of the future supply and demand in the market. He

---

[1] Professor Cairnes (p. 50), after quoting a long passage from Mill, in which this sentence occurs, states that "the conception of cost which it suggests is radically unsound, confounding things in their own nature distinct and even antithetical, and setting in an essentially false light the incidents of production and exchange."

explains this briefly, perhaps too briefly, at the beginning of the third book of his *Political Economy*, and again in the following sentence[1]:—"The influence even of cost of production depends on supply; for the only thing which compels price, on the average, to conform to cost of production, is that if the price is either above or below that standard, it is brought back to it either by an increase or a diminution of the supply." The true nature of this doctrine would have been more manifest had not Mill, after Ricardo, judged it important to use terms that should bring into prominence the properties which distinguished rather than the properties which united the various propositions of the theory of value. The charges of inconsistency and confusion which have been brought against his account, as it now stands, by writers as learned as Mr McLeod, and as powerful as Professor Jevons, establish, I think, conclusively, that his position would have been improved if he had adopted the other alternative. I propose, then, to speak of the form of exposition of Mill's central doctrine, which I have given above, as the "Law of Free Production and Average Demand" (the word free being introduced in order to indicate that the law does not hold for the produce of a monopoly); and to speak of Mill's Laws of Cost of Production[2] (or as I should now say, "Expenses of Production") as corollaries from it.

One advantage of this mode of stating Mill's doctrine would be that it would render more clear his use of the terms "supply" and "demand." The circumstances of a market determine the particular exchange value, the expectation of which will suffice to induce producers to supply on the average any particular amount of a given commodity during a given period. These circumstances determine also the particular exchange value which will induce purchasers to demand on the average any particular amount of it during this period; the demand of each person being dependent upon[3] his means and the value in use

---

[1] *Fortnightly Review*, vol. v, N.S., p. 507.

[2] Mill, Book III, chap. iv, paragraphs xiii and xiv. Mr Carey proposes to say that the value of a commodity is equal to its cost of *reproduction*. He would thus avoid many small difficulties, but he would do serious mischief by diverting attention from the forces which govern supply in the first instance and value in the second.

[3] In mathematical language "a function of." I hold that much of what Professor Jevons says about "final utility" is contained, implicitly, at least, in Mill's account: but he has brought out with excellent distinctness many vital points connected with this notion, and has thereby made one of the most important of recent contributions to Economics.

to him of the commodity. Thus we must "mean by the word demand the quantity demanded, and remember that this is not a fixed quantity, but in general varies according to the value[1]." Although Mill puts this statement in the most prominent place possible, and repeats it, some of his critics have not seen its full force[2]. Thus we are to regard the average exchange value as under normal circumstances equating supply and demand; in this sense, that the circumstances of the market being supposed to be approximately uniform, the average exchange value will be such that the expectation of their obtaining this value for their commodity will cause producers on the average to supply just that amount which consumers are, on the average, just willing to purchase at that exchange value.

I do not think that Mill made his decision lightly when he determined, in his theory of values "in an isolated country," to measure the transaction which he describes in terms of the quantity of the commodity in question[3]. Some years ago, under the influence of Cournot's thought[4], I spent a long time in experimenting with various modes of expression for this theory, and for the theory of international values. I found that, for the more elementary problems of either theory, almost any mode of expression would answer: but that for the more complex problems, that mode of expression which Mill has selected in the former theory is the best adapted for it, and that which he has selected for the latter theory is the best adapted for it; and the experience of others who have concerned themselves with quantitative analysis tends, as far as I can gather, in the same direction[5].

[1] Mill, Book III, chap. ii, § 4.

[2] This is a striking instance in which Cairnes presents his readers with one portion only of Mill's account. He says (p. 23), "Demand as there" [*i.e.* in the chapter from which I quote] "defined, is to be understood as measured, not, as my definition would require, by the quantity of purchasing power offered in support of the desire for commodities, but by the quantity of commodities for which such purchasing power is offered." He does not notice that Mill insists that the quantity demanded "varies according to the value." There is a great difference between the statements "I will buy twelve eggs," and "I will buy a shilling's worth of eggs." But there is no substantive difference between the statement "I will buy twelve eggs at a penny each, but only six at three halfpence each," and the statement "I will expend a shilling on eggs at a penny each, but if they cost three halfpence each I will spend ninepence on them."

[3] As mathematicians would say, to select this quantity for his independent variable.

[4] *Recherches sur les Principes Mathématiques de la Théorie des Richesses*, Paris 1835.

[5] This is one of many instances in which Professor Cairnes might, I think, have appreciated Ricardo's and Mill's work more truly if he had not given his chief attention to qualitative analysis, to the neglect of quantitative analysis.

We must, of course, always bear in mind the fundamental truth, that, to use Mill's words, that

which constitutes the means of payment for commodities...is simply commodities. Each person's means of paying for the productions of other people consists of those which he himself possesses. All sellers are inevitably, and by the meaning of the word, buyers. Could we suddenly double the productive powers of the country, we should double the supply of commodities in every market: but we should by the same stroke double the purchasing power. Everybody would bring a double demand as well as supply[1]:

that is to say, the amount of each commodity which each person would be willing to purchase at a given exchange value would in general be doubled; and the amount which each producer of the commodity would be willing to supply at a given exchange value would be doubled.

Exactly corresponding is his account of market value. The amount which dealers offer for sale at any particular value is governed by their calculations of the present and future conditions of the markets with which they are directly and indirectly connected. There are some offers which none of them would accept: some offers which none of them would refuse. But those who can least afford to wait, and those whose expectation of the future condition of the market are the least sanguine, will just be induced to accept offers which others will just refuse. There is a particular exchange value at which each particular amount will be offered for sale, a particular value at which each particular amount can find purchasers. The higgling and the bargaining of the market tend to force the exchange value to that position which will just equate supply and demand: i.e., to make the exchange value such that the amount which dealers are willing to sell at that value is equal to the amount which can find purchasers at that value.

It is true that Mill does not explain this carefully in his *Political Economy*. The theory of market values was considered by economists as of slight importance, until Mr Thornton's book *On Labour* appeared. Mr Thornton's work is not free from faults; but he has not received his due meed of gratitude for having led men to a point of view from which the practical importance

---

[1] Book III, chap. xiv, § 2. Professor Cairnes insists upon this truth, *e.g.* p. 27. But he has not observed that a recognition of it governs the whole course of Mill's reasonings.

of the theory of market values is clearly seen. In particular he led Mill to give an exposition of his views on the subject[1].

Mill, following Adam Smith, insisted on the doctrine, that fluctuations of the market price, above and below the average price, are injurious to the community[2]. Some of the subtlest arguments for and against "protection to native industry" turn on the principles involved in these doctrines; but such arguments have not, as far as I am aware, received attention in this country.

A few words may be said on Mill's use of "cost of production" in his theory of international values. It has been argued above that, when he speaks of the machinery of exchange as causing the values of commodities freely produced at home to bear to one another on the average the ratio of their costs of production, it would be certain, even without the explanation which he supplies, that he is speaking not of the efforts and sacrifices that were required for the production of the several commodities, but of their exchange measures. The pure theory of international values is based on the hypothesis, that there is no migration of labour or capital from one country to another, and that therefore there exist no artificial and precise common measures of efforts and sacrifices undergone in different countries. Therefore the machinery of exchange knows nothing of any comparison between the costs of production of commodities produced in different countries. When, therefore, Mill makes any sort of comparison between such costs, we may be certain (1) that he is speaking of the efforts and sacrifices themselves, and not of their measures, and (2) that he is not professing to make an exact quantitative statement. And this is the fact[3]. He repeats indeed from Ricardo the remark that, on the hypothesis that capital and labour do not circulate freely between countries,

---

[1] I am unable to conjecture how Cairnes has managed so to misinterpret him as to make the startling statement (p. 117), "We desire to know the circumstances which determine price; and we are told that the selling price is always such that the quantity of a commodity purchased in a given market is equal to the quantity sold in that market. The statement is incontrovertible, but I fail to see how it helps us to understand the facts."

[2] What Professor Cairnes says on this subject (pp. 123, etc.) appears to me to be in substance true, as far as it goes, and important. But he seems to me again to have overlooked some of the work of his predecessors.

[3] Cairnes appears not to have noticed this: hence he charges Mill with grave inconsistencies.

a commodity may exchange for another produced in a different country, though the efforts and sacrifices involved in the production of the one have been much greater than those involved for the other; and the remark that a commodity may be systematically imported into a country which has greater natural facilities for producing it than are possessed by the country from which it is obtained. But these are merely negative statements: they are not constituent portions of the theory. The functions which they discharge do not require that the terms in which they are expressed should be capable of precise quantitative interpretation. We have not to decide what is the number of sugar-canes the labour of cutting which under a tropical sun is to be regarded as equivalent to that of getting a ton of iron ore, in order that we may be able to assent to the proposition that the production of the sugar we obtain in exchange for our iron *may not* have cost just as much labour as the production of the iron did, but may have cost either more or less labour. Whenever, in the constructive portions of the theory, mention is made of a ratio between costs of production, reference is had to two commodities produced freely in the same country; the machinery of exchange is exhibited as weighing the expenses of production, as I propose to say, of the two commodities. It is true, doubtless, that Mill has not guarded against mistaken renderings of his words with sufficient fulness of iteration, but what he has written suffices logically to exclude false renderings; and there are few thoughtful students who fail to perceive the main drift of his reasonings[1].

There is much to be said of the manner in which the pure theory of values in an isolated country and the pure theory of international values are intended to supplement each other in

[1] Great as is the value of Professor Cairnes's constructive and explanatory remarks on this subject, he does not seem to me to have fully entered into Mill's position. For instance, when speaking of the American protectionists, he says (p. 57), "they ask, how can we, with our high-priced labour, compete with the pauper labour of Europe? I must frankly own that, accepting the point of view of the current theory of cost, I can find no satisfactory reply to this question." Mill's answer is, of course, that if American producers generally should be unable to compete with English producers at the present rates of wages, a flow of gold (Cairnes here regards wages in America as measured in gold) from America to England would set in; by which ultimately a general fall in the prices of labour and commodities in America would be effected, until American producers gained possession of the market with regard to those commodities, in the production of which they are at the greatest advantage or the least disadvantage.

Mill's system; the powers of the two theories being combined for the solution of problems relating to the trade, that is actually carried on between (say) two different sets of people in England, or between England and America. But I must content myself here with calling attention to the hints and the facts bearing on this subject that are contained in Mr Cliffe Leslie's eminently instructive and suggestive writings on wages and prices.

WATER AS AN ELEMENT OF NATIONAL WEALTH (1879)[1]

IT is a more difficult task than at first sight appears to estimate correctly the real wealth of a nation. We can find, with tolerable care, a money measure of it. But, unfortunately, it cannot be measured accurately in money. The ordinary way of estimating the wealth of a nation is to calculate separately the money values of all things that have money values and add them together. This, for instance, is what Mr Giffen did in the admirable paper he read a year ago, in which he proved that the wealth of England had risen between the years 1865 and 1875 from about £6,100,000,000 to 8,500 millions—that is, had increased at the rate of about 240 millions a year. This method of calculating is very useful for many purposes, but it is a treacherous method. For it takes no account of such facts as that a bright, clear sky and beautiful scenery are as real a source of enjoyment as the expensive furniture which takes a large place in the inventory of England's wealth. And it takes no account of such facts as that land counts for but very little in countries where there is an abundance of it, and for a great deal in England, where it is scarce. When the value of land rises owing to its scarcity, the landowner does really become richer; the increased amount for which land enters in the inventory of his wealth is not delusive. He becomes richer, but at the expense of his neighbours. The vast sum of 2,000 millions for which land enters in the inventory of England's wealth is delusive. It is nearly as large an amount as is entered in the inventory of the wealth of the United States for the total value of their farms, including farming implements and machinery and live stock; and yet the United States contain nearly twenty times as much fertile land as there is in the United Kingdom. Thus we see that, in estimating a nation's wealth, mistakes are likely to be made—firstly, because many of Nature's best gifts to man are not included at all in the inventory; and, secondly,

---

[1] Gilchrist lecture at Bristol, 1879. Reproduced from the *Bristol Mercury and Daily Post*, March 6, 1879.

because the inventory underrates the importance of everything which is so plentiful as to have a low market value. It is particularly important to be on our guard against these mistakes when we are inquiring to what extent water is an element of national wealth. We may begin this inquiry with observing that water, or at least some fluid, is, so far as we can tell, a necessary condition of life, and therefore wealth, not only on our planet, but on every other. A world without water may not be devoid of motion, for the wind may blow about the dust in it. But it can have, it seems to us, no organic life. There is no life and no wealth on the nearer side of the moon. There is scarcely any life and scarcely any wealth in the Sahara. At the silver mines in Nevada, where the chief supply of water is brought in wooden troughs from a distance of twenty-four miles, there is some wealth; but not nearly so much wealth as one might guess from being told that no one works there for less than four dollars a day; for if a man there should happen to want a cabbage he is not unlikely to have to pay one of his four dollars for it. Next, if we look over the inventories of England's wealth, we find that those places in which every one can get as much pure soft water as he wants for nothing, just those places which are really richest in water are not credited with any wealth at all under this head. But the privileges of the London water companies enter for a very large sum. Yet the Londoners are really so poor in water that they cannot get any at all without paying for it; and they cannot get any that is fit to drink unless they buy it in bottles at a high price. Most of their water is not only unfit to drink, but unfit for other purposes. It has been calculated that if they could change their hard water into soft they could save 3 million lbs. of tea, and as many pounds of soap a year; and that in these and other ways they would save £1,000,000 a year. But London and other places where people are poor in water have water companies whose property, including their plant and their privileges, enters for no less than 400 millions into the inventory of national wealth. Yet this sum, large as it is, represents but a small part of the benefit which our water companies confer on us. Until the reign of James I, when Hugh Middleton brought the New River to London, the Londoners used to buy Thames water of carriers who went about the streets with two buckets

each, just as milkmen do now. A great deal of the water used
in Plymouth was brought five miles by land till Sir Francis
Drake made a "Leet," to bring water from Dartmoor; and the
citizens of Hull used often to have to fetch water in boats across
the Humber from Lincolnshire. Some villages are as badly off
now as these towns used to be. Stories are told of "more than
a hundred people waiting round one pump, and of poor women
rising in the early morning three hours before working time in
order to be first at the tiny stream on which their village
depended for water." The water companies do a much greater
service to the people than is represented by the small charge
they have to make in order to pay fair dividends on their capital.
For, while water carried in the wrong way is a very awkward
burthen, it is, when pumped by steam and carried by pipes, by
far the most portable of all commodities. It is calculated that
the cost of bringing 220 million gallons of water daily from
North Wales to London would be less than £11,000,000; the
cost of buying up the plant and the privileges of the existing
companies would amount to about the same. The saving that
London would make in tea, soap, etc., would pay the interest
on this outlay, and the improvement in the health of Londoners
would be all net gain. It is said with truth that the water supply
of every place should, if possible, be drawn from the river basin
in which it is. But this principle cannot be acted on consistently;
for the underground reservoirs of our chalk and greensand
formations pay no attention to the surface water basins. And
the principle will probably be further broken through by
supplying Liverpool with soft pure water from Lake Bala, and
many other northern towns from the English lakes. Perhaps
we are too careless about letting private persons spoil, or what
is nearly as bad, exclude the public from the enjoyment of our
most beautiful scenery. But I think the waterworks could be
managed so as to do no harm to scenery. And anyhow, it must
be remembered that a man who has the good health that comes
from drinking first-rate water will enjoy second-rate scenery
more than he would first-rate scenery if he were in the indifferent
health that comes from drinking second-rate water. Also, that
while comparatively few visit the lakes, and those only for a few
days, many millions drink the water every day, and more than

a million people want to use it for manufacturing purposes, for which impure or hard water is not fit. Many New Englanders, who have migrated to the rich soil of the Mississippi Valley, come home, giving as the chief reason their longing for the pure water of the barren granite rocks of their native land. This is not the time for discussing the influence of climate on national wealth. But I may notice that the moist winds of England so temper the climate that a man can work hard here for many more days in the year than he can in most other countries. If we suppose he can do only ten per cent. more work here than he could elsewhere, and this is a low estimate, we find that the direct money value of England's invigorating climate is 100 millions a year. Again, the difference between a good and a bad harvest for all kinds of crops cannot be much less than 100 millions in this country, while in France it amounts to nearly as much as the whole value of the indemnity which France paid to Germany. Next with regard to water power. The foundation of England's manufacturing greatness was laid by water power; and a time may come, probably will come in less than a thousand years, when more factories will be driven by water power than by steam. I can find no estimate of the total amount of water power that is theoretically capable of being obtained from all the streams and rivers of the United Kingdom. But the area of the hilly part of the kingdom is about 60,000 square miles, and if we suppose that throughout a third of this area we could utilise thirty-six inches of annual rainfall through a descent of 300 feet on the average, that would give us a force sufficient to raise about two thousand billion pounds one foot high every year; in other words, it would give us about the force that the Americans have in their falls of Niagara. The force of Niagara is, as Siemens has told us, about equal to that which the total annual output of coal would give us if burnt in steam engines of average efficiency, but if burnt in the best steam engines the coal would give about twice as much force as Niagara, while if the whole force of the coal could be utilised, it would be about twenty times as great as that of Niagara. Again, England has a great source of power in the rise and fall of the wind-driven waves of the sea, and in the rise and fall of her tides. If, for instance, we chose to put a dam across the mouth of the Avon and use it as a big water engine, we might, I think, without any great difficulty get it to do work equivalent to raising two hundred thousand million pounds a foot high every day. This work is about equal to the labour of the muscles of two hundred thousand men. One pound of coal in a good engine will do about as much work as a man can do in a day; and the force obtained from the Avon would be about equivalent to that of one hundred tons of coal a day. The Avon engine would be a cumbrous engine to work, as well as an expensive engine to make and keep in repair, and as the capital sum of the water power would, with the present price of coal, be not more than £600,000, I do not think we are likely to use it for a long time. Of course the river could bring ships up to Bristol while it was doing the work of a water engine. It remains to consider water as a carrier. Canals are entered in the inventory of England's wealth for 20 millions. Before Brindley made them for us coal and other heavy things used to be carried on horses' backs at a charge of one shilling per ton per mile. They can be carried for about a fiftieth of that by canal. But they can be carried more cheaply still by river; and by sea a shilling will carry a ton two hundred miles. But the inventory of England's wealth says nothing of her rivers, nothing of her seas. And yet many of the greatest nations of the world have owed more to their rivers and their seas than they have to their land. A steady industry and a sturdy discipline have grown up in places far away from the sea. But I think that most of the world's genius and enterprise owe their origin directly to the sea. I think indeed that it is not too rash to assert that among the greatest calamities that have befallen the world in the course of her troubled history has been the overthrow of a nation that has breathed in genius from the sea by one which has learnt discipline on the land. I cannot now attempt more than a few illustrations of what I mean. Let us look first at the history of Greece. It has often been remarked that the earliest civilisations have been in countries so warm that man required but little food and clothing; so fertile that the labour of his hands left a large surplus over the necessaries of life; countries in which a patient and industrious race has been disciplined by a ruling caste who have themselves gradually acquired culture. Such countries were

Assyria and Egypt, whose civilisation belong not to the sea but to the land. But even they owed great debts to their rivers, and they made great use of canals, for they were good civil engineers. They were astronomers also, and the Egyptians knew a little geometry. Then came the Phœnicians, a maritime nation, who spread their colonies along the Mediterranean, and made many inventions useful for commerce, particularly a written language and arithmetic. Thus most of the best fruits of the world's work were gathered round the head of the Mediterranean, to which the Greeks came when they emigrated from their inhospitable home in Asia. They were a race of energetic barbarians, knowing nothing but ready to know everything. They came to a country which consisted almost entirely of mountains and sea coast. Each little group when it had settled on the sea shore was cut off from its neighbours by the land, but united by the sea to the enterprise of Phœnicia, and the wisdom of Egypt. Phœnicia received them with open arms at once: a new impulse was given to Greek life in the year B.C. 670, when Egypt removed the artificial barriers that secluded her from the world. Thus each city marked out its own thoughts and aspirations, its own business and pleasure, its own political and social life by itself and for itself. It was continually receiving new ideas and new suggestions from over the sea. Each city was stimulated by the broad sympathy of multitudes of other cities around it. But there was no overpowering force to constrain it to grow in this way, or that; there was perfect freedom of the individual mind, and perfect freedom of the State's life, and Greece grew with wonderful growth. First of all came the cities on the coasts of Asia Minor and Italy. They sent out colonies that established themselves along the sea. One of them, Miletus, had eighty such colonies, and each of these was a new home for independent life, a new source of fresh ideas and suggestions for others. The first great misfortune of Greece was the conquest of the free cities of Asia Minor by the army of Crœsus. His sway lasted a short time; the second great misfortune was his overthrow by the army of the great inland empire of Persia. From this time Asia Minor ceased to lead Greek thought; the intellectual supremacy of the world passed to Athens, which the land power of Persia tried in vain to enslave. The third great misfortune of Greece was the overthrow of Athens by Sparta. Sparta, which alone of all true Greeks hated the sea, which preferred strength of body to mental culture, and sacrificed individual genius to discipline. But from that time the life of Greece was domineered over by the discipline of the soldiers of Sparta, of Thebes, of Macedonia, of Epirus, and of Rome; and so the highest energy of Greece passed away. The great law of the world's history has been that energy has moved westwards, dying down in each place after a time under the influence of tyranny, and then causing new energy to spring up from its decay to the west of it: just as in the fairy ring on the grass as each ring dies down a wider ring springs up from its decay. After Greece came Italy, but unfortunately it was not one of those cities of Italy full of genius breathed in from the sea that led the way; but an inland city, another Sparta, a city of warriors, a city of brute force where there was but little originality and no geniality of spirit. But discipline conquered, and it conquered so thoroughly, as to dry up the sources of individual enterprise and self-reliant mental energy throughout the world, and therefore the civilised world, when it was once overthrown by the barbarians, had no power of recovery. I do not think that the dark ages of Europe are fairly to be attributed to the barbarian invasion. For if the civilised world, though defeated in arms, had had more strength of character than its conquerors, it would speedily have obtained ascendancy over them. But strength of character and intellectual energy had been crushed out by the dominion of the military discipline of Rome, that gloried in war and hated the sea. But let us look hastily at the revival of genius in the middle ages. Where was it found? In the great maritime cities of Italy and the Netherlands. In cities that attained in some measure to the glory of Greek life, because they also were free from the tyranny of a great land army, because in them also the enterprise of their most restless spirits, instead of being crushed down by discipline, was able to expand in perfect freedom over the sea, because they, like the early Greeks, breathed in genius from the sea. It is true that some of the greatest cities of mediæval times were inland, and that in particular Florence owed but little to the sea. But, as a rule, these cities owed their first impulse to their intercourse with towns that owed everything to the sea. Without the aid of the maritime towns, they would have been unable to retain their civil freedom, and their enterprise, as long as they did, in opposition to the brute force of the armies of Austria and Spain. The ultimate conquest of the cities by these inland powers was one of the great calamities of the world's history. What England owes to her seas and rivers there is no time to tell now. But he who runs may read how she owes her free institutions to the protection that her seas have given her; how she owes her mental and moral, as well as her commercial greatness to the mighty work which her seas have given her to do. It must, indeed, be admitted that in this present age, those who live far inland have many advantages that used to be almost the exclusive property of those who lived close to the sea. The broadening of civil liberty has enabled individual enterprise and originality to flourish, even in the centre of a great inland and military power. But into this I cannot enter now. I trust I have shown that, as the physical life of man would be dried up without water, as without rain our fair fields would be a desert, so man's mental and moral life requires freedom of movement and freedom of communication with others, by land or by sea. And I trust I have shown that the drinking water, the water power, and the water highways of a country have so great an influence on her destiny, that water may be truly said to be an important element of national wealth.

V

WHERE TO HOUSE THE LONDON POOR (1884)[1]

WHATEVER reforms may be introduced into the dwellings of the
London poor, it will still remain true that the whole area of
London is insufficient to supply its population with fresh air and
the free space that is wanted for wholesome recreation. A remedy
for overcrowding of London will still be wanted. The purpose
of this paper is to suggest that there are large classes of the
population of London whose removal into the country would be
in the long run economically advantageous—that it would benefit
alike those who moved and those who remained behind.

The first effect of the mechanical inventions of the last century
was to scatter the manufacturing industries over the country in
search of water power: the development of steam power made
it possible for them to come back to the towns. Early in this
century the advantages of a town life were very great for the
manufacturers; for communication of all kinds was slow and
dear, and every branch of industry was changing its form and
methods rapidly. Those who lived out in the country had great
difficulty in keeping themselves acquainted with all that was
going on in their trades. Even if they knew what ought to be
done, they could not easily keep their machinery abreast of the
age; employers were at a disadvantage in buying and selling,
and in getting any particular kind of skilled labour they might
suddenly need; and employees found themselves too much in
the hands of individual employers. So the tide set strongly
towards the towns.

But as the century wore on, and communication was opened
up, the special advantages which residence in large towns

---

[1] Reprinted from *The Contemporary Review* for February 1884. [This article was
written before the Garden City movement started and probably gave an impetus to
that movement. The following MS. footnote was appended by Dr Marshall about
1923.] This paper was printed and circulated widely in 1884: since then there has been
a great increase in the number of children who rarely see a green field. It is true that
school playgrounds have multiplied; that commons are now kept in good order; and that
electric tramways and railways enable an ever-increasing number of artisans, and even of
unskilled labourers, to take their families out of London occasionally during the summer.
It is true also that increased care in regard to ventilation and to sanitary arrangements
of all kinds have greatly diminished the evils of urban life. But natural causes tend to
increase the evils, and increased care and energy are needed to combat the evils.

offered to producers gradually diminished. Railways, the cheap post, the telegraph, general newspapers and trade newspapers, and organized associations among employers and employed, all had a share in the change. Meanwhile space in the towns was becoming more and more valuable for trading and for administrative and other purposes; and manufacturers began to doubt whether the special advantages of the town were worth the high ground-rents that they had to pay there. Sir Titus Salt, a pioneer in this as in other ways, saw that he would gain himself and benefit those who worked for him by moving out of Bradford. So he founded Saltaire out in the country, and thus realized at once one of the most wholesome and substantial ambitions that the socialists have set before themselves—that of combining the advantages of the town and the country. Saltaire, itself a considerable town, and within a few minutes' ride of large towns, offers all the quickening influences that man gets from close and varied contact with his fellows. At the same time, it has cheap rents, fresh air, wholesome out-door amusements for young and old; the nerves are not overwrought, and the physique does not degenerate. Saltaire is exceptional in many ways; and it is apt to suffer from too close a dependence on one trade. But this evil is in some measure avoided, while nearly all the advantages of Saltaire are secured, by the semi-rural manufacturing districts that are growing up in many parts of the country, and drawing the manufacturers away from the great towns. Manchester, Leeds, and Lyons are no longer the great homes of the cotton, the woollen, and the silk industries. They are the trading centres of manufacturing districts, over which these industries have now scattered themselves. The mere carmen, railwaymen, warehousemen, and messengers in Manchester are far more in number than all the men engaged in the textile industries, and not very much less than those engaged in the textile and iron industries put together.

But there are other producing industries, which are carried on not so much in factories as in workshops and at home, which are not so ready to seek the fresh air. The causes of this are chiefly morbid, and their action is most conspicuous and most calamitous in London.

The industrial condition of London has several peculiarities.

It has grown round many villages which were at one time remote from its boundaries, and which, if its growth had not been so vast, would have become industrial districts interspersed with green fields.

Next, it has special attractions that draw to it from far and wide many different classes of people. Large as its population is, its demand for the best products of the most highly skilled work is very much larger in proportion. And a legitimate ambition brings, and always will bring, many of the finest workers in the country to it. For different reasons it is an attractive field for many at the opposite end of the industrial scale. Crowds of people go there because they are impatient and reckless, or miserable and purposeless; and because they hope to prey on the charities, the follies, and the vices that are nowhere so richly gilded as there.

No doubt those who go to London, taken altogether, are above the average in strength. But residence for many generations amid smoke, and with scarcely any of the pure gladness of bright sunshine and green fields, gradually lowers the physical constitution. It is said that this deterioration is seen even in families where high wages are earned and well spent; that the thoroughbred Londoner is seldom a perfect workman, and that the reputation of London work is maintained chiefly by those who were born, or whose parents were born, elsewhere. Even if this statement be somewhat exaggerated, it is certain that when, through any cause, the income of a family falls off, or when its income is not well spent, the family deteriorates rapidly in London. Doubtless many of the poor things that crouch for hire at the doors of London workshops are descended from vigorous ancestors, and owe their degradation partly to misfortune and partly to the taste for drink that misfortune at once begets under the joyless London sky. But a great many more of them have a taint of vice in their history. The descendants of the dissolute are naturally weak, and especially those of the dissolute in large towns. It is appalling to think how many of the poor of London are descendants of the dissolute.

Thus there are large numbers of people with poor physique and a feeble will, with no enterprise, no courage, no hope, and scarcely any self-respect, whom misery drives to work for lower wages than the same work gets in the country. The employer pays his high rent out of his savings in wages; and they have to pay their high rents out of their diminished wages. This is the fundamental evil.

It is reasonable that those who can earn high wages should work in London, if they happen to like London; because they can afford to live a fairly healthy life there. They can house themselves comfortably in London, or they can in many cases live in the suburbs, and come in to their work. Not nearly all the watchmakers, engineers, etc., who work in London, are really bound to work there; but no great harm is done by their being there.

Again, those large numbers of workmen of lower grades who are really wanted to supply the needs of London must of course live there. If their numbers were not excessive, the ordinary law of competition would keep up their wages as much above those of similar work elsewhere, as the rents they have to pay exceed the rents for similar accommodation elsewhere.

But there are other kinds of labour which are everywhere lowly paid, and which make goods, not to meet the wants of individual consumers, but for the general market: it is unreasonable and a sign of social disease that these should be housed in London. The industries that thus linger on are chiefly those in which the workers are scattered, not able easily to organize themselves, and most at the mercy of the unscrupulous employer; those industries, in short, which are shunned by the hearty and strong, and are the refuge of the weak and broken-spirited.

The distribution of the industries of London is indeed just what would naturally follow from the causes that, as we have just seen, determine the character of its population. First come those whose work is necessary in London. Those engaged in domestic service are nearly 400,000, if we count the 50,000 washerwomen in this class. There are about 150,000 engaged in carrying and storage, and 120,000 in building. There is a large but not easily ascertained number of assistants in shops; and some of the 78,000 general labourers are no doubt bound to be in London. In all these industries the supply of labour conforms itself to the demand, and is not affected by the special character of the population of London.

But in those industries the work of which could, in great part at least, be done out of London, the supply of labour is determined by the character of the population, and the demand follows the supply. In these industries the chief groups are 45,000 in the printing and allied trades, 40,000 in the furniture and decorative trades, 35,000 in the engineering and other branches of the ordinary metal trades, 20,000 workers in gold and makers of watches and other delicate instruments, and 15,000 makers of carriages, ships, and boats. In all these groups, especially in the second, there are some low-waged workers; but in the main they are high-waged, and can afford to live comfortably in London. There are further a great many minor industries, mostly very small; some of them are skilled industries, but the greater part are very poorly paid. They have a prominent place in some recent descriptions of London life. The total number of those engaged in them, though much less than is often thought, is yet very considerable. And, lastly, there is the great characteristic group of London industries—that of the clothes-making trades. Of the 150,000 or more hired workers in these trades, by far the greater part are very poorly paid, and do work which it is against all economic reason to have done where ground-rent is high. There are, including employers, 70,000 milliners, etc., there are 18,000 female tailors, and 26,000 shirtmakers and seamstresses.

It is clear, then, that of the industries in which the supply of labour is determined, not by the demand, but by the character of the population, the great majority are either very highly paid or very poorly paid. The intermediate class, those who cannot afford to live comfortably in London, but yet have not had their spirit crushed out of them, are comparatively few in number; most of them have left London. But the very weak and poorly paid want help. If they were horses they would get it fast enough; a weak horse is sent off into the country, where stable-room is cheap; people cannot afford to have any but strong horses in London. Surely time and money devoted to helping the feeble and timid to move and carry their work with them are better spent than in diminishing some of the evils of their lives in London. In London, even when their houses are white-washed, the sky will be dark; devoid of joy, they will still tend to drink for excitement; they will go on deteriorating; and, as to their children, the more of them grow up to manhood the lower will be the average physique and the average morality of the coming English generation. Meanwhile they take up space which, if they were gone, would give room for those who must remain to breathe more freely, and for their children to play.

Before considering what direct steps may be taken for this purpose, it will be well to look at the effect of the enforcement of sanitary laws. They have been considered chiefly in their bearing on those who have lived and will go on living in London; but account must also be taken of their bearing on the movements of the population.

The population of London is already migratory in a great measure. One out of five of those now living who were born in London has already gone elsewhere. Of those who are now in London more than a third were born elsewhere, and a great many more are the young children of those who have recently come there. There are about 800,000 females living in London who were born elsewhere. Only a small part of them can be domestic servants, for the total number of these is only 240,000. Of these immigrants a great part do no good to themselves or to others by coming to London; and there would be no hardship in deterring the worst of them from coming by insisting on strict regulations as to their manner of living there.

It would be possible to do this, by a just discrimination, without pressing too severely on the old inhabitants, if Mr Llewellyn Davies' proposal as to inspection were acted on. According to this, the most important perhaps of all the suggestions that have been made on the subject, specially bad districts would be "proclaimed"; they would be inspected by a large staff of officers in a rigorous, uncompromising way, that could not be applied universally without involving needless expense and needless vexation. If it got to be known that these officers would enforce the letter of the law rigidly and without mercy on all new-comers, a good many shiftless people who now come to London would stay where they are, or be induced to go straight to the New World, where the shiftless often become shiftful. The old settlement laws were wrong; they were selfish rules for preventing people from going to legitimate employment;

but to hinder people from going where their presence helps to lower the average standard of human life, is no more contrary to economic principle than the rule that, when a steamer is full, admission should be refused to any more, even though they themselves are willing to take the risk of being drowned.

The analogy of the passenger steamer will help us further. It is a hardship to take away the licence of a short-sighted captain for running his vessel ashore; it is a greater hardship not to do it. It is a question whether every house-owner in "proclaimed" districts should not require a licence. Anyhow, those who cannot manage their houses properly, and exercise a due control over the sanitary habits of their tenants, should be fined till they sell them to others who can. But all changes must be gradual; it is a mistake to propound regulations that cannot be enforced. The house-room insisted on for each person, and the free space insisted on between the houses, should start from a workable level, and increase steadily and surely till a high standard is attained.

The thorough carrying out of such rules, left to itself, would before long rid London of its superfluous population; those only would live there who were really wanted there; and competition for their labour would compel rich London to pay, as it can well afford to do, high enough wages to cover the cost of good accommodation. The suffering caused on the way would be as nothing compared with the ultimate gain; and, if the suffering could not be prevented, it should not be shirked. But there is no more urgent duty, no more truly beneficent work, than to deprive progress of its partial cruelty by helping away those who lie in the route of its chariot wheels.

Even among the landlords there are a few, probably a very few, whose cases afford a plea, not for relaxing the law, but for charitable aid to them. But the chief field for charity will be in helping the poor to live better in London, and to live better out of London.

Nearly all the schemes for enabling the poor to live better in London tend to raise their self-respect as well as to make them more comfortable, and by so doing help them indirectly to live out of London. But such schemes, admirable as they are, require to be worked in conjunction with other schemes for directly helping the poor to move out.

This task gives special facilities for attack in detail, chiefly because there is so little fixed capital in the industries to be attacked; no one experiment need involve great outlay or great risk. There might be great variety in method; but the general plan would probably be for a committee, whether formed specially for the purpose or not, to interest themselves in the formation of a colony in some place well beyond the range of London smoke. After seeing their way to building or buying suitable cottages there, they would enter into communication with some of the employers of low-waged labour. They would select at first industries that use very little fixed capital; and, as we have seen, it fortunately happens that most of the industries which it is important to move are of this kind. They would find an employer—and there must be many such—who really cares for the misery of his employees. Acting with him and by his advice, they would make themselves the friends of people employed, or fit to be employed, in his trade; they would show them the advantages of moving, and help them to move both with counsel and money. They would organize the sending of work backwards and forwards, the employer perhaps opening an agency in the colony. The committee might well keep up permanently a friendly connection with the colony. But after being once started it ought to be self-supporting; for the cost of carriage, even if the employees went in sometimes to get instructions, would be less than the saving made in rent—at all events, if allowance be made for the value of the garden produce. And more than as much again would probably be saved by removing the temptation to drink that is caused by the sadness of London. They would meet with much passive resistance at first. The unknown has terrors to all, but especially to those who have lost their natural spring. Those who have lived always in the obscurity of a London court might shrink away from the free light; poor as are their acquaintanceships at home, they might fear to go where they knew no one. But with gentle insistance the committee would urge their way, trying to get those who knew one another to move together, by warm patient sympathy taking off the chill of the first change.

It is only the first step that costs: every succeeding step would be easier. The work of several firms, not always in the same business, might in some cases be sent together. Gradually a prosperous industrial district would grow up, and then mere self-interest would induce employers to bring down their main workshops, and even to start factories in the colony. Ultimately all would gain, but most the landowners and the railroads connected with the colony.

Railway shareholders belong to the class of people most of whom wish to do something practical for the London poor, and do not know how to do it. There is a thing that wants doing, and that they alone can do; it is to put pressure on their directors to act generously in the matter of carrying the poor. The beneficent Act just passed as to workmen's trains will much depend for its efficiency on whether the railway authorities meet it in a liberal or a higgling spirit. The actual cost of running an extra train is often not very great; and there is scarcely any other direction in which a very little unselfishness will purchase so much good for others; will cause so much happiness unalloyed by any harm; will do so much to raise the quality of human life.

If railways and some at least of the employers will cooperate, the committees will soon be able to provide all whom the gradual improvement need drive out of London with healthy homes without separating them from their employment. Some members might give only time, and others only money. Some committees might be small, and go shares in a colony with others; but some parts of the work could be done only by large and strong committees. A municipality or other public body could not safely do the work—there would be too much room for jobbery and imposture; but, whenever the dwelling-houses of the poor were cleared away for any purpose, public or private, the requirements of conscience or of the law might in many cases be satisfied by handing over to a properly-chosen committee money enough to move the displaced poor out into the country. If such plans as these be carried out, the car of progress may roll on till every one in London is properly housed, and every house has adequate free space around it; and yet its wheels may crush under them none of the industrious poor.

Other provision must be made for those who cannot or will not work. Probably this will never be done satisfactorily till we have braced ourselves to say that being without the means of livelihood must be treated, not as a crime, but as a cause for uncompromising inspection and inquiry. So long as we shrink from the little pain that this would give, we are forced to be too kind to the undeserving, and too unkind to the unfortunate. This inspection would be facilitated by the adoption of Mr Llewellyn Davies' proposal. It would be a part of the great movement towards bringing public and private charity into system and into harmony. Till this is done our treatment of the poor cannot cease to be tender where tenderness is the parent of crime, and hard where hardness is unmerited.

VI

THE PRESENT POSITION OF ECONOMICS (1885)[1]

TWELVE years ago England possessed perhaps the ablest set of economists that there have ever been in a country at one time. But, one after another, there have been taken from us Mill, Cairnes, Bagehot, Cliffe Leslie, Jevons, Newmarch and Fawcett. And, not content with these, death has stricken down also one of the noblest of the rising generation, Arnold Toynbee. Never was there a science more urgently in need of all the work that all her best sons could give her than Economics is now; and few there are to give it.

Different from the rest, and in some respects greater than all the rest, was he in whose place I unworthily stand. He was unique; all history tells of none who have achieved greatness exactly as he did. His genius showed itself in his character as well as in his thought. His courage and tenderness, his self-devotion and simplicity were as great a source of strength as his marvellous force and clearness of thought. And thus he was able to take a position which no other economist has held; he was able to tell the people unpalatable truths and to earn their hearty thanks for doing so. The working classes saw in him the friend of the weak and the oppressed, the chivalrous pleader for the agricultural labourer and the Indian ryot; and they listened to him with something more than forbearance when he taught the hard doctrine that they must in the main work out their own social salvation by their own efforts. He was leading them as he was leading us all to think seriously and patiently about our economic evils and the remedies for them.

And the teacher was always learning. As successive editions of his *Political Economy* appeared, as one work after another came from his pen, they told of the constant growth of his mind. His latest work was always his best work, the strongest, the most original, the most suggestive that he had ever done. And yet after reading all, there remained something more: it was to

[1] An inaugural lecture given by Professor Marshall after election to the professorship at Cambridge in 1885 in succession to Professor Fawcett.

talk with him, and by him to be led to see. That same magic power, that almost enabled him to see the things around him when his eyes were dark, enabled him to bring before those to whom he talked the real bearings of practical economic questions, with a vividness such that I at least have never known the like. But he is gone; and we who remain must carry on, as best we may, his work, guided by his clear thoughts and cheered by his brave example.

It will be my endeavour to-day to give a short account of the province of the economist as I understand it, and of what it seems to me that Cambridge may best do in it.

It is generally known that Economics has to some extent changed its front during the present generation; but the nature of the change is much misunderstood. It is commonly said that those who set the tone of economic thought in England in the earlier part of the century were theorists who neglected the study of facts, and that this was specially an English fault. Such a charge seems to me baseless. Most of them were practical men with a wide and direct personal knowledge of business affairs. They wrote economic histories that are in their way at least equal to anything that has been done since. They brought about the collection of statistics by public and private agencies and that admirable series of parliamentary inquiries, which have been a model for all other countries, and have inspired the modern German historic school with many of their best thoughts.

And as to their tendency to indulge in excessively abstract reasonings, that, in so far as the charge is true at all, is chiefly due to the influence of one masterful genius, who was not an Englishman, and had very little in common with the English tone of thought. The faults and the virtues of Ricardo's mind are traceable to his Semitic origin; no English economist has had a mind similar to his.

The change that has been made in the point of view of Economics by the present generation is then not due to the discovery of the importance of supplementing and guiding deduction by induction, for that was well known before. It is due to the discovery that man himself is in a great measure a creature of circumstances and changes with them; and the importance of this discovery has been accentuated by the fact that the growth of knowledge and earnestness have recently made and are making deep and rapid changes in human nature.

At the beginning of the nineteenth century the mathematico-physical group of sciences was in the ascendant. These sciences, widely as they differ from one another, have this point in common, that their subject-matter is constant and unchanged in all countries and in all ages. The progress of science was familiar to men's minds, but the development of the subject-matter of science was strange to them. As the century wore on the biological group of sciences were slowly making way, and people were getting clearer ideas as to the nature of organic growth. They were learning that, if the subject-matter of a science passes through different stages of development, the laws which apply to one stage will seldom apply without modification to others; the laws of the science must have a development corresponding to that of the things of which they treat. The influence of this new notion gradually spread to the sciences which relate to man. In different ways Goethe, Hegel, Comte and other writers called attention to the development of the inner character and outward institutions of man, and worked their way towards the notion of tracing and comparing the modes of growth of the different sides of human nature.

At last the speculations of biology made a great stride forwards: its discoveries fascinated the attention of all men as those of physics had done in earlier years. The moral and historical sciences of the day have in consequence changed their tone, and Economics has shared in the general movement. The change is not chiefly attributable to any particular attacks that have been made on economic doctrine, nor to the influence of individual writers whether in England or other countries, though some exception may indeed be made in favour of List. The change is mainly due to the irresistible forces of the age affecting at once all the rising generation in all parts of the world.

The chief fault, then, in English economists at the beginning of the century was not that they ignored history and statistics; but that Ricardo and his followers neglected a large group of facts, and a method of studying facts which we now see to be of primary importance.

They regarded man as, so to speak, a constant quantity, and

gave themselves little trouble to study his variations. The people whom they knew were chiefly city men; and they took it for granted tacitly that other Englishmen were very much like those they knew in the city. They were aware that the inhabitants of other countries had peculiarities of their own; but they regarded such differences, when they thought of them at all, as superficial and sure to be removed as soon as other nations had got to know that better way which Englishmen were ready to teach them. The same bent of mind, that led our lawyers to impose English civil law on the Hindoos, led our economists to work out their theories on the tacit supposition that the world was made up of city men.

This did little harm so long as they treated of money and foreign trade, but great harm when they treated of the relations between the different industrial classes. It led them to regard labour simply as a commodity without throwing themselves into the point of view of the workman; without allowing for his human passions, his instincts and habits, his sympathies and antipathies, his class jealousies and class adhesiveness, his want of knowledge and of the opportunities for free and vigorous action. They therefore attributed to the forces of supply and demand a much more mechanical and regular action than they actually have; and laid down laws with regard to profits and wages that did not really hold even for England in their own time.

But their most vital fault was that they did not see how liable to change are the habits and institutions of industry. In particular they did not see that the poverty of the poor is the chief cause of that weakness and inefficiency which are the cause of their poverty: they had not the faith, that modern economists have, in the possibility of a vast improvement in the condition of the working classes.

The perfectibility of man had indeed been asserted by Owen and other early socialists: but their views were based on little historic and scientific study; and were expressed with an extravagance that repelled the business-like economists of the age. The socialists did not always attempt to understand the doctrines which they attacked; and there was no difficulty in showing that they had often failed rightly to apprehend the nature and efficiency of the existing economic organization of society. It is therefore not a matter for wonder that the economists, flushed with their victories over a set of much more solid thinkers, did not trouble themselves to examine any of the doctrines of the socialists, and least of all their speculations as to human nature.

But the socialists were men who felt intensely, and who knew something about the hidden springs of human action of which the economists took no account. Buried among their wild rhapsodies there were shrewd observations and pregnant suggestions from which philosophers and economists had much to learn. And gradually their influence began to tell. Comte's debts to them were very great; and the crisis of John Stuart Mill's life, as he tells us in his autobiography, came to him from reading them. The influence which they have exercised on economists in England and Germany has been, I think, for the greater part wholesome; even though the association with fervid philanthropy may perhaps cause some tendency to rapid and unscientific reasoning.

Among the bad results of the narrowness of the work of English economists early in the nineteenth century perhaps the most unfortunate was the opportunity which it gave to sciolists to quote and misapply economic dogmas. These dogmas were taken away from their context and set up as universal and necessary truths; although a little care would often have discovered that they were originally put forward, not at all as independent truths, but as the outcome of particular illustrations of a scientific method of inquiry. Ricardo and his chief followers may be blamed for what they omitted to do; but they did not commit, to the extent that is generally supposed, the fault of claiming universality and necessity for their doctrines. They did not, however, make their drift obvious. They did not make clear to others, it was not even quite clear to themselves, that what they were building up was not universal truth, but machinery of universal application in the discovery of a certain class of truths.

Adam Smith is most widely known for his argument that Government does harm by interfering in trade. He admitted that self-interest often led the individual trader to act injuriously to the community: but he thought that Government, even with the best intentions, nearly always served the public worse than the enterprise of the individual trader did, however selfish he might happen to be. This doctrine it is which some German writers have chiefly in view when they speak of Smithianismus. But it was not his chief work. His chief work was to indicate the manner in which value measures human motive.

Possibly the full drift of what he was doing was not seen by him: certainly it was not perceived by many of his followers who approached economics from the point of view of business rather than of philosophy. But the best economic work which came after the *Wealth of Nations* is distinguished from that which went before, by a clearer insight into the balancing and weighing, by means of money, of the desire for the possession of a thing on the one hand, and on the other of all the various efforts and self-denials which directly and indirectly contribute towards making it. Important as had been the steps that others had taken in this direction, the advance made by him was so great as to make an epoch. He showed the need of analysing the causes that determine the difficulty of attainment of various economic results; of inquiring which of them are so far uniform in their mode of action that they can be reduced to law and thus made the basis of scientific measurement.

These causes often lie deep below the surface and are likely to be overlooked by the ordinary observer. But he saw that they are in the long run of predominant importance; and, since they are in some measure capable of scientific treatment, he rightly judged it best to give them his chief attention. The fitful and irregular incidents of the market cannot for the greater part be reduced to order, and brought directly within the grasp of scientific machinery. But, when those causes which act with tolerable uniformity are understood, and their effects allowed for, then the residuary effects of other causes stand out prominently. The investigation of the results that can be brought under law[1] thus helps towards the understanding of those which

---

[1] They are now called Normal. Adam Smith called them Natural. But he had not completely freed himself from eighteenth century metaphysical notions as to Nature, and, though on this point greatly in advance of his French contemporaries, he did not always distinguish perfectly between the causal laws of Nature in the indicative mood and her ethical laws in the imperative.

cannot; and thus science is able indirectly to lend her aid in unravelling the tangled skein of the events of actual life. Adam Smith's point of view has been gradually developed by Ricardo, Cournot, Hermann, Jevons and others.

The outward form of economic theory has been shaped by its connection with material wealth. But it is becoming clear that the true philosophic *raison d'être* of the theory is that it supplies a machinery to aid us in reasoning about those motives of human action which are measurable. In the world in which we live, money, as representing general purchasing power, is so much the best measure of motives that no other can compete with it. But this is, so to speak, an accident, and perhaps an accident that is not found in other worlds than ours.

When we want to induce a man to do anything for us, we generally offer him money. It is true that we might appeal to his generosity or sense of duty; but this would be calling into action latent motives that are already in existence, rather than supplying new motives. If we have to supply a new motive we generally consider how much money will just make it worth his while to do it. Sometimes indeed the gratitude, or esteem, or honour which is held out as an inducement to the actions may appear as a new motive: particularly if it can be crystallised in some definite outward·manifestation; as for instance in the right to make use of the letters C.B., or to wear a star or a garter.

In this world such distinctions are comparatively rare, and connected with but few transactions: they would not serve as a measure of the ordinary motives that govern men in the acts of everyday life. But even here political services are more frequently rewarded by such honours than in any other way; so we have got into the habit of measuring them not in money but in honours. We say, for instance, that A's exertions for the benefit of his party or of the State, as the case may be, were fairly paid for by a knighthood: while knighthood was but shabby pay for B; he had earned a baronetcy.

It is possible that in other worlds than ours there may be no private property in material things, no wealth as it is generally understood by us; but that public honours are meted out by graduated tables as rewards for every action that is done for another's good. If these honours can be transferred from one to another without the intervention of any external authority, they may serve to measure the strength of motives almost as conveniently and exactly as money does with us. In such a world there may be a treatise on economic theory very similar to the present, even though there be very little mention in it of material things, and no mention at all of money.

It seems well to insist on this; for a misleading association has grown up in people's minds between that measurement of motives, which is the chief task of economic science, and an exclusive regard for material wealth, to the neglect of other and higher objects of desire. The only condition required for a measure for economic purposes is that it should be something definite and transferable. Its taking a material form is practically convenient in this world, but is not essential.

But, while attributing this high and transcendent universality to the central scheme of economic reasoning, we may not assign any universality to economic dogmas. For that part of economic doctrine, which alone can claim universality, has no dogmas. It is not a body of concrete truth, but an engine for the discovery of concrete truth, similar to, say, the theory of mechanics.

The theory of mechanics contains no statement of fact as to the greatest strain which bridges will bear. Every bridge has its peculiarities of construction and material: and mechanics supplies a universal engine, which will help in determining what strain any bridge will bear. But it has no universal dogmas by which this strain can be determined without observation of the particular facts of the case.

Suppose that all the bridges over the canals of Venice were, as indeed most of them are, very nearly of the same material and general construction: suppose that there were a number of general dogmas roughly true with regard to all of them; and suppose that some engineers had applied these dogmas to bridges built under different circumstances and in other places. When the breaking down of the new bridges had shown the folly of claiming universality for the practical dogmas of mechanics, impetuous people would rush to the conclusion that there was no universal organon of mechanical reasoning. This is exactly the mistake which seems to me to have been made by the extreme wing of the "real" or historical school of German economists.

Ultimately part of this organon will no doubt be presented as a perfectly pure or abstract theory[1]. But at present, while we are feeling our way, it seems best to sacrifice generality of form to some extent, and to conform to the modes of expression adopted by the older economists.

For, indeed, when they spoke of the "economic man" as governed by selfish or rather self-regarding motives, they did not express their meaning exactly. For example, Mill says that in economic phenomena "the psychological law chiefly concerned is the familiar one that a greater gain is preferred to a smaller[2]"; and argues that science gets a better hold in economics than in other social phenomena because it deals with motives that can be compared quantitatively and measured one against another. It is this notion of measurability that he really takes as the basis of his work, though he does not sufficiently emphasize it.

Whenever we get a glimpse of the economic man he is not selfish. On the contrary he is generally hard at work saving capital chiefly for the benefit of others. The fact is that the desire to make provision for one's family acts in a very regular way and is eminently capable of being reduced to law: it is prominent in all economic reasoning, because, though unselfish, it is measurable. Again, if, with Cliffe Leslie[3], we analyse all the infinite variety of motives that are commonly grouped together

---

[1] The ambition to work out a purely abstract theory in some form or other has probably come to many students of the subject: Mill had it, when he wrote (1829) his essay on *The Method of Political Economy*. But he had moved very far away from it by the time he came to write his *Principles of Political Economy with some of their applications to Social Philosophy*. There remained to the last some inconsistency in his use of the term Political Economy. But his view of the way in which economic matter should be studied was never narrowed to mere abstractions and ultimately became very broad; broader indeed than his own practice though that was not narrow. Much that has been written by the newer schools in England and Germany in favour of treating economic affairs on as wide a basis as possible was anticipated by him (see in particular *Logic*, Book VI, and his review of Comte). But he also pointed out difficulties which are often overlooked even now by those writers on method who have not themselves grappled with difficult problems. Mr Walker, in his admirable *Political Economy*, § 19, while quoting the full title of Mill's *Principles of Political Economy*, gives a short extract from his essay on method, which may, I think, have a misleading effect. Mr Walker implies that it is narrower and less philosophic than Cairnes' doctrine; whereas in my opinion it includes Cairnes' doctrine and shows a wider range of philosophic insight.

[2] *Logic*, Book VI, chap. ix, § 3.

[3] *Essays in Political and Moral Philosophy*, pp. 1–8.

under the term "love of money," we see that they are of all kinds. They include many of the highest, the most refined and the most unselfish elements of our nature. The common link that binds them together is that they can be more or less measured; and in this world they are measured by money.

But, though in wording our economic organon this idea of measurability should be always present, it should not, I think, be prominent. For practical purposes, and in order to keep the better our touch of real life, it will be best to go on treating it as chiefly concerned with those motives to which a money price can be directly or indirectly assigned. But motives that are selfish or self-regarding have no claim to more consideration than others except in so far as they may be more easily measurable and may more easily have a money-price assigned to them.

The organon then must have reference to an analysis of the positive motives of desire for different goods, and of the negative motives of unwillingness to undergo the fatigues and sacrifices involved in producing them.

The analysis is difficult chiefly because both classes of motives act in a great measure indirectly. There are many steps between our demand for the coals that are brought to us by railway and the demand by other people for the locomotive engines and the engine-drivers that bring them. There are many steps between the sacrifice of a parent, who sends his son to an expensive school, and the ultimate production of a carpet from the designs of that son when he is grown up. So difficult is this analysis, so subtle are the processes of reasoning involved in it, so many are the different factors mutually modifying one another of which account must be taken, so numerous are the wheels within wheels in the reasoning involved, that up to the present day the task is but half-mastered.

In popular discussions on economics one event is represented as determining a second, which determines a third, which determines a fourth, and so on. Reasoning of this kind can be followed without effort by anyone; but it does not correspond to the facts of nature and has been the source of much confusion. In human conduct one condition does not control another, but altogether they mutually determine one another. To grasp at one view this manifold mutual action is a very difficult task.

This organon deals with the play of measurable motives for and against one another, balancing one another and being substituted for one another, though the persons concerned may be in classes or even in countries that have little direct intercourse. And it sets out that most complex play of human motives that changes the purchasing power of money, and thus alters the measure of all motives.

Lastly, taking account of the fact that the same sum of money measures a greater pleasure for the poor than for the rich, it helps in determining the relations between the money gain that a nation gets from any given social or industrial change and the total increase of happiness arising from it. This task most properly belongs to the economic organon, though it has been much neglected by economists till recently. If more attention had been paid to it, we should have avoided many of those unintelligent applications of the doctrine of *laisser-faire*, which assume that whatever increases wealth must necessarily increase well-being. By a natural reaction many of the social reformers of to-day, in their desire to improve the distribution, are reckless as to the effects of their schemes on the production of wealth. They argue that, if the distribution of wealth were somewhat improved, its inequalities being somewhat diminished, the present or even a rather smaller national income would suffice for all the reasonable needs of man. But statistics prove that this is not the case.

There is scarcely any limit to the developments of economic theory which are possible: but of those which are possible only a small part are useful in having a direct relation to practical issues. Ricardo, who added more to the theory than anyone else, was not fortunate in his choice of cases to be worked out in detail. It is true that many problems of his, though they seem to us to have little practical bearing, yet corresponded very closely to the actual facts of his time. It requires, for instance, some effort to remember what a shifting there has been since his time of the causes which govern the prices of agricultural produce in England. But, after making every allowance of this kind, we must admit that he did not make a very good selection.

Since his time many improvements have been made in the choice and arrangement of cases to be worked out: so that the organon is becoming better fitted to actual conditions. But the work requires a constructive thinker of calibre similar to Ricardo's. Jevons might have done a great part of it, if his life had not been cut short. As it is, a great deal remains yet to be done. There are very few fields which offer so important and rich a harvest to scientific enterprise.

Such then is the work to be done by the economic organon. But two closely allied objections have been raised to it. The first finds fault with any attempt to separate the study of economic from that of other social phenomena. The second urges that we ought to reason direct from facts to facts, without the intervention of any formal theory; that for the solution of modern economic problems we should refer ourselves straight to the teachings of history.

Both of these objections seem to me to turn on a misconception of the nature and province of economic theory. They assume that the reasoning will somehow be simplified by discarding the theory. But it has been well argued by Mill and others that the work which the organon is applied to do cannot be evaded; it may be done almost unconsciously, but it must be done; and, if the aid of the organon is refused, it is done badly. This argument has, I think, never been fairly grappled with by the objectors, but I will restate it in my own way.

The first objection has been chiefly urged by Comte and his followers. One of the chief debts which we owe to Comte's genius, lies in the clearness and vigour with which he showed how complex social phenomena are, how intricately interwoven with one another, and withal how changeful. Hence he argued against any separate study of one part of them, and was specially vehement in his condemnation of the contemporary English economists.

This was partly to be accounted for by the fact that the Continental followers of the English school exaggerated their dogmatism, as was natural; and Comte's argument is undoubtedly valid as against economic dogmas. But the complexity and intricacy of social phenomena afford no reason for dispensing with the aid of the economic organon in its proper place: on the contrary they increase the necessity for it.

It is vain to speak of the higher authority of a unified social science. No doubt if that existed Economics would gladly find shelter under its wing. But it does not exist; it shows no signs of coming into existence. There is no use in waiting idly for it; we must do what we can with our present resources.

The only resources we have for dealing with social problems as a whole lie in the judgment of common sense. For the present, and for a long time to come, that must be the final arbiter. Economic theory does not claim to displace it from its supreme authority, nor to interfere with the manner nor even the order of its work, but only to assist it in one part of its work. For common sense does not deal with a complex problem as a whole. Its first step is to break the problem up into its several parts; it then discusses one set of considerations after another, and finally it sums up and gives its conclusions. The fact which Comte seems to have ignored is that the human mind has no other method of inquiry than this; that a complex problem is broken up into its component parts, less methodically indeed but no less completely by common sense than by formal analysis. When it is thus broken up each separate part offers a foot-hold to treatment by a special scientific organon, if there be one ready.

In nearly every important social problem, one of these component parts has to do with those actions and sacrifices which commonly have a money price. This set of considerations is almost always one of the hardest, one of those in which un-tutored common sense is most likely to go wrong. But it is fortunately one of those which offer the firmest foot-hold to scientific treatment. The economic organon brings to bear the accumulated strength of much of the best genius of many generations of men. It shows how to analyse the motives at work, how to group them, how to trace their mutual relations. And thus by introducing systematic and organized methods of reasoning, it enables us to deal with this one side of the problem with greater force and certainty than almost any other side; although it would have probably been the most unmanageable side of all without such aid. Having done its work it retires and leaves to common sense the responsibility of the ultimate decision; not standing in the way of, or pushing out any other kind of knowledge, not hampering common sense in the use to which it is able to put any other available knowledge, nor in any way hindering; helping where it could help, and for the rest keeping silence.

Sometimes indeed the economist may give a practical decision as it were with the authority of his science, but such a decision is almost always merely negative or critical. It is to the effect that a proposed plan will not produce its desired result; just as an engineer might say with authority that a certain kind of canal lock is unsuitable for its purpose. But an economist as such cannot say which is the best course to pursue, any more than an engineer as such can decide which is the best route for the Panama canal.

It is true that an economist, like any other citizen, may give his own judgment as to the best solution of various practical problems, just as an engineer may give his opinion as to the right method of financing the Panama canal. But in such cases the counsel bears only the authority of the individual who gives it: he does not speak with the voice of his science. And the economist has to be specially careful to make this clear; because there is much misunderstanding as to the scope of his science, and undue claims to authority on practical matters have often been put forward on its behalf.

The next objection comes from the extreme wing of the modern "real" or historic school of economists.

It would be difficult to overrate the importance of the work that has been done by the great leaders of this school in tracing the history of economic habits and institutions. It is one of the chief achievements of our age, and is an addition of the highest value to the wealth of the world. It has done more than almost anything else to broaden our ideas, to increase our knowledge of ourselves, and to help us to understand the central plan, as it were, of the Divine government of the world: such studies have led directly to some broad generalisations that have greatly illumined our path with a broad diffused light, which has made our notions as to the general bearing of economic problems clearer and truer.

But they do not throw a direct light on particular economic problems of our age. They do not in any way help us to dispense with the use of the economic organon: but rather make use of its aid at every step. And those whose great achievements have made the school illustrious have never attempted to dispense with the aid of economic theory, though in the writings of some of them an occasional piece of inconsequent reasoning may betray a rather careless study of it.

But unfortunately they have sometimes spoken a little disparagingly of it; and their words have been caught hold of and exaggerated and perverted by hangers-on of the science, in the same way as were the careless sayings of the leaders of the Ricardian school in the last generation. As thirty years ago a number of men who had never done any solid work for Economics, and knew nothing of its real difficulties, were confidently proclaiming the solution of the most intricate problems by a few cut-and-dried formulae, so now men of the same class are advocating another short cut in the opposite direction. They are telling us to discard all theories, and to seek the solution of our economic difficulties in the direct teaching of facts. This, then, is the second objection.

The answer is that facts by themselves are silent. Observation discovers nothing directly of the actions of causes, but only of sequences in time. It may find that an event followed on, or that it coincided with, a certain group of other events. But this gives no guidance except for other cases in which exactly the same set of facts occurs over again, grouped in just the same way. And such repetitions never occur in the life of man; nor indeed anywhere save in physical laboratories: history does not repeat itself. In economic or other social problems no event has ever been an exact precedent for another. The conditions of human life are so various: every event is the complex result of so many causes, so closely interwoven that the past can never throw a simple and direct light on the future.

When therefore it is said that a certain event in history teaches this or that, an element of deductive reasoning is introduced, which is the more likely to be fallacious the more persistently it is ignored. For the argument selects a few out of the group of conditions which were present when the event happened, and tacitly, if not unconsciously, assumes that the rest are irrelevant. The assumption may be justifiable: but it often turns out otherwise. Wider experience, more careful inquiry, often show that the causes to which the event is attributed could not have produced it without the aid of other causes; perhaps even that they hindered the event, which was brought about in spite of them by other causes that have escaped notice.

It is chiefly for this reason that the same events in economic history are used by different writers to support opposite theories. Both sides may be perfectly honest, both may wish to tell the truth and the whole truth. But, by grouping the same facts in different ways, by making different parts of the truth prominent, they suggest opposite conclusions. For instance, in controversies between American Protectionists and Free Traders, the same statistics have been used to prove that raising the tariff increases and that it diminishes general prosperity. On inquiry we find that a chief cause of their divergence is that they ascribe different lengths to the period which elapses between a change in the tariff and its maximum result[1]. One disputant ascribes to a recent lowering of the tariff a result which another says was part of the effect of a raising of the tariff that occurred some years before. It is difficult for those without special knowledge to be sure what lessons they ought to deduce from these facts, even though both sides are represented by able pleaders; partly because it is possible that both sides have been too intent on the controversy to take account of causes lying outside its scope. And this seems to have been the fact. It is probable that many of the results attributed by both of them to changes in the tariff were chiefly due to causes that had no connection with it.

Again in disputes as to the rates of wages paid in English trades, we find that much turns on allowances for slack time and over time, for the higher earnings and the over pressure of piece-work and so on. We are at the mercy of the narrator unless we can, so to speak, cross-examine the facts; unless we are able to suggest for ourselves causes that he may have overlooked, and to inquire into their action.

Experience in controversies such as these brings out the impossibility of learning anything from facts till they are

---

[1] See in particular Grosvenor's *Does Protection protect?* and the corresponding parts of Carey's *Social Science.*

examined and interpreted by reason; and teaches that the most reckless and treacherous of all theorists is he who professes to let facts and figures speak for themselves, who keeps in the background the part he has played, perhaps unconsciously, in selecting and grouping them, and in suggesting the argument *post hoc ergo propter hoc.*

In order to be able with any safety to interpret economic facts, whether of the past or present time, we must know what kind of effects to expect from each cause and how these effects are likely to combine with one another. This is the knowledge which is got by the study of economic science; while, on the other hand, the growth of the science is itself chiefly dependent on the careful study of facts by the aid of this knowledge.

For this purpose it is necessary to isolate the action of one cause after another; a difficult task in all cases, and seldom to be done except by one of three familiar scientific methods. The first is to find the same cause working in many different surroundings, and in all producing the same effect. Another is, having already discovered the effects of all causes, save one, at work in any case, to subtract these from the total effect, and by the method of residues to determine the effect of that one. The third is the simplest, but cannot often be applied. It is to find two cases which resemble one another in every respect except that one cause is present in one of them but not in the other. Then by holding the cases up to the light, as it were, against one another, the effect of that cause is made to stand out[1].

None of these methods can be safely used without wide knowledge. The thin thread of facts told to us by chroniclers, or travellers, is quite insufficient for the purpose. We must have access to a vast mass of facts which we can, so to speak, cross-examine, balancing them against one another and interpreting them by one another.

It must be admitted that to do this with regard to distant times is difficult if not impossible. For the social and economic history of early times stands on a different footing from their political history. That has some advantages over the political

---

[1] Compare the short but masterly essay, "Die Kathedersocialisten und die statistischen Congresse. Gedanken zur Begründung einer nationalœkonomischen Statistik und einer statistischen Nationalœkonomie," by Prof. Laspeyres.

annals of our own age; while in its turn posterity will understand, say, the policy of Prince Bismarck better than we do, because they will know documents that are now secret. But, in spite of all the print we shall leave them, posterity will not be able to settle a disputed question as to the economic facts of our time as well as we can. And our information as to the economic facts of times long past is so slight and so contradictory, that, if we subject it to the same searching criticism which we apply to disputed statements as to contemporary social facts, much of it crumbles away.

And there is a further difficulty: our present economic conditions are quite unlike any that have existed before. In many kinds of trading the whole world is one market, the chief dealers in every country knowing each day what the dealers in all other countries are doing on that day, and shaping their course accordingly. In some industries bargains between employers and employed are made in one room for many counties together. And—the most important change of all—many of the leaders of the working classes have the knowledge, resource, self-control and dignity which are necessary for carrying through a broad and far-seeing policy. The best parallel that we can find to this state of things in earlier times, though it is very imperfect, is in those trading cities of mediaeval Europe where all were free, and where it was possible to do by word of mouth what is now done by printing press and telegraph.

The study of economic history has done good service in destroying some of the narrower tenets of the older schools; in proving that habits and institutions which had been assumed to be inherent in human nature are comparatively of modern growth: and it has thrown a strong light on the modern problems of oriental countries. But on the other hand economic science has done much and I believe will do a great deal more in applying contemporary observations of the East to explain the economic past. In particular I think it will break up and explain what are called economic customs, very much as the telescope breaks up a nebula.

To say that any arrangement is due to custom, is really little more than to say that we do not know its cause. I believe that very many economic customs could be traced, if we only had knowledge enough, to the slow equilibration of measurable motives: that even in such a country as India no custom retains its hold long after the relative positions of the motives of demand and supply have so changed that the values, which would bring them into stable equilibrium, are far removed from those which the custom sanctions.

Where economic conditions change but little in one generation, the relative values of different things may keep very near what modern economists would call their normal position, and yet appear scarcely to move at all: just as, if one looks only for a short time at the hour hand of a watch, it seems not to move. But, if the preponderance of economic motive is strong in one direction, the custom, even while retaining its form, will change its substance, and really give way.

For instance I believe that rents seldom diverge much for a long time from their Ricardian level in the East, except when there really is a divided ownership of the land[1]. They often appear to do so, but on inquiry it will generally be found that they are really brought back near to it by the adjustment of quasi-feudal dues, or *abwabs*. In other cases the adjustment is effected by slightly altering the character of the commodity without changing its name. In fact after examining in detail the prices of the chief purchases made by the peasants in some parts of India, I have come to the conclusion that fixed custom has less to do with them than is the case with the agricultural labourer in the south of England. It is frequently said that economists have assigned too much influence to the action of competition (or as I prefer to call it the equilibration of measurable motives) in backward countries. I am gradually drifting to the opinion that in many cases too little force has been attributed to it, but that a mistake has been made in assuming that it would take the same outward form as with us, and that our own methods of dealing with it could be applied unaltered to backward countries.

We are able to cross-examine the facts of modern India; and

---

[1] Divided ownership is as much within the scope of Ricardian reasoning as single ownership. It is often said that our chief mistake in dealing with the land of Celtic and Indian peoples has been the applying to it the Ricardian theory of rent. No doubt we did make a mistake in this direction, but I believe our chief error has been legal rather than economic, and has consisted in our refusing to recognize the facts of divided ownership.

I believe that our science working on those facts will gradually produce a solvent which will explain much that is now unintelligible in mediaeval economic history.

Greedy then as the economist must be for facts, he must not be content with mere facts. Boundless as must be his gratitude to the great thinkers of the historic school, he must be suspicious of any direct light that the past is said to throw on problems of the present. He must stand fast by the more laborious plan of interrogating facts in order to learn the manner of action of causes singly and in combination, applying this knowledge to build up the organon of economic theory, and then making use of the aid of the organon in dealing with the economic side of social problems. He will thus work in the light of facts, but the light will not be thrown directly, it will be reflected and concentrated by science.

Such then is the work that lies before economic science: let us consider the relation in which Cambridge stands to it. There is wanted wider and more scientific knowledge of facts: an organon stronger and more complete, more able to analyse and help in the solution of the economic problems of the age. To develop and apply the organon rightly is our most urgent need: and this requires all the faculties of a trained scientific mind. Eloquence and erudition have been lavishly spent in the service of Economics. They are good in their way; but what is most wanted now is the power of keeping the head cool and clear in tracing and analysing the combined action of many combined causes. Exceptional genius being left out of account, this power is rarely found save among those who have gone through a severe course of work in the more advanced sciences. Cambridge has more such men than any other University in the world. But, alas! few of them turn to the task.

Partly this is because the only curriculum in which Economics has a very important part to play is that of the Moral Sciences Tripos. And many of those who are fitted for the highest and hardest economic work are not attracted by the metaphysical studies that lie at the threshold of that Tripos. Economics is a science of human motives, and, since some grouping is necessary, it could not be better grouped than with the other Moral Sciences. Tested by its fruits the Tripos is an excellent one.

It may claim a share, very much larger than in proportion to its numbers, of those who have increased the fame of Cambridge and her power in the world; and what it has done for Economics has certainly not been the least of its achievements. But may I not appeal to some of those who have not the taste or the time for the whole of the Moral Sciences, but who have the trained scientific minds which Economics is so urgently craving? May I not ask them to bring to bear some of their stored up force; to add a knowledge of the economic organon to their general training, and thus to take part in the great work of inquiring how far it is possible to remedy the economic evils of the present day?

For indeed the work is urgent. Material wealth has ever had but slight charms for the Academic mind. Our best men both young and old have found their joy in doing the best work of which they are capable, and have cared but little whether its money gain would be great or small. Secure themselves of being able to live a refined and cultured life, and with a just and noble scorn of those who hunt after superfluous riches, they have often drifted into an attitude of philosophic indifference to wealth and all its concerns. But this has been a great and disastrous mistake.

For why are so many lives draggled on through dirt and squalor and misery? Why are there so many haggard faces and stunted minds? Chiefly because there is not wealth enough; and what there is, is not well distributed, and well used. Much has been said of the physical suffering and ill-health caused by over-crowded dwellings, but the mental and moral ill-health due to them are greater evils still. With better house-room and better food, with less hard work and more leisure, the great mass of our people would have the power of leading a life quite unlike that which they must lead now, a life far higher and far more noble.

It has often been observed that one cause of the marvellous achievements of the Greeks was the directness with which they addressed themselves to the problems of their own time. Never was there an age so full of great social problems as ours; surely they are not unworthy of the best efforts of the best minds among us. Think of the force that University men might bring to bear by their personal influence, if great numbers of them had learnt to think clearly and had studied the subject-matter of the age in which they live. They might then take a wise and active part in relieving misery without making pauperism; in helping the people to educate themselves and rise to a higher level; to become not only more efficient producers but also wiser consumers, with greater knowledge of all that is beautiful, and more care for it.

And, lastly, if more University men looked upon their life here as preparing them for the higher posts of business, what a change they might make in the tone of business! Just and noble sentiments might be introduced into counting-house and factory and workshop, without the dangers which weak benevolence runs of turning sentiment into sentimentality, of courting ruin and increasing the common prejudice that a pleasant looking house of business is likely to be financially unsound. If our Universities were more in sympathy with business, charitable England would not have left to other countries so much of the work of pioneering the way towards making factory life pleasant and beautiful[1].

Why should it be left for impetuous socialists and ignorant orators to cry aloud that none ought to be shut out by the want of material means from the opportunity of leading a life that is worthy of man? Of those who throw their whole souls into the discussion of this problem, the greater part put forth hastily conceived plans which would often increase the evils that they desire to remedy: because they have not had a training in thinking out hard and intricate problems, a training which is most rare in the world and plentiful only in Cambridge. The great scientific strength of Cambridge is not indeed indifferent to social problems; but is content to treat them in an amateur fashion, not with the same weighty seriousness that it gives to other studies.

Partly this may be because Economics is yet so much in its infancy that it has but little to teach. But then those who are already masters of scientific method can learn that little quickly; and, when they have learnt it, they will wonder how much insight they have got, with but a little labour, into the real nature of the problems that have to be solved.

[1] Compare *Old World Questions and New World Answers* by D. Pidgeon.

It will be my most cherished ambition, my highest endeavour, to do what with my poor ability and my limited strength I may, to increase the numbers of those, whom Cambridge, the great mother of strong men, sends out into the world with cool heads but warm hearts, willing to give some at least of their best powers to grappling with the social suffering around them; resolved not to rest content till they have done what in them lies to discover how far it is possible to open up to all the material means of a refined and noble life.

VII

THE GRAPHIC METHOD OF STATISTICS (1885)[1]

THE graphic method of statistics, though inferior to the numerical in accuracy of representation, has the advantage of enabling the eye to take in at once a long series of facts. It has many forms: but its chief form is generally called "the method of curves." Its defects are such that many statisticians seldom use it except for the purpose of popular exposition: and for this purpose it has some dangers. I would however venture to suggest the inquiry whether the method has had a fair chance. It seems to me that, so long as it is used in a desultory and unsystematic manner, its faults produce their full effect, but its virtues do not. I believe that if thoroughly organised, its special virtues will make it a great engine of scientific inquiry, and that a plan may be devised for obviating in a great measure its chief defects. The advantage of being able to take in at a glance the general bearing of many detailed facts is not of first-rate importance when we are considering only one set of facts: accuracy is then more important than ease and rapidity of representation; and in accuracy the graphic method is inferior to the numerical. But ease and rapidity are essential when we want to compare many sets of facts together; because, if the mind is delayed long in taking in the general effect of one set, it meanwhile loses full count of others: a chief function of the graphic method is to facilitate the comparison of different sets of statistics.

A simple table of statistics represents in one vertical row of figures a series of quantities of one kind, and in a parallel row a series of quantities of another, each horizontal pair standing in some definite relation to one another. In the method of curves each of these pairs is represented by a point; the vertical distance of the point from a fixed base line representing one of these figures, and its horizontal distance from a fixed base line representing the other. The statistical "curve" is, strictly speaking, a jagged line formed by joining these points. The most important class of statistical curves, at all events for the

[1] A Paper read at the International Statistical Congress 1885, published in the Jubilee volume of the *Journal of the Royal Statistical Society*.

present purpose, is that in which one set of distances, generally the vertical set, express periods of time; they may be called *historical curves*.

We often speak of observing that certain causes produce a certain result. But what we really do is to observe that the result happened at a certain time and that the causes were in existence at that or some earlier time; and then by a process of, perhaps unconscious, reasoning we infer that the result is rightly to be attributed to the causes in question. History says an event happened "at the same time as the cause," or "after this cause," and reason infers "therefore because of this cause." It suggests *post hoc* (or *cum hoc*) *ergo propter hoc*. But history has not done its work unless it suggests not merely some, but all the causes, or at least all the chief causes which occurred at such a time that they may probably have had a part in bringing about the result. I wish to argue that the graphic method may be so applied as to enable history to do this work better than it has hitherto.

Great use has already been made of the plan of arranging on the same sheet of paper a group of curves, each of which tells one of the constituent parts of a piece of history, the measurement of time being the same for each of the curves. Such for instance is a diagram of the iron trade, in which one curve represents the British exports of iron and steel, another the total production of them, another the stocks of Scotch pig iron, and others the prices of different kinds of iron and steel. It enables us to see at a glance, not only the general character of the change in each of these amounts, but also the relations in which the changes in one element stand to those in another. It calls our attention to sequences and coincidences of time, and prompts us to seek for the causal connection between them. For instance, it suggests an inquiry by calling attention to the fact that the stocks of iron begin to diminish a year or two before each crisis, and go on diminishing for a year or two after, and then begin to rise again. The same plan is applied elsewhere, as for instance in Jevons' *Investigations of Currency and Finance*, for the broader purposes of economics, and its usefulness has been approved by a wide experience.

My proposal is to extend this plan, to apply it not merely

to one sheet of paper, but to a great many pages, which may be bound into one large book, or from which by proper selection many books may be made for special purposes. The sheaf of corn which the Statistical Society has chosen as its emblem is a broad one. A few stalks of corn bound together may just manage to stand up on a still day, but the sheaf that is to be firm and strong must have a broad basis. An isolated sheet of historical curves seems to me like a very slender sheaf.

On this plan, identical columns of figures represent successive years on each of a great many consecutive pages, so that the same horizontal line stands for one and the same year on every page. Each page contains as a rule a group of allied historical curves, while sometimes a page supplements the curves on the adjacent page by a record of facts, that cannot well be expressed by statistics, together with perhaps some subsidiary tables of figures. Some pages are given to vital statistics, others to those of banking, railways, shipping, emigration, poor law, education, crimes, etc., and so on. Some would represent the broad features of England's trade with foreign countries, some would analyse its trade with particular countries, while others would analyse its foreign and domestic trade in particular commodities, and so on.

Were this done for England alone, it would suggest a great many new empirical laws to be analysed by reason and tested by experience. Without such assistance the historian is needlessly at the mercy of accident; he ascribes each event to the causes that he thinks of in connection with it. But possibly, if he had turned over the pages of such a book as this, keeping his eye fixed at each horizontal level on each page, and noticing when any of those showed much irregularity in form, he might have been led to see that the explanation which had at first occurred to him was at all events not the whole of the truth. The value of such a book would increase much more rapidly than its size, because the numbers of ways in which the curves could be grouped together would increase much more rapidly than the numbers of the curves.

But valuable as such a book would be if it related to one country only, its highest use would be for international statistics: and that is the reason why I venture to submit it for discussion to-day. For the whole civilized world is more closely bound together for many purposes than the different parts of England were some time ago; we cannot now understand the events of one country unless we know something of the parallel events in others. Sometimes the necessary facts can be got from handy books such as our own statistical abstracts; but more often they must be hunted up from many books in many languages. And, even when they are found, they are not so arranged that a general survey of them can be taken at once. But this would be done by the book I am pleading for.

For instance, if the history of the English iron trade is being investigated, after looking at the page containing the curves specially relating to it, one can turn in the first instance to those showing the history for England of the money market, of the purchasing power of money, of coal, of railways, of ship building, of foreign trade, of the price of corn and other necessaries, and so on. And lastly, one would look at the pages giving the history of the iron trades of other countries. Not only would these last pages supply important causes for English history that might have otherwise been overlooked, but they would help us to test our explanations of English history by applying them to parallel events in foreign history. For one thing, it would be useful to know how far the rule observed as to England, that large stocks of iron diminish in the years just before and the years just after a crisis, holds of other countries also.

Of course such a work must be expensive; but that is another reason for discussing the plan to-day. It could be so arranged as to be adapted for use in many countries: the edition published in each country having supplementary pages with such detailed information as was only of local interest. Again, by a proper selection of plates, books might be made up of special interest to particular classes of people, as, for instance, to agriculturists, to ship owners, to the iron trade, and so on. I hope that the international society which we are to discuss to-morrow will in the course of time fix a standard gauge for the thickness of the strip allotted to each year, say a depth of five millimetres. It might also adopt a normal size for the page, though occasionally other sizes might be adopted for special purposes without very great inconvenience. Special provision could be made for those statistics which take as their unit of time any other period than a year.

The system of standard gauges and interchangeable parts has recently revolutionized many industries; and I think it may do great good to the statistical industry, rendering possible in it, as it has in other industries, the use of mechanical appliances, whose cost would otherwise have been prohibitive.

Let us then suppose that we have a large collection of historical curves on a standard gauge, perhaps bound up in a book or books, and containing in appropriate places pages of general history: I mean some of its pages deal with such changes as cannot well be expressed by figures, and record them as nearly as possible in the horizontal lines that are appropriated to the period in which the changes have occurred. Let us then inquire more carefully what aid such a system of historical curves can give towards interpreting the past and anticipating the future, and what it cannot give.

The observation of the present and the experience of the past tell us what things happened, at what times and places, and nothing more. By themselves they explain nothing, but they supply materials from which we must ourselves infer the connection of cause and effect. We may do it with the formalism of elaborate science, or in the rough and ready language of ordinary life; but in substance our method is always the same. To explain an event we always consider what causes are likely to have brought it about; we inquire into these causes one after another to see what was the state of each of them at and before the time of the event, and then we use our judgment to decide what part of the result we shall attribute to each cause. Facts are the bricks out of which reason builds the edifice of knowledge. This system claims to do nothing more than to give, ready to the hand of the builder, a full supply of those particular bricks which he wants for any purpose.

Suppose an event A happened in the year 1880, and we think it may have been due to causes B, C, D, etc.; this system will show what were the states of B, C, D, etc. in that year, and the previous years. Also, by calling attention to a remarkable change at about that time in some other cause, K, it may put us on the track of a causal connection that might otherwise have been overlooked. What it cannot do is to tell directly the nature of the dependence of A upon B, C, D, etc. That must be done by reason making use of that abstract and essence of past experience which is on one side science, and on the other practical instinct. But every fresh study of the curves helps to strengthen us in this work, and to verify and improve our estimates of the nature of the effect to be assigned to each cause.

All this can be put more clearly and definitely if we borrow the language of Mathematics. Statistics organize the collection and arrangement of particular statements as to quantity. Mathematical language enables us to express general statements as to quantity with the utmost brevity, precision, and force; and mathematical theory reasons on the basis of these statements. It is true that the results obtained by statistics generally, and in particular the economic branch of statistics, are seldom sufficiently definite and trustworthy to afford much useful material for mathematical *theory* to work on: but they are sufficiently definite to be able often to gain a great deal by having their general tenor stated in the mathematical *language*. Every statistical table suggests the expression of the thing, whose quantities it shows in one column, as a function of the thing whose quantities it shows in another. A historical table of statistics suggests the expression of something as a function of time, and in the corresponding historical curve this suggestion takes a geometrical form which brings it one step nearer to the language of mathematics.

If, for instance, U be the quantity of the effect A in any year, then the increase of U during that year is its rate of growth at that time expressed as $\dfrac{dU}{dt}$. So if X, Y, Z, ... be the quantities at that time of B, C, D, ..., the curves tell us their rate of growth, expressed as $\dfrac{dX}{dt}$, $\dfrac{dY}{dt}$, $\dfrac{dZ}{dt}$, ... Now, A being a function of B, C, D, ..., the rate of growth of A is made up of that part which is due to B, that part which is due to C, and so on. The part which is due to B is the product of the rate of growth of B into the dependence of A on B, that is, $\dfrac{dU}{dX}$; and so for C, D, etc. The whole growth of A is then made up of the sum of these products: that is

$$\frac{dU}{dt} = \frac{dU}{dX} \cdot \frac{dX}{dt} + \frac{dU}{dY} \cdot \frac{dY}{dt} + \frac{dU}{dZ} \cdot \frac{dZ}{dt}.$$

It is of course to be understood that $\frac{dU}{dt}$ on the right hand of the equation is "partial" and on the left is "total."

This is merely writing out explicitly the implicit process by which every thinking man reasons, whether he uses statistics or not. It is, for instance, the way in which a farmer analyses his experience of the advantages of feeding his stock with oil cake; though no doubt it would take him some time to recognise his own offspring in this attire.

Thus, the system of historical curves claims to supply in the most convenient possible form one set of the factors used in every explanation of the past and forecast of the future, in so far as it is based on an estimate of quantity. They supply the rates of growth of the possible causes; reason by aid of theory, which is the abstract of past experience, supplies the other set of factors, viz. the nature of the dependence of the result observed on the several causes. The curves tell us

$$\frac{dX}{dt}, \frac{dY}{dt}, \text{ etc.; reason supplies } \frac{dU}{dX}, \frac{dU}{dY}, \text{ etc.}$$

It must however be admitted that the method of historical curves labours under some just discredit in consequence of its often suggesting misleading notions as to the comparative rates of growth of different things. The difficulty would not be so great if we were concerned chiefly with the absolute amounts of increase; it is not difficult to infer from the historical curve for shipping clearances that they have increased by so many thousand tons. But for the purposes of comparison with other curves, as for instance that of train mileage, this is not what we want to know. What we want to know is the percentage of increase. Though there is not much interest in comparing so many extra tons of shipping clearances with so many extra miles of train mileage, there is great interest in comparing an increase of one-tenth in the tonnage of shipping clearances with an increase of one-sixth or one-twelfth in the train mileage during the same period. In other words, we want to compare what we may call their *proportional rates of increase.* For I would define the proportional rate of increase of a thing to be *the ratio which the increase during, say, a year bears to the amount at the beginning of the year.*

It cannot be denied that the suggestions which historical curves give as to the comparative rates of increase of different things depend very much on the scales on which they are drawn. This evil is considerable even in the case of such prices of commodities and securities as practically oscillate about a fixed level.

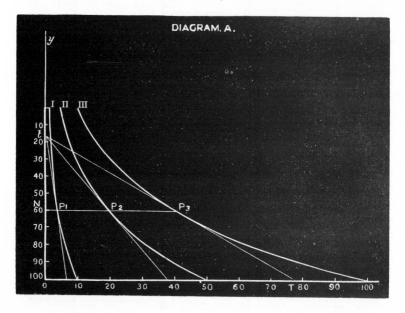

It is greatest in the case of things that increase very rapidly, whether at a fixed rate or not.

For instance, it requires a trained eye to see that the same proportional rate of increase is represented at every point on Curve II in Diagram A. Not only is this the case, but Curve II is identical with Curves I and III. Each of them represents the growth of the population of London on the supposition that, starting at one million, it had increased for a century uniformly at about its actual mean growth during the last thirty years. That is to say, each of them represents the growth at the annual rate of about one forty-third annually, so that it doubles in about thirty years, and is multiplied exactly ten fold in one hundred years. The only difference between the curves is that the horizontal scale is five times as large for the second curve, and ten times as large for the third curve, as it is for the first.

Again, in Diagram B the consumption per head of tea and sugar in the United Kingdom for the years 1860 to 1883 is represented to the same scale in pounds in Curves I and II. The danger of the popular use of statistical curves is illustrated by the fact that an orator might perhaps carry his audience with him while he argued that they showed a much more rapid

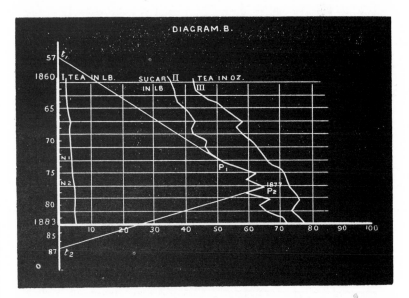

growth of the consumption of sugar than of tea. But really there is very little difference between the two, as is seen on comparing Curves II and III, in which a pound of sugar is compared against, not a pound, but an ounce of tea. Again, in Diagram C, Curves I, II, and III represent the marriages, deaths, and births in England and Wales in each year of the present century. But it is difficult for the eye without some artificial aid to compare the rates of increase at different parts of the same or of different curves.

For this class of difficulties several remedies have been proposed. Expert arithmeticians sometimes translate the curves back into columns of figures; others acquire a considerable skill in measuring and comparing lines with the eye. Sometimes a curve is drawn to a new scale for special purposes; one instance of this has been seen in the case of the tea curve, but a better instance can be seen in Curve IV in Diagram C, which represents marriages on four times as large a scale as the births. From this we see that the ratio of births to marriages has been nearly steadily increasing from something less than four to something more than four.

Another method that can be occasionally used is to draw supplementary curves showing for each year or decade the rate of growth during it. Again, another method is to make the distances horizontally represent the logarithms of amounts. On this plan lines of equal slope denote equal ratios of increase, and therefore the three curves on Diagram A would become parallel straight lines. But this last plan labours under the disadvantage of not presenting quantities as they are, but only their logarithms; and for ordinary use this far more than outweighs all its advantages. Moreover, many of these advantages may be secured by a plan which can be applied at once to the ordinary historical curves, and it is to this that I want specially to draw your attention.

If a ruler be placed so as to touch a historical curve at P (see Diagram A), tN being the vertical distance above P of the point t at which the ruler meets the vertical base line, then the proportional rate of increase at P is the *inverse of the number of years represented by* tN. It will be found on trial that tN is the same number 43 (or more strictly $43\frac{1}{2}$) for every point on each of these curves, which, when interpreted, means that each curve, throughout the whole of its length, represents an annual increase of $\frac{1}{43}$. Whatever be the scale on which the curve is drawn, this plan gives at once an exact measure of the proportionate rate of growth[1].

If the curves had shown a diminishing population, t would

---

[1] The law is that if $x = f(y)$ be the equation to the curve, y being measured downwards from a fixed horizontal line to represent time, and x being measured along Ox to represent quantity, the rate of proportionate increase is $\dfrac{1}{\Delta y} \cdot \dfrac{\Delta x}{x}$, or in the limit $\dfrac{1}{x}\dfrac{dx}{dy}$, *i.e.* $\dfrac{1}{Nt}$. In this case the equation to each curve on its appropriate horizontal scale is $x = 10^{\frac{100}{y}}$, $\therefore Nt = 100 \log_{10} e = 43 \cdot 5$ approximately, and is the same for all points on the curve.

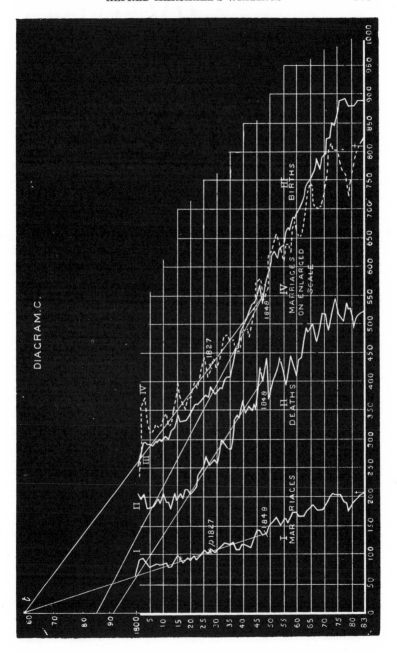

have been below N, and then the inverse of the numbers of years represented by Nt would have been the annual *proportional rate of diminution* at P.

But, instead of wanting to know the rate of growth at a point on the curves, we may want to examine the growths between two somewhat distant points, or periods: it is this that we nearly always want to do in the case of discontinuous, or broken, curves such as those in Diagrams B and C. A strict geometrical mean of the proportionate rate of growths between the two periods requires the use of logarithms; but an arithmetical mean, which can be found by a simple rule, is sufficiently accurate for most purposes. For instance, when we are considering the increase of births in England and Wales between say 1827 and 1848, it will be sufficient for most purposes to know what fraction of the births in 1827 will have to be added in each of the twenty-one years from then to 1848 in order to get the number in 1848. This fraction may be called the *average proportionate rate of increase*, in order to distinguish it from the geometric mean.

The rule to determine this is: first find the point on the curve corresponding to these two years 1827 and 1848; draw a straight line through the two points, and see where it cuts the vertical base line Oy. This point is at the year 1785, that is forty-two years before 1827. Then the rule gives us $\frac{1}{42}$ as the fraction required.

Applying the same rule to the curve of deaths for the same years 1827 and 1848, we find that the straight line joining the corresponding points cuts Oy in the year 1791, thirty-six years before 1827; therefore the average proportionate rate of growth of births between 1827 and 1848 is $\frac{1}{36}$. If we do the same by the two curves representing marriages, we find that they meet (as of course they must) in the same year: this is 1755, showing that the average proportionate rate of increase of marriages for the period is $\frac{1}{72}$[1].

This simple rule enables us with but little pains to escape from the bewildering influence of changes in the horizontal scale to which historical curves are drawn. We have only to

---

[1] If the quantities observed had been diminishing instead of increasing between these two periods, the line joining the two corresponding points would have cut Oy below them, and the vertical distance of this point of intersection below the upper of the two chosen points gives the increase of the average proportionate rate of diminution.

get into the habit of sliding a ruler or a pencil along the curve, and of watching the vertical distance through which it rises between the point at which it leaves the curve and the point in which it cuts Oy; remembering then that the annual proportionate rate of growth varies inversely as the number of years represented by this distance, we shall be able to use historical curves without risk. We shall read them truly, and therefore with the same result, whatever be the scale on which they are drawn, and however misleading would be the notions with regard to the proportionate rate of growth which they would suggest at first sight. We shall thus have got over the chief objection to the general use of historical curves.

It may be added that there is a somewhat similar difficulty in the interpretation of a large family of statistical curves, of which one instance is found in "*demand curves*.' We may want to find a measure of what may be called *the elasticity of demand*: that is, when a fall of price leads to an increase in the amount demanded, we may want to know the ratio in which the percentage by which the amount demanded has increased stands to the percentage by which the price has fallen. If, for instance, in Diagram A the amounts demanded are measured along Ox and the corresponding prices along Oy, so that Curve III becomes a demand curve, then the elasticity of demand represented by the curve at P can be determined by a simple rule. Let a straight line touching the curve at P meet Oy in t and Ox in T, then *the measure of the elasticity required is the ratio of PT to Pt.*

If PT were twice Pt, a fall of 1 per cent. in price would cause an increase of 2 per cent. in the amount demanded; the elasticity of demand would be two. If PT were one-third of Pt, a fall of 1 per cent. in price would cause an increase of $\frac{1}{3}$ per cent. in the amount demanded; the elasticity of demand would be one-third: and so on. I believe that inductions with regard to the elasticity of demand, and deductions based on them, have a great part to play in economic science.

VIII

REMEDIES FOR FLUCTUATIONS OF GENERAL PRICES (1887)[1]

THE purpose of this paper is to inquire whether the greater part of the fluctuations of general prices are not of such a nature as to be incapable of being materially diminished by the adoption of two metals instead of one as the basis of our currency. I shall argue that they are; that the only effective remedy for them is to be sought in relieving the currency of the duty, which it is not fitted to perform, of acting as a standard of value; and by establishing, in accordance with a plan which has long been familiar to economists, an authoritative standard of purchasing power independent of the currency. While admitting that it would be better to base our currency on two metals than on one, I contend that the scheme of opening the mints to gold and silver at a fixed ratio, though commonly called Bimetallism, has no strict title to that name, and that it has not yet established its claim to be the best scheme for attaining those particular ends at which it aims.

I am not an advocate of hurried change. The strong popular prejudice against anything that looks like tampering with the monetary foundations of our business is, on the whole, a healthy prejudice. But the greater the evils of change, the more important it is to inquire thoroughly whether any proposed scheme is the best possible, whether it would attain and sustain the good results which it promises, whether there is any considerable chance that it would have to be abandoned ere long. The evils of our present monetary system are great. A compact body of energetic men advocating a new plan, and proving that it would be, in some respects, an improvement on our present plan, are in a position of advantage. The question they raise is—Shall we continue to endure our present evils, or shall we adopt their plan? But the right issue is not whether their plan would be on the whole better than our present, but whether it is the best of all conceivable plans, account being taken both of the evils of change and of the benefits which will ultimately accrue from it.

[1] *Contemporary Review*, March, 1887.

That is the inquiry on which I start. It is no answer to me to say that change is an evil, and the people are not very likely to submit to a change. For it is certain that one proposal for change has gained an attentive hearing which a few years ago would have been thought impossible. And it is therefore high time to inquire—*If change is to come,* what change will give the greatest surplus of good over evil?

I.—THE EVILS OF A FLUCTUATING STANDARD OF VALUE

The chief functions of money fall under two heads. Money is, firstly, a *medium of exchange* for bargains that are completed almost as soon as they are begun; it is a "currency"; it is a material thing carried in purses, and "current" from hand to hand, because its value can be read at a glance. This first function of money is admirably discharged by gold and silver and paper based on them.

The second function of money is to act as a *standard of value,* or *standard for deferred payments*—that is, to indicate the amount of general purchasing power, the payment of which is sufficient to discharge a contract, or other commercial obligation, that extends over a considerable period of time. For this purpose stability of value is the one essential condition.

Much of the importance of having a good standard of deferred payments is peculiar to modern times. In early stages of civilization business arrangements seldom looked far ahead; contracts to make definite payments at distant times were rare and unimportant. But a great deal of our modern business life is made up of such contracts. Much of the income of the nation goes to its ultimate recipients in the form of fixed money payments on Government bonds, on the debentures of private companies, on mortgages and on long leases. Another large part consists of salaries and wages, any change in the nominal value of which involves great friction; so that as a rule the nominal rate remains unchanged, while the real rate is constantly fluctuating with every change in the purchasing power of money.

And, lastly, the complex nature of modern trade and industry puts the management of business into the hands of a comparatively small number of men with special ability for it, and most

people lend the greater part of their wealth to others instead of
using it themselves. It is therefore a great evil that whenever a
man borrows money to be invested in his business he speculates
doubly. In the first place he runs the risk that the things which
he handles will fall in value relatively to others—this risk is
inevitable, it must be endured. But in addition he runs the risk
that the standard in which he has to pay back what he has
borrowed will be a different one from that by which his borrowing
was measured.

We are vaguely conscious that an element of speculation is
thus unnecessarily introduced into life, but few of us, perhaps,
realize how great it is. We often talk of borrowing or lending
on good security at, say, 5 per cent. If we had a real standard
of value that could be done; but, as things are, it is a feat which
no one performs except by accident. Suppose, for instance, a
man borrows £100 under contract to pay back £105 at the end
of the year. If the purchasing power of money has meanwhile
risen 10 per cent. (or, which is the same thing, general prices
have fallen in the ratio of ten to eleven), he cannot get the £105
which he has to pay back without selling one-tenth more
commodities than would have been sufficient for the purpose at
the beginning of the year. Assuming, that is, that the things
which he handles have not changed in value relatively to things
in general, he must sell commodities which would have then
cost him £115 10s. in order to pay back with interest his loan
of £100; he has lost ground unless the commodities have increased under his hands $15\frac{1}{2}$ per cent. While nominally paying
5 per cent. for the use of his money, he has really been paying
$15\frac{1}{2}$ per cent.

On the other hand, if prices had risen so much that the purchasing power of money had fallen 10 per cent. during the year,
so that he could get £10 for things which cost him £9 at the
beginning of the year—that is, £105 for things which cost him
£94 10s. at the beginning of the year—then, instead of paying
5 per cent. for the loan, he would really be paid $5\frac{1}{2}$ per cent. for
taking charge of the money.

The consequence of this uncertainty is that, when prices are
likely to rise, people rush to borrow money and buy goods, and
thus help prices to rise; business is inflated, it is managed

recklessly and wastefully; those working on borrowed capital pay back less real value than they borrowed, and enrich themselves at the expense of the community.

Salaries and wages, unless when governed by a sliding scale, generally retain their nominal value more or less fixed in spite of trade fluctuations; they can seldom be changed without much friction and worry and loss of time. And, for the very reason that their nominal or money value is fixed, their real value varies, and varies in the wrong direction. It falls when prices are rising, and the purchasing power of money is falling; so that the employer pays smaller real salaries and wages than usual, at the very time when his profits are largest in other ways, and is thus prompted to over-estimate his strength, and engage in ventures which he will not be able to pull through after the tide begins to turn.

When afterwards credit is shaken and prices begin to fall, every one wants to get rid of commodities and get hold of money which is rapidly rising in value; this makes prices fall all the faster, and the further fall makes credit shrink even more, and thus for a long time prices fall because prices have fallen. At such a time employers cease their production because they fear that when they come to sell their finished product general prices will be even lower than when they buy their materials; and at such times it would often be well for both sides and for the community at large that the employees should take rather less real wages than in times of prosperity. But, in fact, since wages and salaries are reckoned in money which is rising in value, the employer pays higher real wages than usual at such a time unless he can get money wages reduced. This is a difficult task, partly because the employees, not altogether unreasonably, fear that when nominal wages are once let down they will not be easily raised. So they are inclined to stop work rather than accept a nominal reduction even though it would not be a real one. The employer, on his part, finds a stoppage his easiest course; at all events, by diminishing production he will help to improve the market for his own goods. He may not happen to remember that every stoppage of work in any one trade diminishes the demand for the work of others; and that, if all trades tried to improve the market by stopping their work together, the only result would be that every one would have less of everything to consume. He may even think that there is a fear of general over-production, not because he is prepared to say that we could have too much of anything at once, but because he knows that, when a long period of peace and invention has increased production in every trade, the volume of goods rises relatively to that of money, prices fall, and borrowers, that is, men of business, generally lose.

The want of a proper standard of purchasing power is the chief cause of the survival of the monstrous fallacy that there can be too much produced of everything. The fluctuations in the value of what we use as our standard are ever either flurrying up business activity into unwholesome fever, or else closing factories and workshops by the thousand in businesses that have nothing radically wrong with them, but in which whoever buys raw material and hires labour is likely to sell when general prices have further fallen. Perhaps the bad habits of mind and temper engendered by the periods of business fever do more real harm than the periods of idleness; but it is less conspicuous and less easily traced. In times of stagnation he who runs may read in waste and gaunt faces a degradation of physique and a weakening of energy, which often tells its tale throughout the whole of the rest of the lives of the men, women, and children who have suffered from it.

II.—The Precious Metals cannot afford a good Standard of Value

A distinction must be made between fluctuations of general prices which come and go quickly and those whose period is long. Short-period fluctuations practically efface themselves when we compare the mean prices of successive decades, but are conspicuous when we compare prices in successive years. Long-period fluctuations do not show themselves clearly from year to year, but stand out prominently when the mean prices of one decade are contrasted with those of other decades. They are chiefly caused by changes in the amounts of the precious metals relatively to the business which has to be transacted by them, allowance being of course made for changes in the extent to which the precious metals are able at any time to delegate their functions to bank-notes, cheques, bills of exchange, and other substitutes. And they would certainly be much mitigated if each decade's supply of the metallic basis of our currency could be made uniform—*i.e.* to grow proportionately to our commercial wants. Bimetallism would tend somewhat in this direction, but it would not go very far; for at best it would substitute the mean between two fluctuating supplies in place of one fluctuating supply.

In old times a disputed frontage used to be measured by the judge stepping heel-to-toe over it. Variations in "the length of the judge's foot" caused great uncertainties, which would have been diminished if two judges had stepped the distance, and the mean of their measurements had been taken. But the improvement would have been small unless there had been some security that if one were a short man the other would be a tall one. And there is no security that the yield of the silver mines will be great when that of the gold mines is small: history shows that the probability is the other way. For, indeed, when a new country is prospected, silver mines are often found in one part and gold in another, while some mines produce both gold and silver.

But, after all, the fluctuations in prices from decade to decade are small in the aggregate as compared with those from year to year, and contribute but a very small share to those uncertainties of business which are the cause of so large a share of human suffering and degradation. No remedy for long-period fluctuations, however perfect it might be, would go any considerable way towards freeing us from these great evils, unless it at the same time greatly diminished the rapid fluctuations of general prices from year to year. These rapid fluctuations are but to a very slight extent caused by variations in the production of gold and silver; for never, not even in 1852, has the increased annual production of gold exceeded a hundredth part of the existing stock, and the annual variations of production have seldom amounted to a thousandth part of the existing stock. So slight is the influence of changes in the apparent fertility of mines on variations of general prices from year to year, that the purchasing power of gold has sometimes risen when its production has been increasing, and fallen when its production has been diminishing. Whatever be the metallic standard of our currency, inflations and contractions of credit and prices will always be caused by wars and rumours of wars, by good and bad harvests, and by the alternate opening out of promising new enterprises, and the collapse of many of the hopes founded on them.

A striking evidence of the fact that these causes have been far more influential in determining the movements of prices than any fluctuations in the supplies and relative values of the precious metals is to be seen in the accompanying diagram. The dark curve shows the variations of the index number, which represents the average prices of the leading wholesale commodities during the last hundred years, estimated in gold alone; while the dotted curve shows the same index number estimated in terms of the two metals, gold and silver in equal shares. On comparing these, we find that the fluctuations shown by the second curve are not very much less than those shown by the first; and, what is of even more significance, that the fluctuations in the index number during the period when the gold value of silver was nearly stationary are greater than they have been since 1873, when its value has been much disturbed[1].

Since 1873 there has been a great fall of gold prices—not, indeed, so great as that between 1809 and 1816, or even that between 1818 and 1832. But, while in the earlier instances silver prices fell as fast as gold prices, or faster, in this latest fall silver prices have had but little share. And this fact is one of the chief arguments urged by Mr Barbour and others in favour of bimetallism. But, when examined closely, the argument appears to be weak. The comparative steadiness of silver prices during the last thirteen years is due to a coincidence which has never happened before and may never happen again.

In 1873 there set in one group of causes tending to raise the value of both gold and silver. During the two preceding decades exhausting wars in America and Europe had held in check the tendency of modern invention and modern habits of saving to increase the production of commodities. The wars had taken

---

[1] The gold prices from 1782 to 1820 are Jevons'; those from 1820 to 1885 are Mr Sauerbeck's. The bimetallic prices are the mean between the gold and the silver prices; the latter being found from the gold value of silver given by Mr Del Mar for the years 1782 to 1820, and by Mr Sauerbeck for the remaining years.

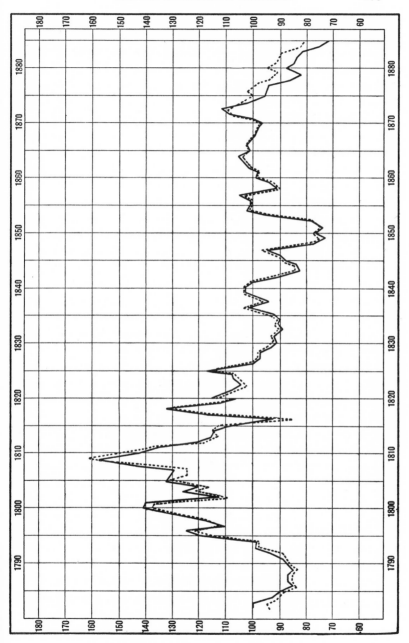

men away from the workshops, had killed some, and unfitted
others for their work; they had diverted industries to supply
the materials of warfare, and had destroyed vast quantities of
commodities of all kinds. Since then invention has gone faster
than ever; the habits of saving are stronger than ever, and
commodities have increased by leaps and bounds. Meanwhile,
the use of bank-notes and of bills of exchange had not kept pace
with the growth of business, and the confident expectations that
were cherished before 1873 of the extension of the English cheque
system in Austria and elsewhere have been signally disappointed.
These and minor causes have tended to raise the values of both
gold and silver.

But, by a strange accident, there happened at the same time
another group of causes which tended further to raise the value
of gold, but to lower the value of silver. The production of gold
diminished, and that of silver increased. Nations ran a race to
see which could most quickly substitute gold for silver as the
staple of their currency; and, partly as a consequence of these
changes, war ministers, Indian peasants, and American negroes
began to hoard gold and showed indifference to silver. The
recent comparative steadiness of the value of silver is due to
the coincidence of these two sets of causes, of about equal force
and acting in opposite directions. The diagram shows that no
such coincidence is hinted at by the statistics of the past: reason
forbids us to expect it in the future.

I maintain, then, that there is no reason to believe that a
bimetallic standard would give us in the long run much more
stable prices than we have now. No doubt it would do some good,
and, if no other course were open to us, it would be worth while
to go through a great deal in order to gain even the small
additional steadiness that would result from a stable bimetallism.
But I contend that, before taking so great a step as entering
into treaties with other nations for the establishment of a new
currency, we ought to inquire whether our standard of value
ought not to be altogether independent of our currency.

The industrial arts generally have progressed by substituting
several specialized instruments for one that used to be applied
for many purposes. The chisel and the plane, the hammer and
the saw, are all developments of the primeval tomahawk; they

do their work well, because none of them is expected to cover a wide range of work. And so, if we have one thing as a medium of exchange, and another as a standard of value, each may be able to perform its share of the work thoroughly well, because it is specially fitted for it. The currency will retain a material form, so that it may "run" from hand to hand as a medium of exchange, while the amount of the currency which is required to discharge a contract for deferred payment will be regulated neither by weight nor measure, but by an authoritative table of figures issued from time to time by a Government Department.

III.—A Standard of Value independent of Gold and Silver

Leaving some difficulties of detail to be discussed at the end of the article, let us suppose that (as was suggested long ago by Joseph Lowe, Poulett Scrope and others[1]) a Government Department extends to all commodities the action taken by the Commissioners of Tithes with regard to wheat, barley and oats. As they, having ascertained the average prices of grain at any time, state how much money is required to purchase as much wheat, barley and oats as would have cost £100 at certain standard prices, so this Department, having ascertained the prices of all important commodities, would publish from time to time the amount of money required to give the same general purchasing power as, say, £1 had at the beginning of 1887. The prices used by it would be the latest attainable; not, as in the case of tithes, the mean of the prices for the last seven years. This standard unit of purchasing power might be called for shortness simply THE UNIT.

From time to time, at the beginning of each year or oftener, the Department would declare how much of the currency had the same purchasing power as £1 had at the beginning of 1887. If, for instance, it declared in 1890 that 18s. had this purchasing power, then a contract to pay a unit in 1890 would be discharged by paying 18s. If it declared in 1892 that 23s. had only the same purchasing power as £1 had in 1887, or 18s. in 1890, then any contract to pay a unit in 1892 would require for its settlement the delivery of 23s.

---

[1] Some account of their suggestions is given in the chapter on "A Tabular Standard of Value" in Jevons' *Money*.

When a loan was made, it could, at the option of those concerned, be made in terms of currency, or in terms of units. In the latter case the lender would know that whatever change there might be in the value of money, he would receive when the debt was repaid just the same amount of real wealth, just the same command over the necessaries, comforts and luxuries of life as he had lent away. If he bargained for 5 per cent. interest, he would each year receive money equal in value to one-twentieth of the units which he had lent; and however prices might have changed, these would contribute a certain and definite amount to his real means of expenditure. The borrower would not be at one time impatient to start ill-considered enterprises in order to gain by the expected rise in general prices, and at another afraid of borrowing for legitimate business for fear of being caught by a general fall in prices.

Of course every trade would still have its own dangers due to causes peculiar to itself; but by the use of the unit it might avoid those heavy risks which are caused by a rise or fall in general prices. Salaries and wages, where not determined by special sliding scales, could be fixed in units, their real value would then no longer fluctuate constantly in the wrong direction, tending upwards just when, if it changed at all, it should fall, and tending downwards just when, if it changed at all, it should rise[1].

Ground-rents also should be fixed in general units, though for agricultural rents it would be best to have a special unit based chiefly on the prices of farm produce. The reckoning of mortgages and marriage settlements in terms of units of purchasing power, instead of gold, would remove one great source of uncertainty from the affairs of private life, while a similar change as to debentures and Government bonds would give the holders of them what they want—a really constant income. The ordinary shareholders in a public company would no longer be led to take an over-sanguine estimate of their position by a period of prosperity, which, besides enriching them directly, diminished

---

[1] Sliding scales, admirable as is their general effect, perhaps err by being too simple. A sliding scale in the iron trade, for instance, should, I think, take account not only of the price of the finished iron, but also, on the one hand, of the prices of iron ore, coal, and other expenses of the employer, and, on the other, of the prices of the things chiefly consumed by the workmen. Trades in which sliding scales are possible could arrange special units for themselves, by aid of the statistics on which Government would base its general unit.

the real payments which they have to make to debenture holders and perhaps to preference stock holders. And, on the other hand, they would not be oppressed by the extra weight of having to pay more than their real value on account of these fixed charges when prices were low and business drooping.

The standard unit of purchasing power being published, the Law Courts should, I think, give every facility to contracts, wills, and other documents made in terms of the unit; and Government itself might gradually feel its way towards assessing rates and taxes (except, of course, such things as payments for postage stamps) in terms of the unit, and also towards reckoning the salaries, pensions, and, when possible, the wages of its employés at so many units instead of so much currency. It should, I think, begin by offering, as soon as the unit was made, to pay for each £100 of Consols a really uniform interest of three units, instead of a nominally uniform but really fluctuating interest of £3. The public, though at first regarding the new notion as uncanny, would, I believe, take to it rapidly as soon as they got to see its substantial advantages. Their dislike of it even at first would be less than was their dislike of coal fires, of railways, and of gas. Ere long the currency would, I believe, be restricted to the functions for which it is well fitted, of measuring and settling transactions that are completed shortly after they are begun. I think we ought, without delay, to set about preparing for voluntary use an authoritative unit; being voluntary it would be introduced tentatively, and would be a powerful remedy for a great evil. This plan would not cause any forced disturbance of existing contracts, such as would result from a change of our currency. It would give a better standard for deferred payments than could possibly be given by a currency (as ordinarily understood), and therefore would diminish the temptation to hurry on impetuously a change of our currency with the object of making its value a little more stable; and it could be worked equally well with any currency.

IV.—Is Fixed-ratio-mintage a Stable Bimetallism?

But next, assuming that our currency must be based on one or both of the precious metals, because these two metals alone are sufficiently durable, rare and generally useful, to be fitted for being handled by bankers and for being the balances of international trade; assuming also that gold and silver give a more stable basis, though perhaps only a very little more stable one than gold alone, I propose to investigate the best way of basing a currency on them. I desire, not to advocate any immediate change in our currency, but only to inquire in what direction it would be best to move if we had decided that the time had come for a fundamental change.

Firstly, is so-called bimetallism really bimetallism? Would the opening the mints of the leading commercial countries of the world to gold and silver at a fixed ratio ensure that the value of our currency would be permanently based on the combined values of gold and silver?

I believe there is not, and has not been for a long time, any great difference of opinion on fundamental economic doctrines between the ablest monometallists and the ablest bimetallists. A statement of the broad conditions of the problem may, I think, be taken almost equally well from such a monometallist as Jevons, or such a bimetallist as Professor Walker or Mr Hucks Gibbs. Both sides are agreed that, if the leading commercial nations were to open their mints freely to the coinage of gold and silver at the ratio of $15\frac{1}{2}$, or 18 or 20, the relative values of the metals would be fixed thereby for a long time at all events; and that meanwhile the fluctuations in the general purchasing power of money and in the exchanges with the East would be somewhat less than they are now. There is some difference as to the extent of this last benefit, but the main point at issue is the probable length of time during which the system would sustain itself. There is agreement as to the *qualities* or general tendencies of the causes under discussion, but not as to the relative *quantities* of these tendencies.

I do not urge, as some have done, that fixed-ratio-mintage is an attempt to substitute an artificial for a natural level of the gold price of silver. For I agree with Mr Hucks Gibbs that, as things are, gold and silver have no natural value. They are so durable that the year's supply is never more than a small part of the total stock, and therefore their values do not conform closely to their costs of production. And, in so far as their values are regulated by the relations between the demands for them and the existing stocks of them, their value is artificial, because the demand for them as currency is itself artificial. I think, however, that cost of production acts on the values of the precious metals more rapidly now than it used to, because the mining finance of the whole world is now the common property of the whole world, and a fall in the cost of production of silver lowers its value almost at once by diminishing the demand for it. The belief that the cost of production of silver is falling relatively to that of gold has spread all over the world. Not only sharp business men but ignorant peasants are ridding themselves of their stocks of silver and buying gold instead. India itself is absorbing as much gold as silver. Mr Norman has shown some *primâ facie* case for believing that, at all events when proper machinery and methods are used in the South American mines, the cost of production of an ounce of silver will be very much less than a twentieth—he says a fiftieth—part of that of an ounce of gold. The question is fairly under discussion; if the general opinion should go any considerable way in Mr Norman's direction, silver hoarding will almost cease.

Next, the consumption of gold for purposes of the arts and for hoarding is increasing at an unprecedented rate. In the West gold watch chains are superseding silver watch chains, and in the East gold bangles are superseding silver bangles. The causes of this increase are likely to continue, because they are based on the modern tendency to the accumulation and diffusion of wealth, which themselves are sure to continue, in spite of the occasional retrogressions caused by great wars, because they are founded on that progress and diffusion of knowledge which cannot go backwards.

I conclude, then, that the consumption of gold for the arts, which is already quite half the total production[1], is likely very soon to exceed the total production, unless its value rises so as to induce much additional capital and labour to go into gold mining. But it is this very rise in the value of gold which the

---

[1] Dr Soetbeer calculates that out of a total production of gold of about £20,000,000 annually, more than £12,000,000 are used in the arts, and more than £3,000,000 go to India, leaving less than £5,000,000 for the needs of the currency. M. Ottomar Haupt's estimates are nearly the same. Professor Nicholson, in his able argument in favour of the stability of fixed-ratio-mintage, seems to me to overlook its tendency to increase silver mining at the expense of gold mining, and to make insufficient allowance for the many causes which are increasing the demand for gold.

fixed-ratio-mintage scheme aims at checking, by coining $15\frac{1}{2}$ or 18, or even 20 ounces of silver into money which has the same legal value as an ounce of gold. Under that scheme, if Mr Norman's estimate is anywhere near the truth, capital and labour would migrate as fast as they could from gold to silver mining. For the miner wants a high value for his produce straight away; the promise of a rise when the bimetallic convention had broken up would not weigh with him. But the hoarders, whether peasants or those responsible for bank reserves and army chests, would look forward to the ultimate rise in the value of gold, and would between them absorb many millions a year.

If these forecasts should in any considerable measure be borne out by the event, the gold coinage would very soon be insufficient for the chief business of the civilized world. The six or seven hundred millions that are now available for the purpose would soon perceptibly diminish. No doubt the system of payment by cheques is increasing, but the habit of buying things for cash is increasing also. People all over the world are getting into the habit of carrying about with them a greater amount of purchasing power, but not into a habit of carrying about heavy purses. So the new silver could not be added to our effective currency; it could only be the basis of some sort of paper currency. I anticipate, therefore, that the fixed-ratio-mintage scheme would result in the almost immediate issue in England of £1 notes, and I think it is not very improbable that after a few years more either the international mintage convention would be dissolved or gold would disappear from circulation. In the latter case the currency would thereafter fluctuate with the supplies, not of the two metals combined, but of silver alone; we should be landed in a paper currency on a silver basis.

It is not necessary for my argument to assume that this forecast has a balance of probability on its side. If there is a chance of one in three of its turning out to be anywhere near the truth, it would, I submit, be most unwise to rush precipitately into so violent a change without having carefully examined every possible alternative. And that has not yet been done, because the belief that the popular feeling was set against any change of our currency had caused the question of new currency systems to be neglected until the able and determined advocates of the fixed-ratio-mintage scheme obtained possession of the popular ear.

But really there is no urgent cause for haste. No doubt the persistent fall of prices is a great evil, but, if it is indeed the duty of Governments to alter the currency to prevent creditors from getting too much from their debtors, they can issue more convertible paper money; the issue of £1 notes in England alone would have a considerable effect. If, in order to pay sufficient salaries to its officials, or for other purposes, the English Government wants to get more taxes from the Indian people, it can surely have the honesty to say so. An ounce of silver is worth now more commodities, whether in India or in England, than it has been on the average of the last hundred years; and if it is necessary that we should take for the purposes of government a larger part of the wealth which has come to them under our rule, we may do it openly. It is not necessary to change our currency in a hurry in order that we may pretend that we are not doing what we are doing.

Before very long our foreign trade will, I hope, be simplified by the adoption of some kind of international currency. But I make bold to say that economic science shows no justification whatever for the doctrine that the permanent fall in the gold value of the rupee causes a permanent dislocation of trade with the East. The fluctuations of the exchanges are no doubt a serious evil; they afford a strong argument for reconsidering calmly the basis of our currency, but not for adopting hurriedly a new currency without giving ourselves time to make sure that it will not falsify the hopes founded on it.

Fluctuations in the relative values of gold and silver are only one of many causes of fluctuations in the rate of exchange between England and India, as is proved by the fact that the annual variations were as great before 1873 (even omitting the disturbed period of the Mutiny) as they have been since 1873, when the gold value of silver has no longer been stationary. The disturbing influence of changes in the gold value of silver has not been too great to be overborne by the steadying influence of the telegraph, steam, the Suez Canal, etc.[1]

[1] The diagram is based on the figures supplied by the India Office, and published in Mr Palgrave's important Memorandum appended to the third *Report of the Commission on the Depression of Trade and Industry.*

V.—A Proposal for a Stable Bimetallism

It is with great diffidence that I suggest an alternative bi-metallic scheme. I am not sanguine enough to hope that I have found the best possible solution of the difficulty; but my plan, whatever its faults may be, seems to have this claim for consideration—that it would be a genuine and stable bimetallism. It would therefore give a slightly better standard of purchasing power than our present currency; and, what is more important, it would form a basis of international currency. An international gold coinage would disturb trade by causing a violent fall of prices: an international silver coinage would have even greater evils. But a system of currency based on both silver and gold could become international; and that is, to my mind, the chief reason why it is worth while to inquire what is the best possible form of bimetallism.

Ricardo suggested that we should use a paper currency resting on a basis, not of coin, but of stamped gold bars weighing twenty ounces each. If, he argued, the currency were in excess and showed signs of falling below its gold value, it would be taken to the Mint, and exchanged for gold bars for exportation; if it were deficient, gold bars would be brought to the Mint and currency demanded. Within the country the paper would be a perfect medium of exchange; while for the payment of the balances of foreign trade, stamped gold bars are better suited than coins.

The currency scheme which I wish to submit for consideration differs from his only by being bimetallic instead of monometallic. I propose that currency should be exchangeable at the Mint or Issue Department not for gold, but for gold and silver, at the rate of not £1 for 113 grains of gold, but £1 for $56\frac{1}{2}$ grains of gold, together with, say, twenty times as many grains of silver. I would make up the gold and silver bars in gramme weights, so as to be useful for international trade. A gold bar of 100 grammes, together with a silver bar, say, twenty[1] times as

---

[1] This number twenty, or whatever it might be, would be fixed on arbitrarily once for all. If we wished the value of the currency to be regulated chiefly by gold we should have only a small bar of silver, if chiefly by silver we should have perhaps fifty or one hundred times as heavy a bar of silver as that of gold. But if we wished the two metals to have about equal influence, we should, taking account of the existing stocks of the two metals, probably choose our silver bar about twenty times as heavy as that of gold

heavy, would be exchangeable at the Issue Department for an amount of the currency which would be calculated and fixed once for all when the scheme was introduced. (It would be about £28 or £30 according to the basis of calculation.)

Any one who wanted to buy or sell gold or silver alone in exchange for currency could get what he wanted by exchanging gold for silver, or silver for gold, at the market rate. Government fixing its own rates from day to day, so as to keep its reserves of the two metals in about the right proportion, might safely undertake this exchange itself; and then any one could buy or sell either gold or silver for currency in one operation.

To insure convertibility the currency would not be allowed to exceed, say, three times the bullion reserve in the Issue Department[1]. The country would save so much on the cost of its currency that it could well afford to keep, as a normal reserve, bullion worth, say, £30,000,000 in excess of this limit, and thus prevent the sudden stringencies which we now suffer whenever there is even a small foreign drain of bullion[2]. There would be, as now, token coins of silver and bronze, but none of gold; because even a small percentage on the value of a gold coin is sufficient to pay the illicit coiner.

Ricardo's proposal was made at a time when the mismanagement of paper issues at home and abroad had made the notion of a paper currency repugnant to all prudent people. But now there is a greater tendency to discriminate between paper money, which has no sound basis, and which may fairly be called soft money, and paper whose convertibility into hard metal is properly secured. The strangeness of the scheme will make many refuse to examine it closely; but those who can overcome their natural repugnance to the use of paper money will, I think, find that it has the following advantages:—(1) It would be

---

[1] Except in times of emergency, when the minimum rate of discount was, say, 10 per cent.; and then the rule might be broken, either, as now, by the authority of the Government, or, which I think would be better, by a self-acting rule.

[2] Thus, if the currency consisted of notes for £120,000,000 besides silver and bronze token coins, the normal reserve would be £70,000,000. The management of the reserves might be entrusted to the Bank of England, or a Government Bank, which would act directly, as now, on the rate of discount, so as to keep the supply of gold and silver at about the right level; or a Government Department with no general banking functions might exercise an indirect pressure on the rate of discount by selling Consols for currency when the reserve was getting too low, and buying them in again so as to let out the currency when the reserve was getting too large.

economical and secure; (2) Though economical, the largeness of its reserve would obviate the sharp twinges that now frequently occur in the money market; (3) It would vary in value with the mean of the values of gold and silver; (4) As it would in no way attempt to control the relative values of gold and silver, and would not be affected even if an ounce of gold became worth fifty ounces of silver, it could be begun at once and without risk by any one nation; (5) If adopted by several nations it would constitute at once a perfect international basis of currency and prices[1]; (6) Lastly, it has, in my eyes, an advantage which may appear fanciful, and on which I do not wish to lay any great stress—viz., that it is a movement in the direction in which we want to go of a tabular standard for deferred payments. If there should ever exist any other commodities besides gold and silver, which, like them, are imperishable, which have great value in small bulk, and are in universal demand, and which are thus suitable for paying the balances of foreign trade, then they could be added to gold and silver as the basis of the currency.

It has the one great disadvantage of being a paper currency, but this is, I contend, shared to a great extent by the fixed-ratio-mintage scheme; for under that paper would probably have to begin to take the place of gold almost at once, and before long would be very likely to extrude it altogether[2].

[1] France could, if it chose, still reckon in francs, England in pounds, and America in dollars; but every twenty-franc note would state on its face how many francs were exchangeable for a standard pair of bars of 100 grammes of gold and 2000 grammes of silver; and therefore the equivalent in £ s. d. of 100 francs would be settled once for all. There would be nothing to be allowed as now for seignorage or for wear and tear of coins. Francs, pounds, or dollars would alike give a definite command over bars of gold and silver, which would form a perfect medium for international payments.

[2] M. Walras has proposed to steady the value of gold by issuing or withdrawing token silver coins according as gold rose or fell in value. His scheme is able and ingenious. But, as he admits, it would, like any other scheme for regulating the value of gold and silver, require an international agreement. And I do not see how this could be managed, because, to say nothing of minor difficulties, there cannot be a common unit of purchasing power for all countries. Every plan for regulating the supply of the currency, so that its value shall be constant, must, I think, be national and not international.

I will indicate briefly two such plans, though I do not advocate either of them. On the first plan the currency would be inconvertible. An automatic Government Department would buy Consols for currency whenever £1 was worth more than a unit, and would sell Consols for currency whenever it was worth less (the ordinary issue and withdrawal of Consols which takes place when the Government wants to borrow or to pay off its debt would be arranged independently, perhaps, by another Department which had no power to issue or cancel currency). Those who had to pay balances to foreign countries would buy gold or silver in the open market; they would be certain of getting in exchange for this money gold and silver that had a fixed purchasing power in England. The researches of Mr Palgrave and Dr Soetbeer show that a unit of fixed

VI.—How to Estimate a Unit of Purchasing Power

Before concluding it will be well to consider how a unit of purchasing power should be estimated. If we demand an ideally perfect unit we are met by the preliminary difficulty that the effective purchasing power of money to each individual depends partly on the nature of his wants. A rise in the price of meat, accompanied by an equivalent fall in that of bread, adds to the purchasing power of the wages of those who are unable to buy much meat in any case. To a well-to-do bachelor the price of the necessaries of life is of very little importance, while, if with the same income he had to find food and clothing for a large family, he might regard a fall in the price of luxuries, accompanied by even a small rise in that of necessaries, as a diminution in the purchasing power of money. It is chiefly for this reason that an absolutely perfect standard of purchasing power is not only unattainable but even unthinkable. What we mean by a unit of purchasing power for, say, the United Kingdom, is that which will give a uniform means of satisfying his wants to the average consumer, that is, to a person who consumes a 37,000,000th part of the total of every commodity that is consumed by the 37,000,000 inhabitants of the country[1].

This, then, is the unit that we are in search of. But for the present we must be content with very rough methods, and improve them gradually as our Statistical Departments get their work into shape. It is enough that even in its simplest and most easily workable form the unit gives a tenfold better standard of value than that afforded by the precious metals.

This simplest plan is to select a number of representative wholesale articles and to add together their prices at different

purchasing power in England would give a more nearly uniform purchasing power in any other civilized country than would an ounce of gold or an ounce of silver. On the whole, this currency would, I believe, give more stability to our foreign trade than our present one.

The other plan is that of a convertible currency, each £1 note giving the right to demand at a Government Office as much gold as at that time had the value of half a unit, together with as much silver as had the value of half a unit. The necessary provisions for keeping a proper reserve of gold and silver would be a little intricate, but would involve no great practical difficulty. Under either of those plans contracts for deferred payments might be made fairly well in terms of the currency. But they are complex; and they would hinder rather than help the adoption of an international currency.

[1] But perhaps with a view to increase the steadiness of business we should count in all the products of British industry, even though these are exported. This would lead us to regard the annual supply of cotton manufactures as worth about £110,000,000, though about £80,000,000 worth of this are exported.

times [1]. The next step in advance is to estimate the importance of each commodity by the mean of the amount spent on it at the different periods under investigation. This importance or *weight* is then multiplied into the change in price of the commodity. For instance, if the value of the pepper consumed in an average year in England is £500,000, and that of the tea is £11,000,000, then a rise in the price of tea by 1 per cent. counts for as much as a rise in the price of pepper by 22 per cent. [2] If the weight of pepper is taken as equal to 1, that of tea must be 22.

The next step is to allow in the weights of particular commodities for the values of things whose prices are governed in the main by the same causes, but which change in character so that there can be no continuous record of their prices. Thus, for instance, the weight allowed for cloth of a standard quality might well include the values of many woollen and worsted manufactures, which change their forms with every breath of fashion. Or, on another plan, we might count the wool instead of the things made of it (for of course we ought not to count both), and take the change in the cost of weaving a yard of standard cloth as typical of changes in the cost of other branches of the manufacture.

The next step is to take account of the price of personal services which are not already reckoned for. It has already been noted that we count in either the price of our cloth, or the price of our wool, together with that of manufacturing it. On the same principle, if we count the value of our bread we must not count the cost of baking it; but, if we count in only the price of the flour, we ought to allow separately for the cost of baking it, whether done by a baker or by a domestic servant. However, since

---

[1] This method was followed by Jevons and the earlier workers, and is still used by the *Economist* newspaper and by Mr Sauerbeck and others, in conjunction with more advanced methods.

[2] This method has been adopted by Mr Giffen with regard to our imports and exports, by Mr Palgrave, and, as he has pointed out, by the French Commission Permanente des Valeurs, by Mr Sauerbeck and by Mr Mulhall. The notion of aiming at ascertaining what may be called the movements of the centre of gravity of prices is so obviously just, that, though there is great room for improvement in detail, the principle may be regarded as thoroughly established. Jevons proposed to take the mean of the logarithms of the changes; but I venture to regard this as due to his overlooking dangers connected with the geometric mean which, though less obvious, are more fatal in extreme cases than those of the arithmetic mean—the one flaw in his unrivalled contributions to the theory of money and prices. The weights of the commodities would be estimated not oftener than once a year, even if, as is very likely, it should be found best to alter the unit itself once a month.

personal services are the most important group of things which are rising in price relatively to the average of commodities, it is perhaps best that they should continue to be omitted until we are ready to take some account of those subtle refinements in manufacture which are ever changing their form, while with every change their real price is falling fast relatively to the average.

This brings us to consider the great problem how to modify our unit so as to allow for the invention of new commodities. The difficulty is insuperable, if we compare two distant periods without access to the detailed statistics of intermediate times, but it can be got over fairly well by systematic statistics. A new commodity almost always appears at first at something like a scarcity price, and its gradual fall in price can be made to enter year by year into readjustments of the unit of purchasing power, and to represent fairly well the increased power of satisfying our wants which we derive from the new commodity[1].

This difficulty has been commonly recognized; but there is another closely connected with it, which seems to have escaped notice. It is that of a thing which is supplied at a time of the year at which it used not to be available. The best plan seems to be to regard it as a new commodity when it first appears out of its old season. Suppose that at one time strawberries were to be had only in June, their average price being 6d. Suppose better knowledge enables us to get them in June at 3d., in May and July at 6d., and during the rest of the year at prices from 1s. up to 10s. Their average price for the year, if made up on the plan followed in some price lists, would be about 5s. as against 6d. in the olden times; whereas, in fact, the change would have more than doubled the purchasing power of money in the matter of strawberries. This class of consideration is of much more importance than at first sight appears; for a great part of modern agricultural and transport industries are devoted to increasing the periods of time during which different kinds

[1] No notice of the new commodity would be taken in fixing the unit on the first occasion of its appearance in the price list. Suppose this to be on the first of January, 1890; then the unit for 1890 would be made up so as to give the same purchasing power of commodities, other than the new one, at these prices as the last unit did at the prices of a year ago. But, before making up the unit for 1891, the weights in the unit for 1890 would be shifted a little, so as to allow for the new commodity, and then the unit for 1891 would be made to give the same purchasing power of all commodities, including the new one, as did that for 1890.

of food are available. Neglect of this has, in my opinion, vitiated the statistics of the purchasing power of money in mediæval times with regard to nearly all kinds of food except corn; even the well-to-do would hardly get so simple a thing as fresh meat in winter. And, again, in backward civilizations, even when things are in season, the supply of them is fitful. Those who have kept fowls for their own eating, find that they often have more than they want at one time and less at another. In many cases it is better to pay 3s. for a fowl to a modern middleman, who, drawing his supplies from a wide area, can furnish any number that may be ordered at a short notice, than 2s. 6d. or even 2s. to one whose resources are smaller. The dealer who makes the supply accommodate itself to our wants really sells a superior commodity, and his price, though nominally higher, may really be lower; just as a coat which fits well and costs £4 may be cheaper than a similar coat that fits badly and costs only £3.

The above difficulty relates to an increase in the time during which a thing is procurable; there is a similar difficulty with regard to place. When fresh sea fish could be had only at the seaside its average price was low. Now that the railways enable it to be sold inland, its average retail price includes much higher charges for distribution than it used to do. The simplest plan for dealing with this difficulty is to take, as a rule, the wholesale price of a thing at its place of production, and to allow full weight to the cheapening of the transport of goods, of persons and of news as separate and most weighty items.

For many reasons it would be better to take retail than wholesale prices; but that would often be impracticable, because the retail price corresponds to different kinds of services at different times and places. The greengrocer who has to keep a large and varied stock of vegetables, to send out once for orders, and a second time with a cabbage, may very likely lose on the transaction, though he sells for 2d. what he bought for a farthing. The poor woman who pays ½d. for the cabbage which she fetches home herself may be really a more profitable customer. Thus retail prices among advanced peoples, and especially among the wealthier portions of them, include the prices of many personal services which in a more primitive state the consumer dispenses with.

The next point is to allow for changes in things which at first sight appear to have remained unchanged. An ox or sheep weighs now more than twice as much as it used to; of that weight a larger percentage is meat, of the meat a larger percentage is prime meat, and of all the meat a larger percentage is solid food, and a smaller percentage is water. Again, an average ten-roomed house is, perhaps, twice as large in volume as it used to be; and a great part of its cost goes for water, gas, and other appliances which were not in the older house. For these reasons we ought, I think, to strike off a very great deal from the ordinary estimates of the purchasing power of money in backward countries, and in the earlier history of our own country.

But ought we also to allow anything for the increased requirements of society? For instance, 10,000 rupees give the retired Indian officer more power of purchasing the necessaries, comforts, and luxuries of life, whether in India or in England, than it would when he entered the service, and yet he finds himself pinched because his income is worth less than the £1000 of his English brother-officer, which he used to regard as its equivalent. I think there is no doubt that this consideration must be entirely ignored in estimating our unit of purchasing power. We want to use our unit for measuring payments of material wealth. If any class of people, whether postmen, or clerks, or Indian officials, have not shared in the general increase of real income, that is a reason for reconsidering their payments. If the Government has so worded its contracts with its officials as really to promise that every ten rupees of their pay shall be always equivalent to £1, it must fulfil the contract; but that can be done without changing our currency.

It is true, then, that we cannot hope to get a standard of purchasing power which is free from great imperfections. But it is equally true that a perfect standard of length baffles all the resources of science; and, though the best standard of value that we can get is not nearly so good for its purposes as an ordinary yard measure is for its purpose, yet it is a great advance on using as our standard the value of gold or even the mean between the values of gold and silver. It is an advance of the same kind, though not nearly as great, as the advance of substituting a yard measure for the length of the foot of one judge, or for the mean between the lengths of the feet of two.

IX

A FAIR RATE OF WAGES (1887)[1]

THE term "remuneration," is here used broadly, so as to include the money equivalents of all the net advantages of an occupation, as well as the money-payments which belong to it. An absolutely fair rate of remuneration belongs to Utopia: but there is much to be learnt from trying with the socialists to ascertain how far it is thinkable, and how far it is attainable. But in fact all socialist schemes, which have any claims to be practical, avowedly involve a compromise: they do not venture to dispense entirely with material reward as an incentive to industrial energy; though they rely less on it, and more on the sense of duty than our present system does. But this compromise prevents them from claiming to be logically thought out schemes of absolute fairness.

Fairness then cannot be absolute, but must be a matter of degree. Even for the purpose of day-dreams we must deliberately frame our notions of equity in the distribution of wealth, with reference to the methods of industry, the habits of life, and the character of the people for whom we are trying to discover a realizable ideal. And much more must we do this when we are trying to construct a working plan, which will so accommodate itself to the actual conditions of business as to be accepted in preference to the excitement of conflict by people as they are, with all their hot impulses, their combative instincts, and their inherited selfishness.

There may indeed be a question whether there is room within these narrow limits for any useful definition of "a fair rate of wages." But the phrase is constantly used in the market place; it is frequent in the mouths both of employers and of employed; and almost every phrase in common use has a real meaning, though it may be difficult to get at. Those who use the phrase, when pressed to explain it, often give an account that will not bear examination; but after the matter has been discussed for

---

[1] This essay reproduces the substance of the Preface contributed to Mr L. L. Price's *Industrial Peace*, 1887.

a time, the meaning that is latent in their minds works itself to the surface.

The basis of the notion that there should be given "a fair day's wage for a fair day's work," is that every man who is up to the usual standard of efficiency of his trade in his own neighbourhood, and exerts himself honestly, ought to be paid for his work at the usual rate for his trade and neighbourhood; so that he may be able to live in that way to which he and his neighbours in his rank of life have been accustomed. And further, the popular notion of fairness demands that he should be paid this rate ungrudgingly; that his time should not be taken up in fighting for it; and that he should not be worried by constant attempts to screw his pay down by indirect means. This doctrine is modified by the admission that changes of circumstances may require changes of wages in one direction or the other: and again, the rule may be held not to apply to cases such as that of needlewomen, where the customary wages are too low to support a healthy life. But substantially it is accepted and acted on in ordinary life.

For instance, if a carpenter has made a box, or a surveyor has made a map of some land for us, we consider that he acts fairly by us, if he does not attempt to take advantage of our not having made a bargain beforehand, or of our ignorance, or of any special hold he may have over us: that is, if he charges us the price of his services at about the rate at which he would expect to be able to dispose of them to those who understand his trade. In this we are not trying to settle, according to an absolute standard of justness, how much of a carpenter's labour ought to be paid as highly as an hour's work of a surveyor. We are not inquiring whether the social system which permits great inequalities in their usual rates of remuneration is the best possible: but taking the present social system as it is, we want to know whether those with whom we are dealing are doing their part to make it work smoothly.

The average rate of earnings of a surveyor is limited on the one hand by the demand for a surveyor's work: but it is determined chiefly by the difficulty and expense of acquiring the knowledge and skill required for his work: the rate of earnings which are required to induce a sufficient number of people to become surveyors is the "normal" rate of surveyors' earnings. This normal rate has no claim to be an absolutely just rate; it is relative to the existing state of things at a particular place and time.

The normal earnings of a carpenter and a surveyor might be brought much nearer together than they are, by even so slight and easy an improvement on our present social arrangements as the extending to all persons of adequate natural ability the opportunity of receiving the training required for the higher ranks of industry. But we have to take things as they are; and, as things are, the price at which a man in any trade can expect to get steady employment, from those who are good judges of the value of his work, is a tolerably well-known normal rate. The surveyor or the carpenter who always charges about this rate to any customers, however ignorant, and without putting them to the trouble of beating him down, is said to do his business fairly.

Similarly a fair employer, when arranging for the pay of a carpenter, does not try to beat him down, or take any indirect advantage of him; but, at all events under ordinary circumstances, offers at once whatever he knows to be the "normal" rate of pay for that man's work: that is the pay which he would expect to have to give in the long run for an equal amount of equally good work if that man refused to work for him. On the other hand he acts unfairly if he endeavours to make his profits, not so much by able and energetic management of his business, as by paying for labour at a lower rate than his competitors; if he takes advantage of the necessities of individual workmen, and perhaps of their ignorance of what is going on elsewhere; if he screws a little here and a little there; and perhaps in the course of doing this, makes it more difficult for other employers in the same trade to go on paying straightforwardly the full rates. It is this unfairness of bad masters which makes trades unions necessary and gives them their chief force: were there no bad masters, many of the ablest members of trades unions would be glad, not indeed entirely to forgo their organization, but to dispense with those parts of it which are most combative in spirit. As it is, though at great expense to themselves and others, they succeed tolerably well on the whole in preventing individual masters from taking unfair advantages of individual men.

The starting point then in our search for the fair rate of payment for any task, in the limited sense of the word "fair" with which alone we are here concerned, may be found in the average rate that has been paid for it during living memory; or during a shorter period, if the trade has changed its form within recent years. But this average rate is often very difficult to determine; and therefore for practical purposes it is generally best to take in lieu of it the rate actually paid in some year when, according to general agreement, the trade was in a normal condition. This gives very nearly the same result, and is more definite and less open to dispute. It is then assumed as a starting point that the rate at that time was a fair rate, or in economic phrase that it was the normal rate; that is, that it was about on a level with the average payment for tasks in other trades which are of equal difficulty and disagreeableness, which require equally rare natural abilities and an equally expensive training. And accepting this year as a normal year for the trade implies an admission that the current rate of profits in the trade was also normal. Differences in ability or in good fortune may have been causing some employers to make very high profits while others were losing their capital; but taking one with another it is supposed that at this standard time their net receipts gave them interest on their capital, and earnings for their own work in managing the business, at the same rate as work in other trades which was equally difficult and disagreeable, and which required equally rare natural abilities and an equally expensive training.

Problems of a time at which general economic conditions are changing quickly

Changes in the course of trade may of course require considerable departure from this starting point. These changes are of many different kinds. Some are gradual in action, and work slowly for a long time in one direction. For instance a new trade has at first normal wages higher than other trades of equal intrinsic difficulty; it is difficult because it is unfamiliar. Gradually it becomes familiar, a great many people have been brought up to it, and its wages slowly sink to a lower level. Or again, improvements in machinery, which cause it to work more smoothly and with less care, may lower the strain required for performing the same nominal task, and thus lower the nominal rate of wage, even though the payment for work involving a given strain is stationary or rising. Or again, the mean level of the general purchasing power of money may be moving slowly upwards or downwards, in consequence of changes in the supply of the precious metals, or of gradual changes in the volume and character of banking and general business. All these are slow changes; there may be disputes as to the facts of the case: but when once they are clearly ascertained, the course is generally clear. Setting aside all questions as to the right of some to be rich while others are poor, it is "fair" that full effect should be given to these changes. For they have on their side natural forces so powerful that opposition to them cannot be successful for long: and it cannot as a rule be maintained even for a short time without recourse to the harsher measures of trade combinations—measures that involve war open or concealed between employers and employed, or between both and the purchasers of their wares. Industrial wars like other wars involve so much waste, that the net gain which they bring to the winners, if any, is much less than the net loss to the losers. And therefore the side which adopts measures of warfare in opposition to changes that are irresistible is generally acting not only unwisely, but also unfairly.

It is, however, often difficult to know how far any set of tendencies is irresistible; how far the causes now acting in one direction are likely to be overborne before long by others acting in the opposite. The presumption that it is part of the employer's business to undertake the risks of the trade, makes it very difficult to know how soon and how far he ought in fairness to concede to his men the full advantage of any improvement in the condition of trade, which may after all last but a short time; and how soon and how far he may require of them a fall in wages to meet a drooping condition of trade which may be but temporary.

In the ordinary course of things the first benefit of an improvement in the demand for their wares goes to the employers; but they are likely to want to increase their output while prices are high, and make high profits while they can. So they soon begin to bid against one another for extra labour; and this tends to raise wages and hand over some of the benefit to the employed. This transfer may be retarded, though seldom entirely stopped, by a combination among employers, or it may be hastened on by the combined action of the employed. As a general rule employers will be bound in fairness to yield at once in such a case a considerable part of their new profits in higher wages, without waiting till their men force it from them by warlike measures, which necessarily involve waste. Even if they succeed temporarily they will set going a spirit of contentiousness, and check the inflow of additional supplies of labour into their trade; the net gain which they get from refusing to yield will probably be small, while the net loss to the employed will be great; their action will be unfair. Fairness requires a similar moderation on the part of the employed. If they try to force wages so high as to leave a very scanty profit for their employers just at the time when they might expect to make their best harvest, capitalists will be discouraged from entering the trade; probably even many of those in it will leave it when work gets slack, even if they do not fail when the first touch of depression comes. The men will then find it difficult to get employment, and will probably thus lose more than all they have gained by their extreme demands, even if they should be successful in the first instance; the net gain to themselves will be little if any, the net loss to their employers will be very great; their claims will be unfair.

When trade declines, the loss in the first instance falls on employers; as prices generally rise before wages rise, so they fall before wages fall. The duties of the two sides are now reversed. The men ought in fairness to yield something without compelling their employers to fight for it; and nothing short of absolute necessity will make it fair for the employers to demand a reduction of wages so great as to cause much suffering to the employed, and drive many of them out of the trade. For such extreme demands will bring them, even if temporarily successful, a very small net gain in proportion to the net injury done to the employed.

Sometimes indeed, for tactical reasons, either side will demand at first more than it expects to get; but, though this may be inevitable in a state of suppressed industrial warfare, it is injurious to the common interests; it is fair only in the sense in which everything is fair in war; it is unfair from the point of view of industrial peace.

From that point of view again it is unfair for the men to spring claims for an advance on an employer suddenly, when he has just taken important time contracts under heavy penalties; it is unfair for the employer to take advantage of the fact that the men have had irregular employment and are short of money, and to use this as a lever for compelling them to work at a lower rate than the necessities of the case demand.

These are typical instances of what is unfair; there are many other classes of action which are ungenerous, and others again which would be avoided by an employer who acted up to the highest standard of unselfishness. But with these we are not directly concerned just at present. We have before us now only the narrow and limited inquiry, how far it is possible for frank dealing in a friendly spirit between employers and employed to remove those unfair dealings, and suspicions of unfair dealings, which are the chief causes of industrial war.

Boards of Conciliation

The best method is that of Conciliation. Delegates of employers and employed meet from time to time with the intention of speaking with perfect openness, avoiding everything like special pleading; each side trying to put itself into the point of view of the other side, and being careful not to make a demand which appears unreasonable when considered from that point of view.

They have two kinds of inquiry before them. In the one they move, so to speak, horizontally: they bring under comparison different kinds of work at the same time. Thus, in mining, different rates have to be made for different kinds of coal, and even for different seams of the same coal: while in some trades, as, for instance, the hosiery trade, prices for many kinds of work have to be agreed on. And, the most intricate matter of all, allowance has sometimes to be made for differences in the condition of the plant of different manufacturers; a rate, which is fair in a factory which has all the latest improvements, may be unfair in a badly organized factory with antiquated machinery. But, complex as these details are, this horizontal levelling of prices is comparatively easy; an agreement is often obtained with surprising quickness where there is a frank and genial disposition on both sides. The difficulty is much greater when the exigencies of the time require the price of the standard task—whether paid by the day or by the piece—to move above or below its standard level, and the calculations have to be made vertically instead of horizontally.

Since working men get less good from a temporary rise of their wages above their usual level than they do harm from an equal fall below it, therefore the fluctuations of wages should be less in proportion than those of the profits of the employers as a body. But here it may be right to make some difference between specialized and non-specialized workmen. Skilled miners cannot turn to other work when mining is depressed without great loss, and their numbers cannot be quickly increased when there is a great demand for their work: their fortunes are more intimately bound up with mining than those of the labourers and others who work on the surface of the mines. It is therefore in accordance with sound principle that the wages of under-ground men should follow the fluctuations of the trade more closely than those of "surface men." Next it is not fair that the workmen should share in the good or ill fortunes of the particular firm by which they are employed, unless they have made a special agreement to do so. Profit sharing arrangements, when well managed, are a gain to all concerned: but it is difficult to make them, and more difficult to keep them up. They require a good deal of mutual knowledge and confidence on the part of employers and employed; they are essentially matters for individual dealing, and not as a rule suitable for management by Boards of Conciliation, which often have to deal with very wide areas.

Speaking generally Boards of Conciliation have nothing to do with the profits of particular employers. But they are very much concerned with the profits of employers taken as a body: for these are the chief measures of the prosperity and adversity of the trade; and in some cases where the relations on both sides are thoroughly confidential, it may be possible to explain to the employed the general course of profits. Often, however, all that can be done is to enable actuaries appointed by them to examine the books of the firms concerned, and to ascertain from them the mean prices got for the goods sold, and in some cases a few other broad facts; holding the rest of the knowledge thus acquired under the oath of secrecy. These results are communicated by them to the Board, and are made the basis of the adjustment of wages; because they indicate better than any others, which are equally definite and easy of access, the amount of the common net fund available for division between employers and employed.

If the arrangement agreed on at any meeting is intended to last only for a short time, and to be revised as soon as there is any change in the circumstances of the trade, its details may be handled with great freedom; many of them may be determined in some measure by general impressions; they need not be calculated by rigid arithmetical processes from definite numerical data. Account may be taken of special circumstances which press heavily on employers or employed, or any group of them. In particular when irregular employment and low wages have caused much suffering among the employed and their families, the employers may be willing to trench on their reserve funds, and allow for a time wages to stand in such a relation to prices as would, if adopted as the basis of a permanent arrangement, soon land them in bankruptcy. If the meetings are frequent, and managed with frankness and kindliness, the future, though unknown, may cause no anxiety; it is nearly as good for either side to know that a fair concession will be made by the other whenever circumstances require it, as to know what that change will be. And the elasticity of this plan gives it great advantages over the rival plan of a "sliding scale"; that is a scale which determines beforehand how great a rise or fall in wages is to be accepted as the result of any given movement of prices upwards or downwards.

These advantages are of great importance in the case of a Board which represents only a small area; for then frequent meetings involve no great expense or loss of time; the delegates can quickly ascertain the views of those whom they represent on any new turn of the situation. But, if the area represented by a Board is very wide, it must proceed on general rules; the delegates may be authorized to act frankly and fairly, but seldom to act generously; therefore the elasticity gained by frequent meetings of the Board will not be of much avail. For the settlement, then, of a price list for a wide area, a well thought out sliding scale seems to be the best means attainable under our present social conditions.

In some trades, as for instance in coal mining, there is very little outlay for raw material, the circulating capital of the employers goes almost wholly in wages, perhaps in "royalties" to owners of land in which the mineral strata lie: so the price of the product is the best simple index of the prosperity of the trade. The plan therefore of fixing wages in the coal trade at a fixed sum together with a certain percentage of the price of coal is both usual and satisfactory. The profits or net receipts of the employers of course oscillate more violently than their gross receipts; these vary, as a rule, roughly with the price of coal. So this plan secures, as it should, that wages should generally rise when profits rise, and fall when profits fall; but with oscillations of less amplitude, rising less when they rise, and falling less when they fall, than profits do. In the iron trade the cost of raw materials is heavy: and probably the best simple scale for it is based on the excess of the price of a ton of iron of a certain quality over the sums of the prices of the coal and ironstone used in making it. As however these latter prices are often subject to very much the same influences as that of iron, the plan of basing the scale on the price of iron simply seems not to work badly. But in the textile and some other trades the prices of the raw materials depend on a great variety of causes (such as the weather in America or Australia), and the standard must be, not the price of the finished material, but the excess of that over the price of the raw material of which it is made.

Of course money is a bad measure in which to express any arrangement that is intended to last long: because the purchasing power of money is always changing. When trade is good and prices are high, the employer's fixed charges are light, and he borrows with a light heart: when trade is bad the consequent fall of prices increases the burden of his fixed charges, and if called on to repay his debt he must make very great sacrifices of his goods. A perfect standard of purchasing power is unthinkable: even a nearly perfect standard is unattainable. But Government could easily publish from time to time the money value of a unit of purchasing power which would be far more nearly constant than the value of money is.

I think it ought to do that. And then nearly all wage arrangements, but especially all sliding scales, should be based on that unit. This would by one stroke make both wages and profits more stable, and at the same time increase the steadiness of employment. It would perhaps be a further improvement if a special unit could be made for wages: that should be based on the general unit, but differ from it by giving greater weight to the prices of the commodities chiefly used by the working classes. Details of this kind might, however, be arranged gradually and tentatively; and in fact this part of the work would probably best be done not by the government, but by boards of conciliation making use of the data supplied by government, and taking account of conditions special to their trade and locality.

So far it has been assumed that everything works smoothly. But, even when there is the best intention on either side of a board of conciliation to be frank, and to look at things as much as possible from the point of view of the other side, there may be differences of opinion which cannot be removed by discussion. A stage may indeed be reached, at which further explanations only accentuate a deep seated difference of opinion. Therefore provision must always be made for referring some points to an independent arbitrator. But here is a dilemma. If he is connected with the trade he is likely, even though he has no personal interest in the questions at issue, to enter on them with a certain bias: if he knows nothing of the trade, a great deal of time will be taken up in explaining to him the position, and after all he may not understand it rightly. There has been much discussion as to which of these two evils is the greater. When there is mutual confidence and good temper and the suspicion of partisan bias is not likely to be strong, it may be best to have an arbiter who already understands the trade, and can give his decision more promptly and more in detail than an outsider could. But, if angry and jealous feelings have already been roused, and there is already a tendency on either side to impute unfairness to its opponents; then it is more important to know that the arbiter comes to the question without bias, than that he will understand it quickly, and be able to enter into all its details.

The action of the arbitrator must in some respects depend on the temper in which the case is presented to him. Sometimes the true facts of the case will be put before him at once, neither side making *ex parte* statements; and, what is even more important, neither side so mistrusting the other as to refuse to make concessions lest they should be taken to indicate weakness and fear, and encourage the other side to be the more aggressive. Sometimes also he will be given to understand that he should determine what is fair with reference only to the general tendency of economic forces, and that he is not to take account of the extent of the preparations for war ready on either side. In other cases, in which hostile feelings are already roused, the leaders may be unable to guarantee that the rank and file will accept a decision that awards them much worse terms than they could get for themselves by a sharp strike or lock-out. The arbitrator then is compelled to take some account of the fighting forces of the two sides; the necessity to be practical may compel him to go further than he would otherwise have done away from an absolute standard of fairness. In such cases, too, he must take for granted that the statements made by either side will be *ex parte*, and conduct his inquiry more or less after the manner of the law courts. This method of investigation is so cumbrous and slow that it cannot be very often resorted to; but, if it does its work thoroughly in a typical case, the indirect influence of its final award may extend very far: it may help many other differences to be settled quickly and quietly in private conversation or by boards of conciliation, and thus may be well worth the time and trouble it requires.

An arbiter, even if he starts with a knowledge of the trade, cannot deal with a detailed price list as easily as a board of conciliation, in which there is a healthy spirit, and which can appoint sub-committees to draw up the first drafts of portions of the price lists relating to special branches of the trade. Therefore, when there is a great variety of detail, any other course than that of conciliation seems hopeless; there is little room even for the action of trades unions, except in the matter of accustoming the workers to know and trust one another, to select able delegates, and to submit bravely to their decision. But this is a most important exception: independently of any direct effect on wages, trades unions have done an inestimable service by teaching members of the same trade to know and trust one another, to act together, and to discuss under the guidance of the ablest minds among them questions of wide and far-seeing policy.

The considerations on which the decision of an arbitrator must be based are as various as human life itself. But yet there is one broad principle which must underlie his work. He must, as the earlier economists would have said, conform to Nature. That is, he must not set up by artificial means arrangements widely different from those which would have been naturally brought about. For, if he does, his work will be in strong conflict with natural forces, and it will be destroyed. He must follow the example of Rennie, who, when he had to construct a break-water in Plymouth Sound, first set himself to discover the slope on which the natural action of the waves of the sea would arrange a bank of stones. He then let stones drop into the water so as to form such a slope: and the force of the waves, instead of overthrowing his work, only built it compact together and strengthened it. He controlled Nature because he guided her forces, while conforming to her laws: and this is the proper work of industrial conciliation and arbitration.

Of course there is a Normal value about which the wages of each kind of labour tend to fluctuate. This value changes with the growth of civilization and the progress of invention, and with changes in man's habits and character: but, at any given place and in any given age, the general relations of the wages of one trade to those of others are determined by the operation of broad causes; and any attempt to keep wages much above or much below their natural level will be opposed by strong natural forces, and will fail.

Such awards should follow the tendency of natural laws to

raise wages when trade is good, and lower them when it is bad. But the fluctuations in the wages of labour are naturally less violent than those in the prices of many goods; and, as variations of wages introduce a harmful uncertainty into the workman's life, conciliators and arbitrators should aim at making these fluctuations as small as they safely can, without holding out to either side a strong inducement to repudiate or evade the award. Mischief almost always results in the long run from an award which gives to one side terms much worse than those which it has good reason to believe that it could obtain by a strike or a lock-out.

Conciliation and arbitration are, indeed, helpless to secure for the feeblest and most ignorant class of workers a decent wage. The "sweater," who, as some sweaters do, works hard himself, earns but a moderate income, and pays promptly and ungrudgingly the highest wages that his trade will bear, cannot be said to act unfairly; but yet few are bold enough to say that he pays fair wages. The fact is that the root of this difficulty is not so much in our methods of business, as in those of education in the broadest sense of the term. Production is at fault, but it is the production of human beings. For this evil the ultimate remedy is in the higher education of the mass of the people. School work is useful as a foundation: but by itself it reaches only a little way. Trades unions increase the intelligence of the workman, by opening his mind to broader problems: boards of conciliation, together with the great co-operative movement, are carrying his education further. They are giving him an acquaintance with the real problems of business, which is the one thing wanted, provided he has good natural abilities, for enabling him to do high work in organizing the world's production. Every increase in the ranks of those who have this power increases the competition of employers for the aid of the employed, and diminishes the toll which has to be paid by the working classes to those who organize the work of the community. And further, anything that widens the intelligence of working men of ordinary ability, who have no natural capacity for the highest work, improves the prevailing tone with regard to the manner of expending the family income, and the responsibilities of parents towards their children.

Though, however, for helping the lowest class of workers we must look elsewhere than to systems of conciliation, these systems are, as has been shown above, a powerful means of raising the working classes as a whole. They are scarcely less powerful a means of raising their employers. The frank and free intercourse at the boards is helping employers to look at their business on its human side, to see that sometimes what is little more than a mere move in a game to them, may affect the whole future of many families; may help happy lives to expand in full vigour, or may turn them into a sour and stunted feebleness. The knowledge and sympathy thus gained by the employers raise those even of the rich who are not in business, widen their notions of justice, and aid them in realizing the responsibilities of wealth.

All these are steps upwards. They have not the rapid pace of a revolution: but a revolution sometimes rushes backwards faster and further than it had moved forwards; and steps such as these move steadily onwards.

X

CO-OPERATION (1889)[1]

GENTLEMEN,—Your two last annual Congresses were opened by two veteran co-operators—Mr Holyoake and Mr Neale. They have spent long lives in the centre of your movement; they have cared for it, and worked for it; they have earned your affection and your gratitude; and they could speak to you words of wise counsel, based on thorough knowledge. But I cannot do that. I can do nothing more than lay before you a sample of the way in which your movement presents itself to an academic economist, and trust to your kind indulgence to pardon my lack of special knowledge of the subject of which I have to treat.

Co-operation is many sided, and can be looked at from many points of view. There are, in consequence, many definitions of it, all having much in common, but each bringing into special prominence some aspect of it which appeals with special strength to some one or other of the many different classes of minds who are attracted by it. It is of course necessary to agree provisionally on some formal definition of a co-operative society for administrative purposes. But a movement, which, though so great, is yet so young, is in danger of being cramped by the too rigid insistence on any hard and fast formula; and I would wish, instead of defining it, to describe the general notion which I have formed of it. I regard it as the typical and most representative product of the age; because it combines high aspirations with calm and strenuous action, and because it sets itself to develop the spontaneous energies of the individual while training him to collective action by the aid of collective resources, and for the attainment of collective ends. It has points of affinity with many other movements; but it is like no other. Other schemes for developing the world's material resources are equally practical and equally business-like, but they have not the same direct aim to improve the quality of man himself. Other schemes for social reform have equally high aspirations, but they have not the same broad basis of patient action and practical wisdom.

[1] Presidential Address, delivered on the occasion of the Twenty-first Annual Co-operative Congress, held at Ipswich, Whitsuntide, 1889.

What distinguishes co-operation from all other movements is that it is at once a strong and calm and wise business, and a strong and fervent and proselytizing faith.

The cardinal doctrines of its faith are, as I have said, not peculiar to it: they are shared more or less by other movements. They are, I take it:—First, the production of fine human beings, and not the production of rich goods, is the ultimate aim of all worthy endeavour. Secondly, he who lives and works only for himself, or even only for himself and his family, leads an incomplete life; to complete it he needs to work with others for some broad and high aim. Thirdly, such an aim is to be found in the co-operative endeavour to diminish those evils which result to the mass of the people from the want of capital of their own; evils which take the two-fold form of insufficiency of material income, and want of opportunity for developing many of their best faculties. Lastly, the working classes, though weak in many ways, are strong in their numbers. They have a great power in their knowledge of one another, and their trust in one another; and they can much increase this force, for by joint action they can make their little capital go a long way towards getting a free scope for their activities, and towards emancipating them from a position of helpless dependence on the support, and the guidance, and the governance of the more fortunate classes. And, though the beginning of such a movement may be small, it has in it the seeds of growth, because it will educate the working classes in business capacity, and in the moral strength of united and public action for public purposes.

Now this co-operative faith, as I understand it, differs from the faiths of many social reformers in two respects. On the one hand it is more prosaic, and more ready to take facts as they are; it does not substitute for them brilliant products of a poetic imagination. And on the other hand, the virtues to which it appeals are the virtues of those who hold the faith. It is not a claim that the virtues of others should induce them to divide equally all round the advantages which they have already acquired.

I do not mean that the co-operator is very likely to consider the existing arrangements with regard to property as the best possible. He may probably think, as I myself certainly think, that the rich ought to be taxed much more heavily than they are, in order to provide for their poorer brethren the material means for a healthy physical and mental development; and he may think, as I certainly do, that the rich are in private duty bound to contribute freely to public purposes far more than the taxgatherer ought by force to take from them, and to confine within narrow bounds their expenditure on their own personal enjoyment, and that of their families. But the point I want to insist on is that any beliefs which the co-operator may hold on questions of this sort do not enter into the co-operative faith, because that relates to the duties of co-operators themselves, and not to the duties of others towards co-operators. The co-operative faith is a belief in the beauty and the nobility, the strength and the efficiency, of collective action by the working classes, employing their own means, not indeed suddenly to revolutionize, but gradually to raise, their own material and moral condition.

But now let us turn to the other side of co-operation, and regard it as a business. As a business it has succeeded, by economizing the efforts required to obtain certain desirable ends, and by utilizing a great waste product. For in the world's history there has been one waste product, so much more important than all others, that it has a right to be called THE Waste Product. It is the higher abilities of many of the working classes; the latent, the undeveloped, the choked-up and wasted faculties for higher work, that for lack of opportunity have come to nothing. Many a fortune has been made by utilizing the waste products of gas works and of soda works; it has been very good business. But a much greater waste product than these is at the foundation of the fortunes of co-operation. Let us then take stock of the resources of co-operation in this country.

The habit of association is specially characteristic of the Teutonic race; and our historians are proud to show how those who settled on these shores were, in this respect at all events, among the most Teutonic of the Teutons. But the exclusiveness of our claims has been somewhat lessened by recent studies of association in the form of village communities, etc., among other races, and especially among the Slavs, and our own near cousins and fellow-subjects in India. And quite recently we have been told that those associations for co-operative production, in which, if liberty is a little wanting, yet law and order are most perfectly developed, are to be found among those extremely distant relations of ours, the Chinese in California[1].

The fact is that the co-operative productive society in its rudimentary form is a product of all ages, and all races, and all places; and the independent productive societies, which we find now scattered sporadically over the whole of Great Britain, are representatives of a very ancient race. In a few cases, as, for instance, in some local institutions connected with quarrying and with fishing, they have an unbroken descent from remote antiquity till now.

But much that is most interesting in the recent history of productive co-operation comes from France, America, and other countries. Those features of it which are most characteristically British are found in its relation to the other sides of the co-operative movement. No other country has anything to compare with our great distributive retail and wholesale societies, or with that great Central Co-operative Union, the Congress of which I have the honour to address to-day. And I will, therefore, begin at that end.

You know well, and the whole world has heard, the figures that tell the growth of the trading business done by co-operation. But I may notice in passing that your figures are a little too modest. They record the number of sovereigns or counters that you have used in your sales; but they take no account of the fact that a thousand of these counters represent a great deal more business than they did a few years ago. The real growth of your trade is the increase in the volume of groceries and draperies, and other things that you have sold. Suppose now that the gold mines had given a richer yield, and the use of bank notes and silver and other substitutes for gold had increased faster than they have, in that case more counters would have been used in your trade: and, if there had been just so many more used that £1000 would have bought throughout the whole period the same amount of goods in general—taking one thing with another— then the figures which you publish would have shown the real

---

[1] See the *History of Co-operation in the United States*, published for the Johns Hopkins University, pp. 478–481.

growth of your business, and not, as they do now, much less than the real growth.

Using Mr Sauerbeck's figures, which are fairly applicable to this case, we find that if £1000 counted for only as much now as it did in the average of the years 1867 to 1877, the sales made by the English Wholesale Society last year would amount, not to six-and-a-quarter millions, but to nearly nine millions, while the sales of all the co-operative societies in the United Kingdom for 1887 (the last year for which I have the figures) would amount to fifty millions, and not merely to thirty-four, as your figures show. But the strongest case is got by comparing 1873, when prices were highest, with 1887. In those fourteen years the sovereigns or counters which represent the total sales of your societies had only a little more than doubled; but the amount of commodities sold had been multiplied by three-and-a-half, and, in the same time, the sales of the English Wholesale had been multiplied nominally by three-and-a-half, but really by five-and-a-half.

Well, what is the explanation of this huge trade? It lies chiefly in the fact that more effort was wasted in doing things that it was not worth while to have done at all in the old-fashioned retail trade than in any other business to which working men had access. It is possible that, if a co-operative society of working men had been able to penetrate the mysteries of the trade of law in its application to real property, and had been able to cut away all those complications that are more trouble to everyone, and more cost to everyone but the lawyers, than they are worth, there might have been an even more striking curtailment of wasted effort. But, however that may be, retail trade was the one accessible business in which there were great economies to be effected. Retailers, as a body, kept far more shops than was necessary, spent far too much trouble and money on attracting a few customers, and then in taking care that those few customers paid them in the long run—the very long run—for those goods which they had bought on credit, or, in other words, had borrowed; and for all this they had to charge. The smallest shopkeepers were those that spent most of their time in looking after their customers, and least in handing goods over the counter. It was those who were nearest the

condition of the working men, who performed the most unnecessary services for them, and charged them the most for so doing.
In some cases a retailer would sell at long credit what he himself
bought at long credit from a wholesale dealer, who himself
perhaps bought at credit from the ultimate producer. The
manufacturer had to charge high for the risks and trouble, as
well as the locking-up of the capital; the wholesale dealer,
starting from this raised platform of high prices, piled up a good
percentage more for a similar cause; the intermediate dealer did
the same, and perhaps, finding the retailer in his power, added
a little adulteration extra; the retailer, having the workman in
his power, added on, perhaps, a little more adulteration, and,
anyhow, a great increase of price.

Now the co-operative store bought for cash, and as nearly as
possible at the fountain head; it required no advertisements; in
its earlier stages it paid next to nothing for shop front; and in
its later stages, when it had a somewhat expensive shop front,
it put a great many businesses behind it, or in successive stories
over it. Its customers, regarding it as their own, would not
mind mounting many steps, or waiting a little for the assistants
on a Saturday night, or at any other time, when there happened
to be too few to get through the business quickly. The customers
were the proprietors, and had no inducement to adulterate their
own goods; and the time which they spent on attending meetings
of the society and managing their own business was in a great
measure saved from the time that used to be spent in considering
whether it would not be better to change their shopkeeper, or
perhaps in lamenting that they were in his power and could
not do so.

Now, my object in dwelling on this oft-told tale is to show
that the success of distributive stores does not prove that there
is any magic in co-operation, which will enable the working
classes to undertake difficult businesses without the aid of picked
men of a high order of business ability. Those whom the stores
have thrust to the wall are chiefly men who did not get very
high earnings, although they charged high prices. The system
of co-operative retailing has such great inherent economies that
it is likely to succeed if carried out with good faith and honesty
and average good sense: the more business genius it has the

better it will succeed, but it can flourish fairly well without
business genius.

And now let us pass to the Wholesale Societies. The Scottish
Wholesale is larger relatively to the population of its district
than the English; and it has special claims of its own on our
admiration, especially in the matter of bonus to labour. But
Ipswich is a long way from Scotland; and it will be simpler that
I should speak of the Wholesale in the singular number, and
refer always to that with which most of those present are
directly connected—the Wholesale which has its head-quarters
at Manchester.

Well, the Wholesale has inherent economies almost as powerful
as those possessed by the retail stores. For, though, by buying
for cash, they may get a little nearer to the original producer
than can the small shopkeeper who buys for credit, the Wholesale
can get much nearer. Its purchases are on so vast a scale as to
command every concession and every attention from producers
and importers. And, while thus buying cheaply, it probably has
less expenses in selling, in proportion to the work done, than any
other trader in a similar position. For, while every other trader
has to convince his customers that it is worth their while to deal
with him, the Wholesale Society is owned by its customers. They
have the power of deciding how much shall be added to the
original cost of the goods before they are sold to themselves, and,
if the goods are priced too high, there is only so much more
profit to be divided among themselves at the end of the quarter,
in proportion to their own purchases. And, therefore, the retail
societies would run no great risk if they shut their eyes and
bought what the Wholesale offered at the Wholesale's prices
without demur. It is true that there are exceptional cases in
which the retail societies' buyer can consult the caprices of local
taste better by buying elsewhere, and others in which accidents
of time and place and opportunity may enable him to buy a
particular lot of goods as cheaply as the Wholesale's buyer could
have done, or even a little cheaper. And it is true that that
self-confidence which is inherent in human nature, and which is
a factor in many of our bad deeds and nearly all our good ones,
may sometimes lead him to buy elsewhere when he should not.
All this may be admitted; but it still holds good that there is

no large trader whose way is made as smooth for him in finding a customer for his goods as the Wholesale Societies.

But the advantages of the Wholesale are still further increased, when it produces in one of its own departments the goods which it sells itself to the distributive stores. Such departments as the boot works at Leicester, or the biscuit works at Crumpsall, can avail themselves of the splendid resources of the Wholesale for buying much of their material. The department has a supply of capital which is at once unlimited and never too large; for the great bank in which the Wholesale keeps its own reserves, and those of many distributive societies, will always allow to it as much capital as it wants, and never force it to pay for more. It can offer practical constancy of employment to its workers, for when trade is slack the Wholesale will, of course, give the preference to the goods of its own department, and leave the other producing firms with which it deals to bear their fretting under the ragged edge of inconstant work as best they may. Again, the department need have no very great anxiety about those fluctuations of prices which make the career of most of its rivals so full of strain and stress. If one year it makes a fortunate purchase of raw material, and the Wholesale can credit it with a sale price for its finished commodities, pitched on a much higher basis, the gains all go into the common purse of the Wholesale; and if, at another time, the markets go against its buyers, so that when wages and all other expenses have been paid, and a fixed 5 per cent. allowed for capital, the balance sheet shows a loss, there is no disturbance of the ordinary routine. Departments which, if they had been independent businesses, would have been sunk by accumulated losses in their early years, have been carried through the waters by the strong hand of the Wholesale; and, having emerged safely, with their lessons of failure behind them, are in fair years making high net profits: these profits go to strengthen still more the already strong hand, and enable it to undertake new tasks, and to help other struggling departments through their temporary troubles.

With these advantages the Wholesale has risen to a position unique amongst all the achievements that have been wrought by the working classes in the history of the world. The mere size of the business which they have to control gives a largeness

to their ideas. It compels them to extend the range of their
thought over the whole country, almost over the whole world.
It is an education in itself to any member of a local society to
have to consider whether his representative on the Wholesale
is to advocate a forward policy—whether, for instance, he is to
support a proposal for starting one more new line of ships of
their own, or for opening a new foreign depôt in addition to
those at Calais and at Rouen, at Copenhagen, and Hamburg,
and New York. He feels a healthy pride as he turns over the
pages of his *Annual*, and sees prints of one splendid building
after another of which he is part owner; as he reckons up the
acres of flooring in his warehouses at Manchester, or asks whether
there are many buildings in the city that are finer than his
London branch, with its high clock tower.

And, when he looks forward, his ambition may reach out a long
way unchecked. He may reason that, if the belief should extend
that all goods sold in the stores, whether high class or low class,
are honestly what they pretend to be, that they are sold at
least as cheaply as the tradesman can sell them, and that there
is a dividend of, say, 2s. in the pound thrown in at the end of
the quarter, the sales of the retail stores may perhaps grow to
three or four hundred millions a year. Every increase in their
sales would increase their power of consulting the tastes of a
great variety of customers, and so retaining those who are now
drawn off to shops that follow special lines of their own; and it
would increase the variety of the orders which they could give
to the Wholesale. And, if the growing loyalty to co-operative
principles, which induced individuals to buy more largely of the
stores, induced the retail stores to buy more largely of the
Wholesale, they would by their very increased custom enable
the Wholesale to extend its operations, to sell to them more
cheaply, to provide them with a larger choice of goods, and
thus to increase their inducements to buy almost everything
from it.

The powers of the Wholesale as a dealer would therefore be
increased much; but its powers as a producer would be increased
out of all proportion. For now, though it can vie with any in
buying direct from the packing houses of Chicago and the flour
mills of Minneapolis, it cannot enter upon any manufacture for

which there is not a very large working class demand; since many purchasers when buying manufactured goods prefer the variety offered by a long street of shops to the charms of the dividend at the stores. Not being able to sell largely, the retail stores do not buy largely; and, being themselves compelled to seek for variety, they will, as a rule, buy only very small quantities of any one particular pattern, whether it is a co-operative product or not. Co-operative manufacture on a large and varied scale is thus like a cocoanut: it has a very hard shell; but, when the shell is broken, there is plenty of good food to be got within. There is a charmed circle to be entered if individual co-operators would buy manufactures so largely from their stores, and their stores would buy so largely of co-operative manufacturers, that co-operative manufactures become so various, and the stocks of them held by the distributive stores become so large, that there would be scarcely any temptation to seek variety in the outside shops.

It is a most fascinating picture. The retail societies, if properly supported by the private individual, and the Wholesale, if properly supported by them, have within them greater economies than have ever been claimed by the plausible promoters of those Trusts of which we have heard so much lately. But, while the purpose of those Trusts was to increase the fortunes of the rich, by means which perhaps might be fair, and perhaps might incidentally benefit the consumers, this further development of the great co-operative federation would be a means by which the working classes would help themselves. Its strength would be a moral strength; would rest on a broad basis of democracy and of equity; its gains would be divided out among all consumers, those consumers being in great part the producers themselves, consuming in proportion to their earnings, and earning in proportion to their efficiency. Raising its high head far beyond all other business undertakings, it would stand forth to challenge the admiration of all ages, the glorious product of working men's hands and working men's heads, of working men's providence and working men's enthusiasm for a great and good cause. It would, in a greater or less degree, act up to all the cardinal principles of the co-operative faith, as I understand it.

And yet, magnificent as this scheme is, there are many ardent co-operators who feel that it falls short of their fondest hopes. It would be strong and vast, and would conform to the principles of the co-operative faith more or less; but their most cherished hopes, their warmest affections, go out towards productive societies, which are less completely under the management of a central control, and which are, therefore, in some respects less strong, and which can offer less resistance to the blows of an adverse fortune; but which yet seem to point more directly towards the true aims of the co-operative faith, because they help the ordinary working man to get nearer to responsible work, because they tend more directly to utilise *the* great waste product—the higher abilities that are latent among the working classes. It is bold and hardly indeed for an outsider, such as I am, to express an opinion on a question on which those are not agreed who have borne the burden and the heat of the long day of co-operative work; but I shall ask your kind forbearance while I lay before you the reasons which have led me to think that extreme centralisation, though it might quicken and strengthen the growth of your great movement for the present, would not really conduce to its highest and most permanent interests; and that in the long run your movement will prosper best if care is taken that its more independent parts are not crushed out, but are enabled to survive and to supplement—not to conflict with—the central kernel of the Wholesale.

Perhaps I may explain my position more clearly if you will allow me to digress a little. It is common to hear it said that England is divided into two nations—the rich and the poor. I am not sure that it would not be in some respects better for the poor if that statement were strictly true. I will admit that if everyone born of rich parents were able and virtuous, and everyone born of poor parents were stupid and vicious, the poor would lose much and gain nothing from being isolated from the rich. But, unfortunately for the poor, they have to make room among their ranks for a large accession every year of the most stupid and profligate of the descendants of the rich; and in return they every year give over to the ranks of the rich a great number of the strongest and ablest, the most enterprising and far-seeing, the bravest and the best of those who were born among themselves. Now, it is true that a system of caste so rigid that every one has to stay always just where he is born is a desolating system. Hope and ambition, and some scope for the play of free competition, are conditions—necessary conditions so far as we can tell—of human progress. But the great evil of our present system, which it is one chief aim of co-operation—as I take it—to remove, lies in the fact that the hope and ambition by which men's exertions are stimulated have in them too much that is selfish and too little that is unselfish. After a man's income has put him beyond the fear of pressing want, any further increase adds to his happiness less than he thought it would before he got it. The direct increase of happiness that results from increasing wealth becomes less and less as the wealth increases; and a person who has already a few hundreds a year may, so far as material wealth has anything to do with it, be nearly as happy as he chooses to be. The pleasure derived from any further increase is chiefly the pleasure of acquisition, of victory over rivals, of a consciousness of the proof of one's own strength, of being admired and envied by those whom one has left behind, and of being wondered at and tolerated by those into whose society one has risen.

And, if the rise is very rapid, it is apt to be very bad for a man, and even worse for his children, as our experience at the Universities shows. A working man, who, by brilliant genius and strong energy, has heaped up a large fortune, is likely to send his sons there; and one might have expected that coming from such splendid stock they would have had noble ambitions, and helped to raise the tone of the University. And sometimes they do that; but in too many cases their influence is in the opposite direction: too often their parents have been too busy in struggling with their new social difficulties to instruct them as to the importance of anything higher than mere money; and, when I see such cases, I am filled with regret that most excellent material has been wasted.

It might have been better for himself, for his children, and for the world, that the father should not have moved so far away from his early associations; that he should have found scope for his strength and a goal for his ambition in working, at the head indeed of his comrades, but among them; and should not have suddenly passed over to dwell among strangers, the large capitalist employers of his old friends. His rank in the social scale would have been nominally lower, but really it would have been much higher. Occupied less with adapting himself— and his wife—hurriedly, and therefore awkwardly, to new conditions, he would have been more truly refined. The able working man who is in no great hurry to terminate his connection with his own class is more often than not a perfect gentleman; and that is what a man cannot be, whatever his nominal rank in life, if he is over-much hasted to get riches. A leader of a great trades union, who has earned the esteem, and confidence, and affection of those around him, has got more of those things for which wealth is really to be desired than if he had accumulated a large fortune; and every sensible man would rather have him for a companion and a friend just as he is, than if he had become a great iron master or cotton lord.

However, those working men who rise to be rich generally do some important service. If they do nothing else, they increase the volume of production; and, when their rise is due to their power of originating new ideas and new methods, their own fortunes represent but a small part, often not a thousandth part, of the increase of material well-being that results from their efforts. And, though some of them may have developed their intellects at the expense of their other faculties, the harm done is not to be compared with the waste of latent abilities on the part of that very much larger number of the working classes, who with fitting opportunities might have been educated to do work as difficult and important as that of the average member of the middle classes, but who have no special genius and no faculty for pushing themselves.

Now, these men want three things—education to fit them for doing higher work; opportunity to do it; and the spur of ambition to rouse them to use the opportunity. This ambition need not be chiefly one for material gain. Theoretically, it might be a mere ambition to be good; but, with human nature as it is, those cases in which men are capable of good actions, but require some other stimulus than the mere desire to be good, are too numerous to be neglected by the practical politician. For practical working there should be added a position recognised as one of trust and of honour; and with every increase in the importance of the work there should be some increase of pay, though it need not always be a very great increase.

Now, there have been at various times a good many schemes proposed for supplying these three wants of education, opportunity, and ambition. Some of these schemes have more poetry than common sense, and some are more violent than just. They are all both entertaining and instructive reading; most of them tend to edify and to elevate the reader. But there is, to my mind, some fatal practical objection to all of them, bar one; and that one is co-operation. As I said just now, other movements have a high social aim, and other movements have a broad and strong business basis. Co-operation alone has both. For it has a broader scope than trades unions or provident societies, or those building societies, which, as your excellent Tenant Co-operators know, are so nearly akin to your own movement. All of these can do something towards bringing out the higher and more unselfish ambition of working men, towards educating and utilising their latent faculties, but it is co-operation alone which has a sufficiently broad business basis to be able to do this great work on a great scale.

It can, however, discharge this high function only by bringing the administrative work close to the people who are to do it. If it organises itself into a vast centralised institution, on the model of a great bureaucratic government, it may have a great force, as such governments often have, but it will miss its highest aims. Looking at the question in this way, we find small profit in the fact that each of the 600,000 co-operators who belong to societies that are members of the Wholesale has an equal vote in determining its policy and that of its productive departments. For, in his capacity of citizen, each has already his voice in controlling the policy of the State. If the co-operator owns a six hundred thousandth part of your warehouses at Manchester, and of the co-operative ship that goes to Hamburg, he also owns a share of all our public buildings and institutions, and of a great navy. The vote which he gives for electing a representative either on the Wholesale or in Parliament has undoubtedly an educating effect; the broader the issues on which his vote depends, the higher is the educative value to him of his vote, provided he knows well what the issues are. But, if the issues are so remote that he does not attempt properly to grapple with them, the volume of his education is but slight. It is a better training in seamanship to sail a fishing-boat, than to watch a three-masted ship, the tops of whose masts alone appear above the horizon.

I do not overlook the fact that, even under a centralised co-operative system, there would be a great deal of local government. Of course, every distributive store would retain its autonomy; and, though the Wholesale would aim at saving it all trouble in deciding as to the ultimate source from which its various supplies should come, its management would offer a good deal of work for a good many active minds; it would continue to give education and opportunities, and a scope for a worthy ambition to the ordinary co-operator. That is true—may the retail store thrive, and continue this good work; there is nothing to be said against it except that it does not give scope for all kinds of business ability, and that there is not enough of it.

But you may say that the local store would still be able to start productive departments of its own, such, for instance, as the little farm which our Ipswich friends have here close by. That brings administrative work to the doors of the private co-operator—work which concerns him nearly, and in which he takes a keen interest; he watches it carefully, and learns a great deal from it, even though he may have no direct part in its management. And further, if little movements of this sort are multiplied, they may become fairly numerous relatively to the whole body of co-operators, and so a considerable part of those who have faculties above the average may find the education and the opportunity and the spur to a worthy ambition of which they are in need. That is true; and local stores can enable splendid results of this kind to be attained in spite of a certain amount of centralisation: all I wish to point out is that they vary in inverse proportion to the extent to which centralisation is pushed.

And, when we come to look at the centralised part of a centralised system of co-operation, we find that the opportunities which it offers to people for doing what I am doing now—making speeches—are out of all proportion to those which it offers for any other work except manual work. I am not one of those who think that the tone of politics is lower than it was; but I do think there is one growing evil in the fact that statesmen have to spend so much time in convincing others of the correctness of their views, and the excellence of their administration, that they have not enough time for administrative work, and for studying carefully the matters committed to their trust. And I gather that your general committee, on whom everything would depend, has a great deal of talking to do. Its present members, including its most able president, were educated under a less centralised system. But I cannot help asking myself whether there is adequate security that in the competition for a post on the committee a man of great administrative force, but not a fluent speaker, would always be sure to get the better of a less able man who had a great faculty of persuasiveness, and had perhaps learnt a thing or two about the great machine which American politicians are perfecting.

But, suppose that danger to be avoided, and your central committee to remain as able, as energetic, and as upright as they are now. It would still be true that, when once elected, their powers and their procedure would necessarily resemble more or less those of the directors of a large joint-stock company; and, if those methods should prevail, which I understand to be most in favour with the advocates of centralisation, the resemblance would be very close. There would be heads of departments, as in any ordinary business, responsible to them and to no one else; and with high authority in matters of detail. There would be, as I have said, a strong executive. Moreover, many of these leading officers probably would have been educated in the co-operative movement. Their abilities, which might otherwise have remained latent and been wasted, would have been turned to good account. So far good. But there is one flaw, a grave flaw from my point of view. It is that the total number of men of that kind—the total number of men to whom the system so organised could point proudly as the high products of co-operation—would be very small in proportion to the capital employed.

There are, then, three reasons for my venturing to hope that co-operators will hesitate before they accept the argument, that the right way of deciding whether the centralised system of production under the auspices of the Wholesale or the inde-

pendent system is the better, is to let the two have a fair field
and no favour, and to cry at the end, "The devil take the
hindmost!" First, I feel sure that the centralised system is
stronger than the independent system, with its present organisation, or lack of organisation; and that, with a fair field and no
favour, the former would win. Secondly, the more loyal the
retail societies are to the Wholesale, the more difficult will it be
to arrange a field which is quite fair, and in which the independent
societies are not at some disadvantage. And, lastly, if success in
the struggle for survival in a fair field is the sole test of excellence,
what is the use of co-operation at all? Surely the direct effect
of the struggle for survival in the animal kingdom is to cause
those animals to flourish which are fittest to derive benefits from
the environment, and so strengthen themselves; not those which
are fittest to confer benefits on the environment. It is true that,
in the higher world of man's action, those plans which benefit
the environment most are likely to have a moral strength which
will enable them to prevail in the long run. But is it not the
special function of co-operation to give them a helping hand,
and enable them to prevail early, or at all events to secure that
their career is not cut so short that they have no "long run" in
which to prevail?

Let us then turn to the independent productive societies.
There is no doubt that they labour under great difficulties. The
management by working men of the businesses in which they
are themselves employed is neither as efficient nor as free from
friction as it would be if we social reformers had been able to
arrange the world just to our own liking. It has often been said
that an army led by a capable general can give odds of twenty
per cent. and a beating to one managed by a committee of able
men, if they commit the one folly of discussing at length all
details. The worst of several possible manœuvres, if adopted
promptly, will often turn out better than the best of them if it
is delayed till its *pros* and *cons* have been well talked out. And
the fact that the employees on the committee of such a co-
operative business are able to hold their own against their
managers in matters of the minutest detail, may often go a good
long way towards wrecking the concern. Moreover, there is a
good deal of human nature in most men, working men not

excepted: and most men's eyes can see pretty keenly when they are looking in the direction of their own merits. The manager and a committeeman may occasionally differ a little about the merits of the committeeman, even though they don't say so; and then it is not always well for the manager. And, if the manager and the committeeman happen to be agreed on the point, but some of the committeeman's fellow-workers take a different view of his merits relatively to their own, then they are likely to remark that a committee is a very good thing, at all events, for those who are on it: and the remark, even though it may be true, does not help the concern to work smoothly.

Then, again, managing a business is a very difficult matter. There are some people who think it easy, and are constantly telling us that there is nothing much that the employers as a class do for industry that the working people properly organised could not equally well do for themselves. Such people remind me of Charles Lamb's friend, who complained that too much fuss was made about Shakespeare; "he could have written that sort of thing himself if he had had the mind." "Ah!" said Charles Lamb, "I suppose it was only the mind that was wanting." To carry on a great business nothing much is wanted except to organise it properly; but then that is just the difficulty. It is as easy as beating the big drum in an orchestral concert. Nothing more is needed than that you should do the right thing at the right time, but there are not many people who can do it.

I have already laid stress on the fact that the success of the distributive societies is no proof of the efficiency of working men as undertakers of business enterprises. Their inherent advantages are so great that they may sometimes prosper fairly even though their management is but second-rate; and there is no question that some of them have done so. Their success gives no ground for anticipating that a productive society would succeed when it had to run the gauntlet of competition with private firms managed by business men quick of thought and quick of action, full of resource and of inventive power, specially picked for their work and carefully trained. And of men thus picked a great number fail; it is said that in some businesses more than half of those who start fail within the first five years. Some of them come to the surface again, but many sink altogether; the waters close over them; everyone takes it as a matter of course; they are heard of no more; but no fuss is made about them. When, however, a co-operative society undertakes a business harder than it can manage, the trumpets which sounded at its christening sound again a little louder at its funeral; and some faithful friend writes out a tender obituary notice, which the careful historian of co-operation epitomises for his necrological chapter—a perpetual warning as to the vanity of human hopes.

And then there is another difficulty. Nearly every kind of business requires every year a larger capital to carry it on; and the working man has seldom much capital. It has been commonly said that in competition capital employs labour and pays it a fixed wage; but that in co-operation labour employs capital, and pays it a fixed rate of interest. But that is more easily said than done. It is easy enough to borrow a thousand millions at four per cent., if the four per cent. is sure—quite sure. But it is not nearly so easy to borrow £1000 at ten per cent., if the ten per cent. is only moderately sure. And most of us know the sorrows of that society of which all co-operators are so fond and proud, the fustian society at Hebden Bridge, which borrowed at $7\frac{1}{2}$ per cent. when its security was not so good, and the current rate of interest was higher, but now finds itself much hampered by having to pay so high a rate.

But, in fact, it is not true that under competition labour is hired by capital; it is hired by business ability in command of capital: and it is not true that in co-operation capital is hired by labour; it may be hired by the business ability that lives in the heads that the working men have on their shoulders; but, if they have not much business ability, they will not get much capital, either of their own or of anyone else's; and, if they get it, they will not keep it long: and it all comes back to that.

Next, after the difficulty of making things is overcome, that of selling them begins; and often the latter is the greater of the two. To say nothing of advertising, private firms spend a great deal of their energy on getting hold of the right kind of travellers and agents for pushing their goods, and a great deal of money on paying them; and this is a thing that co-operative societies cannot do very well; and there is much of it to which, to their credit be it said, they do not take very kindly.

Lastly, a productive society often owes whatever success it has had almost entirely to a few men, perhaps to one man, of exceptional ability, fervent and strong in the co-operative faith. And then it is constantly at the mercy of cruel Death. He snaps the threads of a few lives, or perhaps only of one, and the society dwindles and decays, or is converted into a greedy joint-stock company; and so cherished hopes are once again disappointed, and the proud boasts of confident co-operators are brought to naught.

Well, then, productive co-operation is a very difficult thing, but it is worth doing. When I was an undergraduate, I once took to my mathematical tutor a long face and an unfinished problem. I told him I had worked at it the whole of the preceding day, and yet not done it, though the day before I had done twenty that did not look a bit harder. He was a wise man—Dr Parkinson was his name—and he looked at me cheerily and said, "Well, then, yesterday's work probably did you much more good than that of the day before. There is not much good in doing things you can do; but there is great good in trying to do those that you can't do, but that are worth doing." And it seems to me that the difficulties of non-centralised co-operative production are just those at which it is best worth while to take a long pull, and a strong pull, and a pull all together. I believe that some of them are not so tough as they look, and can be broken through; and that those which are very tough have a corner at no great distance, which you can turn, and so get round them.

In this matter you have a very great advantage from the elasticity of independent productive societies. There must be one spirit in them all, they must all rest on a common principle; but they may have the largest variety of detail. Sometimes, for instance, it may be best not to have employees on the committee at all; but even then the employees may attend the general meetings of the society, and may be represented on the committee by others who are and have been employed in the same or in allied trades. My friend Mr Jones intends, I believe, to call your attention to the co-operative element in the Oldham spinning mills; and I may well leave that subject in his most able hands. But I should like to point out that those mills owe a great deal to the facts that Oldham is the chief centre for manufacturing cotton spinning machinery, and that many of those interested in the mills are or have been mechanics engaged in making that machinery. And there are many cases in which the advice of a workman engaged in an allied trade is of great use to a co-operative society, while the opportunity for giving it is a gain for him.

It is a subject on which I must speak with very great diffidence. But, after hearing a good deal of what can be said on both sides, I incline to think that the real advantages of having employees on the committee are greater, and the disadvantages less, than they are likely to appear at first both to the shareholders and the manager. I think that in this matter the co-operative spirit has a high, though difficult duty, the brave performance of which would ultimately bring its own reward. One reason for thinking that the difficulties arising from having employees on the committee are not so great as they look, is that, though they have had much to do with wrecking many enterprises, that has been because, in any new undertaking, people are apt to mis-understand one another at first. Partly it is that the wrong people are apt to be put on the committee at first; partly that there is no tradition or precedent to which to appeal in disputed cases, but every difference of opinion has to be fought out; partly that some of those who are most quick to start a new movement are least able to bear and forbear when the time of pressure comes. Experience, I believe, shows that difficulties of this kind, if once tided over, are likely to recur, if at all, in a somewhat milder form: they are rather like measles. Difficulties of this kind need not discourage us: they rather show that many of the failures of independent productive societies are due to causes which can be removed by co-operative aid and guidance. They are arguments against the complete isolation of such societies, but not in favour of their being consolidated under a rigid centralised government.

And it is much the same with regard to the other difficulties. No doubt many productive societies have failed through en-gaging in unsuitable businesses; but co-operative experience may guide them away from tasks in which it is necessary to run great risks, to act with great vigour and decision, to have a wide range of technical and commercial knowledge, to be well posted in the latest news and to get it nearly at first hand, to be constantly devising new schemes and new methods of manufacture, and appealing to and creating new tastes. Co-operative production may occasionally come across a man who has the rare qualities required for such work. But, unless his co-operative virtue is very strong, the large gains which he can make in the outside world will draw him away. And for the present, at all events, productive societies need to be guided towards those industries that do not require rare talents; towards industries in which punctuality, and order, and neatness, and careful economy in matters of detail, and a steady resolute tread along a well-beaten path, are the things chiefly wanted. There are plenty of men latent among the working classes who have the capacity required for this work, and who would be content with a moderate income and a good position among those who know them.

Industries which satisfy these conditions seldom want a very large capital. Such as do must of course be avoided; and no doubt many productive societies have failed partly through under-estimating the capital required for what they have undertaken. Here co-operative counsel on the one side and co-operative capital on the other will be of good service. Productive societies that are in other respects on the right lines can generally get what capital they want at a reasonable rate of interest: though I do not say that distributive societies can make a good business by undertaking to pay five per cent. on an unlimited number of new shares, and lending out the money at a moderate rate to a more or less risky business. But I would venture to ask in passing whether there is not a pressing need for prompt action in the matter of accepting new capital at five per cent.? Is it not an anachronism?

Here, then, we see again an argument against the isolation of productive societies. And we find still another argument in the difficulties that they have in marketing their goods; and another in the need for continuity of management. For marketing is just the business in which co-operation is most effective; and the crisis through which a society passes when its best members are removed by death or in other ways may often be tided over by a little co-operative aid from outside.

Does not all this point to the conclusion that in order to give co-operative production in this country a fair chance of doing its best, there is required some broad-based organisation for helping it? I say in this country, because the industrial qualities of this country are peculiar, and not like those of any other. Englishmen are not particularly quickwitted, or specially adapted for contriving sporadic productive associations, each fighting entirely for itself, each trying some new experiment, depending on its own resources, and heedless of what others have done or are doing.

And, on the other hand, Englishmen have no liking for things controlled and drilled by a central government. What suits their character best is to have a broad and solid association based on many smaller associations, not controlling and directing them, not interfering with their freedom without absolute necessity, but acting as a common centre for help and advice; serving as a channel by which any member that is in special need may receive the aid of others, and taking perhaps an active part in administering aid and the wholesome advice by which it may perhaps have to be accompanied. It seems to me that the three great features of English social life, trades unions, provident societies, and co-operation, owe their success to adopting this plan. Broad-based, highly-organised freedom of action is characteristically English: and the true future of English co-operation lies, I am convinced, in adhering to these lines.

If co-operation, which has made its great position by fostering freedom, should throw its strength into developing departments of the Wholesale governed by a central authority, is there any certainty that this new departure, so seemingly at variance with the traditions of the English people, would be supported by them permanently? I spoke just now of the great strength of a productive department of the Wholesale; but does not the permanence of the strength of the Wholesale itself depend upon its adhering to English traditions of freedom and local autonomy? Even though centralised departments may be the strongest and fittest to thrive on their environment for the present, are they the fittest to benefit it, are they even the surest to flourish themselves in the long run? And would it not be, on the other hand, equally un-English to continue to allow the independent productive societies to fight their hard fight, to struggle, and too often to die an early death, for the want of a guiding and a helping hand, for the want of those advantages, those economies, and those powers which come from broad-based association and co-operation? Do not many of your discussions point in this direction? Your schemes for propaganda, and the cordial reception given to Mr Gray's excellent papers on "Co-operative Production," seem all to do so. Your Co-operative Guild, your Co-operative Aid Association and your Labour Association are evidences that you recognise a want of this kind.

Is not, however, your Co-operative Union itself the right body for the work? But is it at present strong enough? Ought you not to develop it and to put more of your funds at its disposal? I speak here with the greatest hesitation. I do not mean to suggest that the funds for this purpose should be levied compulsorily on all societies, whether in favour of the movement or not; but I think that many societies would favour it. And it is just that part of the movement in which outsiders would be most willing to help, if they were sure that the funds contributed would be spent under the authority of the Union, and therefore wisely. I do not know whether anyone would raise an objection on the ground that the constitution of your Union permits joint-stock companies and other external associations to become members of it, though none have yet done so. In that case you might perhaps think it best to create a new body for the purpose; but it is to be hoped that this would not be necessary. Might you not give to your Union the means and the duty to help productive societies with guidance and with funds, leaving them the greatest liberty of detail, subject to the condition of their adhering closely to high co-operative principle, under which of course would be included securing a full share of the profits to the workers? Might not it further undertake to act as a common centre of information as to their special wants, and to warn them against pressing into a field that was already full; to take part in acquainting distributive societies with what they are doing; in acquainting them with the needs of distributive societies; in organising arrangements for depôts, exhibitions, commission agents, and travellers; and, lastly, might it not act as a kind of board of arbitration and conciliation for troubles that may arise either within a society, or between it and others?

It would, of course, nominate members on the committees of those associations which sought its pecuniary aid; but probably many other societies would ask it to do this, just as many schools and local colleges are glad to have members on their councils nominated by the Universities, partly because they can give good advice, partly because they bring an impartial judgment to the decision of any internal difficulty that may arise, and, not least, because their presence gives prestige and attracts the confidence of the outside world. And might it not be instructed to choose these representatives from as wide a circle as possible, and so to give to many men the opportunity of showing what they are worth as administrators; not, of course, putting untried men into responsible posts, but always finding for a man who had done one task well something more responsible to go on with? Is this a Utopian dream? Is not the tendency of your whole movement really in this direction; and has not the time now come, not, indeed, for prompt action, but for steadfast deliberation, that may prepare the way for resolute action? And the last question of all—can you forgive me, an ill-informed outsider, for my presumption in asking these bold and intrusive questions?

I have come to the end of my time, and yet have touched the fringe of only a small part of the great problems which you have set yourselves to solve. The days of romantic chivalry are past. Knights-errant no longer rescue imperilled maidens from the castles of terrible giants, or slaughter dragons that vomit volcanoes of flames; but there is as loud a call as ever for courage and a chivalric self-sacrifice for great and worthy ends. Those who are full of the co-operative faith have to endure the disappointment of seeing themselves out-voted by numbers who care for little that is co-operative except the dividend; and still they have to keep their courage, and to keep their temper, and to fight the good fight time after time till they win. I am told by those who know, what I should have otherwise expected, that there will be in this hall to-day many of the truest and bravest knights of that great order of modern chivalry—co-operation; and they must sometimes wish that the doors had not been held so widely open for those worshippers in their great temple whose devotions are exclusively paid at the shrine of dividend, who stay eagerly watching to see whether the golden image that dwells there will hold up its fingers at the end of the quarter to signify 2s. 3d. or 2s. 4d.; and care for very little else. But to them I would repeat the noble motto of the English Wholesale: "Labour and Wait."

They and others who are not here to-day may wonder that I have not put more into the foreground the great issue as to whether the employees of a co-operative society should share in its profits. I have not done so, partly because my time was short, partly because there seems some danger of its over-shadowing what I regard as a still more fundamental question. Profit-sharing is a great end, but it is also a means to an even greater end. It certainly tends to award to the worker a better and juster share of his work than he would otherwise get; but, taken by itself, it does not go very far towards that end. Unless it is used also as a means towards a better organisation of industry it is apt to become little more than a change of form, nearly as much being taken off wages at one end as is added on at the other under the name of profit-sharing. But even so it compares not unfavourably with the best result that can be reached without it, even if the spirit of the employers is liberal, and they try to pay not as low wages as they can, but as much as the business will bear; and if as their business extends they promote their old employees as rapidly as possible to higher posts at higher salaries. It is true that those employees who have been more than five years with one firm are, taking all England together, much better off than they would have been if the firms for which they had worked had barely kept their heads above water; and there is much more indirect profit-sharing, and solidarity of interest between employer and employed in the non-co-operative world than at first sight appears. And I must further confess that, when any abstract or "metaphysical" principle—the term is not mine—is applied to settle rigidly what share of the profits should go to labour and what to capital, and what to the consumer, I find myself unable to follow it; whether it is put forward in the interests of labour or of the consumer. Nevertheless, I regard the movement towards the direct participation by the employee in the profits of the business as one of the most important and hopeful events of modern times, and as one of the best and most valuable fruits of the co-operative spirit.

It is the most convincing outward sign and symbol, and the most efficient means, of a true desire to associate the worker in the business, to keep warm his interest in it; to induce him to take a pleasure in advancing its prosperity by all means, whether they fall within the technical limits of his ordinary work or not; to offer him, as far as may be, education, and opportunity and scope for a worthy ambition to act not merely as a hand, but as a thinking and thoughtful human being. Profit-sharing is a good means towards this great end; and he has not lived in vain who has helped to overcome the obstacles which impede its general adoption.

The term profit-sharing is, however, sometimes applied to the case in which labour, or rather "the business ability that lives in the heads that working men have on their shoulders," endeavours to hire capital at a fixed rate of interest, and in favour of that I have nothing to say now, because I have been speaking for it all along. I must, however, confess to some partial agreement with the advocates of the present system of the Manchester Wholesale, when they argue that their employees in any productive department cannot be regarded as hiring capital on these terms. They argue that the Wholesale undertakes to market their goods for them, as well as to superintend their general management, and that an arbitrary element is introduced in the charge which has to be made for their services, and therefore that the profits to be divided among the employees, if that system were adopted, could not be determined by any abstract principle. I admit it; but I still wish that the Manchester Wholesale would follow the example of its Scottish sister; and, accepting the fact that there is an arbitrary element, calculate it as best it can, and share the net profits with the employees. As, however, I have already said, I should much prefer that the Union should perform for the independent co-operative societies many of the services which the Wholesales perform for their productive departments. Then the societies could approach as near as existing conditions will allow to the ideal of "labour employing capital."

This is, however, only one of many tasks that lie before the true knights of co-operation. There are others in which the path of duty, if not more easy, seems yet more clearly marked in its general outline, though even in them there is a fringe of debatable ground.

You have, for instance, still to fight the old fight against giving credit. The wily trader is developing a fresh line of attack, by new modifications of the old plan of payment by instalments. He claims to give his dividend at the beginning instead of at the end; and I am told that there are a great many silly flies who walk into the pretty parlour of that shrewd spider.

Again, you have the old battle for honesty in dealing. You have been hampered a good deal by the reaction against undiscriminating attacks on adulteration. The term is often used so as to include open and undisguised changes in the character of goods to suit the wants and the tastes of consumers. But you seem to me to have a clear duty; it is to explain to consumers what things are cheap and what things only appear to be cheap; to give them for their money as high class goods as you can afford, and as much truthful information about them as you possess. Gradually they will care less and less to buy show instead of substance.

And you have—the most difficult task of all, because that in which you are most likely to be suspected of jealous motives—to keep the field clear of those who would use it for their own selfish purposes. Co-operators may be as generous as they please; but they must not be merciful either to wrong-doing or to incompetency. They should try to give to every man a better scope for his abilities, and therefore the opportunity for earning a better income than he would have got if his best faculties had not been turned to account; but they must not allow people to prey on the movement. If the manager of a store does his business so negligently or with so little skill that he could not keep his customers together were it not for the prestige which his store derives from co-operation, he must take a lower place. This is your hardest and most bitter task: there is none more repugnant to the spirit of the true co-operator; but there is, I believe, none which it is more imperatively his duty to perform, none which is more vital to the continued prosperity of the movement.

It is also a duty to pay to those who are doing their work with exceptional ability salaries high enough to prevent any excessive strain on their allegiance to co-operation arising when they receive tempting offers from outside. This is a pleasant, but not an easy task. It is said that successful business men owe much to their knowing when to pay very high salaries; and co-operators must keep their wits well about them in order to find out when to do it.

Thus, in every direction there is plenty of work for the heads as well as for the hearts of co-operators. They hold a most responsible position; it lies with them to control the future of that scheme for social reform which is the greatest because its business basis is the strongest; and of that business undertaking which is the greatest because its aims are the noblest and the most aspiring. Those co-operators who, caring little for themselves, labour hard and earnestly to turn to good account the knowledge that working people have of one another, their power of wise trust and sober confidence in one another, their sympathy and affection; those who work steadfastly towards the aim of giving education and opportunity and spur of a worthy ambition to that latent ability of the working classes which is the great waste product of the world; they will

> Live
> In pulses stirred to generosity,
> In deeds of daring rectitude, in scorn
> For miserable aims that end in self,...
> Enkindle generous ardour, feed pure love,
> Be the sweet presence of a good diffused,
> And in diffusion ever more intense.
> So shall they join the choir invisible,
> Whose music is the gladness of the world.

XI

SOME ASPECTS OF COMPETITION (1890)[1]

I. LIMITATION OF THE SCOPE OF THE PAPER TO A STUDY OF SOME FORMS OF COMPETITION IN COMMERCE, AND OF CHANGES IN THE MENTAL ATTITUDE OF ECONOMISTS WITH REGARD TO IT

I UNDERSTAND that the function of an Opening Address to a Section of the British Association is to give an account of the advances made in some part of the field of study with which that Section is specially concerned. The part of our field to which I would direct your attention to-day is the action of competition. We cannot, in the short space of time allotted to us, make an adequate study of the progress that has been made even in this part of our field; but we may be able to go some way towards ascertaining the character of the changes that are going on in our own time in the mode of action of competition, and in the attitude of economists towards it.

I do not propose to speak of changes in the moral sentiments of economists with regard to competition—though these, also, are significant in their way—but of changes in their mental attitude towards it, and in the way in which they analyse and reason about its methods of action. And partly for this reason, partly on account of the limitation of the time at my disposal, I propose to confine my remarks to some aspects of competition in commerce, and not to enter upon the subject of competition and combination in the buying and selling of labour. For in relation to that subject, the change in the moral attitude of economists is in some ways more marked and more important than that in their mental attitude; and it is therefore not so well fitted as that of competition and combination in commerce to illustrate the change in the methods of economic science to which I would invite your attention.

[1] Presidential Address to the Economic Science and Statistics Section of the British Association, at Leeds, 1890.

The abandonment of Dogma; the development of Analysis

The change may, perhaps, best be regarded as a passing onward from that early stage in the development of scientific method, in which the operations of Nature are represented as conventionally simplified for the purpose of enabling them to be described in short and easy sentences, to that higher stage in which they are studied more carefully, and represented more nearly as they are, even at the expense of some loss of simplicity and definiteness, and even apparent lucidity. To put the same thing in more familiar words, the English economists of fifty years ago were gratified, rather than otherwise, when some faithful henchman, or henchwoman, undertook to set forth their doctrines in the form of a catechism or creed; and the economists of to-day abhor creeds and catechisms. Such things are now left for the Socialists.

It has, indeed, been an unfortunate thing for the reputation of the older economists, that many of the conditions of England at the beginning of this century were exceptional, some being transitional, and others, even at the time, peculiar to England. Their knowledge of facts was, on the average, probably quite as thorough as that of the leading economists of England and Germany to-day, though their range was narrow. Their thoroughness was their own, the narrowness of their range belonged to their age; and, though each of them knew a great deal, their aggregate knowledge was not much greater than that of any one of them, because there were so few of them, and they were so very well agreed. In these matters we economists of to-day have the advantage over them.

Their agreement with one another made them confident; the want of a strong opposition made them dogmatic; the necessity of making themselves intelligible to the multitude made them suppress even such conditioning and qualifying clauses as they had in their own minds: and thus, although their doctrines contained more that was true, and new, and important than those promulgated by almost any other set of men that have ever lived—doctrines for which they will be gratefully remembered as long as the history of our century retains any interest—yet, still, these doctrines were so narrow and inelastic that, when they were applied under conditions of time and place different from those in which they had their origin, their faults became obvious and created a reaction.

Perhaps the greatest danger of our age is that this reaction may be carried too far, and that the great truths which lie embedded in these too large utterances may be neglected because they are not new, and we are a little tired of them: and because they are associated with much that is not true, and which has become, not altogether unjustly, repugnant to our sentiments.

I propose to illustrate this danger chiefly by reference to that point at which it assumes its gravest form just at present, viz., the relations between competition and combination in domestic trade. But the relations between Protection and Free Trade in foreign commerce have a longer and more fully developed history; and I will begin by referring briefly to them because they throw a clear light both on recent changes in economic thought, and on the warnings which the experience of our forefathers, in dealing with the problems of their age, gives us with reference to those problems which are more specially ours.

II. First illustration. The policy of Protection

Englishmen used to underrate the differences between the influences of Foreign Trade on an Old and a New Country

It is a constant source of wonder to Englishmen that Protection survives and thrives, in spite of the complete refutations of Protectionist arguments with which English economists have been ready to supply the rest of the world for the last fifty years or more. I believe that these refutations failed chiefly because some of them implicitly assumed that whatever was true as regards England, was universally true; and, if they referred at all to any of the points of difference between England and other countries, it was only to put them impatiently aside, without a real answer to the arguments based on them. And further, because it was clearly to the interests of England that her manufactures should be admitted free by other countries, therefore, any Englishman, who attempted to point out that there was some force in some of the arguments which were adduced in favour of Protection in other countries, was denounced as unpatriotic. Public opinion in England acted like the savage monarch who puts to death the messenger that comes running in haste to tell him how his foes are advancing on him; and, when John Stuart Mill ventured to tell the English people that some arguments for Protection in new countries were scientifically valid, his friends spoke of it in anger—but more in sorrow than in anger—as his one sad departure from the sound principles of economic rectitude. But killing the messengers did not kill the hostile troops of which the messengers brought record; and the arguments which the Englishmen refused to hear, and therefore never properly refuted, were for that very reason those on which Protectionists relied for raising a prejudice in the minds of intelligent and public-spirited Americans against the scientific soundness and even the moral honesty of English economics.

The first great difficulty which English economists had, in addressing themselves to the problems of cosmopolitan economics, arose from the fact that England was an old country—older than America in every sense, and older than the other countries of Europe in this sense, that she had accepted the ideas of the new and coming industrial age more fully and earlier than they had. In speaking of England, therefore, they drifted into the habit of using, as convertible, the two phrases—"the commodities which a country can now produce most easily," and "the commodities which a country has the greatest natural advantages for producing," that is, will always be able to produce most easily. But these two phrases were not approximately convertible when applied to other countries; and, when List and Carey tried to call attention to this fact, Englishmen did little more than repeat old arguments, which implicitly assumed that New England's inability to produce cheap calico had the same foundation in natural laws as her inability to produce cheap oranges. They refused fairly to meet the objection that arguments, which prove that nothing but good can come from a constant interchange of goods between temperate and tropical regions, do not prove that it is for the interest of the world that the artisans who are fed on American grain and meat should continue always to work up American cotton for American use three thousand miles away. Finding that their case was not fairly met, the Protectionists naturally thought it stronger than it was, and honestly exaggerated it in every way. One of my most vivid recollections of a visit I made, in 1875, to study American Protection on the spot, is that of Mr Carey's splendid anger, as he exclaimed that foreign commerce had made even the railways of America run from east to west, rather than from north to south.

Difficulties of American manufacturers fifty years ago

England had passed through the stage of having to import her teachers from other lands. But her genius for freedom had attracted to her shores the pick of the skilled artisans of the world; she had received the best lessons from the best instructors, and seldom paid them any fee, beyond a safe harbour from political and religious persecution. And modern Englishmen could not realise, as Americans and even Germans could fifty years ago, the difficulties of a manufacturer taking part in starting a new industry, when he came to England to beg or steal a knowledge of the trade, and to induce skilful artisans to come back with him. He seldom got the very best; for they were sure of a comfortable life at home, and were perhaps not without some ambition of rising to be masters themselves. He had to pay their travelling expenses, and to promise them very high wages; and when all was done, they often left him to become the owners of the 160 acres allotted to every free settler; or, the bitterest pill of all, they sold their skill to a neighbouring employer who had been looking on at the experiment, and, as soon as it showed signs of prosperity, stepped in, improved on the first experiments, and reaped a full harvest on a soil that had been made ready by others.

Again, the pioneer manufacturer had to bring over specialised machinery, and specialised skill to take care of it. If any part went wrong, or was superseded, the change cost him ten times as much as his English competitor. He had to be self-sufficing: he could get no help from the multitude of subsidiary industries, which in England would have lent him aid at every turn. He had a hundred pitfalls on every side: if he failed, his failure was full of lessons to those who came after; if he succeeded, the profits to himself would be trivial, as compared with those to his country. When he told the tale of his struggles, every word went home to his hearers; and when the English economists, instead of setting themselves to discover the best method by which his country might help him in his experiment, said he was flying in the face of Nature, and called him a selfish schemer for wanting any help at all, they put themselves out of court.

The Action of the Laws of Diminishing and Increasing Return intensifies the evils of Protection in England, but lessens them in America

But the failure of English economists to allow for the special circumstances of new countries did not end here. They saw that Protective taxes in England had raised the price of wheat by their full amount (because the production of wheat obeys the Law of Diminishing Return; *i.e.* increased supplies can be raised in an old country, such as England, only at a more than proportionately increased cost of labour); that the high price of bread had kept a large part of the population on insufficient rations; that it had enriched the rich at the expense of a much greater loss to the rest of the nation; and that this loss had fallen upon those who were unable to lose material wealth without also losing physical, and even mental and moral strength; and that even those miseries of the overworked factory women and children, which some recent German writers have ascribed exclusively to recklessness of manufacturing competition in its ignorant youth, were really caused chiefly by the want of freedom for the entry of food. They were convinced, rightly, as I believe, that the benefits claimed for Protection in England were based, without exception, on false reasoning; and they fought against it with the honest, but also rather blind, energy of a religious zeal.

Thus they overlooked the fact that many of those indirect effects of Protection, which aggravated then, and would aggravate now, its direct evils in England, worked in the opposite direction in America. For, firstly, the more America exported her raw produce in return for manufactures, the less the benefit she got from the Law of Increasing Return (*i.e.* that manufacture on a large scale is more economical than on a small); and thus her case was contrasted with England, who could manufacture more cheaply for her own use the more of her manufactures she sent abroad; and, for this and other reasons, a Protective tax did not nearly always raise the cost of goods to the American consumer by its full amount. And, secondly, Protection in America did not, as in England, tax the industrial classes for the benefit of the wealthy class of landlords. On the contrary, in so far as it fell upon the exporters of American produce, it pressed on those who had received large free gifts of public land; and there was no *primâ facie* injustice in awarding to the artisans, by special taxation, a small part of the fruits of that land, the direct ownership of which had not been divided between farmers and artisans, as it equitably might have been, but had been given exclusively to the former.

General conclusions as to Protection

I have touched on but a few out of many aspects of the problem. But perhaps I may stop here, and yet venture to express my own opinion on the controversy. It is, that fifty years ago it might possibly have been not beyond the powers of human ingenuity to devise schemes of Protection which would, on the whole, be beneficial to America, at all events, if one regarded only its economic and neglected its moral effects; but that the balance has turned strongly against Protection long ago. In 1875 I went to America to study the problem of Protection on the spot. I discussed the Protective policy with several of its leading advocates, I visited factories in almost every first-class city, and compared as well as I could the condition of the workers there with that of similar workers at home, and I walked up and down some of the streets of nearly all the chief American cities, and said to myself as I went: "The adoption of Free Trade, so soon as its first disturbances were over, would strengthen this firm and weaken that"; and I tried to strike a rough balance of the good and evil effects of such a change on the non-agricultural population. On the whole it seemed to me that the two were about equally balanced, and that the abandonment of Protection would injure the lower rather than the higher classes of manufacturing industries; that those metal and wood trades, for instance, which give the best scope for the special genius of the native American artisan would gain by the change. Taking account therefore of the political corruption which necessarily results from struggles about the tariff in a democratic country, and taking account also of the interests of the agricultural classes, I settled in my own mind the question as to which I had had some doubt till I went to America, and decided that, if an American, I should unhesitatingly vote for Free Trade. Since that time the advantages of Protection in America have steadily diminished, and those of Free Trade have increased; I can see no force in Professor Patten's new defence of Protection as a permanent policy. I have already implied that I believe that many of those arguments that tell in favour of Protection as regards a new country tell against it as regards an old one. Especially for England a Protective policy would, I believe, be an unmixed and grievous evil[1].

In Economic discussions absolute frankness is in the long run the best Policy

But this expression of my own opinion is a digression. My present purpose in discussing Protection is to argue that, if the earlier English economists had from the first studied the conditions of other countries more carefully, and abandoned those positions that were at all weak, they could have retained the controversy with their opponents within those regions where they had a solid advantage. They would thus have got a more careful hearing when they claimed that, even though labour migrated more freely between the west and the east of America than between England and America, yet it was unwise to spend so much trouble on protecting the nascent industries of the East against those of England, and none on protecting the nascent industries of the West against those of the East; or, again, when

---

[1] P.S.—I do not include under the head of a Protective policy any of the many ingenious schemes that have been propounded for "Retaliation" on those countries that impose high duties on imports from England, or for taxing imports from foreign countries, in order to be able to allow some differential advantage to the goods of our colonies, on condition that they grant corresponding advantages to English goods. It is true that many of these schemes have been advocated by arguments of a most unscientific character, such as find their proper place only in the crudest forms of Protectionism. But it is not necessary to base their claims on arguments of this kind. Arguments of some force can be given for the belief that some of these schemes, if they could practically be carried out under certain conditions, might on the whole do a little more good than harm to England. But there seems at present to be no probability that the proposed conditions will be realized in practice.

they urged that the younger an industry was, and the more deeply it needed help, the more exclusively would its claims have to stand on its own merits, while its older and sturdier brothers could supplement their arguments by a voting power which even the most honest politicians had to respect, and by a power of corruption which would tend to make politics dishonest.

Had the English economists been more careful and more many-sided, they would have gradually built up a prestige for honesty and frankness, as well as for scientific thoroughness, which would have inclined the popular ear to their favour, even when their arguments were difficult to follow. Intellectual thoroughness and sincerity is its own reward; but it is also a prudent policy when the people at large have to be convinced of the advisability of a course of action against which such plausible fallacies can be urged as that "Protection increases the employment of domestic industries," or that "it is needed to enable a country in which the rate of wages is generally high to carry on trade with another in which it is generally low." The arguments by which such fallacies can be opposed have an almost mathematical cogency, and will convince, even against his will, any one who is properly trained for such reasonings. But the real nature of foreign trade is so much disguised by the monetary transactions in which it is enveloped, that a clever sophist has a hundred opportunities of throwing dust in the eyes of ordinary people, and especially the working classes, when urging the claims of Protection as affording a short cut to national prosperity; and, to crown all, he contrasts America's prosperity with English prophecies of the ruin that Protection would bring on her[1].

---

[1] P.S.—Some of these prophecies have been repeated with reference to the recent McKinley Bill. But, even if all the rest of the world were submerged under the ocean, the United States, without any foreign trade at all, would remain a great and a prosperous nation; and, even though it be true—as I myself think it is—that the Act is a part of a policy which is on the whole mischievous to America, and is itself a mistake; and though the plans which it adopts for promoting the growth of American tin plate, lace, etc., industries do not seem to be the best possible; and though their good effects for America will probably be overweighed by much greater evils, yet those good effects can scarcely fail to be very important. On the other hand an old fallacy has reappeared in a new form in an argument, which has attracted much attention both here and in America, that the Act must have benefited America, because it has led to the investment of a few hundred thousand pounds of English capital in starting tin plate and lace works, etc., in America. Protection always puts capital into some industries: that movement "is

It is true that Ricardo himself, and some of those who worked with him, were incapable of supposing that a doctrine can be made more patriotic by being made less true; and, so far as their limits went, they examined the good and evil of any proposed course, and weighed the good and evil against one another in that calm spirit of submissive interrogation with which the chemist weighs his materials in his laboratory. But they were very few in number, and their range of inquiry was somewhat narrow, while many of those Englishmen who were most eager to spread Free Trade doctrines abroad had not the pure scientific temper.

Now at length, however, there seems to be the dawn of a brighter day in the growth of large numbers of many-sided students in England and other countries, and notably in America itself, where the problems of Protection can be studied to most advantage—students who are not, indeed, without opinions as to what course it is most expedient to follow practically, but who are free from party bias, and have the true scientific delight in ascertaining a new fact or developing a new argument, simply because they believe it to be new and true, and who welcome it equally whether it tells for or against the practical conclusion which, on the whole, they are inclined to support.

III. Second illustration. Trusts and other forms of Combination

But I must leave the subject of competition from outside a nation and pass to that of competition within. Here the past counts for less, the present and the future have to work for themselves without very much direct aid from experience. For, rapid as are the changes which the last few years have seen in the conditions of foreign trade, those which are taking place in the relations of different groups of industry within a country are more rapid still and more fundamental. The whirligig of

seen"; but, before we can regard it as a net gain, we must make sure that there is not an equal or greater, though "unseen" leaking of capital out of other industries which the new tariff indirectly injures; and for every hundred thousand pounds that the Protection policy causes to be sent from England to be invested in American factories, it probably keeps away at least a million pounds that would otherwise have been sent there to be invested in railways and agriculture. And indeed the adoption of free trade by America would probably give a great stimulus to the immigration of English capital and labour to avail themselves of America's vast natural resources for almost every branch of industry.

Time brings its revenges. It was to England's sagacity and good fortune in seizing hold of those industries in which the Law of Increasing Return applies most strongly, that she owed in a great measure her leading position in commerce and industry. Time's revenge was that that very Law of Increasing Return furnished the chief motives to other countries, and especially America, to restrict their commerce with her by Protective duties to home industries. And Time's counter-revenge is found in this—that England's Free Trade has prevented the Law of Increasing Return from strengthening combinations of wealthy manufacturers against the general weal here to the same extent as it has in countries in which Protection has prevailed, and notably America.

American and English Business contrasted

The problem of the relations between competition and combination is one in which differences of national character and conditions show themselves strongly. The Americans are the only great people whose industrial temper is at all like that of the English, and yet even theirs is not very like. Partly because of this difference of temper, but more because of the differences in the distribution of wealth and in the physical character of the two countries, the individual counts for much more in American than in English economic movements. Here few of those who are very rich take a direct part in business, they generally seek safe investments for their capital; and, again, among those engaged in business the middle class predominates, and most of them are more careful to keep what they have than eager to increase it by risky courses. And, lastly, tradition and experience are of more service and authority in an old country than in one which, like America, has not yet even taken stock of a great part of her natural resources, and especially those mineral resources, the sudden development of some of which has been the chief cause of many recent dislocations of industry.

In England, therefore, the dominant force is that of the average opinion of business men, and the dominant form of association is that of the joint-stock company. But in America the dominant force is the restless energy and the versatile enterprise of a comparatively few very rich and able men who rejoice in that power of doing great things by great means that their wealth gives them, and who have but partial respect for those who always keep their violins under glass cases. The methods of a joint-stock company are not always much to their mind; they prefer combinations that are more mobile, more elastic, more adventurous, and often more aggressive. For some purposes they have to put up with a joint-stock company; but then they strive to dominate it, not be dominated by it. Again, since distances in America are large, many local monopolies are possible in America which are not possible in England; in fact the area of a local monopoly there is often greater than that of the whole of England. A local coal combination, for instance, means quite a different thing there from what it does in England, and is more powerful in every way.

Again, partly, but not solely, because they are so much in the hands of a few wealthy and daring men, railways, both collectively and individually, are a far greater power in America than in England. America is the home of the popular saying that, if the State does not keep a tight hand on the railways, the railways will keep a tight hand on the State; and many individual railways have, in spite of recent legislation, a power over the industries within their territories such as no English railway ever had, for the distances are great, and the all-liberating power of the free ocean befriends America but little.

The pressure of Combinations is becoming more Extensive, but less Intensive

It is this change of area that is characteristic of the modern movement. In Adam Smith's time England was full of trade combinations, chiefly of an informal kind, indeed, and confined to very narrow areas; but very powerful within those areas, and very cruel. Even at the present day, the cruelest of all combinations in England are, probably, in the trades that buy up small things, such as fish, and dairy and garden produce in detail, and sell them in retail; both producers and consumers being, from a business point of view, weak relatively to the intermediate dealers. But even in these trades there is a steady increase in the areas over which such combinations and partial monopolies extend themselves. New facilities of transport and communication tell so far on the side of the consumer, that they diminish the *intensity* of the pressure which a combination can exert; but, at the same time, they increase the *extension* of that pressure, partly by compelling, and partly by assisting, the combination to spread itself out more widely. And in England, as in other Western countries, more is heard every year of new and ambitious combinations; and of course many of them remain always secret.

The success of American Trusts has been brilliant, but perhaps not very solid

But it is chiefly from America that a cry has been coming with constantly increasing force for the last fifteen years or more, that in manufactures free competition favours the growth of large firms with large capitals and expensive plants; that such firms, if driven into a corner, will bid for custom at any sacrifice; that, rather than not sell their goods at all, they will sell them at the Prime Cost—that is, the actual outlay required for them, which is sometimes very little; that, when there is not enough work for all, these manufacturers will turn their bidding recklessly against one another, and will lower prices so far that the weaker of them will be killed out, and all of them injured; so that when trade revives they will be able, even without any combination amongst themselves, to put up prices to a high level; that these intense fluctuations injure both the public and the producers; and the producers, being themselves comparatively few in number, are irresistibly drawn to some of those many kinds of combinations to which, nowadays, the name Trust is commonly, though not quite accurately, applied; and that, in short, competition burns so furiously as to smother itself in its own smoke. It is a Committee of the American Congress that reports that "combination grows out of, and is the natural development of, competition, and that in many cases it is the only means left to the competitors to escape absolute ruin."

The subject is one on which it would be rash to speak confidently. We of this generation, being hurried along in a whirl of change, cannot measure accurately the forces at work, and it is probable that the best guesses we can make will move the smiles of future generations; they will wonder how we could have so much over-estimated the strength of some, and under-estimated the strength of others. But my task is to try to explain what it is that economists of this generation are thinking about competition in relation to combination; and I must endeavour to reproduce their guesses, hazardous though this may be.

To begin with, I think that it is the better opinion that popular rumour, going now as ever to extremes, has exaggerated some features of the movement towards combination and monopoly, even in America. For instance, though it is said that there are a hundred commodities, the sale of which in America is partly controlled by some sort of combination, many of these combinations turn out to be of small proportions, and others to be weak and loose. Again, the typical instances which are insisted on by those who desire to magnify the importance of the movement are nearly always the same, and they have all had special advantages of more or less importance.

This is specially true of the only Trust which can show a long record of undisputed success on a large scale—the Standard Oil Trust. For, firstly, the petroleum in which it deals comes from a few of Nature's storehouses, mostly in the same neighbourhood: and it has long been recognized that those who can get control over some of the richest natural sources of a rare commodity are well on their way towards a partial monopoly. And, secondly, the Standard Oil Trust has many of those advantages which enable large railway companies to get the better of their smaller neighbours; for, directly or indirectly, it has in some measure controlled the pipe lines and the railways which have carried its oil to the large towns and to tidal water.

The strength of a moderate policy

On the other hand, we must remember that the future of a young and vigorous movement is to be measured, not so much by what it has achieved, as by what it has learnt; and that every unsuccessful attempt to hold together a Trust has been a lesson as to what to avoid, taught to men who are wonderfully quick to learn. In particular, it is now recognized that a very large portion of the failures in the past have been due to attempts to charge too high a price; that this high price has tempted those on the inside to break faith, and has tempted those on the outside

to start rival works, which may bleed the Trust very much
unless it consents to buy them up on favourable terms; and,
lastly, that this high price irritates the public: and that, especially
in some States, public indignation on such matters leads to rapid
legislation that strikes straight at the offenders, with little care
as to whether it appears to involve principles of jurisprudence
which could not be applied logically and consistently without
danger. The leaders in the movement towards forming Trusts
seem to be resolved to aim in the future at prices which will be
not very tempting to any one who has not the economics which
a large combination claims to derive, both in producing and in
marketing, from its vast scale of business and its careful organization; and to be content with putting into their own pockets
the equivalent of these economies in addition to low profits on
their capital. There are many who believe that combinations of
this kind, pursuing a moderate policy, will ultimately obtain so
great a power as to be able to shape, in a great measure, the
conditions of trade and industry.

*Difficulty of combining central responsibility and individual energy:
a pooling of gains often drifts into complete consolidation*

It may be so, but these eulogists of Trusts seem to claim for
them both that individual vigour, elasticity, and originating
force which belong to a number of separate firms, each retaining
a true autonomy, and that strength and economy which belong
to a unified and centralized administration. Sanguine claims of
this kind are not new; they have played a great part in nearly
all the bold schemes for industrial reorganization which have
fascinated the world in one generation after another. But in
this, their latest form, they have some special features of interest
to the economic analyst.

They have a certain air of plausibility, for the organizers of
Trusts claim that they see their way to avoiding the weak points
in ordinary forms of combination among traders, which consist
in the fact that their agreement can generally be evaded without
being broken. For instance, the most remarkable feature in the
history of English railways during the present generation is, not
their tendency to agree on the fares and freights to be charged
over parallel lines—for that has long been a foregone conclusion

—it is the marvellously effective competition for traffic which such railways have maintained, both of a legitimate kind, by means of improved conveniences offered to the public as a whole, and of an illegitimate kind, by means of those special privileges to particular traders which we are now, at last, seriously setting ourselves to stop by law.

It is difficulties of this kind which the modern movement towards Trusts aims specially at overcoming. Trusts have very many forms and methods, but their chief motive in every case is to take away from the several firms in the combination all inducements to compete by indirect means with one another[1].

The chief instrument for this purpose is generally some plan for pooling their aggregate receipts, and making the gains of each depend on the gains of all, rather than on the amount of business it gets for itself. But here the dilemma shows itself. If each establishment is left to its own devices, but has very little to lose by bad management, it is not likely long to remain well managed, and anyhow the Trust does not gain much of the special economy resulting from production on a very large scale. For this a partial remedy can sometimes be found in throwing as much of its work as possible on to those establishments which are best situated, have the best and most recent appliances and the ablest management, and, perhaps, closing entirely some of the others. But, when once the pooling has begun, the combination is on an inclined plane, and every step hurries it on faster towards what is virtually complete amalgamation and consolidation. The recent history of Trusts shows a constant tendency to give a more and more absolute power to the central executive, and to reduce the heads of the separate establishments more and more nearly to the position of branch managers. In some cases the only substantial difference between such a Trust and a consolidated joint-stock company is, that it is nominally left open to the several parties contracting to claim their separate property after the lapse of a certain number of years, while some

---

[1] P.S.—Professor Brentano has called my attention to the plan of the German Iron Combination, which does not allow individual firms to sell direct to the consumer, but only through a central office. It fixes the amount of each firm's produce which may be sold, and the price of sale; and each firm gains by every reduction it can make in its own expenses of working. This plan has great elements of strength, and is probably specially suitable for Germany. But it is still on its trial.

are already preparing to dissolve and reconstitute themselves formally as joint-stock companies.

This tendency has been helped on by the action of the legislature and the law courts, and, since this action can be traced back in some measure to the imperfect analysis of competition in the older economic writings, it has a special interest for us here.

IV. A FALSE ANTITHESIS BETWEEN COMPETITION AND COMBINATION

It has led to the favouring of rigid, as against loose forms of Combination

There seems to have been set up a false antithesis between competition and combination. For instance, if 100 workmen agreed to act together, as far as possible, in bargaining for the sale of their labour, they were denounced as combining to limit freedom, even when they did not interfere in any way with the liberty of other workmen, but merely deprived the employers of the freedom of making bargains with the 100 workmen, one by one. But the employer himself was allowed to unite in his own hands the power of hiring a hundred or twenty hundred men, and if he had not enough capital of his own he might take others into private, if not into public, partnership with him. Now, no trades union was likely to be as compact a combination, governed by as single a purpose, as a public or private firm, still less as an individual large employer; and, therefore, there was not only a class injustice, but also a logical confusion, in prohibiting combinations among workmen, on the ground that free competition was a good, and that combination, being opposed to free competition, was, for that reason, an evil.

It was an additional grievance to the workmen that employers had all manner of facilities for combination, of which they made full use; as is vigorously urged by Adam Smith, to whom the working classes owe more than they know. And it was this social injustice, rather than the logical inconsistency of economists and legislators, that led workmen to claim—and for the greater part successfully—that nothing should be illegal if done by workmen in combination which would not be illegal if done by any one of them separately—a principle which works well practically in the particular case of workmen's combinations if applied with moderation; though it has no better claim to universal validity than the opposite doctrine.

But at present it is with the latter that we are concerned—the doctrine, namely, that a use of the rights of property which would be "combination in restraint of competition" if the ownership of the property were in many hands, is only a free use of the forms of competition when the property is all in a single hand. This doctrine has resulted in the prohibition of pooling between railways which were allowed to amalgamate, and in the prohibition of combination on the part of a group of traders to coerce others to act with them, or to drive others out of the trade, though all the while no attempt was made to hinder a single very wealthy firm from obtaining the despotic control of a market by similar means.

But to the economists of to-day the whole question appears both more complex and more important than it seemed to their predecessors, so they are inquiring in detail how far it is true that the looser forms of combination are specially dangerous in spite of their weakness, and even to some extent because of their weakness; how far the greater stability and publicity, and sense of responsibility and slowness of growth, of a single consolidated firm make it less likely to extend its operations over a very wide area, and less likely to make a flagrantly bad use of its power; and, lastly, how far it may be expedient to prohibit actions on the part of loose combinations, while similar actions on the part of individuals and private firms are allowed to pass in silence, because no prohibition against them could be effectual.

It is a sign of the times that the American Senate approved, on 8th April last, a Bill of Senator Sherman's, of which the second Section begins thus: "Every person who shall monopolise, or attempt to monopolise, or conspire with any other person or persons to monopolise, any part of the trade or commerce among the several States, or with foreign nations, shall be deemed guilty of a misdemeanour." This clause is interesting to the constitutional lawyer on account of the skill with which it avoids any interference by the central authority with the internal affairs of the separate States; and though, partly for this reason, it is perhaps intended to be the expression of a sentiment that may help to guide public opinion, rather than an enactment which will bear much direct fruit; yet it is of great interest to the economist as showing a tendency to extend to the action of individuals a form of public criticism which has hitherto been almost confined to the action of combinations.

To return, then, to the tendency of Trusts towards consolidation. It is probable that the special legislative influences by which it has been promoted may be lessened, but that other causes will remain sufficiently strong to make a combination, which has once got so far as any sort of permanent pooling, tend almost irresistibly towards the more compact unity of a joint-stock company. If this be so, the new movement will go more nearly on old lines than at one time seemed probable; and the question will still be the old one of the struggle for victory on the one hand between large firms and small firms, and on the other between departments of the Government, imperial or local, and private firms. I will then pass on to consider the modern aspects of this question, ever old and ever new, but never more new and never more urgent than to-day.

V. Modern analysis tends in many cases to justify State Control, but not State Management

To begin with, it is now universally recognized that there is a great increase in the number and importance of a class of industries which are often called monopolies, but which are perhaps better described as *indivisible* industries. Such are the industries that supply gas or water in any given area, for only one such company in any district can be given leave to pull up the streets. Almost on the same footing are railways, tramways, electricity supply companies, and many others. Now, though there are some little differences of opinion among the economists of to-day, as to the scale on which the owners of such undertakings when in private hands should be compensated for interference with what they had thought their vested rights, all are agreed that such right of interference must be absolute. Economists of all schools are eagerly inquiring what form it is most expedient for this interference to take. And here differences of opinion show themselves. The advantages of a bureaucratic government appeal strongly to some classes of minds, among whom are to be included many German economists and a few of the younger American economists who have been much under German influence. But those in whom the Anglo-Saxon spirit is strongest would prefer that such undertakings, though always under public control, and sometimes even in public ownership, should whenever possible be worked and managed by private corporations. We (for I would here include myself) believe that bureaucratic management is less suitable for Anglo-Saxons than for other races who are more patient and more easily contented, more submissive and less full of initiative, who like to take things easily and to spread their work out rather thinly over long hours. An Englishman's or an American's life would involve too much strain to make them happy, while the Englishman would fret under the constraints and the small economies of their lives. Without therefore expressing any opinion as to the advantages of the public management of indivisible undertakings on the Continent, the greater part of the younger English and American economists are, I think, inclined to oppose it for England and America. We are not sure that we could exchange our own industrial virtues for those of the Continent if we wished to, and we are not sure that we do wish it. And, though we recognize that the management of a vast undertaking by a public company has many of the characteristics of bureaucratic management, yet we think the former is distinctly the better suited for developing those faculties by which the Anglo-Saxon race has won its position in the world. We believe that a private company which stands to gain something by vigorous and efficient management, by promptness in inventing, as well as in adopting and perfecting improvements in processes and organization, will do much more for progress than a public department.

Again, while a public company is inferior to a small private firm in its power and opportunities of finding out which among its employees have originating and constructive ability, a department of Government is far inferior in these respects to a joint-stock company, especially in England. And further, such a department is more liable to have the efficiency of its management interfered with for the purpose of enabling other persons to gain the votes of their constituents on questions in which it has no direct concern; and, as a corollary from this, it tends to promote the growth of political immorality, and it suffers from that growth.

There is certainly a growing opinion among English and American economists, that the State must keep a very tight hand on all industries in which competition is not an effective regulator; but this is the expression of a very different tone of thought from that which is leading so many German economists towards what is called State Socialism. In fact, as far as I can judge, English economists at all events are even more averse to State management than they were a few years ago; the set of their minds is rather towards inquiring how the advantages claimed for State management, without its chief evils, can be obtained even in what I have called indivisible industries; they are considering how a resolute intervention on the part of the State may best check the growth of *Imperia in Imperio*, and prevent private persons from obtaining an inordinate share of the gains arising from the development, through natural causes, of what are really semi-public concerns, and at the same time leave them sufficient freedom of initiative and sufficient security of gain by using that freedom energetically to develop what is most valuable in the energy and inventiveness of the Anglo-Saxon temper[1].

But, though we dislike and fear the present tendency towards a widening of the area of public management of industries, we cannot ignore its actual strength. For more forethought and hard work are needed to arrange an effective public control over an undertaking than to put it bodily into the hands of a public department; and there is always a danger that in a time of hasty change the path of least resistance will be followed.

By way of illustration of the inquiries that have had their origin in this fear of public management, as contrasted with public control and public ownership, I would here mention a notion which has been suggested partly by the relations of some

---

[1] Among the younger English economists who have written on the subject of Combinations, Trusts, and Government interference, I would specially refer to Mr Rae and Professor Foxwell. Most of the young American economists have written on it instructively from various points of view, and in Mr Baker's *Monopolies and the People*, to which I am myself much indebted, the English reader will find condensed into a short compass an account of the general position of these questions in America, together with some bold and interesting suggestions for reform. Some useful documents relating to Trusts have recently been published in a Consular Report by our Foreign Office [5896–32].

municipalities to their tramways, gas and water works. At present it is in a very crude form, and not ready for immediate application; but it seems to have occurred independently to a good many people, and it may have an important future. It is that a public authority may be able to own the franchise and, in some cases, part of the fixed capital of a semi-public undertaking, and to lease them for a limited number of years to a Corporation who shall be bound to perform services, or deliver goods, at a certain price and subject to certain other regulations, some of which may perhaps concern their relations to their employees. In order that the plan may have a fair chance of success, it is essential that the capital to be supplied by the private Corporation should not be so large as to prevent there being a real and effective competition for the franchise. But, this being assumed, the special point of the proposal is that, where possible, the competition for the franchise shall turn on the price or the quality, or both, of the services or the goods, rather than on the annual sum paid for the lease. Competition as to quality is, from the consumer's point of view, often just as beneficial as competition as to price, and sometimes more so. And in industries which obey the Law of Increasing Return, as very many of these indivisible industries do, a reduction of price or an improvement of quality will confer on the consumer a benefit out of all proportion to the extra cost involved[1].

VI. The general influence of large Combinations

They economise in bargaining: but it is doubtful whether they render Industry more Stable

But I have lingered too long over those industries which I have called indivisible, and I must pass to those in which competition exerts a pretty full sway. The first point to be observed is that competition in bargaining and competition in production stand in very different relations to the public interest; and that one of the great advances in modern analysis consists in the emphasis which it lays on the distinction between the two. Competition in bargaining constitutes a great part of competition in marketing, but is not the whole of it. For under marketing is included the

---

[1] This belongs to a class of questions relating to monopolies, etc., the more general and abstract aspects of which can be best shown by the diagrammatic method.

whole of the effective organization of the trade side of a business; and most of this performs essential services for the public, and is, in fact, of the same order as production commonly so called. But a great part of marketing consists of bargaining, of manœuvring to get others to buy at a high price and sell at a low price, to obtain special concessions or to force a trade by offering them. This is, from the social point of view, almost pure waste; it is that part of trade as to which Aristotle's dictum is most nearly true, that no one can gain except at the loss of another. It has a great attraction for some minds that are not merely mean; but nevertheless it is the only part of honest trade competition that is entirely devoid of any ennobling or elevating feature. A claim is made on behalf of large firms and large combinations that their growth tends to diminish the waste, and on the whole perhaps it does. The one solid advantage which the public gain from a combination powerful enough to possess a local monopoly is that it escapes much waste on advertising and petty bargaining and manœuvring. But its weakness in this regard lies in the fact that to keep its monopoly it must be always bargaining and manœuvring on a large scale. And, if its monopoly is invaded, it must bargain and manœuvre widely in matters of detail as well as in larger affairs.

Still less can we fully concede, without further proof, the claim which has been urged on behalf of such combinations, that they will render industry more stable and diminish the fluctuations of commercial activity. This claim, though put forward confidently and by many writers, does not appear to be supported by any arguments that will bear examination. On the one hand some industries which are already aggregated into large and powerful units, such as railway companies, give exceptionally steady employment; and others, such as the heavy iron and the chemical industries, exceptionally unsteady. And, when combinations succeed in steadying their own trades a very little, they often do it by means which diminish production and disturb other trades a very great deal. The teaching of history seems to throw but little light on the question, because the methods of regulation which are now suggested have not much in common with those of earlier times, while the causes which govern fluctuations in prices have changed their character completely.

Large Combinations can turn economically to account such knowledge as already exists

Let us then next turn to the economies of production on a large scale. They have long been well known, and our forefathers certainly did not underrate their importance. For, though the absence of any proper industrial census in England prevents us from getting exact information on the subject, yet there seems no doubt that the increase in the average size of factories has gone on, not faster, but slower than was thought probable a generation or two ago. In many industries, of which the Textile may be taken as a type, it has been found that a comparatively small capital will command all the economies that can be gained by production on a large scale; and it seems probable that in many industries in which the average size of businesses has been recently increasing fast, a similar position of maximum economy will shortly be attained without any much further increase in size.

Those reductions in the expenses of production of commodities, which have been claimed by the eulogists of Trusts and other large combinations, as tending to show that their gains are not at the expense of the public, turn out generally to have been at least equalled by the reductions in the expenses of production in similar industries in which there was no combination. And this count in their eulogy, though it may truly stand for something, seems to have been much exaggerated. But after all, what these very large public firms and combinations of firms have done has generally been only to turn to good account existing knowledge, and not to increase that knowledge. And this brings us to the main reason for regarding with some uneasiness any tendency there may be towards such consolidations of business.

But in a multitude of independent undertakers there is more inventive energy

It has always been recognized that large firms have a great advantage over their smaller rivals in their power of making expensive experiments; and in some of the modern "scientific" industries they use part of their resources in hiring specialists to make experiments for them in the technical applications of science. But on the whole observation seems to show, what might have been anticipated à priori, that these advantages count for little in the long run in comparison with the superior inventive force of a multitude of small undertakers. There are but few exceptions to the rule, that large private firms, though far superior to public departments, are yet, in proportion to their size, no less inferior to private businesses of a moderate size in that energy and resource, that restlessness and inventive power, which lead to the striking out of new paths. And the benefits which the world reaps from this originality are apt to be under-rated. For they do not come all at once like those gains which a large business reaps by utilizing existing knowledge and well proven economies; but they are cumulative, and not easily reckoned up. He who strikes out a new path by which the work of eight men is rendered as efficient as that of ten used to be, in an industry that employs 100,000 men, confers on the world a benefit equal to the labour of 20,000 men. And this benefit may in many cases be taken as running for many years. For though his discovery might have been made later by someone else of equal inventive power, yet this someone else, starting with that discovery in hand, is likely to make another improve-ment on it.

I believe that the importance of considerations of this kind is habitually underrated in the world at large; and that the older economists, though fully conscious of them, did not explain with sufficient clearness and iteration the important place which they take in the claims of industrial competition on the gratitude of mankind.

The chemist in his laboratory can make experiments on his own responsibility: if he had to ask leave from others at each step he would go but slowly, and though the officials of a com-pany may have some freedom to make experiments in detail, yet even as regards these they seldom have a strong incentive to exertion; and in great matters the freedom of experimenting lies only with those who undertake the responsibility of the business.

It may indeed be admitted that some kinds of industrial improvements are getting to depend on the general increase of scientific knowledge rather than on such experiments as can only be made by business men. This dependence, however, tells on the side of small firms which have a great managing ability in proportion to their capital, but cannot afford to make expensive experiments for themselves. For nearly all such scientific knowledge, as soon as it is achieved, becomes the public property of the nation, or rather of the world.

VII. Modern Analysis of the Motives of Business Competition

The love of money is only one among many

But the growing importance in business of that scientific knowledge that has its origin in academic studies, relatively to that technical knowledge which has its origin in business work, may serve as a convenient introduction to the next point that I want to make in the analysis of competition. It is that the motives which induce business men to compete for wealth are not altogether as sordid as the world in general, and I am forced to admit, economists in particular, have been wont to assume.

The chemist or the physicist may happen to make money by his inventions, but that is seldom the chief motive of his work. He wants to earn somehow the means of a cultured life for himself and his family; but, that being once provided, he spends himself in seeking knowledge partly for its own sake, partly for the good it may do to others, and last, and often not least, for the honour it may do himself. His discoveries become collective property as soon as they are made, and altogether he would not be a very bad citizen of Utopia just as he is. For it would be a great mistake to suppose that the constructors of Utopias from the time of Plato downwards have proposed to abolish competition. On the contrary, they have always taken for granted that a desire to do good for its own sake will need to be supplemented by emulation or competition for the approbation of others.

But business men are very much of the same nature as scientific men; they have the same "instincts of the chase," and many of them have the same power of being stimulated to great and even feverish exertions by emulations that are not sordid or ignoble. This part of their nature has however been confused with and thrown into the shade by their desire to make money.

The chief reason why the scientific man does not care much for money is that in scientific work the earning of much money is no proof of excellence, but sometimes rather the reverse. On the other hand, in business a man's money-earning power, though not an accurate test of the real value to the world of what he has done, is yet often the best available. It is that test which most of those, for whose opinion he cares, believe to be more trustworthy than the highly-coloured reports the world hears from time to time of the benefits which it is just going to derive from a new invention or plan of organizing that is just going to revolutionize a branch of industry. And so all the best business men want to get money, but many of them do not care about it much for its own sake; they want it chiefly as the most convincing proof to themselves and others that they have succeeded.

Economic progress requires as a condition free individual responsibility, but not the maintenance of those rights of property which lead to extreme inequalities of wealth

These are the very men for whom the older economists were most eager to claim freedom of competition as needful to induce them to do fully their high work for the world. But this seems to involve the error of running together, and treating as though they were one, two different positions—an error which seems to resemble in character the failure to distinguish adequately between the results of Protection in an old and a new country.

The first of these positions is that industrial progress depends on our getting the right men into the right places, and giving them a free hand and sufficient incitement to exert themselves to the utmost; and the second is that nothing less than the enormous fortunes which successful men now make and retain would suffice for that purpose. This last position seems to be untenable.

The present extreme inequalities of wealth tend in many ways to prevent human faculties from being turned to their best account. A good and varied education, freely prolonged to those children of the working classes who show the power and the will to use it well, an abundance of open-air recreation even in large towns, and other requisites of a wholesome life—such things as these might, most of us are inclined to think, be supplied by

taxes levied on the rich, without seriously checking the accumulation of material capital, and with the effect of increasing rather
than diminishing the services which competition renders to
society by tending to put the ablest men into the most important
posts, the next ablest into the next most important, and so on,
and by giving to those in each grade freedom sufficient for the
full exercise of their faculties.

It is quite true that, where any class of workers have less than
the necessaries for efficiency, an increase of income acts directly
on their power of work. But when they already have those
necessaries the gain to production from a further increase of
their income depends chiefly on the addition that it makes, not
to their power of working, but to their will to exert themselves.
And all history shows that a man will exert himself nearly as
much to secure a small rise in income as a large one, provided
he knows beforehand what he stands to gain, and is in no fear
of having the expected fruits of his exertions taken away from
him by arbitrary spoliation. If there were any fear of that he
would not do his best, but if the conditions of the country were
such that a moderate income gave as good a social position as a
large one does now; if to have earned a moderate income were
a strong presumptive proof that a man had surpassed able rivals
in the attempt to do a difficult thing well, then the hope of
earning such an income would offer to all but the most sordid
natures inducements almost as strong as they are now when
there is an equal hope of earning a large one.

The socialists have underrated the difficulty of business work

On all this class of questions modern economists are inclined
to go a little way with the socialists. But all socialist schemes,
and especially those which are directly or indirectly of German
origin, seem to be vitiated by want of attention to the analysis
which the economists of the modern age have made of the
functions of the undertaker of business enterprises. They seem
to think too much of competition as the exploiting of labour by
capital, of the poor by the wealthy, and too little of it as the
constant experiment by the ablest men for their several tasks,
each trying to discover a new way in which to attain some
important end. They still retain the language of the older

economists, in which the employer, or undertaker, and the capitalist are spoken of as though they were, for all practical purposes, the same people. The organ of the German school of English socialists prints frequently in thick type the question, "Is there one single useful or necessary duty performed by the capitalist to-day which the people organized could not perform for themselves?" It would be just as reasonable to ask if there is a single victory to which Julius Cæsar or Napoleon conducted their troops which the troops, properly organized, could not have equally well won for themselves; or whether there is a single thing written by Shakespeare which could not have been equally well written by any one else if, as Charles Lamb said, he happened to "have the mind to do it." It is quite true that many business men earn large incomes by routine work. It is just in these cases that co-operation can dispense with middlemen and even employers. But the German socialists have been bitter foes of co-operation, though this antagonism is less than it was.

The world owes much to the socialists, as it does to every set of enthusiasts among whom there are noble men, and many a generous heart has been made more generous by reading their poetic aspirations; but, before their writings can be regarded as serious contributions to economic science, they must make more careful and exact analysis of the good and the evil of competition. They must suggest some reasonably efficient substitute for that freedom which our present system offers to constructive genius to work its way to the light, and to prove its existence by attempting difficult tasks on its own responsibility, and succeeding in them; for those who have done most for the world have seldom been those whom their neighbours would have picked out as likely for the work. They must not, as even Mr Bellamy and other American socialists do, in spite of their strong protestations to the contrary, assume implicitly a complete change of human nature, and propound schemes which would much diminish the aggregate production, but which they represent as enabling every family to attain an amount of material well-being which would be out of reach if the aggregate income of England or America were divided out equally among the population.

VIII. The Growing Importance of Public Opinion as an
Economic Force

But though the socialists have ascribed to the virtues inherent in the human breast, and to the regulating force of public opinion, a much greater capacity for doing the energizing work of competition than they seem really to have, yet, unquestionably, the economists of to-day do go beyond those of earlier generations in believing that the desire of men for the approval of their own conscience and for the esteem of others is an economic force of the first order of importance, and that the strength of public opinion is steadily increasing with the increase and the diffusion of knowledge, and with the constant tendency of what had been regarded as private and personal issues to become public and national.

Public opinion acts partly through the Government. But, though the enforcement of the law in economic matters occupies the time of a rapidly increasing number of people, and its administration is improving in every way, it fails to keep pace with the demands resulting from the growing complexity of economic organization and the growing sense of responsibility of public opinion. A part of this failure is due to a cause which might easily be remedied; it is that the adjustment of punishment to offences is governed by traditions descending from a time when the economic structure of England was entirely different. This is most conspicuous with regard to the subtler, or, as they are sometimes called with unconscious irony, the more gentlemanly forms of commercial fraud on a large scale, for which the punishment awarded by the law courts is often trivial in comparison with the aggregate gains which the breakers of the law, whose offences can seldom be proved, make by their wrongdoing; and it is still more trivial in comparison with the aggregate injury which such wrongdoing inflicts on the public. Many of the worst evils in modern forms of competition could be diminished by merely bringing that part of the law which relates to economic problems of modern growth into harmony with that which relates to the old-fashioned and well-matured economic questions relating to common picking and stealing.

But at best the action of the law must be slow, cumbrous, and inelastic, and therefore ineffective. And there are many matters in which public opinion can exercise its influence more quickly and effectively by a direct route than by the indirect route of first altering the law. For of all the great changes which our own age has seen in the relative proportions of different economic forces, there is none so important as the increase in the area from which public opinion collects itself, and in the force with which it bears directly upon economic issues.

And in this connection I may perhaps transgress a little beyond the bounds I have set myself in this paper, and may glance rapidly at combinations of labour on the one side and o employers on the other. They are now able to arrange plans of campaign for whole trades, for whole counties, for the whole country, and sometimes even beyond; and partly on account of the magnitude of the interests concerned, partly because trade disputes are being reduced to system, affairs which would be only of local interest are discussed over the whole kingdom.

Many turbulent little quarrels which centered more often about questions of individual temper, than of broad policy, are now displaced by a few great strikes; as to which public opinion is on the alert; so that a display of temper is a tactical blunder. Each side strives to put itself right with the public; and requires of its leaders above all things that they should persuade the average man that their demands are reasonable, and that the quarrel is caused by the refusal of the other side to accept a reasonable compromise.

This change is increasing the wisdom and the strength of each side; but the employers have always had fairly good means of communication with one another; it is the employed that have gained most from cheap means of communication by press, by railway, and by telegraph, and from improvements in their education and in their incomes, which enable them to make more use of these new and cheaper facilities. And while the employers have always known how to present their case to the public well, and have always had a sympathetic public, the working classes are only now beginning to read newspapers enough to supply an effective national working class opinion; and they are only now learning how to present their case well, and to hope much from, or care much for, the opinion of those who are neither employers nor of the working classes.

I myself believe that in all this the good largely predominates over the evil. But that is not the question with which I am specially concerned at present. My point is that, in the scientific problem of estimating the forces by which wages are adjusted, a larger place has to be allowed now than formerly to the power of combination, and to the power of public opinion in judging, and criticizing, and aiding that combination; and that all these changes tend to strengthen the side of the employees, and to help them to get a substantial, though not a great, increase of real wages; which they may, if they will, so use as to increase their efficiency, and therefore to increase still further the wages which they are capable of earning, whether acting in combination or not.

Public Opinion needs to be Educated for its new Responsibilities

And thus public opinion has a very responsible task. I have spoken of it as the opinion of the average man; that is, of an average member of one of those classes of society that is not directly and immediately concerned in the question at issue. But he is very busy, and has many things to think about. He makes great mistakes; but he learns by all of them. He has often astonished the learned by the amount of ignorance and false reasoning which he can crowd into the discussion of a difficult question; and still more by the way in which he is found at last to have been very much in the right on the main issue. He is getting increased power of forming a good and helpful opinion, and he is being educated in mind and in spirit by forming it, and by giving it effect. But in the task which he is undertaking there are great difficulties ahead.

In an industrial conflict each side cares for the opinion of the public at large, or as we have said of the average man. But they often care especially for the good opinion of those whose sympathy they are most likely to get: in the late South Wales strike, for instance, the railway companies were specially anxious about the good opinion of the shippers, and the engine drivers about that of the colliers. And there is some fear that, when party discipline becomes better organized, those on either side will again get to care less for any public opinion save that of their own side. And, if so, there may be no great tendency towards agreement between the two sides as to what are reasonable demands.

It is true that there is always the action of outside competition tending to visit with penalties either side which makes excessive use of any tactical advantage it may have obtained. As we have just noticed, the shrewdest organisers of a Trust are averse to raising the price of its wares much above the normal or steady competition price. And the first point which courts of Conciliation and Arbitration have to consider is, what are the rates of wages on the one hand and of profits on the other, which are required to call forth normal supplies of labour and capital respectively; and, only when that has been done, can an inquiry be properly made as to the shares in which the two should divide between them the piece of good or ill fortune which has come to the trade. Thus the growth of combinations and partial monopolies has in many ways increased, and in no way diminished, the practical importance of the careful study of the influences which the normal forces of competition exert on normal value.

But it must be admitted that the direct force of outside competition in some classes of wages disputes is diminishing; and, though its indirect force is being increased by the increased power which modern knowledge gives us of substituting one means of attaining our ends for another, yet on the whole the difficulty of deciding what is a reasonable demand is becoming greater. The principles on which not only the average man but also an expert court of Conciliation or Arbitration should proceed in forming their judgments, are becoming, in spite of the great increase of knowledge, more and more vague and uncertain in several respects.

And there are signs of a new difficulty. Hitherto the general public has been enlightened and its interests protected by the fact that the employers and employed when in conflict have each desired to enlighten the public as to the real questions at issue; and the information given on one side has supplemented and corrected that on the other: they have seldom worked together systematically to sacrifice the interests of the public to their own, by lessening the supply of their services or goods, and thus raising their price artificially. But there are signs of a desire to arrange firm compacts between combinations of employers on the one side and of employees on the other to restrict production. Such compacts may become a grievous danger to the public in those trades in which there is little effective competition from foreign producers: a danger so great that if these compacts cannot be bent by public opinion they may have to be broken up by public force.

It is, therefore, a matter of pressing urgency that public opinion should accustom itself to deal with such questions, and be prepared to throw its weight against such compacts as are injurious to the public weal, that is, against such compacts as are likely to inflict on the public a real loss much greater than the gain to that trade; or in other words, are of such a nature that if their principle were generally adopted in all trades and professions, then all trades and professions would lose as buyers more than they would gain as sellers.

IX. Conclusion

To sum up. It seems that one cause of the present strength of Protection in other countries is that the earlier English economists lessened the force of the valid arguments against it, by mixing them up with others, which, though valid as regards England, did not apply without great modifications to new countries; but economists of the younger generation, however fervent their devotion to free trade, seldom speak of Protection in new countries with the old unmeasured bitterness. The change of mental attitude towards competition in this aspect is in a great measure accomplished; and similar changes in the attitude of economists to monopolies and combinations are now in progress. It is clear that combinations and partial monopolies will play a great part in future economic history; that their effects contain much good as well as much evil, and that to denounce them without discrimination would be to repeat the error which our forefathers made with regard to Protection. If we do not take time by the forelock, and begin early to consider how their evil effects may be minimized and their possible good developed, we shall miss an opportunity that will never recur. For a later generation will find it more difficult to extricate the good from the evil than those who are contemporary with that great growth of the facilities of communication which are giving to the forces of combination and monopoly a new character, and in some directions a new strength.

So far nearly all the younger economists appear to be agreed; but, while some would not be sorry to see small firms displaced by large, large firms by Trusts, and Trusts by Government departments, others, in whom the Anglo-Saxon spirit is stronger, regard these tendencies with very mixed feelings, and are prepared to exert themselves to the utmost to keep Government management within narrow limits. They are most anxious to preserve the freedom of the individual to try new paths on his own responsibility. They regard this as the vital service which free competition renders to progress, and desire on scientific grounds to disentangle the case for it from the case for such institutions as tend to maintain extreme inequalities of wealth; to which some of them are strongly opposed. In order to preserve what is essential in the benefits of free competition, they are willing to have a great extension of public control over private and semi-public undertakings; but, above all, they look to the extension of the new force of public opinion as a means of eliminating much of the evil effects of competition, while retaining its good effects.

I have spoken of some aspects of competition, but those of which I have said nothing are more numerous and certainly not less important. I have put aside, as belonging to a different order of inquiry, the moral aspects of competition, and all study of its bearing on those who are least able to help themselves. But I should have liked, if time had sufficed, to compare the tendency towards the formation of vast Trusts with that towards national or even international federation of Trade Unions; and again with the growth of the centralized force of the Co-operative Wholesale Society. I should have liked to examine the new forms of indirect competition between industrial groups, each of which is in direct competition with a third one, and so on.

I have however taxed your patience too long already, and must ask you to be lenient in your judgment of this imperfect and fragmentary study. I have endeavoured to give some illustrations of the changes which are coming over economic studies. I believe that the great body of modern economists think that the need of analysis and general reasoning in economics is not less than our predecessors supposed, but more. And this is because we think economic problems more difficult than they did. We are recognizing more clearly than they did that all economic studies must have reference to the conditions of a particular country and time. Economic movements tend to go faster than ever before, but, as Knies pointed out, they tend also to synchronize; and the economists of our own country have much more to learn now than fifty years ago from the contemporary history of other countries; but, in spite of the many great benefits which we are deriving from the increase of our historical knowledge, the present age can rely less than any other on the experience of its predecessors for aid in solving its own problems.

Every year economic problems become more complex; every year the necessity of studying them from many different points of view and in many different connections becomes more urgent. Every year it is more manifest that we need to have more knowledge and to get it soon in order to escape, on the one hand, from the cruelty and waste of irresponsible competition and the licentious use of wealth, and on the other from the tyranny and the spiritual death of an ironbound socialism.

XII

BENJAMIN JOWETT (1893)[1]

THE late Master of Balliol made no claim to be an economist in any special sense of the word. But he took great interest in political economy, especially on its social side; and through the younger men who came in contact with him was not without influence over the economic thought of the present generation. Bagehot, as he used to say himself, was the last English writer on economics who had learnt it from Ricardo direct, before the days of Mill's *Political Econony*. The Master was probably the last teacher of economics who had done so. Professor Henry Smith, who took his degree in 1848, and in after years was one of his closest friends, used often to speak of the days when Jowett had taught him political economy; and it would be interesting to know if the record can be carried back still earlier. He had various ways of teaching. Sometimes coming upon some young man of force and promise who had not quite the right training for his mind, or had not found in his other studies the right incentive to hard work, the Master would give him a book on political economy to read, and get him to come in from time to time to talk over his reading. Sometimes he would take one student alone, sometimes two or three together; and he did this up to the end, even in the last year of his life. While Tutor of Balliol he used to give short courses of set lectures on political economy, though he did not continue these after he became Master: and he more than once preached on the right use of wealth. His teaching on the subject was admirably adapted to guide and stimulate: it was full of shrewd common-sense, and pithy hints as to details; and, at the same time, brought home to his hearers the responsibility under which money is spent, and led them towards high ideals in its use.

He took part in most of the questions which agitate modern economists: but his own masters were Plato and Ricardo. Everything that they said, and all that rose directly out of what they said, had a special interest for him. Like them he sought the basis of reality in ideas; like them he was wise and farseeing, but fearless of paradox.

In pure economics his favourite subject was the currency, and he took a keen interest in the recent controversy on it. His views were generally conservative; and he was never converted to bimetallism. But he was ready to follow wherever Ricardo had pointed the way; and in a letter written not long ago he raised the question whether the world would not outgrow the use of gold as its standard of value, and adopt one of those artificial standards which vex the soul of Mr Giffen. And similarly in social matters he was conservative. He did not believe that the face of the world could be changed in a day; and he was not very patient of impatience. But to be earnest in anything, and especially in social reform, was a sure way to his heart. He was deeply interested in working men who were gentlemen in thought and feeling; and he used to say that only thus could they attain their full strength. The economic difficulties in the way of getting a first-rate education pressed heavily on his mind: his public efforts, both at Oxford and in connection with Bristol University College, to diminish them are well known; and a great part of his own income flowed by secret channels towards the same end. But he looked less to academic teaching than to the introduction of a noble spirit in business, as a means of bringing out the best faculties of those whose start in life had not been favoured by fortune. Plato's socialistic ideas possessed his mind; he made a careful study of contemporary socialistic thought when preparing to write the last edition of his introduction to Plato's *Republic*; and there is much that is instructive to the economist in his introductions to others of the *Dialogues*.

But after all, his influence on the economic life of England was quite as much through his faculty of making people want to know the right thing, and to do it, as by his own direct work. His sincerity was infectious. He knew how to get hold of what was best in men, and to make them good citizens. He cared not whether they were of high birth or of low estate, provided only he could see in them a possible power of good in the world after he should have left it. A very great number of those who are forming public opinion to-day, or discharging high duties for the State, have learnt from personal contact with him, that money, though a good servant, is a bad master; and that private advantage is but poor exchange for the sense of having worked faithfully for one's country. His own college responded bravely to the calls he made on it. There are few Foundations, either at Oxford or Cambridge, which have less material resources than Balliol: but he, continuing the good work of others, endowed it with that wealth of unselfish devotion and energy by which it has attained its unique position.

XIII

THE OLD GENERATION OF ECONOMISTS
AND THE NEW (1897)[1]

ON accepting the invitation with which the new Cambridge
Economic Club has honoured me to address its first meeting, it
seemed that, perhaps, my most appropriate subject would be
the relation in which the work of the older generation of economists, which is drawing near the close of its activity, stands to
the work which appears to lie before that coming generation, to
which most of the members of the club belong. I propose
therefore to lay before you some estimate of the preparation
which has been made by the nineteenth century and the old
generation of economists for the new generation of economists
and the twentieth century. The estimate must be fragmentary
and incomplete. The subject is large, and its treatment to-night
must suffer from the shortness of the time at our disposal; but
it will suffer yet more sorely from the limitations imposed by my
own subjectivity. For it is never more difficult to free one's self
from the shackles imposed by one's own bias than when endeavouring to take a survey of the present and to forecast the
future.

Economic science as I first knew it, just thirty years ago, was
more confident than now: partly because it was less active. Its
general propositions and general principles were bold and
peremptory: at all events so long as they kept on this side of
the water. Some of them flourished elsewhere, especially in
France. But most of them were bad sailors; and, if they were
met with in other lands, they generally had a languishing air
as though they had not recovered from sea-sickness. And even
in England they were becoming less robust. Their decadence was
no doubt hastened by academic criticisms, the ultimate source
of which was to be sought in the new German school of history.
But, probably, these criticisms had less influence than the rapid
changes which were taking place throughout the whole Western
World in the economic structure of society, and in the tone and

[1] An Address delivered in Cambridge, England, October 29, 1896. Reprinted from the
Quarterly Journal of Economics, January, 1897.

temper of political thought: while, so far as England herself was concerned, the experiences of administrators and business men in Asia and Africa as well as in America had long been suggesting broader views of the action of economic and other social forces. It is consistent with the general history of English thought and action to believe that Englishmen were more influenced by their own experiences than by the scientific studies of foreigners.

These experiences bore fruit early in the writings of Richard Jones. It is noticeable that he was addressing Indian cadets when he said in 1833,

> We must get comprehensive views of facts, that we may arrive at principles that are truly comprehensive. If we take a different method, if we snatch at general principles, and content ourselves with confined observations, two things will happen to us. First, what we shall call general principles, will be found to have no generality; we shall set out with declaring propositions to be universally true which, at every step of our further progress, we shall be obliged to confess are frequently false; and secondly we shall miss a mass of useful knowledge, which those who advance to principles by a comprehensive observation of facts necessarily meet with on their road.

Richard Jones had not fully grasped the modern distinction between generality of doctrines or dogmas, and generality of analytical conceptions and ideas; and his own position has its defects. But he said just what was wanted at the time: and his influence, though little heard of in the outer world, largely dominated the minds of those Englishmen who came to the serious study of economics after his works had been published by Dr Whewell in 1859.

Thus general economic principles had to justify their existence before a court which no longer had any bias in their favour, and perhaps had some little bias against them. Consequently they became less dictatorial, and more willing to admit their own limitations. Never again will a Mrs Trimmer, a Mrs Marcet, or a Miss Martineau earn a goodly reputation by throwing them into the form of a catechism or of simple tales, by aid of which any intelligent governess might make clear to the children nestling around her where lies economic truth, and might send them forth ready to instruct statesmen and merchants how to choose the right path in economic policy, and to avoid the wrong.

It is now patent, even to those who are in a hurry, that no practical problems can be settled offhand by appeal to general doctrines; for the things of which account must be taken are so diverse, and our knowledge of many of them is so slight, that they yield no firm hold for formal proof. Much must be taken on conjecture; much must be decided by common sense rather than by reasoning on strictly logical lines.

Thus the growing perfection of scientific machinery in economics, so far from lessening the responsibilities of common sense, increases those responsibilities: for it widens and deepens the issues with which the economist has to deal, and for the ultimate decision of which he must, after all, rely mainly on his practical instincts. And on the other hand the retiring disposition of general principles and general propositions has been accompanied not by a diminution but by an increase of their real authority. They no longer wield the big battle-axe and sound the loud war cry like a Cœur de Lion; they keep in the background like a modern general: but they control larger forces than before. They exert a more far-reaching and more powerful influence on ideas: and ideas fashion the course of the world ever more and more.

For, indeed, the progress of knowledge in economics as elsewhere has shown that nature's facts are more diverse and more complex than used to be thought; and hence some have inferred that the more we know of the fundamental forces of economic and social life the more diverse will they appear. But to reason thus is to ignore the experiences of physical science, which has gone over the same ground a little ahead of social science. Physical science has learnt that an increasing knowledge of the variety and complexity of the phenomena of nature has often been accompanied by a diminution in the number of principles required to explain them. It has learnt that a few simple causes can produce an endless variety of results; and that a small change in the strength of any one of the forces, or in its method of combination with others, may alter the result beyond recognition. The discovery of intimate true affinities between things which appear wholly different to the hasty observer has long been recognized as one of the chief tasks of physical science.

Thus we cannot predict results from a mere knowledge of fundamental forces, without making a full investigation of the particular circumstances under which the forces act: a small change in those circumstances may alter the action of the fundamental forces almost beyond recognition. Hence it follows also that increased knowledge of these forces is more likely to stimulate than to check the study of particular facts. And this is what has actually occurred. Newton's law of gravitation stimulated the work of astronomical observatories. Darwin's development of the laws of struggle and survival gave perhaps a greater impetus to the careful and exact study of particular facts than any other event that has ever occurred. Nor is this all. For, when simple and elementary principles have already a fairly strong hold in any body of knowledge, every new fact has a greater opportunity of suggestiveness than before the knowledge was organized. Röntgen's rays are all the more stimulating to thought and to further observation, because of their tendency to modify general principles that have already won their spurs.

As the nineteenth century has worn on, there has been a growing readiness among economists, as among students of physical science, to recognize that the infinite variety and complexity of nature's forms is compatible with a marvellous latent simplicity of her governing principles. The pursuit of particulars has become ever more eager; but what little tendency there once was to dissociate it from the study of general principles has now almost died away. It is now recognized by everyone that an inference from one set of facts to another, whether it be performed by instinctive or by formal reasoning, involves not one process but two. It involves a passage upwards from particulars to general propositions and ideas; and a passage downwards from them to other particulars. We can seldom infer particulars from other particulars without passing in effect through generals, however simple be the subject-matter of our study; and we can never do so in the complex problems of social life.

Parallel with this advance is an increase in the skill with which the partial thoughts of economists of earlier times are interpreted. We have learnt that most of them were true seers, with careful habits of observation; and that what they meant to say was for the greater part true within its limits; though what they said does not always fully suggest to us what was in their own minds until we have supplied the latent premises which they instinctively took for granted. We no longer look to them for quite the same sort of instruction as before; but that which we now seek, we are getting from them.

A further advance is the recognition that in economics we deal with the whole of man's nature, though we lay chief stress on certain special aspects of it. From this it follows that, in so far as we base ourselves upon the history of past times at all, it must be history as a whole. We need more than economic history, more than a history of economic institutions and customs, wages and prices, of trade and finance: we want a history of man himself, and economic history as contributing to that. To take one instance: the history of Socialism has great value, but not of the kind which is commonly ascribed to it. It is of little service as a record of particular events from which specific inferences can be drawn to modern problems. For the socialistic problems of to-day are very different from those of earlier times. The forces of reform and of resistance to change, the relations between different trades and classes in the same nation and the economic relations between nations are all different: the substance of the problem of social reform has changed, the machinery with which it has to be handled has wholly changed; and the success or failure of one particular social experiment long ago is not likely to throw a very strong special light on any experiment that may be tried now. But every such experiment in the past throws light upon human nature. And the history of such experiments throws light on the dynamics as well as on the statics of human nature: it tends to show not only what human nature was at any time, but also how it has developed. It offers us therefore great aid towards estimating the direction and the rate of growth of human nature in the future, and specially of that side of human nature which it is most important for us to understand, when considering daring modern schemes for social reform.

Social science or the reasoned history of man, for the two things are the same, is working its way towards a fundamental unity; just as is being done by physical science, or, which is the same thing, by the reasoned history of natural phenomena. Physical science is seeking her hidden unity in the forces that govern molecular movement: social science is seeking her unity in the forces of human character. To that all history tends; from that proceeds all prediction, all guidance for the future.

It is not for us to complain that the name of history has been sometimes usurped by what is but a fragment of history. Out of that tangled complex which constitutes the history of man, a few prominent threads have been selected and traced out: and much progress has been made towards the correlation of political institutions, and political events. The political branch of history has advanced far ahead of all other branches, because it is important on its own account; because it is definite, picturesque, of general interest, and richly supplied with records specially belonging to it. It throws also incidentally a bright light on the development of human nature; and in this way, as well as through the particular events which it records, it affords great help in tracing the thread of economic history. So great progress has political history already made that for this cause alone the economists of the future will have a much greater command over their work than had the "classical" economists. And they will owe a great debt also to ideas that have done good service for physical science, and are being adapted to some limited and partial aspects of social science.

It was perhaps not fully recognized by the older economists themselves, that in their predilection for a study of tendencies, they were really working to obtain just that mastery of knowledge which has laid the foundation of the successive triumphs of physical science. But, when studying particular facts with the purpose of inferring tendencies, they were conforming to the great canon already noticed that, in passing from particulars to particulars, we must go not directly but by way of generals; and also to a second great canon, that the main importance of the particular facts of nature lies in the light which they throw upon the processes of nature; or, in other words, that from what *is* we have to learn what *is becoming*; from *das Sein* we have to learn *das Werden*.

Economists have in recent years come more nearly into line with physical science by borrowing from it some of those terse and powerful phrases by which it has been long able to describe and explain nature's tendencies more easily and more precisely than is possible in ordinary language. They are facing the fact that at the basis of nearly all modern knowledge there lies a study of tendencies, in the form more or less disguised of a study of the relations between the infinitesimal variations of different things. This study the shrewd ordinary man makes, though he may not know it: the man of science makes it, and knows that he does so: though before he addresses a popular audience he may fitly wrap up what he has done in language that is less terse and clear, but more familiar.

This work of the new methods is far from finished: much remains for your generation to do. But the start has been made; and it will be no hindrance to you, but rather some assistance, that many still look with suspicion on the movement. Their criticisms will help you to be careful not to outrun your positive knowledge and observation, and not to forget the differences in character between the facts and the forces of the physical world and those of the moral world.

To pass then to a rather less technical aspect of analysis:— Speaking generally, the nineteenth century has in great measure achieved *qualitative* analysis in economics; but it has not gone farther. It has felt the necessity for *quantitative* analysis, and has made some rough preliminary surveys of the way in which it is to be achieved: but the achievement itself stands over for you. "Qualitative" and "quantitative" analysis are terms borrowed from chemistry—a science which deals with things as they are, and not with their growth; and therefore the terms are not exactly what we want. But they must serve. Qualitative analysis tells the iron-master that there is *some* sulphur in his ore, but it does not enable him to decide whether it is worth while to smelt the ore at all, and, if it is, then by what process. For that purpose he needs quantitative analysis, which will tell him *how much* sulphur there is in the ore. And so it is also in economics. Every event has many effects; some work good, others evil. Some are permanent, others will quickly pass away. Some affect many, others only a few. Some grow cumulatively, others invite a reaction. Mere qualitative analysis, then, will not show the resultant drift of economic forces. It may show gain here and loss there; but it will not show whether the gain is sufficient to overbalance the loss; whether the gain should be pursued in spite of the loss. And yet, for the purposes of practical action, this decision must be made. It is useless to say that various gains and losses are incommensurable, and cannot be weighed against one another. For they must be, and in fact they are, weighed against one another before any deliberate decision is or can be reached on any issue.

Of course the laws of duty impose boundaries that are not to be passed: just as at chess when a king is already at the right-hand end of the board he cannot move to the right. But the fact that the laws of chess rule some moves out altogether, does not prevent chess from consisting mainly of a balancing of the advantages of one programme of legitimate moves against another, and often weighing the value of a piece against that of an improved position. A piece and a position are logically quite heterogeneous; but he would be no chess-player at all who could not weigh the one against the other. And, though there are some things which no statesman may do, no economist may recommend, yet the action of the statesman and the advice of the economist must be based upon as exact an estimate as may be got of the relative importance of different sets of advantages, each made up of many things that are logically heterogeneous.

Here a distinction must be made between the relative weights which people do in fact assign to the various things which concern their physical, their mental and their moral well-being, and the relative weights which, as philosophers and moralists, we may think they ought to assign to those things. Ethical instincts and philosophy are the supreme authority in deciding what aims are fit to be pursued. But in studying the facts of the past and in devising schemes for the future our first concern is with the things that people have wished and do wish for; and at a later stage we may consider what things they probably can be induced to wish for in the future. No doubt their weighing is often foolish and shortsighted, sometimes ignoble and even wicked. Philosophers as we may strive to be, we surely afford no exception to this rule. We may wish that the ways of all were different; we may exhort ourselves and others to better ways: but we have to study mankind as they are. We must not picture to ourselves an unreal world as it might, or ought to be, and make schemes for it. That way lies social madness, leading to a failure of hot aspirations and thence to cold reaction. Our first duty as economists is to make a reasoned catalogue of the world as it is; and never to allow our estimates as to what forces will prove the strongest in any social contingency to be biased by our opinion as to what forces ought to prove the strongest. A chief part of the work which lies before the economists of the twentieth century is to make that estimate— not well, for that is impossible, but—somewhat less badly than it has been made hitherto.

The older economists were really driving at quantitative analysis when they took it as their special duty to make things stand out in true perspective, in true proportion. They set themselves to lay stress on "that which is not seen" because it is remote or obscure, in opposition to the popular tendency to care chiefly for "that which is seen," because a bright light happens to fall on it, because it is simple and near at hand: and they set themselves to defend the interests of the silent and patient many against the claims of the pushing and clamorous few. For indeed, as Fortrey said more than two centuries ago,

Private advantages are often impediments of public profit; for, in what a single person shall be a loser, there endeavours will be made to hinder the public gain; from whence proceeds the ill success that commonly attends the endeavours for public good: for commonly it is but coldly prosecuted, because the benefit may possibly be something remote from them that promote it, but the mischief known and certain to them that oppose it; and interest more than reason commonly sways most men's affections.

The pushing and clamorous few in an economic controversy are often a group of producers who can put their case well, and who show great energy and resource in making themselves heard. Hence has arisen the tradition that the economist is generally on the side of the consumer as against the producer: he aims at protecting the unvocal many who consume the products of a particular trade, against the vocal few who speak on behalf of the trade.

A good instance of the difficulty of getting your quantities right is found in the inverse claim, which is sometimes put forward nowadays, that the interests of consumers are really less important than those of producers; because the producers are many and the consumers few; the terms consumer and producer being taken again in a forced sense; but in a different one from that of the old. Of course everyone is a consumer, and everyone is a producer (or the dependent of a producer); for income can only be derived from labour that takes part in production, or from the ownership of something that takes part in production. But, when the consumers are said to be few and the producers many, the consumers are taken to be those whose incomes enable them to consume largely; and the producers are generally taken to be those who work for a wage. The claim so interpreted is one which the economist must treat seriously and sympathetically. An instance is offered by the story, which seems to be not entirely without some basis in fact, of the vendor of Oriental tapestry, who excused the high price which he asked for it by the assertion that the stitch was so fine that ten people had lost their eyesight, and many more had been seriously injured, by working on that single piece. The whim or the artistic lust of the rich consumer had outweighed the welfare of the producers in this instance; and other instances nearer home might be obtained from some trades in which the hours of labour are excessive or its conditions unwholesome. Such instances of social discord are facts which the economist must admit: they are the result of natural laws which it is his business to help to counteract.

But they are exceptional instances; and I believe that the statement that the interests of working men are those of producers rather than those of consumers is very seldom true even in the limited and artificial sense in which the words are used. The question is one of relative quantities; and it is misconceived partly because people do not know the right directions in which to look for their quantities.

For instance, when working men think of themselves as consumers, they seldom look in the right directions. They know that they are consumers of food and clothing. But they do not think of themselves as consumers of such things as iron. They look upon the price of iron as the concern mainly of railway and ship companies, and other capitalists who purchase it. But, in fact, a low price of iron is at least as great a benefit to the working man as to anyone else. It is a chief cause of the increase of that purchasing power of his wages which results from the fall in the prices of his food and clothing, while the price of his labour has been maintained. Everyone is apt to take as a matter of course the great benefits which economic progress brings him, and to regard any slight injury that results from it as an unendurable grievance; and thus to see things in a wrong proportion. But progress is *not* a matter of course: it is the result of effort. If there had been no improvement in steam engines and the manufacture of iron during the last fifty years, the purchasing power of Englishmen's wages would be much less than it is now: I do not know how much less, but I guess thirty or forty per cent. less. Some of the quantities in the problem must always remain more or less conjectural; but others could be taken out with tolerable certainty.

Such work as this belongs to the academic economist. For he has no class or personal interests to make him afraid of any conclusion which the figures, when carefully interpreted, may indicate; he accepts the premises of the working classes that the well-being of the many is more important than that of the few. He is specially trained to detect the falsity of the mirage which is caused by the fact that the comfort of a few rich men sometimes has a higher bidding power in the market than more urgent needs of many poor, and will outbid them in the market. Being thus fortified by the consciousness of his own rectitude, the economist, in the coming generation even more than in the past, must dare when occasion arises to oppose the multitude for their own good. He must for instance analyse the methods which people are tempted to take for securing a high minimum wage, falsely called a living wage, in a particular trade; and must show which of them will have indirect effects that will cause to working men as a whole a loss greater than the benefit.

Cries for a living wage have the shouts of the market-place on their side just now: they are raised by dockers and coal miners; by cotton spinners and glass blowers, and by capitalist booksellers. They appear to strengthen one another; because ordinary people do not see that the means most commonly advocated are such as, if generally pursued, would impoverish all. It is true that a great and important principle lies at the root of this movement for a living wage. Economists have fought for it in the past, and your successors may need to fight for it again. But, just as you are entering on your work the movement for a living wage has become so popular, that there is less need to dwell on its merits, than to analyse its latent assumptions as to the relative quantities of losses and gains. "There is money in this branch of discovery," said the professor of pure science, "and we will leave it for those who seek money"; you may parody this and say—"there is popularity in the doctrine of a living wage; so we had better leave politicians to praise it and set ourselves to criticise it."

Again, while taking an attitude of reserve towards movements that are already popular, you will incline to be critical of prophecies that are fashionable. For instance, it is getting to be asserted commonly that collective bargaining is about to displace bargaining between individuals as the main arbiter of distribution and exchange. It may be so; but predictions of this kind have been made much more often than they have been fulfilled. You will need to examine how far the large and obtrusive surface, which collective bargaining presents, rests on a solid foundation; and how far it is hollow. You will not think lightly of the old social discords which it tends to lessen: but you will set against them those new discords which it may introduce. For clearly it tends to make a man work, or sell, not up to that margin at which there is a balance of gain and loss to him, but up to a margin which, if not arbitrary, yet fails of any close adaptation to his individual case. You will need to look at history and see how often collective bargaining, when most elaborately contrived and strong in outward appearance, was honeycombed and weak; you will need to watch the vast network of by-paths by which, when one person is willing to sell a thing at a price which another is willing to pay for it, the two manage to come together in spite of prohibitions of King or Parliament, or of the officials of a Trust or Trade-union. No doubt you may live to see collective bargaining a greater force than I expect, and working in ways which I do not guess. The experience of the past does not foretell the future; but it justifies some scepticism as to the solidity of those forms of collective bargaining which are most ostentatious.

These last remarks illustrate the difficulty of forecasting the nature of the problems which will chiefly occupy the coming generation. But I will take another illustration of this difficulty, the chief interest of which lies in the guesses which past experience prompts us to hazard as to a mode of action of the healing force of nature. For, in social as in physical life, nature modifies old remedies to meet new developments of old evils. And I will venture on a surmise of one way in which your generation may perhaps see this healing force more active than heretofore.

Everyone is aware of the tendency to an increase in the size of individual businesses, with the consequent transference of authority and responsibility from the owners of each business to its salaried managers and officials. This would have been impossible had there not been a great improvement in the morality and uprightness of the average man: for even as late as the seventeenth and eighteenth centuries we find the great trading companies breaking down largely in consequence of the corruption and selfishness of their officials. But, men who are above such gross iniquity as was common then relatively to the few opportunities for it, are yet likely to succumb to subtler temptations, and especially to the temptation to consult their own ease by jogging along quietly in accustomed routes, and avoiding the trouble and worry of new initiative.

And indeed this tendency to an increase in the size of businesses introduces an ever-growing discord into industry. The owner of a business, when contemplating any change, is led by his own interest to weigh the whole gain that it would probably bring to the business against the whole loss; but the private interest of the salaried manager or official draws him in quite another direction. For the trouble of a new experiment will come largely on him. If it fails, he will have to bear much of the blame; and, if it succeeds, only a very small part of the consequent gain will accrue to him. So the path of least resistance, of greatest comfort and least risk to himself is generally that of not striving for improvement himself, and of finding plausible excuses for not trying an improvement suggested by others, until its success is established beyond question.

If this were the whole of the case, then every new advantage that modern changes confer on large businesses in their contests with small would be a source of danger to social progress. For the economies of the large business as against the small are mostly a matter of private concern and bear no further fruit: but the improvement of methods spreads from its first home all over the country, all over the world; and the private gain which results from it to the inventor is seldom a hundredth part, sometimes not a millionth part of the social gain. A strong tendency to ossification of the social organism might therefore be feared as the result of bureaucratic habits of shirking trouble-some initiative, the main benefits of which would accrue to those who had not borne the burden. But this tendency is being counteracted, partially at least, by several forces. The increase in the size of industries goes with the substitution of scientific methods for empirical: and the basis of scientific technique is largely provided by laboratory work to which an ever-increasing number of elastic and enterprising minds are rising from among the people, being stimulated a little by the hope of gain, and much by intellectual ambition, and the sympathy of other students of science. And in addition to this general energizing force, a special force somewhat similar to it is coming into play to preserve from stagnation the more exclusively practical side of business management. For business experts are getting more and more into the habit of writing and reading specialist journals, of holding congresses, and in other ways coming under the judg-ment of one another. The old thankless task of attempting an improvement which may after all turn out badly, and to which a man's official superiors and the public at large may be in-different, assumes a new shape when it is likely to be judged by a critical and appreciative audience who knows the technical difficulties of the problem. The most important improvements often remain for years just short of yielding financial profit: but such an audience applauds the clever and bold endeavour even though its financial fruit is not ripe; even though the interest of a manufacturer in charge of his own business would not impel him to use it. Thus the modern intercourse of expert officials with one another is bringing into the business world some part of that great progressive force which pure science has long derived from the approbation awarded to successful research by audiences fit though few. Such approbation is a reward; and like every other reward, present or deferred, appeals to elements of our nature that are not the very highest of all: and partly for that reason it may be trusted to act steadfastly. But it is not only a reward: it is also a sympathy; and sympathy is the one solid and strong force acting steadfastly throughout the whole of human nature, which has in it nothing sordid. The coming generation of economists will have no more urgent, and perhaps no more pleasant task, than to inquire, with as close an estimate of quantities as may be, how far this class of forces may take the place of the cruder force of the pursuit of private material gain, which is being in some directions weakened by the growth of large businesses, and especially those under public control.

I have trespassed too long upon your patience and must conclude, though I have touched on only the outer fringe of the issue to which I have ventured to address myself. To sum up then:—During the generation that is now passing away it has been made clear beyond doubt by many workers in many lands that the true inductive study of economics is the search for and arrangement of facts with a view to discovering the ideas, some temporary and local, others universal and eternal, which underlie them: and that the true analytical study of economics is the search for ideas latent in the facts which have been thus brought together and arranged by the historian and the observer of contemporary life. Each study supplements the other: there is no rivalry or opposition between them; every genuine student of economics sometimes uses the inductive method and sometimes the analytical, and nearly always both of them together. There is a difference in proportion between different students; as one may eat more solid food and another may drink more fluid: but every one must both eat and drink under pain of starving or dying of thirst.

The generation of economists which is now passing away has worked through controversy as to method, to the extinction of that controversy. It has established the harmony between the study of facts and of ideas; it has shown the need of a catholic spirit in the interpretation of men as well as of facts. It has done much towards completing the main lines of qualitative analysis; but it has not grappled at close quarters with the

difficulties of quantitative analysis. The time has not yet come
for taking stock of the value of its constructive work. But it
has at all events cleared the field for the constructive work of
the larger and stronger strain of economists that are to follow:
and perhaps when people look back a century hence they may
speak kindly of it, not so much for what it achieved itself, as
for the far greater work which it prepared the way for you to
achieve.

The problem of social aims takes on new forms in every age;
but underlying all forms there is the one fundamental principle,
that progress mainly depends on the extent to which the
strongest, and not merely the highest, forces of human nature
can be utilized for the increase of social good. There are some
doubts as to what social good really is; but they do not reach
far enough to impair the foundations of our fundamental
principle. For there has always been a substratum of agreement
that social good lies mainly in that healthful exercise and
development of faculties which yields happiness without pall,
because it sustains self-respect and is sustained by hope. No
utilization of waste gases in the blast furnace can compare with
the triumph of making work for the public good pleasurable in
itself, and of stimulating men of all classes to great endeavours
by other means than that evidence of power which manifests
itself by lavish expenditure. We need to foster fine work and
fresh initiative by the warming breath of the sympathy and
appreciation of those who truly understand it; we need to turn
consumption into paths that strengthen the consumer and call
forth the best qualities of those who provide for consumption.

Other generations, in the heyday of art and literature in the
ancient and mediæval world, have hit upon methods of doing
this more or less successfully; but their aims have had a narrow
horizon, limited to the welfare of a fortunate few. The generation
of students of social science which is now passing away has
striven to deal with the problem on a broader basis; and your
generation is called on to continue that work with greater
knowledge and with greater resources. You are called on to
apply your knowledge of history, and especially of contemporary
history, your powers of analysis and of quantitative measurement, your fancy and your intuition, your instincts and your

sympathies, towards the great task of utilizing the present waste products of human effort for the production of human lives that are joys in themselves and the sources of joy. For the future, as for the past, the chief lever of all is hope, hope for a man's self and hope for those dear to him. And your generation will stand out beyond that which has gone before, as that has stood out beyond its predecessors, as having an increasing power and opportunity of bringing the energizing influence of hope to the homes of what as late as the beginning of this century were called the lower orders of the people.

Your generation, beyond all that has gone before, is called on to inquire in a sanguine, but yet in a critical and analytical temper how far that force of association and sympathy, which we have just noticed as beginning to act powerfully among the expert officials in large businesses, may extend to people generally; how it may *draw* them on to high endeavours, as the good shepherd leads his sheep, without requiring the compulsive force of want to *drive* them forward with cruel blows: how far it may be possible to obliterate the old doctrine that the many must pine in order that the few may pioneer. Your generation will recognize that men are not equal by nature and cannot be made equal by art. It will recognize that some work must be done that is not ennobling. But it will seek to apply the growing knowledge and material resources of the world to reduce such work within narrow limits, and to extirpate all conditions of life which are in themselves debasing. It will expect no sudden improvement in man's conditions of life, because he forms them as much as they form him, and he himself cannot change fast. But it will press on steadfastly towards the distant goal where the opportunities of a noble life may be accessible to all.

XIV

MECHANICAL AND BIOLOGICAL ANALOGIES
IN ECONOMICS (1898)[1]

THE terms Statics and Dynamics are imported into economics from physics; and some discussions about them among economists have seemed to imply that statics and dynamics are distinct branches of physics. But of course they are not. The modern mathematician is familiar with the notion that dynamics include statics. If he can solve a problem dynamically, he seldom cares to solve it statically also. To get the statical solution from the dynamical all that is needed is to make the relative velocities of the things under study equal to zero, and thus reduce them to *relative* rest. But the statical solution has claims of its own. It is simpler than the dynamical; it may afford useful preparation and training for the more difficult dynamical solution; and it may be the first step towards a provisional and partial solution in problems so complex that a complete dynamical solution is beyond our attainment.

The term "relative rest" calls for notice: for it plays an important *rôle* in the so-called stationary state of the economist. "Absolute rest" is an unmeaning term; statical problems deal with relative rest. This fact is perhaps more familiar than he knows to "the man in the train." The train may be running smoothly on straight rails; and then he may be tempted to treat the problem of packing his parcels on the rack as a statical one: for although all the things are moving they are relatively at rest. But experience has taught him that parcels, packed at the top of a railway carriage with reference to statical conditions only, are likely to fall if the movement of the train is checked: it has taught him to look out for the disruptive dynamical element that is latent in the apparently peaceful statical problem.

Many writers have carried over physical conceptions into social science. And it is interesting to note Mill's delight on

---

[1] From an article on "Distribution and Exchange" in the *Economic Journal*, March, 1898.

finding, as he thought, a key to economic method in the fact that "the principle of the Composition of Forces" is applicable to economics. "When the mind applies this principle it performs a simple act of addition. It adds the separate effect of one force to the separate effect of the other, and puts down the sum of these separate effects as the joint effect[1]."

This is true: and in relation to statical problems properly so-called it is the whole truth. For, when considering the equilibrium of things which are strictly at rest relatively to one another, we have but to add by simple arithmetic the forces acting at a point in any direction; and make sure that the sum is zero.

But in dynamical problems, though true, it is not the whole truth. For, when a force moves the thing on which it acts, it thereby changes the force which that thing afterwards exercises. The attraction of the Earth alters the movement of Venus, and thus alters the force which Venus exerts on the Earth: which again alters the movement of the Earth, and therefore the attraction which the Earth exerts on Venus; and so on in endless but ever-diminishing reciprocal influences. Meanwhile both planets disturb slightly the Sun, whose attraction is their chief controller; and all the other planets have a part in the play. For such complications as these arithmetic is useless: they need the strength and delicacy of vast and subtle mathematical engines working out large volumes full of mathematical formulæ and figures. But these engines cannot be applied to economics. The most helpful applications of mathematics to economics are those which are short and simple, which employ few symbols; and which aim at throwing a bright light on some small part of the great economic movement rather than at representing its endless complexities.

Thus, then, dynamical solutions, in the physical sense, of economic problems are unattainable. And, if we are to adhere to physical analogies at all, we must say that statical solutions afford starting points for such rude and imperfect approaches to dynamical solutions as we may be able to attain to. This is in substance what I propose to argue now; but I prefer other words.

---

[1] Mill's *Autobiography*, pp. 159, 160. See also my *Principles*, third edition, Book I, chap. vi, p. 2.

It has been well said that analogies may help one into the saddle, but are encumbrances on a long journey. It is well to know when to introduce them, it is even better to know when to stop them off. Two things may resemble one another in their initial stages; and a comparison of the two may then be helpful: but after a while they diverge; and then the comparison begins to confuse and warp the judgment. There is a fairly close analogy between the earlier stages of economic reasoning and the devices of physical statics. But is there an equally serviceable analogy between the later stages of economic reasoning and the methods of physical dynamics? I think not. I think that in the later stages of economics better analogies are to be got from biology than from physics; and, consequently, that economic reasoning should start on methods analogous to those of physical statics, and should gradually become more biological in tone. Of course a new class of considerations as, *e.g.*, of money, credit, international trade, may be introduced after some others have been carried a long way; and in the first handling of new matter there may be a temporary reversion to physical analogies. But that will soon pass; and, when the new matter is ready to be worked up with the old in an advanced stage, the method will become ever more remote from the physical and more akin to the biological.

Let us then look more closely at the method appropriate for the earlier stages of economic reasoning. Man's powers are limited: almost every one of nature's riddles is complex. He breaks it up, studies one bit at a time, and at last combines his partial solutions with a supreme effort of his whole small strength into some sort of an attempt at a solution of the whole riddle. In breaking it up, he uses some adaptation of a primitive but effective prison, or pound, for segregating those disturbing causes whose wanderings happen to be inconvenient for the time: the pound is called *Cæteris Paribus*. The study of some group of tendencies is isolated by the assumption *other things being equal:* the existence of other tendencies is not denied, but their disturbing effect is neglected for a time. The more the issue is thus narrowed, the more exactly can it be handled; but also the less closely does it correspond to real life.

Each exact and firm handling of a narrow issue, however, helps towards treating broader issues, in which that narrow issue is contained, more exactly than would otherwise have been possible. With each step of advance more things can be let out of the pound; exact discussions can be made less abstract, realistic discussions can be made less inexact than was possible at an earlier stage.

The pound *Cæteris Paribus* is never turned to better service in locking up disturbing causes, which we want to keep out of the way provisionally in the earlier stages of an enquiry, than when it is applied to the famous fiction of "the Stationary State." This state obtains its name from the fact that in it the general conditions of production and consumption, of distribution and exchange remain motionless; but yet it is full of movement; for it is a mode of life. The average age of the population may be stationary; but each individual is growing up from youth towards his prime, or downwards to old age. The average size of the business firms may be stationary; but at any moment almost every business is either rising or falling. The average value of grain may be stationary; but the current price fluctuates with successive harvest flows. The study of such fluctuations about a centre of rest is really a dynamical problem, though the simplest form of it is always included in the study of a "stationary state," and indeed affords the chief inducement to the fiction of such a state.

The fiction does not require that the numbers of the population should be stationary. Nearly all the distinctive portions of the stationary state may be exhibited in a place where population and wealth are both growing, provided they are growing at about the same rate, and there is no scarcity of land: and provided also the methods of production and the conditions of trade change but little; and above all, where the character of man himself is a constant quantity. For in such a state by far the most important conditions of production and consumption, of exchange and distribution, will remain of the same quality, and in the same general relations to one another, though they are all increasing in volume. Thus, to quote from a private letter of Mr Flux, "The term static is not exactly what we want: we want to express the conception of 'steady motion' as familiar in hydrodynamics; or, to take examples from solids, as illustrated by the case of a spinning top or a bicycle."

This stationary state, however, bears less resemblance to the real conditions of life now than it did in past generations. There has even been a perceptible change in this respect since Mill's time. For, though most of the factors at work now were at work then, their relative importance has changed so much as to alter the broad features of the problem.

When Mill was growing up, England was still oppressed by the difficulty of obtaining raw produce; and this was giving a bias to distribution in favour of those who own land, and against those whose income is derived from labour and who have many mouths to feed. The black shadow thus cast over the land reached its second climax in the potato famine. Since then it has dwindled: but Mill was always haunted by the fears which had oppressed Ricardo and Malthus, and they gave a sombre tinge to his study of the "influence of progress of industry and population on rents, profits and wages[1]." That discussion, it may be noted, is free from the fallacies of the wages fund. It examines the distribution of the net produce on national income, regarded as a flow; and from an analytical point of view it is perhaps the most advanced and modern part of his work. A century hence the substance of that chapter may seem more modern than it does to-day; for at the present rate of growth the whole world will be fully peopled ere many generations are passed. But just at present the acreage of fertile land, from which the nations of Western Europe can conveniently draw their supplies of raw produce, is increasing much faster than the population; and in this bright interval the outlines of the influence of progress on distribution and exchange are freed from that particular black shadow.

In our own age pressure of numbers on the means of subsistence does not cause a fundamental readjustment of the notion of equilibrium even for very long periods; we can allow for the growth of population by estimating demand and supply alike, not with regard to a total flow of so many units of produce per annum, but with regard to a flow of so many units *per head* per annum. The remedy is not perfect; some minor corrections will remain to be made: but so far as this change is concerned, the general outlines of our picture will be true to the facts of life; and

---

[1] Mill, *Principles*, Book IV, chap. iii.

in view of the complexity of the whole problem, we can scarcely hope for more than that.

The chief difficulties of economic science are now in another direction; they arise rather from the good than from the evil fortunes of mankind. The increasing command which progress is giving us over the forces of nature is altering the conditions of work and life rapidly and in many various ways. It is altering the character as well as the magnitude of economical and social forces. It is altering them perceptibly in each decade, and it may revolutionize them "in the long run."

Of course there is some analogy to this in mechanics. Our planetary system happens, indeed, to be in stable equilibrium; but a little change of circumstance might make it unstable; might, for instance, after a time cause one of the planets to shoot away from the sun in a very long ellipse, and another to fall into it. Again, though a pendulum will generally swing clean backwards and forwards along the same line; yet, if the clock is standing on an inclined ledge, the vibration of the pendulum may make it slide downwards towards a final catastrophe. Mechanical analogies ought, therefore, not to be abandoned hastily on the ground that economic events react upon the conditions by which they were produced; so that future events cannot happen under exactly the same conditions as they did.

But the catastrophes of mechanics are caused by changes in the quantity and not in the character of the forces at work: whereas in life their character changes also. "Progress" or "evolution," industrial and social, is not mere increase and decrease. It is organic growth, chastened and confined and occasionally reversed by the decay of innumerable factors, each of which influences and is influenced by those around it; and every such mutual influence varies with the stages which the respective factors have already reached in their growth.

In this vital respect all sciences of life are akin to one another, and are unlike physical sciences. And therefore in the later stages of economics, when we are approaching nearly to the conditions of life, biological analogies are to be preferred to mechanical, other things being equal. Other things may not be equal; the mechanical analogy is apt to be the more definite and vivid: the analogy, for instance, of a satellite which is moving around a planet, which is itself moving around another centre, is helpful for special purposes, even in very advanced stages of many economic problems; and wherever helpful it should be used. But as the science reaches to its highest work such occasions become rarer and rarer, and the tone becomes more and more that of a biological science.

Consider, for instance, the balancing of demand and supply. The words "balance" and "equilibrium" belong originally to the older science, physics; whence they have been taken over by biology. In the earlier stages of economics, we think of demand and supply as crude forces pressing against one another, and tending towards a mechanical equilibrium; but in the later stages, the balance or equilibrium is conceived not as between crude mechanical forces, but as between the organic forces of life and decay. The healthy boy grows stronger every year; but with early manhood there is some loss of agility; the zenith of his power is reached perhaps at twenty-five for such a game as racquets. For other corporeal activities the zenith comes at thirty or later. For some kinds of mental work it comes rather late; for statesmanship, for instance, it comes very late. In each case the forces of life preponderate at first; then those of crystallization and decay attain to equal terms, and there is balance or equilibrium; afterwards decay predominates.

Again, with every spring the leaves of a tree grow, attain full strength, and after passing their zenith decay; while the tree itself is rising year by year to its zenith, after which it also will decay. And here we find a biological analogy to oscillations in the values of commodities or of services about centres which are progressing, or perhaps themselves oscillating in longer periods.

The balance, or equilibrium, of demand and supply obtains ever more of this biological tone in the more advanced stages of economics. The Mecca of the economist is economic biology rather than economic dynamics.

.

XV

HENRY SIDGWICK (1900)[1]

As a freshman I learnt that I should "cap" Dr Whewell and the Vice-Chancellor, but no one else outside my own College. A year or two later I learnt that there was in Trinity a younger man whose force resembled Whewell's. If Whewell was Headmaster, Sidgwick became Captain of the whole school. We looked to him for leadership against the obstruction of the elderly: and we thought people became elderly as soon as they were ten or fifteen years older than ourselves. So when we heard that the votes in Trinity of those senior to Sidgwick went one way, and those of Sidgwick and the juniors went the other way, we felt that Sidgwick was leading a band of champions of the new age, who were gradually gaining ground. We took him as our Captain, though he was not of our house, and borrowed our opinions on University reform largely from him. Gradually we were scattered. But to the end my first desire on every new question was to know how Sidgwick would vote and why. One voted confidently and cheerily when led by him; but doubtfully and anxiously when on the other side. For, even when one could not follow him, one knew that his opinions were the embodiment of a great idea. Surely the character of our hero, so gentle and so strong, so various, so honest and earnest in thought and deed, has been foreshadowed in "the noblest Roman of them all." For he lived

> in a general honest thought
> And common good to all......
> His life was gentle; and the elements
> So mixed in him that Nature might stand up
> And say to all the world:—*This was a man!*

[1] From the *Cambridge University Reporter*, December 7, 1900.

XVI

AN EXPORT DUTY ON COAL (1901)[1]

A UNIVERSAL tax on all a country's exports has similar results to those of a universal tax on her imports. Each of them acts in the same way as a special stamp duty on contracts made in connexion with her foreign trade; or, again, as an increase in the cost of carriage across her frontiers (the cost of carriage elsewhere not being affected). Each of them tends to make her goods a little more scarce than they otherwise would be in foreign markets; and so to enable an all-round merchant to bring back a trifle more imports in return for each bale of exports. The main burden of such taxes is borne by the country herself, but other countries are forced to contribute a small share.

To the extent of this small share duties on imports and exports show a balance of advantage, from the purely national point of view, as compared with other methods of levying revenue. And free trade would be a blunder if no one were hurt by taxes except those who ultimately pay them.

But nearly all taxes, and especially taxes on commodities, and most especially "differential" taxes levied on goods passing the frontiers, injure people who do not pay them as well as those who do. For they divert direct consumption from those routes by which human efforts can satisfy human wants most easily; and turn it to others which are naturally less advantageous, but which evade the tax. In so far as this is done, the people suffer and the tax-gatherer gets nothing. If, for instance, in consequence of the charges imposed when passing the frontier, imported wool were partially displaced by home-grown wool of inferior quality, or at a higher cost, then those who used this wool would be injured by the tax, though they did not help to pay it.

There is no absolute à priori proof that these evils must necessarily outweigh the advantages of shifting a part of the direct burden of a country's taxes on foreigners. And it is not

---

[1] A letter to the *Times*, April 22, 1901.

by trained economists—not even by those who are the most ardent free-traders—that the defence of free trade is based on absolute *à priori* reasoning.

On the contrary, it is based on a study of details. For that shows that, as the world is constituted, an attempt to make other nations contribute to a country's revenue on any considerable scale is foredoomed to failure; and especially that England cannot now do it. Again, a study of detail shows that the waste and friction and indirect consumers' loss caused by differential duties on the frontier are always greater than they appear at first sight; and especially in the case of a densely-peopled country which has limited natural resources and must trust mainly to a highly efficient organization of her industry and trade.

One may indeed amuse one's self by imagining a small country, whose sole exports consist of rare minerals which other countries are ready to buy from her at almost any cost. She might restrict her output, or levy high duties either on her exports or on her imports. All three courses would come to much the same in the long run, and, in any case, she would enrich herself at the expense of her neighbours by refusing free trade.

But, as this world is made, no case of this kind on a large scale is possible. There is not, and there cannot be, any large country the greater part of whose exports are free from effective competition. And, therefore, a heavy general tax either on a country's imports or on her exports would merely make foreigners take out their purchases from her in those goods which were important for them, and they would supply themselves with other goods from elsewhere. That is, she would fail in the attempt to make scarce those goods for which foreigners have so urgent a need that they would buy them of her at a high cost rather than dispense with them.

There are thus three classes of frontier taxes which may be economically defensible. First come non-differential import duties on comforts and luxuries, such as those in England on tobacco and spirits; and, in case of need, on tea and sugar. Second come "protective" import duties on things for the production of which a country has great latent facilities that are just ripe for development; as was the case with tin-plates in

America a few years ago. (I am not advocating such taxes, for I believe their end can be attained at less cost in other ways.) The third are special export duties on commodities with which foreigners cannot easily dispense; such seems to be the case with our best steam coal, and, perhaps, our best gas coal.

If Glamorganshire were an independent country, she might possibly gain by an all-round tax either on imports or on exports. But, as it is, the easiest way in which we can charge to foreigners "all that the traffic will bear" as regards Welsh coal is by a special export duty.

But is it worth while to do this? On the one hand, our coal is a chief foundation of our industrial well-being; we are wasting our children's inheritance; and there is much to be said for taking toll from coal in order to lessen our National Debt. On the other hand, a tax on the export of coal appears to present many technical difficulties; and to be not worth the disturbance it must cause unless it is to be permanent. And, what is more important, it is, to a certain extent, a breach of international comity; while we are in a specially defenceless position against some export duties that certain other countries might conceivably levy. It is now five and twenty years since I first thought of writing to advocate an export duty on coal, but was restrained by this last consideration; and I have often taken up the question since. My doubts have never been resolved; but I admire the courage of the Chancellor.

XVII

SOCIAL POSSIBILITIES OF ECONOMIC CHIVALRY (1907)[1]

1. *Different schools of economic thought have shown a marked tendency to convergence as to fundamentals both of method and doctrine during the last thirty years.*

THE Congress which has been opened to-day under the auspices of the Royal Economic Society is one of many recent indications that economic questions are to play a greater part in the life and thought of the present century than they did in that of the past. Parliaments all the world over now spend more than half their time on economic issues, and probably no other serious subject gives so much employment to the printing presses that work for periodicals and general literature. Universities are giving more attention to it, especially in the United States, Germany, and this country. There are said to be 325 professors of it in the United States, where it is richly endowed. But in this country the economic department of almost every University except Manchester, Birmingham, and London is seriously handicapped by a lack of funds.

Much progress has been made recently in economic science, especially on the analytical side. Disputes as to method have nearly ceased; all students accept Schmoller's dictum that analysis and the search for facts are, like the right and left foot in walking, each nearly useless alone; but that the two are strong in combination.

Again, what by chemical analogy may be called *qualitative* analysis has done the greater part of its work—that is to say, there is a general agreement as to the characters and directions of the changes which various economic forces tend to produce. Differences of opinion still exist, of course; and in controversy a small difference is apt to hide a large underlying agreement, and to be overrated by the public at large. But serious students on opposite sides of an economic controversy are now nearly always in fuller agreement with one another on fundamental

[1] This essay reproduces, with some slight alterations, an article in *The Economic Journal*, March, 1907.

matters than they are with those on their own side whose opinions have been formed without careful study.

Much less progress has indeed been made towards the *quantitative* determination of the relative strength of different economic forces. That higher and more difficult task must wait upon the slow growth of thorough realistic statistics. The new Census of Production may, in the course of time, supply one of the many sets of necessary facts; but it must fight its way gradually over great technical difficulties, increased by the present jealousy of the ordinary business man against the publication of any of his affairs.

2. *There has been a similar but less complete convergence as to social ideals and the ultimate aims of economic effort.*

But I will turn aside from these severe matters to one which is perhaps more suitable to a cheerful occasion, and which has very urgent claims on the consideration of economists at the present time. The ideals and the ultimate aims of all our economic work have been the subject of much eager discussion, but not of much careful, thorough, persistent study. I would like to ask you this evening to consider what it is that such study can do towards helping the world to turn its growing resources to the best account for social well-being.

It is a common saying that we have more reason to be proud of our ways of making wealth than of our ways of using it. Even the working classes buy many things that do them little good and some things that do them harm. And the well-to-do classes expend vast sums on things that add little to their happiness and very little to their higher well-being, but which they regard as necessary for their social position. Few people would assert that a man with fifty thousand a year is likely to have a very much happier life than if he had only a thousand; but to climb from the place in society which belongs to £1000 a year to that which belongs to fifty thousand, is a source of almost ceaseless delight to nearly every pattern of man, and to his wife. This satisfaction is, however, not net social gain: for something must be deducted for the chagrin of some of the many men and their wives who will be passed on the way. Of course, anyone who bears heavy responsibilities, and uses his brain much, needs larger house-room, more quiet, lighter and more digestible food, and perhaps more change of scene and other comforts than will suffice for maintaining the efficiency of unskilled work, and even of artisan work; and, from the higher social point of view, it would be bad economy that such a man should cut his expenditure down below these "necessaries for efficiency" for his responsible work. In addition to this outlay, a good deal is spent upon things that yield solid, unostentatious pleasure of a wholesome kind: and only very austere people could condemn some expenditure of this kind, provided it does not absorb nearly the whole of a moderate income, or any considerable part of a very large income. Allowances must be made for these two classes of expenditure by the well-to-do; and also for the one or two hundred millions of their total income which are turned into capital annually, and thus enable us to make nature work for us as an obedient and efficient servant. But there still remains a vast expenditure which contributes very little towards social progress, and which does not confer any large and solid benefits on the spenders beyond the honour, the position, and the influence which it buys for them in society.

Now there is a general agreement among thoughtful people, and especially among economists, that if society could award this honour, position, and influence by methods less blind and less wasteful; and if it could at the same time maintain all that stimulus which the free enterprise of the strongest business men derives from present conditions, then the resources thus set free would open out to the mass of the people new possibilities of a higher life, and of larger and more varied intellectual and artistic activities.

Opinions are not likely to agree as to the amount of private expenditure which is to be regarded as socially wasteful from this point of view. Some may put it as high as four or even five hundred millions a year. But it is sufficient for the present that there is a margin of at least one or two hundred millions which might be diverted to social uses without causing any great distress to those from whom it was taken; provided their neighbours were in a like position, and not able to make disagreeable remarks on the absence of luxuries and of conventional "necessaries for social propriety" which are of little solid advantage.

3. *The temporary suspension of the pressure of the Law of Diminishing Return from land on the population of this country gives special opportunities for social reform to the present generation, and throws corresponding responsibilities on them.*

Cheap transport by land and sea, combined with the opening up of a large part of the surface of the world during the last thirty years, has caused the purchasing power of wages in terms of goods to rise throughout the Western world, and especially in Britain, at a rate which has no parallel in the past, and may probably have none in the future. The Law of Diminishing Return is almost inoperative in Britain just now, but after a generation or two it may again be a powerful influence here and nearly all over the world. Wages in Britain are now but very little affected by the rate of growth of population and the pressure on the means of subsistence. The restraining forces which prevents their rise from being even faster than it is, is the fact that countries whose large expanse offers very high returns on investments in railways, in building, in developing mines and new agricultural land can outbid British enterprise in the demand for capital. The progress of the arts of production and transport has increased British prosperity fast, in spite of this. But the world is really a very small place, and there is not room in it for the opening up of rich new resources during many decades at as rapid a rate as has prevailed during the last three or four. When new countries begin to need most of their own food and other raw produce, improvements in transport will count for little. From that time onward the pressure of the Law of Diminishing Return can be opposed only by further improvements in production; and improvements in production must themselves gradually show a diminishing return. Great, therefore, as has been the rate of social progress of Britain during the last generation, we may not be contented with it. There is an urgent duty on us to make even more rapid advance during this age of economic grace, for it may run out before the end of the century[1].

---

[1] There are some who hold that, though nature may be niggardly in her return of raw produce, compensation may be found in the more liberal supply, by aid of electricity, of the power that aids man's efforts. But this belief appears to involve a technical misapprehension. Electricity facilitates and cheapens the distribution of power, both in bulk over large distances and in detail to individual machines; and it economises power

4. *Progress is in the long run delayed by exaggeration of the evils inherent in present economic conditions.*

Men of certain types of mind, which are not morbid, delight now, as in previous generations, in vehement indictments of existing social conditions. Their efforts may rouse a passing enthusiasm, which is invigorating while it lasts; but they nearly always divert energies from sober work for the public good, and are thus mischievous in the long run. Let us consider a few figures.

First, it may be noted that the use which is being made of increasing wealth is not, in the main, sordid or selfish. Recent changes in the distribution among different callings of those who are "occupied"—that is, working for profits, salary, or wages— show no great increase in those who supply material comforts and luxuries; but they do show a great increase in those who are working on behalf of Government or on their own account to check disease and mitigate its sufferings, and to develop the intellectual and artistic faculties of the people: the increased output of each worker in occupations which can avail themselves of improved mechanical appliances accounts for a part, but not the whole, of this contrast. Again, if the present age were as selfish as it is often represented to be, we should find that the chief expenditure of public money for improving the conditions of life and work had accrued to the benefit of those who can enforce their will at the polling-booth. But, on the contrary, it has gone chiefly to the benefit of women and children; and meanwhile young people's wages have risen faster than those of women, and those of women have risen faster than those of men. And, again, our age has reversed the old rules that the poor paid a larger percentage of their income in rates and taxes than the well-to-do, and that the Treasury was more generous in

by lessening the amount of it that runs to waste in machines not fully employed. But electricity has done relatively little to economise the use of water power *in situ*. Partly on account of its inconstancy, it is, in general, far less economical than it appears at first sight for almost every purpose; the chief exceptions being in some chemical industries in which work can proceed throughout the twenty-four hours and be curtailed without great loss (since relatively little labour is employed), when the water supply runs low. There is not very much available water power in this country. Tidal power would not pay its expenses, save in a very few estuaries. It may be noted that the price of continuous power supply to large consumers is the same at Newcastle-on-Tyne as at Niagara. Electricity generated by water may enlarge the resources of Italy: but it cannot go far towards maintaining Britain's resources when her coal has become scarce.

providing sinecures for the well-to-do than in lessening the ignorance, the disease, and the sufferings of the poor.

Another exaggeration, arising out of a careless reading of Mr Charles Booth's statistics, states that a third of the people of this country are on the verge of hunger. He estimated that a million people in London are poor in the sense that they belong to families, the aggregate income of which does not exceed 21s. a week all the year round—that is, £54. 12s. annually. Now 21s. is the price of three-quarters of a bushel, or twenty-four pecks, of good wheat; while the average wage of English labour throughout recorded history from the beginning of the Middle Ages till quite recent times was less than six pecks of wheat a week, often mouldy; it never rose for any considerable time beyond nine pecks. I may state that one of the few things which every German knows for certain about England is that there are a million people in London living in extreme poverty on the verge of hunger. But they open their eyes when they learn that under this misleading title are included all members of families with a less aggregate income than twenty-one marks all the year round. For twenty-one marks will buy much less food than 21s. will; and 70 per cent., if not more, of the German working-class families have a less annual income than 1100 marks.

Again, the reasonable dissatisfaction, with which every thoughtful person must regard the existing distribution of wealth, is in danger of being perverted towards ill-considered measures of reform by Utopian schemers; who imply, if they do not explicitly state, that, if wealth were equally divided, everyone would have access to means of comfort, refinement, and even luxury which are far out of the reach of any of the working classes at present. But the fact is that very many prosperous artisans' families, certainly many more than a hundred thousand, already enjoy a larger income than they would if the total of £1,700,000,000, at which the income of the United Kingdom is estimated, were divided out equally among its population of forty-three million—that is to say, they would lose by an equal distribution of income[1].

[1] The statistical position may be looked at in another way. The average annual earnings of the men, women, and children employed in the chief manufacturing industries was estimated by the Board of Trade, as the result of a partial wage census in 1888, to be £48. The returns took insufficient account of the high wages earned by many

These facts are consistent with the belief that a vast increase of happiness and elevation of life might be attained if those forms of expenditure which serve no high purpose could be curtailed, and the resources thus set free could be applied for the welfare of the less prosperous members of the working classes; the whole change being so made as not considerably to slacken the springs of productive energy. But they are not consistent with the common suggestion that by retrenching the lavish expenditure of the rich, and dividing income equally, the whole people would be raised to affluence previously unknown to working men. More's *Utopia* and Morris's *News from Nowhere* stimulate aspiration, and are so beautiful in themselves that they will remain a joy for ever. And they work unmixed good, because they do not profess to be practical. But in recent years we have suffered much from schemes that claim to be practical, and yet are based on no thorough study of economic realities; that lack the subtle beauty of a delicate imagination; and that even propose to tear up by the roots family life, the tree whose fruits and flowers contribute much more than half to the sum total of all that is known of beauty and happiness by the people in general, and especially by the working classes.

5. *Chivalry in war and chivalry in business.*

Our age is, then, not quite as wasteful and harsh as it is sometimes represented. Much more than a half, possibly even three-quarters, of the total income of the nation is devoted to uses which make for happiness and the elevation of life, nearly as efficiently as is possible with our present limited understanding of the arts of life. Even so, there is a large margin for improvement; and yet in one respect we seem to be going on wrong lines. For it is easier to make believe, even to oneself, that one looks down on wealth, than to work with energy in order to make wealth a thing of which the world may be proud. But in fact material resources enter of necessity so much into the thoughts and cares of nearly everybody that, if the world is not

piece-workers; and, though they have been criticized as possibly rather too high in some other respects, we may be sure that the average is now over £50. Therefore a family of average ability and average size, all the members of which are employed in manufacture, has now a considerably higher income than it would have under an equal division of income to all persons, including the very young and the very old.

proud of its wealth, it cannot respect itself. Surely, then, it is worth while to make a great effort to enlist wealth in the service of the true glory of the world. And history seems to suggest a route to this end.

War is more cruel even than competition to oust rivals from their work and living; but there grew up around it a chivalry which brought out the noble, emulative side of war, and even something of the finer sympathies. If in the Elysian fields a mediæval warrior be now discussing with late inhabitants of worlds many billions of miles away from our own the experiences of his old world, he may hold up his head as he speaks of the chivalry of war, the thing that occupied people's imagination most in that age.

In the present age our thoughts are occupied with industrial progress, with the marvellous services which we compel nature to render to us in manufacture and transport. But, if the talk should turn in the Elysian fields on the elevation of life which we have won by the new methods of business, we should not hold up our heads as bravely as would the mediæval knight. I want to suggest that there is much latent chivalry in business life, and that there would be a great deal more of it if we sought it out and honoured it as men honoured the mediæval chivalry of war. If we do this for a generation or two, then people bringing the latest news from this world may talk boldly of the chivalry of wealth: they may be proud of the elevation of life which has been achieved by training the finer elements of human nature to full account in the production of wealth and in its use.

Chivalry in business includes public spirit, as chivalry in war includes unselfish loyalty to the cause of prince, or of country, or of crusade. But it includes also a delight in doing noble and difficult things because they are noble and difficult: as knightly chivalry called on a man to begin by making his own armour, and to use his armour for choice in those contests in which his skill and resource, his courage and endurance, would be put to the severest tests. It includes a scorn for cheap victories, and a delight in succouring those who need a helping hand. It does not disdain the gains to be won on the way, but it has the fine pride of the warrior who esteems the spoils of a well-fought battle, or the prizes of a tournament, mainly for the sake of the

achievements to which they testify, and only in the second
degree for the value at which they are appraised in the money
of the market.

6. *The chief motive to the highest constructive work in industry
is a chivalrous desire to master difficulties and obtain recognized
leadership.*

The commonplace and even the sordid sides of business work
obtrude themselves on our notice. Some men are known to
have become rich by foul means. Many more have prospered
by a steady adherence to affairs, largely of a routine character;
with but little use of the higher imagination, and perhaps with
scarcely any romance in their lives except in their family relations. These two classes of business men come into close
contact with the ordinary observer; and, if he rejoices in the
æsthetic expenditure of wealth which he has inherited probably
from a business ancestor, he is likely to declaim in vigorous but
undiscriminating language against those who greedily pursue
wealth.

But there can be no doubt that at least one-half of the best
ability in the Western world is engaged in business. Unless,
therefore, we are convinced that human nature is irredeemably
sordid, we must expect that there is much nobility to be found in
business; and, if we look for it in the right place, we shall find it.

It has indeed been remarked with increasing frequency by
careful observers during recent years that those business men,
on whose work the progress of industry most depends, care for
wealth more as an indication of successful achievement than for
its own sake. Success in science, in literature, and in art can
be judged directly; and a man engaged in these occupations
seldom cares for money beyond a mere competence, unless he
is rather sordid. He wants to be sure that he has worked well;
and if he earns the laurel wreath of approval of the cultivated
public, he is content. On the other hand, if business men were
arranged in order according to the merits of their proposals as
written down on paper and judged *à priori*, it would be a very
bad order. And for that reason, more than for the money it
brings them, the ablest and best business men value success.
Assuming that a man's career is free from the suspicion of fraud,

malign destruction of rivals, and oppression of employees, success is good *primâ facie* evidence of leadership. It is often the only trustworthy evidence that is available to the public, and can be appreciated by those near to him, whose joy in his success is one of his chief rewards.

Men of this class live in constantly shifting visions, fashioned in their own brains, of various routes to their desired end; of the difficulties which nature will oppose to them on each route, and of the contrivances by which they hope to get the better of her opposition. This imagination gains little credit with the people, because it is not allowed to run riot; its strength is disciplined by a stronger will; and its highest glory is to have attained great ends by means so simple that no one will know, and none but experts will even guess, how a dozen other expedients, each suggesting as much brilliancy to the hasty observer, were set aside in favour of it[1].

7. *The need for enlarging the honour given to the highest constructive business faculty is increased by the growth of bureaucratic rule, which is hostile to it.*

There are many kinds of laboratory experiments which a man can be hired to make at a few hundred pounds a year, but the epoch-making discoveries generally come from men who love their work with a chivalrous love. The true significance of such a man's life is often not recognized till he has passed away, but he is fairly sure that he will be honoured at last. Money is wanted to educate scientific men, to supply them with apparatus, and a moderate income earned without oppressive routine of teaching or other fatigue. But that is all that money can do. That being done, creative science can be evoked only by the force which evokes creative art and creative literature—the force of chivalrous emulation.

A chemist requires only a little space in a laboratory. But

---

[1] The imagination of such a man is employed, like that of the master chess-player, in forecasting the obstacles which may be opposed to the successful issue of his far-reaching projects, and constantly rejecting brilliant suggestions because he has pictured to himself the counter-strokes to them. His strong nervous force is at the opposite extreme of human nature from that nervous irresponsibility which conceives hasty Utopian schemes; and which is rather to be compared to the bold facility of a weak player, who will speedily solve the most difficult chess problem by taking on himself to move the black men as well as the white.

many of the most important experiments of a business man require the whole space, the whole material appliances, and the whole staff of a large business to be at his disposal, and often for many years consecutively. If he is working at his own risk, he can put forth his energies with perfect freedom. But, if he is a servant of a bureaucracy, he cannot be certain of freedom; he may be given a little freedom for a while, and then a change in administration, or impatience at his failure to strike the true path of progress at his first trial, may cause him to be pulled up sharp; and his chains clank, even when they do not press tightly.

Difficulties of this kind are met not only in the industrial undertakings of Governments, but also in very large joint-stock companies, and especially the so-called trusts. The chief owners of the trusts have given, and are giving, an extraordinary amount of thought to devising means whereby the heads of departments and others may be allowed a free hand, and emulation may be brought to bear as a stimulus to their energy and enterprise. Their devices are marvellously ingenious, and among the most instructive episodes in recent economic history, but they have attained only a modicum of success. Experience shows ever more and more that the technical economy to be attained by piling Pelion on Ossa in the agglomeration of vast businesses is nearly always less than was expected, and that the difficulty of the human element ever increases with increasing size. Much can be done by various schemes of reward and promotion as regards junior officials, and even the superior officials are stimulated by congresses and other opportunities for submitting their new ideas to the judgment of brother-experts. But no fairly good substitute has been found, or seems likely to be found, for the bracing fresh air which a strong man with a chivalrous yearning for leadership draws into his lungs when he sets out on a business experiment at his own risk.

8. *Economists generally desire increased intensity of State activity for social ameliorations that are not fully within the range of private effort: but they are opposed to that vast extension of State activities which is desired by Collectivists.*

These considerations point towards the watershed which divides the large majority of economists from "Collectivists"—

i.e., those who would transfer to the State the ownership and management of land, machinery, and all other agents of production. We are told sometimes that everyone who strenuously endeavours to promote the social amelioration of the people is a Socialist—at all events, if he believes that much of this work can be better performed by the State than by individual effort. In this sense nearly every economist of the present generation is a Socialist. In this sense I was a Socialist before I knew anything of economics; and, indeed, it was my desire to know what was practicable in social reform by State and other agencies which led me to read Adam Smith and Mill, Marx and Lassalle, forty years ago. I have since then been steadily growing a more convinced Socialist in this sense of the word; and I have watched with admiration the strenuous and unselfish devotion to social well-being that is shown by many of the able men who are leading the collectivist movement. I do not doubt that the paths, on which they would lead us, might probably be strewn with roses for some distance. But I am convinced that, so soon as collectivist control had spread so far as to narrow considerably the field left for free enterprise, the pressure of bureaucratic methods would impair not only the springs of material wealth, but also many of those higher qualities of human nature, the strengthening of which should be the chief aim of social endeavour.

To those who take this view of the dangers of collectivism, it is sometimes thought sufficient to reply that they still wallow in the mire of *laissez faire*. The phrase is ambiguous, and misleading rhetoric abounds with regard to it. Its original meaning was that gilds and *métiers* should not prohibit people from entering a trade for which they were competent; any one should be at liberty to choose his own work. It was not till much later that the phrase was twisted to mean:—Let Government keep up its police, but in other matters fold its hands and go to sleep.

In Adam Smith's time Government was corrupt, and, though he himself, like all his chief followers, was unselfishly devoted to the well-being of the people, experience had taught him to look with suspicion on those who invited the Government to new enterprises for the public weal: for their real motive was generally to increase their own gains, or to provide easy and well-paid posts for themselves or their relatives. Matters improved but slowly during the next fifty years. But honesty and true philanthropy grew apace during the earnest, if somewhat ungainly, beginning of the Victorian era. And J. S. Mill, one of the first to proclaim boldly that Shelley was greater than Byron, made a memorable attempt to combine many of the essential principles of Socialism with an unswerving devotion to individuality and a hatred to mechanical regulations of life[1].

Mill had seen a vast increase in the probity, the strength, the unselfishness, and the resources of Government during his life; and it seems that each succeeding decade had enlarged the scope of those interventions of Government for the promotion of general well-being which he thought likely to work well. One of the chief causes of this improvement was a change of sentiment which had, perhaps, its chief origin in the Wesleyan Revival, as Lecky has well shown. The movement was promoted by Parliamentary reform; by the spread of education, and by increasing zeal in the Established and Nonconforming Churches; by the cheapening and improvement of literature; by the rise of co-operation, itself largely due to Owen, that noble if weird prophet of Socialism; by the writings of Scott and Dickens, of Wordsworth and Tennyson, of Carlyle and Ruskin, of Newman and Maurice; and by the personal influence of Queen Victoria and of Gladstone, and other public men.

These and similar influences have co-operated with technical progress to enlarge the scope for the beneficial intervention of Government since Mill's death even more than during his long life. Government has now many new large and subtle resources for finding out where it can do more harm than good. Partly through the co-ordination and mutual aid of the forces of central and of local authorities, it has a much increased power of putting into effective operation any decision at which it has arrived. And the people are now able to rule their rulers, and to check class abuse of power and privilege, in a way which was impossible

---

[1] If anyone will read Mill's *Autobiography*, his essays "On Socialism," published in the *Fortnightly Review* for 1879, or even his discussions of progress and of the functions of Government in the last chapters of Books IV and V respectively of his *Political Economy*, and compare them with Carlyle's pamphlet on *Shooting Niagara*, he will see that the popular opinion as to the generosity of Carlyle's temper and the hardness of Mill's is incorrect. He may even perhaps think that it should be inverted.

before the days of general education and a general surplus of energy over that required for earning a living. Thus we can now safely venture on many public undertakings which a little while ago would have been technically unworkable, or which would have probably been perverted to the selfish and corrupt purposes of those who had the ear of Government. But, on the other hand, this very enlargement opens out so many and so arduous new public duties that no Government, not even the German, can nearly catch up the work that is specially its own. Thus a new emphasis is given to the watchword, *Laissez faire*:—Let everyone work with all his might; and most of all let the Government arouse itself to do that work which is vital, and which none but Government can do efficiently.

For instance, public authorities are just beginning to awake to the urgency of their duties with regard to mapping out in advance the ground plans on which cities should expand—a task more vital to the health and happiness of coming generations than any other which can be accomplished by authority with so little trouble, while private effort is powerless for it. So I cry, "*Laissez faire*:—Let the State be up and doing"; let it not imitate those people who have time and energy enough to manage their neighbours' households, while their own is always in disorder.

Again, let the Legislature cease to pass any laws the true meaning of which is avowedly uncertain and must be declared by the courts of law; for such laws hamper constructive enterprise, and give an undue advantage to those who can afford the expense of one or more appeals. Let public authorities provide building laws and bye-laws which, while effective for social purposes, are so well thought out and so elastic that no one is compelled to put up walls much stronger than is necessary for his purposes, in order that the automatic working of general rules, unaided by the use of brains on the part of the authorities, may secure adequate strength for other buildings under different conditions. Such reforms do not require any considerable increase of public budgets. But they require that Government should obtain its fair share of the growing intelligence of the country; that this intelligence should be concentrated intensively on work which none but Government can do, and that it should not be spread out thinly and carelessly on any social service that is needed. It is more necessary now than ever to bear in mind that the State alone can order an adequate inquiry where agents betray their trust, or where fraudulent producers or dealers can outwit the consumer; and that no activities of its own that are not absolutely necessary should be allowed to interfere with its imperative duty to inspect and to arbitrate: for that cannot be discharged by anyone else, except it be the ever-ready writers in newspapers. Further, in the interest of the purity of the public service, it should abstain from putting its officials to work where their probity can receive but little external support, except from a system of checks and counterchecks so elaborate and cumbrous that many clerks are needed where one would suffice in private service. The increase of mechanical office work is one of the chief evils of large businesses, even under the comparatively elastic *régime* of joint-stock companies: and it would be grievously increased if public servants were under ever-increasing temptations in relation to those very matters which evade the courts of justice, and in which public servants alone can act as efficient guardians of business rectitude.

9. *Some illustrations of the anti-social influences likely to result from Governmental enterprise in matters where the private hand is competent for action, and the hand of authority is needed to preserve purity.*

Let us look at some illustrations. The careless treatment of milk is an insidious cause of disease, which public authority has hitherto treated somewhat negligently. That is indeed one sin against the true constructive doctrine:—*Laissez faire*; let the Government arouse itself to do energetically its proper work of educating British farmers up to the Danish standard, if not beyond; and of enforcing sanitary regulations in critical matters such as this. No doubt, under present conditions, it may be right to organize municipal depôts to provide specially pure and appropriate milk for those infants whose mothers cannot give them their natural food. But the function of such depôts is purely educational: they ought soon to make way for enlightened free co-operation under stringent public supervision. But high collectivist authority openly advocates them as the thin end of the wedge for pushing all private producers out of the milk trade; and this seems to be anti-social. For it would close a suitable career to many men who were learning the elementary principles of enterprise in a simple business: and it would increase the glaring disproportion between the work that is required of municipal councils and the number of hours which they could give to it; even if they had nothing else to do:—even if none of their energies were demanded for private businesses of their own, or for conciliating the favour of their constituents against the next election.

The milk supply is a relatively simple affair. But Governmental intrusion into businesses which require ceaseless invention and fertility of resource is a danger to social progress the more to be feared because it is insidious. It is notorious that, though departments of central and municipal government employ many thousands of highly-paid servants in engineering and other progressive industries, very few inventions of any importance are made by them: and nearly all of those few are the work of men, like Sir W. H. Preece, who had been thoroughly trained in free enterprise before they entered Government service. Government creates scarcely anything. If Governmental control had supplanted that of private enterprise a hundred years ago, there is good reason to suppose that our methods of manufacture now would be about as effective as they were fifty years ago, instead of being perhaps four or even six times as efficient as they were then. And in that case, if the population of the country had grown to forty-three million, it is probable that the total real income of the country would be about half what it is now; and that, if divided out equally among all families, it would yield less than the average healthy bricklayer or carpenter now earns. It has been well said that if all the material wealth in the world were destroyed by an earthquake, leaving only the land, knowledge, and food enough to sustain life till the next harvest, mankind would in a generation or two be nearly as prosperous as before; but, if accumulated knowledge were destroyed, while the material wealth remained, several thousand years might be needed to recover lost ground.

And yet while Governments are being thus urged in the name of collectivism to an anti-social destruction of the springs of knowledge, a public engineering venture can often make a brave show. For it annexes the best products of that free enterprise which it is stifling. Its vast resources enable it to buy the most up-to-date plant, and to be for the time at least ahead in this respect of some of the very businesses whose brains it is picking. It calls attention to its accounts, and they show a profit. The ordinary observer neglects the fact that in equity every business of such a form as to be unlikely to make inventions of its own ought to pay a subsidy to those whose ideas it is turning to account. And he neglects the fact that, when a Government undertaking becomes obsolete, its accounts drop silently away. There is, indeed, grave doubt whether those of its undertakings which have no exclusive monopolistic advantage would show a fairly good return on the aggregate capital invested in them, if their accounts were made out on the same complete and rigorous system that is required of private business.

A Government could print a good edition of Shakespeare's works, but it could not get them written. When municipalities boast of their electric lighting and power works, they remind me of the man who boasted of "the genius of my *Hamlet*" when he had but printed a new edition of it. The carcase of municipal electric works belongs to the officials; the genius belongs to free enterprise.

I am not urging that municipalities should avoid all such undertakings without exception. For, indeed, when a large use of rights of way, especially in public streets, is necessary, it is doubtless generally best to retain the ownership, if not also the management, of the inevitable monopoly in public hands. I am only urging that every new extension of Governmental work in branches of production which need ceaseless creation and initiative is to be regarded as *primâ facie* anti-social, because it retards the growth of that knowledge and those ideas which are incomparably the most important form of collective wealth.

10. *Social disaster would probably result from the full development of the collectivist programme, unless the nature of man has first been saturated with economic chivalry.*

I venture to think that the able and high-minded leaders of modern collectivism lay too much stress on the technical superiority of their schemes over those of the earlier Utopian socialists and communists. That superiority is indeed beyond question. The earlier ventures, and some even of the more recent experiments in America, disdained the use of modern machinery in the field and in the workshops. They held aloof from great world markets, and they applied almost primitive methods to satisfy little more than primitive needs. They recognized no private property even in house-room and furniture; they allowed no scope for individuality in taste or in the minor affairs of life; they arranged that everyone should share equally in the joint produce of the labour of all; or, if there was any discrimination, it was only that which, within the limits of a family subduing the prairie, allots the hardest work to the strongest and sturdiest members, and assigns to an ailing daughter or sister the choicest food, and the seat nearest to the window in summer and that nearest to the fire in winter. There was neither the opportunity nor the largeness of insight and foresight needed for a classification of workers according to their faculty, combined with special compensation in shortness of hours or otherwise for those who did specially difficult or specially disagreeable work, and so on.

Modern collectivists claim that their schemes are free from all these narrownesses. With earnest emphasis, though perhaps with insufficient appreciation of the difficulties of the problem, they foreshadow more or less distinctly a finely-woven texture, in which the warp of unified central authority and ideas is crossed by a weft of departmental responsibility and free play in detail. They point to administrations such as that of the Prussian railways, where attempts have been made, on lines which have been worked out more thoroughly by giant businesses in America, to devise opportunity and incitement for free spontaneity on the part of each successive grade of officials down to the lowest. They avow themselves to have a loyal zeal for individuality; and some of them have even followed John Stuart Mill in his passionate cry that occasional solitude is so necessary for the health of man's spirit, that a world from which it was crowded out would be already half dead. In view of this technical contrast between the old and the new, it may seem at first sight that the failures of Socialistic enthusiasts in the past have no lesson of warning against the schemes which now hold the field. But I venture to think that a closer view suggests the contrary.

For many of those Utopias were almost ideally perfect experiments for the purpose of investigating how much economic chivalry there is in the breast of the common man—that is, of the man who is not endowed with the qualities of leadership. And the results proved, I think, conclusively that in the common man jealousy is a more potent force than chivalry. The immediate cause of the failure of those Utopias seldom lay in their technical deficiences. It lay rather in the belief on the part of some of the members that others were doing less than their share of hard and disagreeable work, or were getting insidiously more than their share of the comforts and amenities of life. Those who were dissatisfied could not easily move into a neighbouring business and find their level there; for that would have involved the abandonment of those hopes and ideals which had attracted them to the movement, and for which some of them had made sacrifices. Their discontent had not the wholesome outlet which a freedom of movement affords to most people in the modern world; so it remained under the surface, and festered, till at last the whole society was full of sores, and the end came. This was, in fact, the experience of almost every if not every such scheme, except a few in which an ardent devotion to some particular religious creed, positive or negative, completely dominated their lives and thoughts. In those exceptional societies material comforts counted for little, and personal jealousies could be stilled by the counsel and authority of the leaders whom the ordinary members reverenced as prophets, raised above the ambitions and the temptations of ordinary life.

In Germany the dominion of bureaucracy has combined with other causes to develop a bitter class hatred, and occasionally to make social order depend on the willingness of soldiers to fire on citizens; and the case is, of course, much worse in the even more bureaucratic Russia. But under collectivism there would be no appeal from the all-pervading bureaucratic discipline. A man would often think himself unfairly treated: he would believe that others were contributing less to the common fund than he was, and were, through favouritism or even corruption, drawing more from it; and such a man would, if possible, flee to a country where free enterprise still flourished. But if there were no such haven, his disquiet would grow; obedience to authority would be given unwillingly; and, if the discontented were to be kept to their work by force, the resulting tyranny would need to surpass all previous records in minuteness of detail and in the destruction of everything that makes life worth living.

I submit, therefore, that, if collectivism is to work even fairly well, there must be ample provision for enabling anyone who thinks his lot unduly hard to find relief in some way that has not as yet been discovered. It is true that ingenious suggestions have been made for automatically regulating the work and pay in different occupations under a collectivist *régime*: but they are not likely to approve themselves to anyone who has followed closely the working of co-operative and competitive businesses.

Let us, however, suppose, for the sake of argument, that some workable scheme to this end could be devised. Even then we should need to face the difficulty already suggested that those improvements in method and in appliances, by which man's power over nature has been acquired in the past, are not likely to continue with even moderate vigour if free enterprise be stopped, before the human race has been brought up to a much higher general level of economic chivalry than has ever yet been attained. The world under free enterprise will fall far short of the finest ideals until economic chivalry is developed. But until it is developed, every great step in the direction of collectivism is a grave menace to the maintenance even of our present moderate rate of progress.

11. *Social possibilities of economic chivalry on the part of individuals and the community as a whole under existing institutions.*

To conclude:—There is much more economic chivalry in the world than appears at first sight. The most important and progressive business work is scarcely ever without a large chivalrous element, and is often mainly dominated by chivalrous motives. But there is also much getting of wealth that is not chivalrous, and much expenditure that has no touch of nobility. To distinguish that which is chivalrous and noble from that which is not, is a task that needs care and thought and labour;

and to perform that task is a first duty for economists sitting at the feet of business men, and learning from them. An endeavour should be made so to guide public opinion that it becomes an informal Court of Honour. Then wealth, however large, would be no passport to social success if got by chicanery, by manufactured news, by fraudulent dealing, or by malignant destruction of rivals: and that business enterprise which was noble in its aims and in its methods, even if it did not bring with it a large fortune, would receive its due of public admiration and gratitude; as the work of the progressive student of science, or literature, or art does now.

The discriminating favour of the multitude at Athens and at Florence gave the strongest stimulus to imaginative art. And if coming generations were to search out and honour that which is truly creative and chivalric in modern business work, the world would grow rapidly in material wealth and in wealth of character. Noble efforts would be evoked; and even dull men would gradually cease to pay homage to wealth *per se* without inquiring how it had been acquired. Wealth-getting by sordid means would not win its way in society, nor in popular favour; and no political committee, however devoid of high sentiment, would be shortsighted enough to follow a recent example in choosing a candidate who had been proved judicially to owe much of his wealth to base means. Sordid practices would then prevent wealth from yielding that social *éclat* for which sordid men chiefly prize it, and would go out of favour with men of ability and common sense, however devoid of high principle.

The chivalry which has made many administrators in India, Egypt, and elsewhere, devote themselves to the interests of the peoples under their rule is an instance of the way in which British unconventional, elastic methods of administration give scope for free, fine enterprise in the service of the State; and it atones for many shortcomings in forethought and organization. Again, because the dead hand of bureaucracy has stretched but a little way into her affairs, this country is able to call together voluntary committees of men trained in strenuous private enterprise, who freely give good general guidance in some large matters, such as London transport systems and army administration; and this, again, is a form of chivalry in work which has great potentialities for good, and which it is the business of economists and others to study and to praise.

Gradually, it may be hoped, public opinion may be worked up to the point at which a rich man who lives idly will be despised. The increasing strenuousness of life which shows itself in sport may find an ever-increasing vent in solid work for the public weal. As President Eliot suggests, rich men might be led to give themselves specially to tasks which required high faculties and responsible characters, but for which it is not easy to allot large salaries: they might, for instance, take work where an impecunious person, finding large streams of money passing through his hands, might be subject to temptations from which they would be free; and they might set themselves to public tasks which would prepare the way for progress in the future, but would not yield sufficient immediate fruit to secure liberal endowment from a democracy[1].

Thus chivalry in work would run into chivalry in using wealth. Expenditure for the sake of display, however disguised by an æsthetic atmosphere, would be thought vulgar. He who devoted his energies to buying good pictures, especially by artists not yet known to fame, and gave them to the public at his death, if not before, would have reaped a good return from his wealth; and so would he who made his park beautiful, opened it to the public, and perhaps arranged for easy transport to it from neighbouring industrial districts.

Economic chivalry on the part of the individual would stimulate and be stimulated by a similar chivalry on the part of the community as a whole. The two together might soon provide the one or two hundred million a year that appear to be available, without great pressure on the well-to-do, towards bringing the chief benefits which can be derived from our new command over nature within the reach of all.

Equipped with such funds, the State could so care for the amenities of life outside of the house that fresh air and variety of colour and of scene might await the citizen and his children very soon after they start on a holiday walk. Everyone in health and

---

[1] *Great Riches*, 1906. Compare another recent memorable utterance from Harvard University—Professor Taussig's address to the American Economic Association, Dec. 1905, on "The Love of Wealth and the Public Service."

strength can order his house well; the State alone can bring the beauties of nature and art within the reach of the ordinary citizen. But the chivalrous rich man could aid municipalities in such vastly expensive schemes as that of Miss Octavia Hill for gradually opening out several broad bands of verdure at different distances in and about every large town, and for connecting them by transverse avenues along which working men and their wives might stroll, while the children played around them, to a recreation ground. Again, he might help towards removing the reproach that the exceptional natural advantages which London derives from her great river with its high banks cannot be seen by the eye, but only by the imagination. These and similar calls would attract much of his resources while he was alive, and most of his means would go to public uses at his death. For the growing opinion that it is an ignoble use of wealth to leave large fortunes mainly to relations is reinforcing the perception by the rich that the inheritance of great wealth is seldom an unmixed good. Strong men are getting more and more to recognize that a deep full character is the only true source of happiness, and that it is very seldom formed without the pains of some self-compulsion and some self-repression. Those who from childhood upwards have been able to gratify every whim are apt to be poor in spirit.

The rich man would further co-operate with the State, even more strenuously than he does now, in relieving the suffering of those who are weak and ailing through no fault of their own, and to whom a shilling may yield more real benefit than he could get from spending many additional pounds. He would contribute towards the costly organization needed for helping and compelling those who, through weakness or vice, have lost their self-respect, either to reform their own lives, or, at all events, to cease to drag their children down with them. He would, by increased voluntary service, aid the State to abandon the unworthy plea that even a rough discrimination between the just and unjust is so difficult and would require so large an outlay that the same measure must be meted out to all who, in old age or before it, are in urgent need of assistance. Under such conditions the people generally would be so well nurtured and so truly educated that the land would be pleasant to live in.

Wages in it would be high by the hour, but labour would not be dear. Capital would therefore not be very anxious to emigrate from it, even if rather heavy taxes were put on it for public ends: the wealthy would love to live in it; and thus true Socialism, based on chivalry, would rise above the fear that no country can move faster than others lest it should be bereft of capital. National Socialism of this sort might be full of individuality and elasticity. There would be no need for those iron bonds of mechanical symmetry which Marx postulated as necessary for his "International" projects.

If we can educate this chivalry, the country will flourish under private enterprise. Or, should collectivists succeed in showing that human nature had at last been so firmly based in chivalry that their great venture might be tried without running violent risks, some other civilization than that which we can now conceive may take the place of that which now exists. It may, of course, be higher. But those who believe that all the commerce of the world will ere long be carried through the air should make a few aeroplanes carry heavy cargoes against the wind before they invite us to blow up our railway bridges. For similar reasons it seems best that the difficulties of collectivism should be studied much more carefully, before the scope for creative enterprise is further narrowed by needlessly intruding collective administration into industries in which incessant free initiative is needed for progress.

Thus the end before us is a great one. It calls for steady, searching analysis, and for a laborious study of actual conditions. Economists cannot do it alone. Perhaps it may be found that their share in it will not be large, but I myself believe it will be very large. I submit, then, that a most pressing immediate call on us is to associate in our own minds and those of others economic studies and chivalrous effort.

XVIII

THE EQUITABLE DISTRIBUTION OF TAXATION (1917)[1]

UNTIL recently "equity" was thought an adequate guide in the philosophy of taxation: and it was generally considered equitable that every one should contribute "on the joint-stock plan" to the expenses of the State in proportion to the income (or, as was sometimes said, the property) which he enjoyed under it. But further consideration showed that, while a joint-stock company has no responsibility for the number of shares which each individual holds in it, the duty of the State is of larger scope. For equity proceeds on the basis of existing rights, as generally recognized. A joint-stock company must accept them as final: but the State is under obligation to inquire which of them are based on convention or accident rather than funda-mental moral principle; and to use its powers for promoting such economic and social adjustments as will make for the well-being of the people at large. A chief place among those powers is held by its control of the distribution of the burden of taxation. The notion that this distribution should be governed by mere equity was long dominant: but now it is seen that the problem is one of constructive ethics; though, of course, on its technical side, it calls for careful economic and political thought.

This new notion is indeed largely based on observations which were certainly made two thousand years ago, and probably much earlier, that the happiness of the rich does not exceed that of the poor nearly in proportion to the difference in their com-mands of material wealth. Sages have indeed frequently asserted that happiness is a product of healthy activity, family affection, and content; and that it is as often to be found in the cottage as in the mansion.

But yet a lack of the necessaries of life causes positive suffering, which transcends in a way the lack of happiness; and therefore taxes, which trench on the necessaries of life at the command of any stratum of sober, hard-working people, call for special justification.

[1] This essay formed part of an article contributed to *After-War Problems*, 1917, edited by Mr W. H. Dawson.

Again, though the upper strata of society do not enjoy an excess of happiness over the lower strata at all proportionate to their superiority in incomes, yet almost every one derives considerable pleasure from an increase of his income, and suffers annoyance from its diminution. For the increase gratifies, and the diminution disappoints, the hope of some enjoyment or of some ambition which is near in sight. With an increase the man feels himself rising in that social stratum to which he is accustomed: the stratum which knows him, and which he knows; the stratum whose wants and thoughts and aspirations are kindred to his own. A clerk is made proud and happy when he can move from a working-class quarter to one in which untidy clothes are not seen; but he does not fret at being unable to move into a fashionable quarter: he is grieved if unable to take his family to the seaside for their wonted two or three weeks; but he does not greatly repine at being unable to travel round the world.

These considerations point to the conclusion that, while antisocial excess in the consumption of alcohol by any class is rightly subject to heavy taxation, those who apply practically the whole of a small family income to good uses should make little or no *net* contribution to the Revenue. It will not be advisable, or even possible, to exempt from taxation all the things consumed by them: but the greater part of what they contribute directly to the Exchequer should be returned to them indirectly by generous expenditure from public funds, imperial and local, for their benefit. The ever-growing outlay on popular education, old age pensions, insurance, etc., is an expression of the public conscience needed to palliate extreme inequalities of wealth: while enabling even the poorest class of genuine workers to remain full, free citizens, with a direct interest in public finance.

Even if it be true that as much personal hurt is caused by taking £1000 from an income of £10,000 as by taking £20 from an income of £200, yet the hurt caused by obtaining £1000 of additional Revenue by means of levies of £20 from each of fifty incomes of £200 is unquestionably far greater than that caused by taking it from a single income of £10,000. But invalid inferences are likely to be drawn from this fact, unless account is taken of the extent to which excessive taxes on capital react indirectly on the people at large. While special provision is made for those whose incomes fall short of the necessaries of life and vigour, every one else must bear a considerable share of the national burdens. But the shares should be graduated steeply: and this can be effected only by a large use of taxes on income and property: no close approach towards it has been attained by taxes on particular commodities. For, indeed, many such taxes press with the heaviest weight on the poorest classes, and with no great weight on the rich; while those of them, which fall chiefly on the rich, have never been made to yield a very large amount of revenue.

In earlier times nearly the whole of most people's incomes was derived from operations known to their neighbours, and a large understatement of income was not likely to escape detection. But modern methods of investment and other causes had made it almost impossible to detect fraudulent understatements, until the plan, now familiar, was adopted of taxing at the source all British corporate incomes; while incomes from Stock exchange securities issued abroad are now in effect brought under the same discipline by aid of the agencies of the money market. This has enabled the Inland Revenue officials to give most of their attention to the intricacies of small private businesses, a task in which their methods have greatly improved. Thus the percentage of income demanded by the tax rose long ago much above that which it had originally been thought possible to charge with tolerable safety, unless during the emergency of a war; and yet the evasions are believed to have become relatively small. This plan, however, increases the difficulties of direct graduation of the burden of the tax: so recourse is now had to the indirect method of allowing certain abatements to be made from small incomes before they are assessed to the tax.

In order to carry the graduation above the limit at which no abatement was made a Super-tax was introduced in 1909, surcharging all very large incomes. The collection of that tax derives little aid from the practice of charging at the source; but, as the number of incomes which come under it is small, the officials can give a good deal of time to each of them. The great increases in the income-tax and Super-tax levied during the war, together with the Excess-profits-tax, while throwing no direct light on the probable course of taxation after the war, suggest a hope that the various advances towards graduation made before it will be sustained and developed after it. In so far as the graduation is effected by abatements, people have a direct interest in submitting statements of their incomes in detail to the income-tax officials: and in this way graduation tends to promote the accuracy of income-tax returns and to diminish evasions.

The exceptional power of adjustment to special conditions possessed by the income-tax extends some way in the direction of taking account of the fact that two persons with equal incomes may have to bear very unequal burdens. Thus insurance premiums are deducted, subject to certain conditions, from income before taxation: and some further deductions, which might advantageously be enlarged, are made on account of young children. There is much to be said for the present plan of regarding the incomes of husband and wife as a single unit for taxation: but the charge levied on that unit should be less than if it had to support only one person.

This inequality between the burdens of taxation on two persons with equal incomes, but unequal responsibilities, extends below the income-tax paying class; but it is only in that class that a direct remedy is in sight. Among the working classes especially an unmarried man is likely to consume highly taxed alcohol and tobacco in greater quantities than a married man with an equal income; but in regard to most taxed commodities the married man's expenditure is likely to be the larger. It is true that the married operative is likely to derive more aid than the unmarried from public expenditures on health insurance and on schools: but, though the education given by the subsidized schools is as good as that afforded by some relatively expensive private schools, even the lower middle classes are induced by convention to hold aloof from them in this country.

If it were possible to exempt from the income-tax that part of income which is saved, to become the source of future capital, while leaving property to be taxed on inheritance and in some other ways, then an income-tax graduated with reference to its amount, and the number of people who depended for their support on each income, would become a graduated tax on all personal expenditure. Rich and poor alike would be left to select those uses of their incomes which suited them best, without interference from the State; except in so far as any particular form of expenditure might be thought specially beneficial, or specially detrimental, to public interests. The income-tax would levy the same percentage on the rich man's expenditure on coarse tea and on fine tea, on bread and on expensive food; and a higher percentage on each than on the poor man's expenditure on anything, unless it be alcohol and tobacco[1]. The way to this ideal perfection is difficult; but it is more clearly marked than in regard to most Utopian goals.

In pursuing this way, a watchful eye would need to be kept on the danger that excessive taxes on large incomes may check energy and enterprise. It is true that a man of high genius and originating faculty often values his gains less for their own sake, than for the evidence which they afford to himself and others of eminent power. His energy would not be much affected by a tax which lowered his share, provided it did not put him at a disadvantage relatively to others. The zeal of a yachtsman in a race is not lessened when an unfavourable tide retards the progress of all; and the business man of high faculty might not be made much less eager for success by taxation, which took from him and his compeers a considerable portion of their gains. But the average man desires wealth almost exclusively for its own sake; though some little introspection might suggest to him that what he really cares for is an increase in wealth relatively to his neighbours: and thus the problems of a steeply graduated income-tax run into those of graduated taxes on capital.

Heavy taxes on capital, of course, tend to check its growth, and to accelerate its emigration. It is to Britain's credit that she has been able to export a great deal of it before the war: but, if her factories had been equipped with as generous a supply of

---

[1] The "expenditure" which is contrasted with saving is, of course, expenditure for immediate personal consumption on commodities and services of all kinds; for that part of an income which is "saved" is spent, if not by the person who saves, yet by those to whom he hands over its use in return for promised income. Thus all is spent: but that part, which is spent for personal consumption, disappears soon after it is taxed; and that part which is turned into income-yielding capital, is taxed again fully in the long run. Suppose a tax of, say, a shilling in the pound is levied permanently on every income, and £1000 saved yields, say, 4 per cent. permanently: then that £40 of annual income will yield permanently £2 as tax: and the present value of that permanent yield will be £50—the exact amount of a tax of a shilling in the pound levied on the £1000.

machinery as those of America, her industries would probably have been more productive than they were; and, if she is to hold her place in the van of industry after the war, she will need much new capital for her own use. Her natural resources, except in coal and a favourable coastline, are small; and a chief cause of the superiority of the wages of her workpeople over those in other countries of Europe has been the fact that her businesses could obtain the necessary supply of capital at lower charges than anywhere else. Therefore taxes on capital must be handled with caution. Ethical considerations and those of high policy alike make for the preservation of the capital that is needed to sustain the strength of a country in peace and when assailed by hostile aggression.

So far as the rights of property have a "natural" and "indefeasible" basis, the first place is to be attached to that property which any one has made or honestly acquired by his own labour. But the right thus earned does not automatically pass to his heirs: the tardy development of steeply graduated duties on inheritance (or "Death Duties") has approved itself increasingly to the ethical conscience and to the practical counsels of administration: and this in spite of the fact that such taxes are generally paid out of capital, for the heir seldom sets apart a sinking fund out of his income. There are considerable evasions, some technically valid, and others not; but they are said to be less than had been anticipated. The annoyance which a man feels on reflecting that his heirs will inherit somewhat less than he has owned does not seem to affect conduct much; and perhaps some part of the Revenue needed after the war, in excess of that before it, may be safely got by a moderate increase of these duties.

XIX

RETAIL PRICES[1]

A RETAIL dealer when once he has established a good connection has always had a partial and limited local monopoly. If he has used it ill, he has lost it sooner or later. But, so long as he has retained it, he has not been under the necessity of adjusting his charge for each particular service to the cost of that service. His prices may be arbitrary to an extent that is impossible in the case of middlemen or ordinary producers who supply business customers. For a business customer will scrutinize the charge for each individual thing; and, if that charge is above its true cost, he will find some one prepared to supply it at its true cost: if he fails to do this, he is likely to fail in business altogether; since a small percentage on the things which he buys may affect his net profits by a large percentage. But the private consumer has often better things to do with his time than to give it to discovering the cheapest market for each class of purchases; and, not being a good judge of quality, his judgment is often mistaken when he does try. The retailer, knowing this, is apt to adapt his charges not to the cost of the services rendered, but to what the consumer will bear: he is apt to charge highly in those branches of his business in which his clientèle cannot form a good judgment for themselves or are unlikely to trouble themselves to buy in the cheapest market.

For instance the customer seldom knows when the wholesale price of a thing has fallen, and will probably expect to be supplied at his old price; so the retailer, unless for some special reason, is slow to follow a fall in wholesale prices. There may indeed be a special reason to the contrary. He may seize the opportunity of using that commodity as a decoy to attract customers: he may put down its price so low that it no longer pays its share of the general expenses of his establishment, and advertise the price prominently. Or some rival may have done just that and compelled him to follow suit. Sooner or later something of this kind is certain to happen. The longer retailers generally

---

[1] From an unpublished undated MS.

have delayed to follow a fall in wholesale prices, the more striking is the effect which an ambitious firm can attain by prominent offers of large quantities of the commodity at a very low price: and for a long time to come the remaining retailers may find themselves partly crowded out. The fear then that a long delay to lower the price may be disastrous to them partly overcomes their unwillingness to move, even before the general public has learnt that they ought to move. But the unwillingness is strong; the gain to be got by selling at the old price to contented customers is clear; the danger may not seem pressing; the wholesale price may perhaps rise again and a hasty movement may need to be soon retraced. Again, every change is an evil in itself: it does not press only on old-fashioned tradesmen; but is sometimes specially troublesome to progressive retailers, who bring out expensive priced catalogues at intervals, and encourage customers to send orders in writing which can be filled up with great economy of labour in the warehouse without touching the open shop. When therefore the retailer thinks it no longer safe to ignore a fall in wholesale price, he often prefers giving a rather better quality at the old price, to formally lowering his price. He thus pleases his customers, does not bruit about the fact that wholesale prices have fallen, does not disturb his price list; and yet he puts as great a difficulty in the way of a rival, aiming a sensational stroke, as if he had lowered his price.

Lastly the retailer's working expenses are not affected by wholesale price. If that falls by say a quarter, he has made the full corresponding reduction in retail price when he has deducted a quarter of the old wholesale price, a quarter of the insurance against risk that the commodity would depreciate before sale, and rather less than a quarter of his own net profits. Hence the retail price cannot be expected to fall in the same ratio as the wholesale price, unless there has been meanwhile a reduction in the proportion which the retailer's working expenses bear to his turnover. And, though such a reduction may be in progress and in fact has been in constant progress for many years, it would not except by accident make a perceptible advance during a rapid fluctuation of wholesale prices. These seem to be the chief causes of the well-known fact that retail prices seldom fluctuate downwards as far and as fast as the corresponding wholesale prices.

Retail prices are rather quicker to follow upward than downward movements of wholesale prices for several reasons. When, as often happens, there is an understanding among retailers in the same trade as to prices, a rise in the wholesale market is more likely than a fall to stimulate prompt common action; and trade etiquette is apt to condemn as aggressive the action of a retailer who refuses to go with the others, on the ground that he has laid in a large stock before the rise in price. And even where there is no such understanding, the retailer stands to gain something in hand by promptly following a rise, just as he does by delaying to follow a fall.

But on the other hand the customer who is jolted out of his habit, finding the price raised against him, is apt to be set on the inquiry whether he cannot do better elsewhere. So the retailer prefers keeping the price nominally fixed, but supplying a rather inferior quality. And as in the case of falling prices a temporary change, which may need soon to be reversed, is inconvenient; and in any case the rise in retail price corresponding to a rise in wholesale price ought not to be in equal proportion, because working expenses are not affected by the change.

Thus then a fall in wholesale prices tends to raise, a rise in wholesale prices tends to lower, the qualities of the goods retailed under the same name. The real retail price, that is the price account being taken of quality, falls a good deal more slowly than the wholesale price; and it rises rather more slowly. Fluctuations of the nominal price are smaller and slower than those of real retail price, which again are smaller and slower than those of wholesale price. When, as before 1873, prices were generally rising, adulteration was rampant in almost all classes of goods. The following period of almost steadily falling prices saw a general dwindling of the area covered by adulteration. About 1873 "woollen" goods were largely made of cotton: twenty years later cotton was seldom found except in fabrics where it served some useful purpose; or again, in fancy dress materials, the fashion for which had extended downwards to strata which demanded cheap stuffs for occasional wear during the short life of the fashion. Of course there are numerous exceptions: the progress of chemical and mechanical science is always bringing cheaper substitutes, which are more taking or will really answer the purchasers' purposes better than the earlier substitutes: and they will make their way in spite of a fall in the price of the genuine commodity. But this does not impair the truth of the broad proposition that a rise in price increases and a fall in price diminishes the inclination of retailers to offer inferior goods to their customers, rather than to tempt them with better goods than they have bought before.

It stands to reason that retail prices follow wholesale prices the less closely the larger the elements of partial monopoly and of expenses of working that enter into them; and therefore, other things being equal, the smaller the quantities in which they are retailed. The retail price of milk scarcely fluctuates at all: a fall of fifty per cent. in the price of tea is not likely to be reflected in the charge made for a cup of afternoon tea at a fashionable hotel. Railway companies, the largest of retail dealers, do not revise their list of passenger fares to meet a fluctuation in the price of coal; unless they had nearly decided on that course on other grounds, and the rise in the price of coal serves to pre-cipitate their action, as a heavy shower of rain may bring down a rock that is already almost on the move.

Again in commodities such as beer and tobacco, which are sold by the quart or ounce for a few pence, a small variation in nominal price is not possible. So small alterations in wholesale price (or in cost, for the retailer is often an agent of the producer), including those due to taxation, work themselves out in changes of quality, unless it happens that a change in nominal price had already been impending. Things which are not sold by measure, but by name, are altered quickly in quantity; and, since selling by name is the rule in backward districts, retail prices in them are often astonishingly sensitive[1].

Further, there must always be a good many movements of retail price which stand in no relation to changes in the wholesale trade, or are even in opposite directions. They are like snow flakes which rise as they fly past a house in a strong wind, not because gravitation is in abeyance, but because it is overborne

---

[1] For instance, in 1878, when the taxes on salt were readjusted throughout India, being raised in the southern half and lowered in the northern, it was expected by many that the rule of custom and the smallness of retail purchases would prevent the raiyat from feeling the change for a long time to come. But the result was opposite. Salt was retailed by the pinch. And from the day when the new rule came into operation, the pinch was increased in size in the northern, and diminished in the southern half.

by the force of wind eddies. Thus, when fashion changes, average retail prices of dress stuffs may fall while wholesale prices are rising; because in the former goods that are going out preponderate and in the latter goods that are coming in. When a harvest of high quality is followed by one in which much of the grain was spoilt, old flour will be worth more than new; and retailers may be raising the prices of their remaining stocks, while wholesale prices show a decline. Again, an individual retailer may move the price of a certain commodity apparently at random, when he or a neighbouring rival begins or ceases to make it a catch article; or when the stock he has laid in turns out to be in bad condition and must be cleared out at a sacrifice; and so on. But all cases of this kind put together cover a very small part of the transactions of life: and, it would not have been worth while to call attention to them at all, were it not that they have furnished sensational material to writers who have argued that retail prices generally are arbitrary and scarcely at all subject to economic law.

XX

FRAGMENTS

I think a young man's autobiography has seldom much interest: but observations by old men on the response of their own phases to changes in the prevailing phases of political and social ideas and sentiments during half a century or more have interested me: and, if time and strength favour, I should like to leave behind me some general notes as to my mental and socio-ethical experiences. But I think time and strength will *not* serve for this. (1921.)

In the years of my apprenticeship to economic studies, between 1867 and 1875, I endeavoured to learn enough of the methods of operation of the greater part of the leading industries of the country, to be able to reconstruct mentally the vital parts of the chief machines used in each, neglecting, of course, all refinements and secondary complications. This endeavour was associated with an attempt to form a rough estimate of the faculties and training needed for working each, and the strain involved therein: and, my guide—if, as generally happened he was the employer or a foreman—would generally answer my inquiries as to the wages which each was receiving. After continuing on this course for some years, I began to ask my guide to allow me to guess the wages. My error did not very often exceed two shillings a week on one side or the other: but, when it did, I stopped and asked for an explanation. Sometimes my mistake was due to the fact that the work was easier or more difficult than it appeared to me: sometimes to the fact that the demand for the work was largely seasonal, or liable to variations due to fashion and other causes: sometimes that a high grade operative was being set to rather low grade work, because his proper work was not on hand just then, and was of course being paid the wages of his proper work: sometimes that the work was a blind alley, rather low grade and not leading up to higher work; and so on. These explanations were specially conclusive when I inquired why men were doing work which seemed within the range of women. In almost every such case, it was shown that the work was more difficult, or required more strength or more prompt resource and judgment, than appeared on the surface: or that it extended on occasion into hours that were forbidden to women by law; or—and this was no uncommon occurrence in those industries in which the large majority of the operatives were women—that a man was being paid more highly than a woman would be for the same work, because he seemed to develop the qualities required of a foreman, and the business required a larger number of such men than could find employment in it without some such special arrangements.

A little before 1891 St John's had organized a splendid $\frac{1}{2}d$. post with three times the conveniences, from the 'Varsity man's point of view, of the $1d$. Royal Post. It more than paid its way, though its stamps could only be bought by Johnians. I recollect that, when it was quashed, I was set on the inquiry as to Consumers' Surplus and that I made much use of its experiences. I also went into the dependence of a cheap local parcels delivery on the right to carry local letters: taking account of the fact that it costs as much to send a book from here to Selwyn Gardens or Christ's as to California or Japan. On such bases I guessed the percentage which Consumers' Surplus was of total receipts under a free system; while postal statistics gave me a basis for aggregates. But I have forgotten details and life is short.

Cournot's work is now easily accessible, mainly through the good efforts of Professor Fisher; and anyone who reads it can imagine the influence which it would exert on a young man, accustomed to think in Mathematics more readily than in English, and bewildered on his sudden entry into the strange land of economics, where many of the cardinal doctrines seemed to be mathematical propositions overlaid by the complex relations of real life; and at the same time distorted and stunted because the older economists had not recognized the mathematical conceptions that were latent in their own. I have long ago forgotten Cournot; and I may be wrong. But my impression is that I did not derive so much of the substance of my opinions from him as from von Thünen. Cournot was a gymnastic master who directed the form of my thought. Von Thünen was a *bonâ fide* mathematician, but of less power: his blunder as to the natural wage is not of the same order as Cournot's little slips. But, to make up, he was a careful experimenter and student of facts and with a mind at least as fully developed on the inductive as on the deductive side. Above all he was an ardent philanthropist. And I had come into economics out of ethics, intending to stay there only a short while; and to go back, as soon as I was in a position to speak with my enemies in the gate, that is, with those men of affairs who dashed cold water on my youthful schemes for regenerating the world by saying "Ah! you would not talk in that way, if you knew anything about business, or even Political Economy." And I loved von Thünen above all my other masters. Professor Fisher has cared for Cournot. I would that someone would care for von Thünen. He should not, I think, be translated: but an abstract of his work should be given, with translations of a good deal of his second volume.

Prediction in economics must be hypothetical. Show an interrupted game at chess to an expert and he will be bold indeed if he prophesies its future stages. If either side make one move ever so little different from what he has expected, all the following moves will be altered; and after two or three moves more the whole face of the game will have become different. (1922.)

Defoe tells us that an Englishman found salt carried on the Volga in clumsy boats, and proposed an improved plan to the Grand Duke of Moscow. He listened carefully and then said: "'Tis well for you that you are not one of my subjects; do you come hither to set up projects to starve my people? Get you gone forthwith out of my dominions upon pain of death. You would perform that work with eighteen men, on which now one hundred and twenty are employed and get their bread by. What must the hundred and two men do that are to be turned out of their business? Must they perish and be starved for want of employment? Get you gone." In this venerable and malignant fallacy there is a grain of truth: and, partly for that reason, it is quite alive now, though it has been slain a thousand times. What then follows? Only that such doctrines must be slain ten thousand times. For this it is necessary to go into the market place, to study the people, to enter into their ways of thought. It is necessary to watch every twist and turn of agile and seductive but generally honest writers, such as the authors of *Merrie England* and *Coin's Financial School*; and to meet them before the people, so that the people will see what is done; and to slay the old fallacies again and yet again before their eyes.

Railways afford a striking instance of the common rule that the goods made for the few are often produced by cheap machinery and makeshift appliances fitted up for a short occasion and slight wear; but that there is no expense to which it is not worth while to go in preparing the most complex, delicate, durable and efficient machinery for producing things that will be consumed by the great mass of the people. The cheapest things are the cheapest largely because it has been worth while to produce them by the most expensive machinery. The cheapest railway fares and freights are on lines on which there is so incessant a rolling of wheels that the permanent way and all its appliances can profitably be constructed almost regardless of cost and with a sole view to strength and efficiency. And, on the other hand, the highest charges are those of railways made on the cheapest possible manner through sparsely peopled districts. Such railways generally pay very little for their land, and economize in every direction; but they carry so few units of traffic that the total cost per unit is often higher even than the high charge made for it.

Competition is a monster now grown of overwhelming strength. If we were perfectly virtuous, he would now feel himself out of place and slink away. As it is, if we resist him by violence, his convulsions will reduce society to anarchy. But, if he can be guided so as to work on our side, then even the removal of poverty will not be too great a task.

Combination as to production, and to a minor extent as to trading, is itself the source of economies which cannot be obtained without it. There are drawbacks, of course, as regards energy and freedom and elasticity, some of which affect the combines and some the public. But there is generally a kernel of solid gain (not necessarily *net* gain) which arises from natural causes and which could not be reached by any improvement in moral attitude.

Combinations as to employment, on the other hand, bring in no economies that could not be obtained by an improvement in moral attitude: and they necessarily involve waste.

At the same time the evils against which they are directed are *some of them* so vital that, so long as the moral improvement route is not practicable, the combination route may be worth, and indeed is worth, what it costs in many cases: and, in some cases, more.

There are a few narrow occupations in which blind people can earn in full self-respect a moderate living: if people whose eyesight gives them a larger choice moved into these occupations, the harm done to the blind would outweigh socially any slight gain that consumers might get from the cheapening of the products of those occupations; and any subsidizing of such a movement would be distinctly anti-social. Now it may be asserted that the lower grade industries generally, and especially what are called the "sweated industries," offer the only refuge for those who, being weak in body or character or both, desire to live an independent life: and that, when women belonging to well-to-do or artisan families do work at home or elsewhere for such industries, the injury which they do to the poor and weak producers outweighs the benefit which they render to consumers, as well as their own pecuniary gains. Such an argument needs to be carefully constructed. There is a danger that a few sensational cases of hardship may be multiplied by iterated reports, and loom much larger than they should: and therefore every item in the argument should be set out in quantity and not merely in quality. When that has been done, when the best figures to be had, whether based on actual enumeration or largely conjectural, have been analysed and criticized and rectified, it may conceivably be found that the intrusion of well-to-do people into low grade industries is on a sufficient scale to alter materially the relations of supply to the demand for labour of that grade, and to depress its wages. But the chance that this result will emerge appears at present very small, and it may be provisionally neglected.

If an industry is temporarily depressed, an accident that gives it some employment may do good, even though it is in itself an evil: *e.g.* if part of a sea-wall is washed down at a place where some huge failures (probably due to over-confident enterprise) have caused much idleness, the result may be a net social good. For those who are set on it will consume things that otherwise might have been consumed by the rate- or tax-payers: and that is in itself no harm. And they will help to put into gear the local trade and industry. But that merely shows that, when a machine is out of gear, the rules for its ordinary use are not necessarily the best. Such exceptional cases are therefore to be set aside.

The function of Government is to govern as little as possible; but not to do as little as possible. When it governs it so far fails, as an army fails when it fights. But an army to succeed must be active; and a Government to succeed, must be ceaseless in learning and diffusing knowledge, in stimulating and co-operating.

The Government, especially in a free country, is not an entity outside the nation, but a considerable part of the nation; and it can discharge its duties to the nation only by so arranging and developing its work as to make government itself a great education. This involves an extension of local responsibilities wherever possible. But devolution under rigid superior control is in danger of becoming mechanical and formal. The devolution that makes for organic evolution must not be limited to responsibility for carrying out details of schemes devised by the central authority: it must extend to the thinking out and the carrying out of appropriate constructive schemes in which the central ideas of the national scheme are adjusted to particular local conditions and requirements.

A country, which has no considerable supply of mineral oil, must always jealously guard her supplies of coal for use at sea. But it seems probable that the greater part of the uses to which coal is now applied in furnaces, fireplaces, etc. will ultimately be handed over to electricity, generated by coal consumed near the mines, with a careful preservation of by-products. Future developments of technique will decide how far gas will hold its own for special uses: but the direct consumption of coal, the most cumbrous of heavy products that travel over the whole country, will in the main be largely superseded by that of electricity, which carries itself at no expense, when adequate wires have once been set up. Such an arrangement would give scope for monopolies so powerful as to require thorough control by the State; and might seem at first sight to be suitable for a State monopoly. But the utilization of the by-products of coal is a most important matter; and it is in urgent need of the elastic energies of private enterprise in order to secure that each decade may see a great advance on that which went before it. Therefore it seems best that the State should cautiously but firmly control the charges made in each district for the standard "Board of Trade Unit"; and leave the process of obtaining it in private hands.

Gilds of various kinds exercised much zeal and some wisdom in regulating the affairs of many industries during the Middle Ages. Most of these regulations were designed to promote the interests of a particular group of artisans or traders, without any considerable injury to other people: but they became obstructive when the conditions, to which they had been fitted, passed away. Some of them became unworkable when the conditions of an industry changed greatly. For a considerable time they suffered much from the substitution of machines driven by water power for those which had relied on the force of the human hand or foot. Many industries moved from their old seats in town or country to the neighbourhood of streams rushing down the sides of hills: and by moving they became free from the pressure of obstructive rules made in times when the powers of horses and of human feet were the chief sources of the movement of mills, looms, and other machines.

These changes in the methods of industry and in its geographical distribution caused much hardship, and many unwilling movements from old homes to inhospitable banks of falling streams. Industry itself might seem to have had a pitiless joy in the discomfort of mere individual men and women. But the glory of the streams was soon to be dimmed. A monster force, derived from the sun long before mankind had appeared on the earth, soon laughed to scorn the power of such small streams as those of Britain: and industries began to settle near coal mines, and in other places to which coal could be conveniently conveyed.

Coal-engendered steam not only displaced water power from its first place as a prime-mover; it also displaced rivers and canals from their dominating influence over long-distance movements of ores, coal, grain and other weighty materials. But the great paths of the ocean gradually gained far more traffic than the rivers had lost: for coal became the chief source of man's power of massive movements over considerable distances, as well as of most of the mechanical work that had been effected not very long ago by wind and water and by the muscles of horses and of men, women and children.

These changes in technique are still increasing their influences on the characters of mankind. They are enabling children to spend for their own benefit much time and energy which used to be spent in hard bodily toil, that developed scarcely any valuable qualities save those of patience and endurance.

I think that in the distant future there may be an international concert for the regulation of discount in order to diminish short period fluctuation of general prices: but I do not think that discount can control the rate of interest permanently: of course it might conceivably have a great effect under imaginary conditions; but not, I think, under real conditions. I don't like notes printed on gold: and, on the whole, I incline to think that no effective regulation of general prices, that is consistent with the maintenance of an international currency based on gold (to that limited extent to which it is carried now), is possible without international agreements as to taxes on gold output, rising when gold is in too quick supply and falling in the converse case: the proceeds of the tax to be so distributed that the countries directly affected by it will not be losers. I think that might probably suffice: for the tendency to use gold merely as a reserve is on the increase I fear, and the notion of gold running short seems to go into the background. But, if it did, a few kilogrammes of silver might be brought to the aid of a gold kilo. (1916.)

Wealth exists only for the benefit of mankind. It cannot be measured adequately in yards or in tons, nor even as equivalent' to so many ounces of gold; its true measure lies only in the contribution it makes to human well-being. Now, when bricks and sand and lime and wood are built up into a house, they constitute a greater aggregate of wealth than they did before; even though their aggregate volume is the same as before: and, if the house is overthrown by an earthquake, there is indeed no destruction of matter; but there is a real destruction of wealth, because the matter is distributed in a manner less conducive to human well-being. Similarly, when wealth is very unevenly distributed, some have more of it than they can turn to any very great account in promoting their own well-being; while many others lack the material conditions of a healthy, clean, vigorous and effective family life. That is to say the wealth is distributed in a manner less conducive to the well-being of mankind than it would be if the rich were somewhat less rich, and the poor were somewhat less poor: and real wealth would be greatly increased, even though there were no change in the aggregate of bricks and houses and clothes and other material things, if only it were possible to effect that change without danger to freedom and to social order; and without impairing the springs of initiative, enterprise and energy. There is unfortunately no good ground for thinking that human nature is yet far enough improved away from its primitive barbarity, selfishness, and sloth, to be ready for any movement in this direction so rapid and far reaching as to effect with safety any great increase in real wealth by a mere redistribution of material wealth.

It is probable that a future Social Order may greatly surpass the present in justice and generosity; in the subordination of material possessions to human well-being; and even in the promptness of its adjustments to changing technical and social conditions. But a grateful memory will always attach to the excellence of the work, which free exchange has done and is doing, in turning to account the combative and predatory energy of the present crude nature of man: it has supplied much of the driving force, by which crowded districts in the western world have been endowed with material comforts and intellectual training beyond those which were attained a few centuries ago even in places where nature's bounties were large relatively to the number of people whom they were called on to support.

The main cause of this success has been the simple and almost mechanical action of the forces by which the modern social order has built up an organization of effort so intricate that it could not be described adequately in a long study; while yet it works smoothly; and its wastes through friction and maladjustments are small in proportion to its achievements. It turns to account the faculties of forecast and contrivance and business courage. But yet a great part of its work is automatic in this sense, that its chief and sufficient motive is the reasoned expectation of net gains resulting from its pursuit with sound judgment and courage.

Work is not a punishment for fault: it is a necessity for the formation of character and, therefore, for progress. (1922.)

Effort is essential to us; therefore, unless we are to be transformed in nature (as well as faculty), there must be something in heaven that we can accomplish, is worthy of accomplishment, and requires effort. Therefore *either* heaven must be a different place from that which Oriental quietism has imagined; *or* our nature must be so fundamentally changed after death that there is something like a breach of continuity in it. In the latter case, there would be little apparent reason in holding the future representative of a man responsible, in good and evil, for that man's life. These considerations seem to point to the conclusion that the old Saxon ideal of heaven (as a place where the "hunting grounds" are more noble in scope and character than those of this earth) is more true to the fundamentals of human nature than Asiatic, or even semi-Asiatic, conceptions of it. (1921.)

I have come to the conclusion that the Unknown probably has concerns in which this world plays a part almost as insignificant as that played by a single small insect in the history of this minute world....Every year my reverence for the Unknown becomes deeper; my consciousness of the narrow limitations of all the knowledge in this world becomes more oppressive; and my desire to add to that quantity something that will count, though it is a microscopic fraction of that microscopic whole, becomes stronger. (1916.)

My wife has counselled and aided at every stage of my every outpouring: and given the best part of her life to aiding me by counsel in all matters large and small at every stage. She refuses to allow her name to appear on the title page: but that is its proper place. (From the draft of a preface to a proposed final volume, dated 19. 3. 23.)

PART III
LETTERS

1, Glen Oran Villas, Apsley Road, Clifton

30 *June*, 1879

Dear Professor Jevons,

I take up the pen with some shame to acknowledge your letter of May the 12th, and the safe arrival of "Rau." When your letter came I was in an unusual press of work which, as I was not very well, I could hardly get through; and when the pressure was over I forgot your letter till just now.

I am looking forward with the greatest interest to the new edition of your book. During the last two years I have been too much occupied with practical work to do any considerable amount of study or writing. I hope better days are in store, and I think soon I may begin on a book of curves of which the papers sent you by Mr Sidgwick will form the basis. The pure theory of international values I don't much care about. I don't think it can be made easy without curves, and I think I shall leave it very much as it stands; but in the rest of the book I propose to give only a subsidiary place to curves, and to develop the application of the theory somewhat. In this way I hope to contribute my mite towards that work of "real"-ising the results of abstract quantitative reasoning in Economics of which I recognize in you the chief author. The *Economics of Industry*, the 2*s*. 6*d*. book which my wife and I are writing, is nearly finished. You may be sure that one of the first copies that are bound will find its way to Hampstead.

Yours faithfully,

A. MARSHALL.

To A. H. D. ACLAND

17 Chesterton Road, Cambridge
26 *Feb.* 1886

My dear Acland,

I don't think my views on Labour Statistics are worth much: but as you ask for them, here they are.

American experience shows, I think, that a Labour Statistics Bureau may be of great service provided it does not attempt too much. I would have it aim at collecting only a few results at first, but subjecting those to a severe ordeal. It would be slow work at first: but nothing trustworthy can be got till certain disputed points of principle have been settled. When this has been done for a few representative trades, the work can easily be extended to others.

My own plan would be to issue to employers and employed at the chief centres of, say, the machine making trades, forms to be filled up, shewing not only the rates of wages in each branch, but the proportion of workers who get each rate, with separate columns for additions through overtime and piece work, and for deductions through short time. On this basis a draft Report for each such centre should be issued; local papers would no doubt gladly print it. Then notice should be given that a representative of the Bureau would hold a court at a certain time, say in the town hall; and hear arguments to shew that the figures in the draft Report were too high or too low: reporters being present. Then the Bureau should sum up and deliver judgment in its final report.

The process would at first be tedious; but I have so many hundred square yards of wage statistics which I don't much believe, that I would gladly exchange some of them for as many square inches of figures that had been tried in open court in this way.

I agree with you that lists of blue books ought to be more accessible.

Yours very truly,

A. MARSHALL.

To Rev. J. LLEWELLYN DAVIES

Balliol Croft, Cambridge
Feb. 1886

....I have gradually become convinced that the main evil of our present system of aid of the poor is its failure to enlist the co-operation of the working classes themselves. It is because I believe that the working classes alone can rightly guide and discipline the weak and erring of their own number that I have broken silence now.....

But the feeling that the Residuum ought not to exist and that they will exist till the working classes themselves have cleared them away....has coloured my whole life and thought for the last ten years. I care about it more than about all other political questions put together.....

The peril is really very great. Soon the control of the working classes over Imperial and Local Government will cease to be nominal and become real. If they had learnt to look for guidance to the C.O.S. people, they could have been shown how to use out-relief rightly, and not to abuse it. As it is, I believe they *will* abuse it.

I remain,

Yours most respectfully and sincerely,

ALFRED MARSHALL.

I do not think undeserving people often get out-relief: but I think that the House is in many ways less disagreeable to them than to those of clean minds.

To JAMES BONAR

Balliol Croft, Cambridge
4. ii. 1891

My dear Bonar,

....Do you think I should ignore those reviewers who complain that I overweight what I say with qualifying and explanatory clauses, and that it would be better if I put what I had to say broadly, and left the corrections to come in gradually? I am like an ass between two bundles of hay—not stationary, but—wagging my head first towards the aim of (moderate) simplicity, and then, as a new critic like yourself comes down on me for inaccuracy, craning out again towards the aim of having every statement (taken with its immediate context) completely accurate as far as it goes. You are so careful and exact a writer on these subjects, and yet your style is so pleasant, that I should value your opinion on the point very much.

So far I have found some refuge in the unsatisfactory compromise of retaining and even increasing the repetition of qualifying clauses, but relegating them to footnotes....

Yours very sincerely,

ALFRED MARSHALL.

Balliol Croft, Cambridge
27. ix. 1898

My dear Bonar,

May I venture on the rashness of a definition? I do not myself hold a classical author to be one who more than others has said things which are true, as they stand. I don't feel myself bound to agree with him on many points, not even on any point. But he is not for me classical unless either by the form or the matter of his words or deeds he has stated or indicated architectonic ideas in thought or sentiment, which are in some degree his own, and which, once created, can never die but are an existing yeast ceaselessly working in the Cosmos. With that definition I can to my own satisfaction say pretty well whom I regard as classical economists. I think such a large proportion of them wrote in the half-century 1770–1820 that that is rightly called the classical epoch. I incline to regard Petty and Hermann and von Thünen and Jevons as classical, but not Mill....

Balliol Croft, Cambridge
6. iii. 1899

My dear Bonar,

Blandford's death is a loss to progress. I had not realized how much he was bound up with you....

I do not want people to study Indian currency! I want them to have studied the economics of industry and trade; fluctuations of commercial prosperity; good and evil of international indebtedness, of paternal policies in railway matters and so on. I am using currency reserves as my peg; because currency reserves happen to be under discussion. But I am never weary of preaching in the wilderness "the only very important thing to be said about currency is that it is not nearly as important as it looks."

Yours ever,

A. M.

Balliol Croft, Cambridge

18. vi. 1912

Dear Bonar,

.... Speaking generally I may say that the chief interest in Symmetallism departed with the collapse of Fixed-ratio-mintage: and that the changes in the arts of extracting gold from the earth, etc., in which it is embedded have been so great, and the discoveries of gold fields so extensive, that the facts of a quarter of a century ago—with which my evidence was largely concerned—are mostly obsolete. As to the analytical part of the evidence [Gold and Silver Commission] I have not consciously changed my position. It is set out in some directions more fully in my evidence before the Committee on Indian Currency of 1899....

Yours ever,

A. M.

Balliol Croft, Cambridge

8. viii. 1919

My dear Bonar,

I have just returned home, and found your letter of August 2nd. I agree that no very large indemnity can be got from Germany by any *one* of the routes you mention: but I think they might be used simultaneously. I am however opposed on principle to every sort of attempt to exact a sum approaching to ten thousand million pounds, even though the greater part of it might in fact be paid in *territory*. If—as appears to be the case—Germany must be forced to cede much territory in Africa as well as in Europe, I think that such territory should be accepted at the very high money value which she would naturally set on it: and the remainder of our demands on her might be covered mainly by the transference of securities representing command over property in various parts of the world.

In any case, I think, no transfer should be enforced which cannot be put through quickly. For the military occupation of Germany, which would be required to enforce large payments spread over many years, would involve so much expenditure and so greatly retard that quenching of the military spirit, which is needed to restore British industry to its sober, earnest habits of work, that its net effect might probably be an economic loss. The hatred which it would cause, even among those numerous though not specially vocal Germans, who try to see our side of the conflict, would, I think, be an enduring calamity.

I have not read Giffen's article on the payment of the French 1873 indemnity in recent years, but I recollect that I thought it exaggerated the harm which the purely economic side of the inflation did to Germany. The main source of the mischief appeared to me to be the enormous increase of influence which the results of the war (geographical, political and economic) gave to the German jingoes. In 1869, they were, I believe, a relatively small minority of the population of Germany, except in the North East provinces; but the war set school teachers, among others, to wallow in jingoism; and the average German as he entered manhood was very much more jingoistic than he would have been if born a little earlier. And, though the milliards were an important contributory cause to this deterioration of quality, I think that a similar, if milder, madness would have spread over the people without it.

In fact the milliards did this good; that they made German business men so over-confident as to intensify the subsequent depression of trade. That depression was a wholesome medicine and mitigated much of the evil influences which the indemnity exerted on German business; though it did not check the domination of the military caste over society, over the universities, and—partly through them—over the schools.

I therefore oppose the demand for a *huge* indemnity in the interests of the British nation, even more than on ethical grounds: but I think that, if liberal allowance be made for Germany's property in land and its fixings in Africa and elsewhere, even £M10,000 might be got out of her.

I don't go into detail: but I do not regard a compulsory gift of German goods to us as necessarily a danger. Any violent disturbance of a *particular* British industry is of course an evil: but most of the goods which Germany could send us would be such as she might have exported to other countries in Europe or outside of it. It would probably not be well to export those goods: but we might export similar goods of our own to the markets to which they would have gone if Germany had been free in the matter. Again our agriculturists could do with any amount of German potash. German sugar is also in elastic demand; but of course no vast quantity could be handled in the next few years: and so on.

I have recently been much tempted to publish some of my opinions on current financial and social problems: and also on the strange compound of good and evil in the character of the German population—most people who write on the subject seem never to have associated, as comrades, with Germans, and to recognize only the evil. But my strength fails fast; and I have much half-ready material, belonging to my special province, which will need to be cremated on my funeral pyre. So I dare not write controversy on matters as to which I have no direct responsibility: and indeed I have to cut down even my reading of current events rather severely.

I live so much out of the world that I did not know you were in England: that good Mother must rejoice in your return even as does one of her humbler sons.

Yours very sincerely,

ALFRED MARSHALL.

From THOMAS BURT, *Miner* and *Privy Councillor*

The Reform Club

May 10th, 1892

My dear Professor Marshall,

I have not till this morning had time to carefully read your paper on State aided pensions &c. in the *Economic Journal*. I have read it carefully and with great satisfaction. It is to my mind one of the most thoughtful, and altogether one of the best, things I have read on the subject. I agree with it all. You spoke of having got into "hot water" over it, or some portion of it. I really cannot understand why. The tone of your article from beginning to end is judicial, and not a word of censure is applied to man or institution. Of course the "hot water" I only take to mean that rather strong exception has been taken to some of the opinions you express.

Our conversation the other day was conducted under rather unfavourable conditions, and probably I have not dealt specifically with the point you wished to bring before me. In that case I shall gladly forward a supplementary epistle should you so desire—though perhaps the entire agreement I have expressed will suffice.

With kind regards to Mrs Marshall and your dear self—

I am very truly yours,

THOS. BURT.

To L. L. PRICE

Balliol Croft, Cambridge

19. viii. 92

.... In the early seventies, when I was in my full fresh enthusiasm for the historical study of economics, I set myself to trace the genesis of Adam Smith's doctrines. I have long ago forgotten all details, but the general impressions are very fresh in my mind. On the business side I thought he was entirely British (Scoto-English): as regards philosophy and "tone," I thought he was not so Scotch as was commonly supposed nor did I think he was French. In these respects he seemed to me to have been markedly under the influence of Locke. But as regards analysis, and the development of economic science proper, he seemed to me entirely French. (There were great lacunae in my reading. Foxwell says Mirabeau was very important: I know nothing of him even now and probably Foxwell is right. I knew next to nothing of Petty and nothing of Cantillon: but I know them now, and I do not agree with Foxwell about them.) I found so much in the Physiocrats which I had thought to belong to Adam Smith, that at first I got quite set against him. But afterwards I thought that many of these things were in substance older even than the Physiocrats; and that it was the form of his thought rather than the substance that he owed specially to them. And then I grew to think that the substance of economic thought cannot well be to any great extent the work of any one man: it is the product of the age. Perhaps an exception should be made for Ricardo: but everything of importance that was said in the five generations 1740–65, 1765–90, 1815–40, 1840–65, 1865–90, seems to me to have been thought out concurrently more or less by many people. And so I began to look for Adam Smith's originality more in the general conspectus which he presented than in particular doctrines. And as regards this, the more I knew of him, the more I worshipped him. It was his balance, his sense of proportion, his power of seeing the many in the one and the one in the many, his skill in using analysis to interpret history and history to correct analysis (especially as regards the causes that govern human nature, but also in other matters), that seemed to mark him out as unique; very much as similar qualities have more recently given a similar position to Darwin....His high prerogative comes from his having shown how inseparable induction and deduction are. In answer to those who say that he was inductive and his followers strayed from his example into the paths of deduction, I say that he was never *purely* inductive, but that there was an element of deduction in all his work: and that he never argued from a crude enumeration of particular historical instances. I think he was always inductive, but never *merely* inductive....

To Professor E. C. K. GONNER

Balliol Croft, Cambridge

9. v. 94

My dear Gonner,

You ask me to tell you something about my own work in connection with the post-graduate study of Economics in Cambridge. I understand that you will get direct from Foxwell and others an account of their work; and that the Cambridge Calendar and Reporter, supplemented by the detailed prospectus of lectures in Moral Science, for the typical year 1887–8, give you all the necessary information as to the general scheme of Cambridge teaching, examination, scholarships, &c.

I do not think it can be said that Cambridge offers very high inducements to graduates or undergraduates to study Economics. Those who do study it have generally a strong interest in it: from a pecuniary point of view they would generally find a better account in the study of something else. In particular the ablest students for our great Triposes—Mathematics, Classics and Natural Sciences—often think that they would rather diminish than increase their chance of a Fellowship by taking up a new line of study: and they are generally advised to try to do some original work in that with which they are already familiar.

Methods of teaching, of course, vary, but I will explain my own private hobbies. That of course does not come to much by itself. But it seems to be what you want in this particular letter.

I recognize the existence of students whose minds are merely receptive; and who require of their teachers to render plain their path in the systematic study of a text-book; or even to speak an elementary text-book at them if they cannot or will not find the time to read a text-book for themselves. But I always warn such students away from my lecture room.

Even my more elementary teaching makes no pretence at being systematic, but aims at treating certain dominant ideas and representative problems more fully than would be possible if every side of the subject had to be discussed equally. If I think the class are merely listening and not thinking for themselves, I try to shake them out of the rut. If they are thinking for themselves, I try to lead them on until they have got pretty well into the middle of a real difficulty and then help them to find their way out. I say very little about method; but I endeavour in every advanced course of lectures to work out rather fully a difficult example of almost every important method, having generally set, a week before, a question bearing on the example, so that they will know its difficulties before I begin.

My aim is thus to help them to acquire a delicate and powerful machinery for scientific investigation, without requiring them to attend long courses of lectures. For that is what graduates generally do not care to do. Some people say that books have superseded oral teaching, at all events for able students; I don't think they have. But I think able students are injuriously treated when a chapter of a book is spoken at them. It ough' to be printed, and given to them to read quietly. But the best way to learn to row is to row behind a man who is already trained; the learner's body moves by instinctive sympathy with his. And so the trained teacher should, I think, work his own mind before his pupils', and get theirs to work in swing with his. The graduate picks up the swing quickly. But he often wants a good deal of personal advice. I am "at home" for six hours in every week to any student who chooses to come to see me; and graduates generally come more frequently than others. The initiative in the conversation rests with the student; but if he is interested in any matter, I pursue it at length, sometimes giving an hour or more to a point which is of no great general interest, but on which his mind happens to be troubled; and I give much time to detailed advice about reading.

Of course the great hope in the background is that some of them will go on to do original work. But unfortunately more than half of those from whom I have expected most have been carried off by Headmasters to toil for the good of others; and though the spirit is often willing, the flesh is generally too weak to stand the strain of original work while teaching in a school. Such men of course help to form a sound public opinion in those parts of the country in which they settle; but they do not contribute much to that reward of the teacher's work which he loves best. It is those few who are able to persist that he cares for most; and one has two things to fear—on the one hand that they will be weighted down by mere information, or, on the other hand, that they will pursue some special enquiry without adequate general training and knowledge.

I take therefore great pains about the choice of books for graduates to read. I never recommend the same list to any two. Nor will I give a man any advice at all till I know a good deal about his mind, and have formed some opinion as to those things in which he is likely to excel. My first aim is to stimulate his enthusiasm for knowing and perhaps for doing something in particular. But as time goes on, I begin to look out for his weak points and, where necessary, to put pressure on him to read a few sterling books that are good for his mental health—that will perhaps give him important knowledge that he does not particularly care for, or will exercise his mind in difficult analysis and reasoning for which he has no special aptitude. The severe examination in Mathematics at large, which most Cambridge graduates prepare for, is a useful tonic in this regard, and greatly as any English economist must envy the large quantity of original work which German students put out at about the time of their degrees, I think it is possible that even German universities have just a very little to learn from Cambridge practice in this matter. Our students seldom write when they should: theirs perhaps occasionally write when they should not. I will add that I think Cambridge is not without some disadvantages as compared both with Oxford and the provincial colleges. The habits of mind fostered by the Mathematical Tripos have indeed induced Cambridge students generally to be more certain whether they know what they mean than most others. But Cambridge suffers much from the narrowness of the studies of all except those choice students who are able to think and read both for their Tripos and outside of their Tripos; and she suffers much from the lack of men who can put important truths in easy language that is attractive to able men who are not specialists. In these respects Oxford has a great advantage over her. Oxford gains too from the fact that her students can afford to read a little Economics, without departing from the straight path which leads to success in Greats; whereas in Cambridge Economics does not enter in any way whatever into any Tripos except the Moral Sciences and the Historical. And the provincial colleges have a great advantage over both Oxford and Cambridge, in the directness with which students at them are brought into contact with the problems of social and economic life.

Yours sincerely,

ALFRED MARSHALL.

To Bishop WESTCOTT

Balliol Croft, Cambridge

23. ii. 97

My dear Bishop,

I have read with the greatest interest the Addresses you have so kindly sent me. Everything you say draws me towards forms of belief, which are not altogether my own, but the substance of which I am in some measure able to hold fast; strengthened by holy influences such as yours.

Yours most sincerely,

ALFRED MARSHALL.

Dosses Gasthaus, Grödner Tal, South Tirol

23. vii. 98

My dear Bishop,

The best things that I know of, the only tolerably good things, about Consumers' Leagues, are American. But I cannot send you references to them till I get home in September.....

My own views are that Consumers' Leagues are good things in their way: but dangerous. They are apt to get into the hands of those who want to do a great deal for humanity at small cost to themselves. Such people delegate the making of their white and black lists to trade-unionists and others; who have really two sets of motives. One is the same as that of the Consumers' League. The other is to keep up wages by making their labour scarce. The former motives they avow: the latter they keep in the background, perhaps being scarcely aware themselves how far they are governed by those considerations that touch their own pockets most closely. So the social enthusiasts make themselves in effect agents for what is perhaps the most malignant of all social evils—the exclusion of the masses of the people from the best work which they are capable of performing. That is what the Gilds did as soon as ever they had got power and reputation and, above all things, the influence of the Church on their side. They put into their public declarations the most noble protestations of zeal for the public good and of zeal for true religion: and by that means they seem to have deceived the best men of their own time and many worthy historians of modern times, especially those who approach the subject from the Church point of view. But what did the Gilds really do? They checked improvements lest these should render their skill obsolete: they kept the masses of the people forcibly in occupations so low in grade and so overcrowded relatively, that the hunger and filth and the skin diseases born of the two lasted on in England for centuries after the people might have been fairly well-to-do if the free action of economic causes had not been checked by the Gilds, with their sanctimonious preambles.

....."Masters" do not often profess philanthropic motives, when they combat the restrictive influences of Trades Unions. But in effect they often do fight the battle of the masses against class selfishness, from which no set of people were ever free— not even artizans. They prevent the few from entrenching their position by regulations that hinder the many from doing the best work of which they are capable, and from bringing up their sons to better work than their own. Consequently trade-unions —unlike the gilds in their later days—have exercised on the whole a liberating and elevating influence. Also Combinations of Masters—partly because they have been mere selfish movements—have lacked coherence: and have seldom been able for long together to exploit the public for their own interest. But Mr Smith argues, and not without reason, that combinations of masters and men playing into one another's hands will have coherence. If so they will bring to the front gradually the meanest characters among employers and employed, and ere long trade-unions will cease to be on the whole liberating and elevating influences.....

Yours very sincerely,

ALFRED MARSHALL.

Balliol Croft
26. x. 99

My dear Bishop,

Patten's "Consumption" had maliciously hidden himself in *the* thickest of my hundred or more volumes of classified economic tracts. I am in no hurry for the volume; and it is possible that one or two articles in it may interest you. To be in any way of the smallest service to you is a high joy and pride to me.

I have been reading again recently your paper on the Organization of Industry. I think it is a masterly piece of work. I am just now working at the good and evil of Stock Exchange fluctuations. Like everything else which I touch in my second Volume, which will be more concrete than my first, I find it grows in difficulty in my hands. Thence I am to pass to speculation in goods, and that will bring me to think again about Mr E. J. Smith's schemes[1]. I am not inclined to regard them as less anti-social than when I first heard of them; but I incline to think that opposition to them from within the trades themselves can be trusted increasingly to limit their powers for evil. I cannot but think that the attempt to pledge the prestige of the Christian Social Union on behalf of the Standard Trade Union rate of wages, however it has been attained, is much to be regretted on many grounds. Two months ago [in Nürnberg] I was allowed to see one of the largest of those chromo-lithographic works in which English books and journals are "made in Germany." I was shown about by a partner, who was an Englishman, and he talked to me freely. The anti-social side of English Trade-Union regulations for the maintenance of a standard wage seems to be mainly responsible for the result that some tens of thousands of Englishmen are doing unskilled work at low wages in order that a small group of people, by cruel apprenticeship regulations, etc., may sustain their standard rate a few shillings higher than it otherwise would have been. Just those trade-union rules which Mr Smith's movement tends to strengthen have the effect of checking the influx of workers into the higher

---

[1] [The reference is to the Birmingham Bedstead Association, much discussed in the *Economic Review* of 1899, and commented on in *Industry and Trade*, p. 606 n. ED.]

ranks of industry: and, should the movement spread, a rise in the customary wages in the majority of trades might and probably would be accompanied by a great injury to the wages and the general well-being of the working classes as a whole.

I read about the Co-operative meeting at Newcastle. I thought it was splendid. Only the report which I saw did not make Mr Livesey say that his objection to Trade-Unionism was limited to its aggressive forms and especially such as that of the old gas workers' union. He used to say this on the Labour Commission.

Yours very sincerely,

ALFRED MARSHALL.

Balliol Croft, Cambridge

24. i. 00

My dear Bishop,

....I am not ashamed to confess that I know of no simple means by which a fair wage can be assured to all workers. I know of lots of simple means by which a fair wage and more than a fair wage can be assured to any particular group of workers that may be selected for the favour: but they all have unfortunately other effects. Some of them take from the rich and give to those who are less rich: I would promote all such by every means in my power that were legitimate; and I would not be specially scrupulous in interpreting that word. But the transfers of this kind that can be made by legislation, or by any sort of compulsion, seem to me to turn out to be small. The statistics of the incidence of taxation are most disappointing in this respect. One beats one's wings impotently against figures which show that modes of expenditure, which one would select for special burdens, can be disentangled only to a very small extent from others which it would be very unwise to burden: I have spent a very long time on analysing the figures which bear on this question.

Other such remedies take a little from the rich and a good deal from the working classes, and distribute nearly the whole among the working classes. But the inevitable waste of the double interference leads to the result that the rich would be a little worse off, and the working classes none the better. And these again cover a comparatively small area, though larger than the first set.

The main "remedies," which act through regulation or custom or other restriction, prevent people from learning to do high-class work, in order that the few who can do it may be in great demand; and they make every occasion they can for throwing people out of employment as too old—at the age of 50 or lower in many cases—or because they have less than the average stamina. Thus they keep up the rate of wages per hour in each rank by means that diminish regularity of employment in that rank a little, and diminish very much the number in each of the higher ranks. And so they do a little surface good at the expense of many times as great an injury to those whom it is most important to raise.

There is only one effective remedy that I know of, and that is *not* short in its working. It needs patience for the ills of others as well as our own. It is to remove the sources of industrial weakness: to improve the education of home life, and the opportunities for fresh-air joyous play of the young; to keep them longer at school; and to look after them, when their parents are making default, much more paternally than we do.

Then the Residuum should be attacked in its strongholds. We ought to expend more money, and with it more force, moral and physical, in cutting off the supply of people unable to do good work, and therefore unable to earn good wages.

And as private individuals, I think we can do much more. We can find out people who, because they are old, or broken, or perhaps a little stupid, would be avoided by the money-making employer, even if he could get them a good deal below the "standard" wage: and we can pay them a good deal more than the market value of their labour; and help them up. After a while they will often find themselves worth good wages and steady employment; and will leave the rest where they have been sheltered, making room for others. This happens in fact.

These and other little ways seem to me wholly good. Why should I be ashamed to say that I know of no simple remedy? Is the Physician not allowed to say the same? He is asked— "Can you cure me?" "Certainly not at once." "Not by *any* means?" "Not by any right means. I can give you powerful drugs, which will drive away the symptoms which you regard as your illness. But they will undermine your constitution. Patience is better for you."

Why should the economist be ashamed to admit that the more he studies "the mystery of evil" on its economic side, the more he is convinced that the key to the mystery is not in human hands; and that ill-considered remedies for evil—and as such I cannot help describing several of the specific proposals of the Oxford branch of the C.S.U.—are likely to do in the future, as in the past, much harm below the surface, with a little good above it.

As regards professional charges, such regulations as there are, are, I think, designed to protect the consumer against charlatans. For instance stock brokers, the most keenly competitive set of people, are prohibited by their regulations of the Exchange from advertising: and there are rules to govern their charges to private customers, in the absence of special agreement. But they are allowed to charge as much less as they like; and in many cases they charge only a small fraction of their nominal dues.

A "physician" may not take a less fee than £1. 1s.: but he may and often does give several consultations, to well-to-do patients as well as others, for a guinea. But a general practitioner may and often does charge 2s. 6d. or 3s. 6d. even to well-to-do people. And I knew a man in Bristol who made £800 a year by charging sixpence per consultation.

English lawyers are rather fettered by rules: and perhaps, partly in consequence, there is less justice in England, especially for the poor, than in any other country where the judges are upright. Further, these rules and custom seem to keep the average lawyer largely unemployed and poor. Americans say that English lawyers and medical men would be better off on the American plan of sheer freedom: and some English people, I believe, agree with them.

Yours very sincerely and gratefully,

ALFRED MARSHALL.

P.S. I have not stated, because I think you know, my general views about the "Standard wage" movement. But I will try to put their substance as shortly as I can. It is:—

i. The movement has been of the highest value to the working classes and the nation: and was a chief cause of the rapid progress of England in the middle of the century.

ii. It was then unpopular; and therefore, though it was occasionally violent, its range was too limited to enable it to act oppressively on a large scale; and its weakness brought Nemesis speedily when it showed anti-social tendencies.

iii. Now, it is popular and surrounded by a halo. Most of the work for which it was specially fitted is done: and underground evil is growing relatively to the surface good done by it.

iv. But the good is on the whole greater than the evil even now.

v. The standard wage is sometimes an equitable wage: but only by accident. The direct and natural effect of the machinery by which the standard wage is fixed in many trades is a tendency towards inequity.

vi. For instance, though there is a little bricklayer's work that is highly skilled, a good deal of it is such as an intelligent bricklayer's labourer could learn to do in a few weeks, if he were allowed to. Therefore a standard wage of (say) 10d. an hour for bricklayers and 6d. for their labourers—and this is not an extreme case—seems to be not equitable. [I should prefer 1s. for really skilled bricklayers, 8d. for ordinary; 8d. and 6d. for labourers.]

vii. Equity can be claimed with enthusiasm for "equal earnings for all"; or again "for earnings in proportion to needs and not in proportion to services rendered." And it can be claimed, though with perhaps little enthusiasm, for the unmitigated competitive system, which adjusts payments to services rendered more exactly than any artificial system conceived.

viii. But, to claim it for a system of standard wages, in which the standard of each trade is fixed by its strategical skill and resources in excluding competition from below, seems to me an abuse of words, leading to a confusion and even inversion of moral ideas.

ix. An elastic standard does more good and less harm than an inelastic one. E.g. an elastic system in the building trade would bring out the best capacities of operative builders; and would raise the average real wages of working men; without taking account of the fact that, by cheapening building, it would cause them to be better housed, whether in their cottages or workshops.

x. But many trade unionists, and especially those who are most likely to endeavour to use consumers' leagues &c. for their own purposes, are opposed to elasticity on strategic grounds.

xi. Consumers' leagues are at less disadvantage in dealing with the conditions of work than in dealing with wages. And here, if they will give hard and sustained personal work to discovering whether the conditions of work are such as to raise or lower the physical and moral tone of those whom they affect, they can do vast good.

xii. But if, to save themselves trouble, they adopt rigid rules, their interference will differ from that of Government for the worse in many respects, and for the better in none.

xiii. And if, still further to save themselves trouble, they allow these regulations to be drawn up by such employees, or employers, *or both together*, as have an interest in keeping the trade select and privileged, then their interference will, I think, be an unmixed evil.

xiv. Consumers' leagues are often managed by people who have a limited acquaintance with one or two businesses. From this experience they are apt to deduce general rules, and to regard themselves as being "practical." But here, as every where else, the most dangerous of all sweeping general rules are those which are deduced by aid of *a priori* intermediate axioms, (of which the so-called "practical mind" has always unconsciously a large stock), from limited experiences. Such leagues are likely to do more good than harm when they deal with individual cases one by one: but far more harm than good when they lay down general rules. And, when they publish such rules for the guidance of crude young men, they are taking on themselves a very grave responsibility.

xv. My own belief is that in this imperfect world the nearest attainable approach to equity in remuneration must be based, not on any one set of considerations, but on at least 4: viz.

(*a*) the services rendered by the worker;

(*b*) the needs of the worker;

(c) the inducements which it gives to the worker to make the best of his faculties as a worker, as a comrade, and as a free responsible individual;

(d) the inducements and opportunities (or absence of hindrances), which it offers to persons in a lower grade, to rise into or to bring their sons up to the occupations in question.

Auckland Castle, Bishop Auckland

Feb. 3rd, 1900

My dear Professor Marshall,

How can I thank you for your most kind and suggestive letter? As soon as a little time of leisure comes I hope to study it carefully. I have often said that I should have spent my ten years on the revision of the N.T. gladly if the revised version of St Luke xxi. 19 could have gained popular currency, a promise of conquest in place of a command to endurance. It is often hard to be patient, and yet all life is our teacher. Perhaps I shall take courage to ask you further questions in due time. I must not waste your time now.

Ever yours gratefully,

B. F. DUNELM.

Balliol Croft, Cambridge

20. i. 01

My dear Bishop,

Thank you much for your excellent address on progress. It will certainly help to make the world better; it will direct people's thoughts towards the true aims of life; and it will help to reduce mere material wealth to its proper, and very small, proportions in their minds, and so far I am with you, or, I should say, following you, with whole heart.

But, as I know you are so good as to wish me to speak wholly without reserve, I will venture to add that what you say about competition seems to me to cover too large a ground, and to be liable to be used for purposes that are alien to your own, if not opposite to them. I entirely agree that much harm is done by the prestige which the word "progress" gives to movements on behalf of which its name may be fairly invoked in one sense, but that not the highest sense. But I would submit that very much more harm is being done in the present age by uncertainties as to the meaning of "competition." It has base forms; and when you or Carlyle or other great preachers are denouncing it, these forms are chiefly in your minds. But what you say with reference to some kinds of competition which are unwholesome is apt, I think, to be exploited for selfish purposes with reference to other kinds of competition. When a man exerts himself to arrest or diminish competition, his motive may be the public good: but as a matter of fact it very seldom is. In at least nineteen cases out of twenty, his motive is to prevent his being at a disadvantage in spite of his being less energetic as a worker, less ready to throw away obsolete machinery &c. as a capitalist, than those whose competition he finds disagreeable. The Christian Socialists did, I believe, a great deal more good than harm: but they did harm. Their authority has been used with great effect by those mean, lazy and selfish men who since 1860 have done so much to undermine the vigour and honest work of English industry, and have removed her from the honourable leadership which she used to hold among the nations.....

Fifty years ago nine-tenths of those changes, which have enabled the working classes to have healthy homes and food, originated in England. America had a few specialities, and so had France. But, speaking generally, anything which was not English was really dearer than the English, though bought at a lower price. We owed our leadership partly to accidental advantages, most of which have now passed away. But we owed it mainly to the fact that we worked much harder than any continental nation. Now, on the average, we work less long and not more vigorously than our fathers did: and, meanwhile, the average amount of thoughtful work done by the German has nearly doubled; and a similar though less marked improvement is to be seen in other countries. Americans and Germans jeer at the way in which many of our business men give their energies to pleasure, and play with their work; and they say, truly as I believe, "unless you completely shake off the habits that have grown on you in the last thirty years, you will go to join Spain." And when they have said this, it has sometimes occurred to me that Spain did attain, two hundred years ago, to that ideal towards which many of those who claim to be followers of the Christian Socialists are drifting, and which I find in the "weedy" minds of some young members of the Christian Social Union. In consequence it is, I believe, a fact that there is scarcely any industry, which has changed its form during the last ten years, in which we are not behind several countries; and that every Teutonic country, whether behind us or in front of us, is on the average growing in vigour of body and mind faster than we; and that, because there is none of them that is not less self-complacent than we are, less afraid to meet frankly and generously a new idea that is "competing" for the field.

And now as to international trade competition. Of course the popular notion that a country can be undersold all round in-volves a contradiction in terms: it would mean that other countries were sending her presents in goods and not accepting payment for them. In fact our nominal imports exceed our nominal exports very much: but, as has been shown over and over again by statisticians and economists, that is to be ex-plained partly by differences in the methods of reckoning the money value of the two; and partly by the fact that many of our real exports are services rendered to foreigners, especially in the form of continual loans, and which could not be reckoned among our exported goods, whatever system were adopted by custom house officials. Our real danger is that we shall be undersold in the product of high class industries, and have to turn more and more to low class industries. There is no fear of our going backwards absolutely, but only relatively. The danger is that our industries will become of a lower grade relatively to other countries: that those which are in front of us will run farther away from us, and those which are behind us will catch us up. This might be tolerable if peace were assured; but I fear it is not. Here I am very sad and anxious.....

So, recollecting that we are vulnerable in all parts of the world, and are not self-sufficing either in raw material or in food, I believe that London will ere long be held to ransom if we continue to allow the average efficiency of other nations per head to grow faster than our own. Our times of leadership were times when an hour of an Englishman's work was worth more than that of almost anyone else, and the Englishman worked as many hours as he could without overworking himself; we bore hard work and we forbore from that ὕβρις which is goading the Continent into dangerous enmity. Above all we were respected because it was known we respected the love of freedom even against our own material interests. We were then stronger than we seemed and might have afforded to sacrifice some strength for the graces of life. But now this seems no longer the case. German soldiers have always thought we overrated our strength: and now they tell me that their own estimates had been far too high. I think therefore that the first step towards a right use of wealth within the country is the taking an unaggressive position among nations. If we provoke war, we must be prepared to fit ourselves for war—in plain terms to spend £100,000,000 on our army and navy, before long, when at peace.

Now in "competition," as it is commonly understood, I find something crude, ugly, harsh; but with this evil, which can and ought to be diminished, I find very much good that has hitherto been attained by no other route. Till another route has been found, I think it is dangerous and even wrong to speak of competition as though it were an evil touched with good.

In my view Freedom *is* life: the virtues which the Christian Socialists so excellently fostered *elevate* life. And they took it for granted that it was easy to diminish the evil side of competition by attacks on competition generally, without seeing that in this way they were working against freedom and therefore against life. No doubt they thought that competition was not essential to freedom: and in a sense that is so. In ideal freedom there is no competition, except perhaps emulation in doing good for its own sake. But in that ideal state there is no need for private property, nor policemen nor any of our social burrs. And my complaint against Kingsley and Maurice is that, though virile themselves, their teaching tended in some degree to emasculate character; because so much of it was negative. When they praised in positive terms the virtues of gentleness and unselfishness, when they urged that we were only trustees for wealth, when they spoke on the lines of most of the address on "Progress," they could not be misunderstood. But they were misunderstood when they attacked competition: indeed they misunderstood themselves, because they had not thought out a way of checking competition generally without lessening freedom: they did not know how hard that is. They did not foresee how their teaching would be applied to strengthen the hands of those who want to keep out competition from below— that is to subordinate the interests of the many to the privileges of the few, and to suppress pushing men, who insisted on making things by such improved methods of machinery, organisation, &c., that old-fashioned firms had no choice save either to fail or to adopt modern improvements.

Economists are in a sense always studying the value and limits of competition. But they seldom talk of competition in general: because general propositions must be vague; and they work at definite parts. But occasionally they write of it broadly. Cooley's book which I send is a good specimen I think.....

Yours in sincere devotion,

ALFRED MARSHALL.

I admit that the desire to "best" B and C is neither a noble force in any way, nor a very strong force generally. But the emulative desire to do better than—not B and C in particular, but—others in general, is, I think, one of the strongest and most persistent forces in history, working perhaps one-tenth for evil, but nine-tenths for good.

Auckland Castle, Bishop Auckland
Jan. 22nd, 1901

My dear Professor Marshall,

How can I thank you as I ought to do for this fresh proof of your kindness? What you say is very helpful and I think that I can fully agree with all that you say of the necessity of competition for us, being what we are, as a stimulus. What I fear is the growing tendency to make personal distinction and personal gain, measured by money, human ends. After all οὐ διακονηθῆναι ἀλλὰ διακονῆσαι is the only rule in which we can rest. The wilful restraining of power for selfish purposes, which must fail, by some trade unions is one of the saddest things I know; yet even this answers in part to a generous thought. I wish that you could say something at length on the Unions. The time has come, I think, for wise and sympathetic criticism.

The Essays which you have sent me will, I am sure, be suggestive, and I will study them carefully.

I ought perhaps to say that, shocked as I was by the Jameson raid and by the way in which it was received in London, I cannot regard the S. African war as other than inevitable. The declaration of war by Kruger seemed to me to reveal the whole policy of his party. Up to that point I thought peace possible. Indeed I had always reckoned Majuba amongst our triumphs till Lord Kimberley told us how the peace came about. You will forgive me if you condemn me.

I often wish that I could consult you about the Christian Social Union: probably some of our Cambridge friends do. There is much serious work among the members, and those whom I know desire the truth. All my love and hope for Cambridge was stirred by a very short visit to the Trinity Commemoration. I said a few words in Chapel which the Master asked me to print. You will feel what I failed to express.

With sincere gratitude,

Ever yours,

B. F. Dunelm·

Balliol Croft, Cambridge
23. i. 01

My dear Bishop,

Section IV of your address at Trinity seems to me one of the noblest and truest things ever said: I heartily subscribe to every word of it.....

My notion as to the proper work of the academic student with regard to Trade Unions is that he should treat them as a special case of association in which the good of individual unselfishness is ever surrounded and apt to be vitiated by the evil of class selfishness. I think that, when the academic student takes on himself the rôle of a preacher, he is generally less effective than when he treats the problems of life objectively; that is when he assumes no major premises based on his own views of duty, his own ideals of social life. So I am leading up to my discussion of Trade Unions by studies in which the Trade Unionist is invited to pass judgement on problems of combination in which he has no direct interest. Then I want to imply, when I come to his problems:—*De te fabula narratur.*

This is one reason for abstaining, now for many years, from saying anything publicly on labour questions.

I am not satisfied with the result. For the work is very long; and my life is ebbing away. But I think the notion was right in the main; and anyhow it would be a mistake to change my plans at this late stage.

Your devoted follower,

ALFRED MARSHALL.

Auckland Castle, Bishop Auckland
St Paul's Day 1902

My dear Professor Marshall,

No doubt you can decide better than any one what ought to be the course of your work. Yet I long for some words from you on Labour combinations. The most suggestive remark which I have found in Dr Cooley's book is that parts of men, and not men, unite in combinations. And may one not say that we are all of us in danger of becoming parts of men in the pursuit of special aims. How rarely we see a whole man. Again and again Matthew Arnold's words ring in one's ears: "Thou art a living man no more, Empedocles, nothing but a devouring flame of thought." The Universities must train men.

As my thoughts go back to the past in this stillness, I cannot but recall very vividly my visit to you just before I came here. You showed me then sure lines of work and thought, and you have never failed me in my difficulties since.

May I not then call myself not only gratefully but affectionately yours,

B. F. DUNELM.

To EDWARD CAIRD, *Master of Balliol College*
(*re* Engineers' strike)

Balliol Croft, Cambridge
22. x. 97

My dear Master,

I have followed this strike with an interest amounting to excitement. I am very much of an 8 hours man: I am wholly a trade-unionist of the old stamp. For the sake of trade unionism, and for that of labour as a whole, I hope that the employers will so far get the better of the leaders of the modern unionism, that the rank and file of the workers will get to see the futility as well as the selfishness of the policy which their new leaders are pressing. Everywhere the tried men, who had made modern unionism the greatest of England's glories, have been pushed aside—sometimes very cruelly. For a time the Engineers adhered to moderate and unselfish courses. But lately they have used their grand prestige, I hold, for England's ill.

In Belgium, Germany, Bohemia, Hungary and Japan, crowds of men are learning to manage machines which a few years ago required high skill, but which have been now so improved that they will do excellent work in the hands of a mere "ploughman." This tends of course to open out new kinds of mechanical work that require high skill: but England cannot keep much of that work, unless she is also able to grow with the age in the application of the more abundant lower skill to suitable work.....

There is no fear whatever, not the very least, that the A.S.E. will be broken up. No one wishes it: and it could not be done. But unless the A.S.E. *bonâ fide* concedes to the employers the right to put a single man to work an easy machine, or even two or more of them, the progress upwards of the English working classes, from the position of hewers of wood and drawers of water, to masters of nature's forces will, I believe, receive a lasting check. If the men should win, and I were an engineering employer, I would sell my works for anything I could get and emigrate to America. If I were a working man, I would wish for no better or more hopeful conditions of life than those which I *understand* to prevail at the Carnegie works now (there may be evils there, of which I do not know, but I have watched for some account of them and have found none).

The 8 hours question is of course not the real issue *at all*. The real issue lies entirely in the question whether England is to be free to avail herself of the new resources of production. I think, however, that, while Americans and Germans work longer hours than we do, the most expensive machinery will not be freely used here except on the plan of double shifts. With double shifts, proper machinery, and the application of each man to "just that work which is the highest of which he is capable," I believe a 7 hours day would be long enough, and wages (real and not money wages) may be doubled in the coming generation as they have been in the past.

I have marked this as "confidential" because I have decided —not without hesitation—to take no public part in the controversy just now. If all employers were like Sir Benjamin Browne and Colonel Dyer I would speak out. But of course many of them are as great enemies of "the good" as some of the new-unionists are. And, as I am saying nothing publicly, I do not want to speak half-publicly.

Yours very truly,

ALFRED MARSHALL.

Balliol Croft, Cambridge
5. xii. 97

My dear Master,

In brief, I *think* that:—

i. This is the crisis of our industry. For the last twenty years we have indeed been still progressing; but we have been retrograding relatively to the Americans and to the nations of central Europe (not France, I think) and to Eastern lands.

ii. The causes are partly natural, inevitable, and some are, from a cosmopolitan point of view, matters for satisfaction.

iii. But one is unmixed evil for all, and a threat to national well-being. It is the dominance in some unions of the desire to "make work," and an increase in their power to do so.

iv. And there is another like it. It is the apathy of many employers and their contentment with inferior methods, until driven out of the field or threatened severely, at least, by more enterprising foreigners.

v. The present distresses are an insignificant price to pay for remedying these evils, if so be that the remedy comes. If the men retort on the employers even more strongly than they have done—"part of our weakness lies at your doors anyhow," so much the better.

vi. The employers' terms disappoint me: but less on second reading than on first. The tone is harsh: but this may mean nothing. The condition that the prices for piece work shall be fixed by individual agreement seems a great step backwards. But looking at the history of the recent past, I do not see what else is to be done. Agreement on generous lines, such as under the Mundella hosiery scheme, or the North of England Iron schemes, is an immense advance on individual bargaining. I have often said that T.U.'s are a greater glory to England than her wealth. But I thought then of T.U.'s in which the minority, who wanted to compel others to put as little work as possible into the hour, were overruled. Latterly they have, I fear, completely dominated the Engineers' Union. I want these people to be beaten at all costs: the complete destruction of Unionism would be as heavy a price as it is possible to conceive: but I think not too high a price.

If bricklayers' unions could have been completely destroyed twenty years ago, I believe bricklayers would be now as well off and more self-respecting than they are: and cottages would be 10 or 20 % larger all round. And, meanwhile, healthier brick-layers' T.U.'s would have grown up. Till recently the Engineers' Union was one which was contrasted with the bricklayers' union (or some of its worst-minded branches); now they seem to be as bad.

vii. In this I find no sign of deterioration of character. I think the Engineers have been under exceptional temptations, and have yielded to the seductions of those semi-socialists who have captured them.

viii. Mr Sinclair's letter in the *Times* of yesterday (Dec. 4) seems to me to go to the root of the matter. He illustrates one side—the American as distinguished from the Continental—of the causes that are at present making England move relatively backwards. The balance against us, allowing for the superior weight of American locomotives, comes out at about 3 : 1, i.e. 3 Glasgow men needed to do the work of 1 American. I should put (say) a quarter of this to account of our employers, a half to account of new-unionism, and the remaining quarter to no account at all. I mean that, when a man works in a leisurely way and for relatively short hours, he does get some gain which may be set off against the loss in his efficiency.

ix. Leisure is good, if it is well used. But the laborious laziness, which has come into many English Government work-shops, and some private ones, engenders a character to which leisure is useless.

x. So long as our foreign policy aims at pushfulness, especially in those directions in which we imitate other nations with least benefit to ourselves—as in Egypt.—I think we are bound to increase our expenditure on Army and Navy at an ever-increasing rate. If then we go backwards *relatively* in mere production, we court disaster. Were it not for this, I should be fairly contented with our making progress absolutely, even though most other nations were growing faster.

Yours very truly,

ALFRED MARSHALL.

Addendum to vi.

I think it ought to be possible to devise a phrase which shall appear less hostile to the principle of Trade Unionism than that referred to under vi, and which shall yet prevent the use of collective bargaining as a means of hindering new men and new machines from coming into work for which they are needed. I hope some such phrase may be found. I have tried a little and failed.....

Balliol College
Dec. 11th, 1897

My dear Professor Marshall,

I am much indebted to you for giving me so much of your time and so clear a statement of your view of the position.

I can go along with you in all you say of the particular causes of quarrel, and think the masters ought to win on these. But

I cannot think that any good would come of their breaking down the Union. I am afraid it would bring us back to the lawless methods of an earlier time. Of course, if the masters consented to modify their claims in the clauses in which they propose to deal with the individual workman, the difficulty would be got over. If not, I should feel obliged—so far as I see—to give what little support I can to the men. All the same I think it a great pity that men like Colonel Dyer should not be able to carry the rest of the masters with them in devising some less objectionable terms which would secure the particular points on which the masters lay weight, and set up some system like that he has consented to elsewhere.

With many thanks,

I am,

Yours very truly,

EDWARD CAIRD.

Balliol Croft, Cambridge

12. xii. 97

My dear Master,

Many thanks for your letter. You say:—"But I cannot think that any good would come of their (the masters) breaking down the Union." I am not sure whether you suppose me to think so. I emphatically think the opposite. In fact I have some notion— I have not clearly decided yet—of sending the Union a small subscription after the conflict is over. I do not regard the danger to the Union as lying mainly in the exhaustion of their funds. I think it lies in the time given to "masters" to train unskilled men for work which they say is easy, but which the Engineers want to label artificially as skilled and preserve as their own monopoly. If the men are right, then whoever gets the better of *this* struggle, the "masters" must in the long run take on the Engineers practically on their own terms. If, as I believe, "the Masters" are right, then whoever wins now, those of the Engineers who are not really skilled will not be able to find occupation save on the "Masters'" terms. This is, I think, right. If the Engineers are not acting unsocially they will in the long run substantially win. If, as I think, they have been acting unsocially, since they got under the influence of the Socialists, they will anyhow lose. If the "Masters" had published their explanations with their manifesto, much harm would have been averted.

I am not so much afraid as you are of the results of a temporary collapse of a Union. If that should lead to violence, then there should be violence now. For only a very small percentage of those who are most prone to violence are in Unions. The Dockers and the Gas Workers are individually of violent habits: but the collapse of the Dockers' Union, and the South London Gasworkers' branch, has resulted in a diminution, not an increase, of violence, I believe.

Yours very truly,

ALFRED MARSHALL.

To S. D. FULLER

Balliol Croft, Cambridge
21. xi. 97

....To be overkind to the children of the pauper class, relatively to those of the self-respecting poor, would directly frustrate nature's rule that the better strains of population shall have a better chance of moving upwards and multiplying than the inferior strains have. This objection does not tell directly against boarding out the aged.

I am in favour generally of freedom of experiment: and should wish every method which has a *primâ facie* prospect of success to be tried. But it seems doubly important to go slowly in such matters: because I believe that in them the system is of the least importance: nearly all depends on individual character. If a hundred children or aged poor are boarded in well-selected homes, the good may predominate over the evil; and yet, if a hundred thousand homes had to be found, the evil might on the average largely predominate over the good.....

I want discrimination; and to offer to the best people a choice between (A) workhouses with more comforts and freedom than the ordinary house; (B) out-relief, which might take the form of boarding out in some cases. I think this should be done at all costs. Every penny so spent would be fruitful of indirect good as well as direct. It would tend to keep distress from sinking into despair: it would conserve self-respect.....

Yours very faithfully,

ALFRED MARSHALL.

To Professor E. CANNAN

Balliol Croft, Cambridge

7. i. 1898

My dear Cannan,

I have been looking again at the letter you were so very good as to write to me in December; and I have been re-reading part of Fisher's articles. Is this a correct survey of the situation?:

You and Fisher hold that wealth is a stock and a flow: but capital is only a stock.

I take wealth to be a stock only.

So far it would appear that the differences between us is only as to the use of the word "wealth." I can see no advantage in your use: but the matter does not strike me as important, so far.

But I think there is something of more importance behind. I take it we are all agreed that "capital," from the individual point of view, must be used in the common business way; more or less on the lines of what I have called trade-capital; and that it has no scientific justification: that therefore the discussion is all about "capital in general" or "capital from the social point of view."

Assuming that, I want to adhere to the line of division between "Land" or "Free goods," and "Capital." I can't be sure that you and Fisher do.

You see the position taken up in my Ed. III only comes to this, that I have openly adopted as my *standard* definition one which corresponds to what has been *de facto* my main use of the term ever since about 1869, when I used to think in Mathematics more easily than in English. I then adopted the doctrine of the national dividend, its division into the shares of land, labour and capital, governed by the equivalence of differential coefficients of cost of production on the one hand (or disutility), and utility on the other [I did not use those words then]. There remained great lacunae in my theory till about 85; when, on my return to Cambridge, I resolved to try to find out what I really did think about Distribution: and I gradually developed (sufficiently to please my complacent self) the doctrines of substitution between primâ facie non-competitive industrial groups, of quasi-rents, etc. But all this, though vital to my special views, did not affect my use of "capital." That was throughout the stock of things, other than land, which are instrumental in satisfying human wants. (In my first version of distribution in 1879, I did not speak of the National Dividend; because I wanted to get rent out of the way first: and Earnings-and-interest Fund was National Dividend after deducting Rent.)

I did not openly define capital in that way; because I did not dare to set myself in opposition to English tradition. But in practice I nearly always used the term in that way, except when I was talking of trade-capital.

Now I have dotted my i's and crossed my t's; and my position is:

Capital [in general] is a stock.

Wealth is a stock.

But (i) Capital does not include "free goods": this is a matter of principle.

(ii) Capital does not include those trifles, the income from which is neglected by ordinary people and income tax collectors. This is a mere matter of convenience; it corresponds to writing £M437 instead of £437,495,821:14:8¾.

(iii) Though in England (not perhaps in France) wealth and capital consist for the greater part of the same goods, yet when we use the term "capital" we are always thinking of the "productiveness" and "prospectiveness," which mainly affect the demand for and the supply of wealth,....

Now as to inconsistencies between my Preface and Book II, ch. IV. Is not what I say about capital in the Preface contained in what I say on top of p. 143 and on pp. 152–3? [of course

I shall not reprint that Preface, so I propose to copy a part of it in at the end of p. 153 together with a paragraph to the same effect as p. 5 of this letter].

Fisher puts a strange interpretation on the first ¶ of p. 152. I don't want it: and I want space. So I shall omit it.

The first line of § 6 may be clearer as "some writers have thought it specially important," and I admit that the last line of first ¶ of Note 2 on p. 150 is now incorrect. I did not notice it. Of course I shall strike it out.

Is there any other change needed to make me consistent with myself? I cannot alter my definition of wealth to make it include income: for I see only evil in that change. But outside of that, is there anything I can do to free me from reproach in your eyes? You were good in December. Goodness brings its own punishment, in this abominable infliction on you.

Pardon! Yours humbly,

ALFRED MARSHALL.

To Professor A. W. FLUX

Balliol Croft, Cambridge
7. iii. 98

My dear Flux,

What *do* you mean by speaking of "my failure to afford you satisfaction." Human wants are insatiable. Who ever satisfied everybody, unless he was a fool and satisfied himself; or acourting and satisfied *her*? You are doing gloriously; if I may use my grey hairs as a screen behind which to talk somewhat after the manner of an Oracle, you are becoming more realistic, and I would that you did so even faster; and to that extent satiety-point is not reached. But—again the grey-hair-screen—your strength and vigour and elasticity, your productiveness and prospectiveness (*i.e.*, work valid for future times as well as the present) are a good sight for sore eyes..... *Macte Virtute*.

You say that, *à propos* of Increasing Returns, you are inclining to lay stress on the incomplete utilisation of existing productive facilities. That is of course one of my chief hobbies. My confidence in Cournot as an *economist* was shaken when I found that his mathematics *re* I.R. led inevitably to things which do not exist and have no near relation to reality. One of the chief purposes of my Wander-jahre among factories, etc., was to discover how Cournot's premises were wrong. The chief outcome of my work in this direction, which occupied me a good deal between 1870 and 1890, is in the "Representative firm" theory, *Principles*, pp. 348–390, the supplementary cost analysis, pp. 435–8 and 464–470; as well as the parts that directly relate to supply price for I.R.

The supplementary cost question can of course only be touched in Vol. i. It will give a chief motive to a great part of Vol. ii, especially as to Fluctuations of credit and prices. I still think that my term "process" is the best I have met with for covering in a short space all this group of difficulties.

But of course I don't suppose that I have said anything like the last word on the subject. Go ahead, and say a later and a better one.

Very many thanks indeed for your kind and good help.

Yours affectionately,

ALFRED MARSHALL.

Balliol Croft, Cambridge
19. iii. 04

My dear Flux,

I was just settling down to a belated letter of thanks to you for your generous and strong aid on pp. 281–3 of the current *Quarterly Journal of Economics*; and for your article in the *Canadian Bankers' Magazine*, when your letter of the 8th arrived.

I am very glad that you are coming to England and that you will be here at the British Association meeting. We have asked Dr and Mrs Pierson to stay with us for that. I hope you will get put up somewhere in our neighbourhood so that we may see you during the meeting, and that you will be able to look in on us in June. We have taken lodgings in Norfolk for July and the first half of August.

Thank you *very much* for your most kind offer to read the proof of my new book.....The first half, which is only half written, is on the causes and nature of Industrial Leadership treated historically as well as analytically. The second is on International Trade; while at the end is to come an application of the basis thus provided to current issues. The second part is to be as scientific as is compatible with an attempt to catch the general reader; but free use is to be made of appendices throughout. I am going to be a little venturesome in it: and shall be most grateful for your kindly help.

In the last part I am going to give a little freedom to my *sentiment*, as distinguished from my reason; and to speak as a citizen rather than specially as an economist. There also I shall be grateful for help. But sentiment is like a butterfly; no amount of friendly discipline will make him go by a rational bee-line.

Our best regards to Mrs Flux.

Yours very sincerely,

ALFRED MARSHALL.

Balliol Croft, Cambridge
26. v. 04

My dear Flux,

....I have been drawn in for an unusual amount of festivities much against my will. I have not attended a big dinner for ten years, and hoped I might never have to do so again. But I have to be responsible for Leroy Beaulieu, who arrives to-morrow; and so must go to three! straight on end.....Towards the end of June, I have to go to Oxford. Then from 17 to 23 August this house is to be a sort of Hotel with at least one Dependance, for British Association foreign guests—Pierson, Lotz and Dietzel, and probably some others. So I shall not have the repose of the blessed, which the would-be cautious writer so craves.

Consequently I don't know what is to happen to my book. I have got about 150 pp. in type; and I have made special arrangements for having it all set up before I read it. Now, however, it is certain that the book will not be out till the autumn and probably not till later. For the course of events has lessened the demand for short books—there are already several good ones out; and the Tariff Issue will probably not get to a head within the next six or twelve months. Also I find that the further I go the slower I go. Just at present I am getting out of the industrial problems of Germany into those of U.S.A. That will bring my Part I to 200 pp. or more. Only after that shall I begin International Trade, and severe analysis.....

Yours very sincerely,

ALFRED MARSHALL.

To T. C. HORSFALL

Balliol Croft, Cambridge
8. iii. 1900

I am entirely in agreement with your claim that the community is bound to see to it that town dwellers have opportunities for knowing what a full healthy life is. Country folk are less dependent on training and on inspiration derived from their fellow-men. The fresh air and bright sunshine strengthen and stimulate, and at the same time soothe their nervous systems: and the beauty of everchanging nature offers an invitation to reverent and religious feeling, whether it be precipitated in theological forms or not. But town life, with its everincreasing density and extension, shrouds the individual away from himself, and from the Infinite. It keeps up an incessant strain on his nervous strength, and tends to make him forget the blessedness of repose. He is always on the move, and therefore he is seldom entirely himself: he is scarcely ever completely refreshed; and therefore he is apt to seek for excitement by the paths of least resistance, and the excitements to which they lead are seldom altogether pure and healthy.

I think therefore you are right in contending....that the growth of towns increases the urgency of the duty to broaden and deepen education. That duty would have grown anyhow with the increase of our resources and knowledge and with the expansion of our social ideals. But the growth of towns makes it doubly urgent to supply wholesome thoughts and suggestions, lest unwholesome should prevail: and to turn music and painting and other fine arts to account in filling the void in man's life caused by the want of the free light and freshness and beauties of nature. The clatter and the bustle and the nervous strain of constantly jostling amongst a multitude of others must impoverish some sides of his nature; and it is therefore imperatively necessary, if the child is to grow up in any fulness of life, that he should see and hear and read of the brightest ideals that have come to mankind. Strong, vigorous but placid self-control is the bond of life; and the harder of attainment this is made by the physical conditions of town life, the easier should the access be to the restful influences and aspirations of those whose lots have been cast in larger moulds.

Yours very faithfully,

ALFRED MARSHALL.

From Dr N. G. PIERSON, *Prime Minister of Holland*

The Hague
3. iv. 1900

Dear Professor Marshall,

We are getting fairly on in our home politics. The bill for Compensation of accidents has been passed (and it is a grand measure) by the Lower House; so also, the bill introducing Compulsory education. The dwellings'-bill is under examination and I think it will pass.

But we are all much occupied in our minds by that horrid war in South Africa. I do not know what your feelings are in this matter, though I am not inclined to believe you strongly sympathize with Mr Chamberlain's politics. What is all this fighting for? Why could not these small republics be left alone? A curious light upon the so-called Outlander grievance is thrown by the fact that all the Outlanders, not belonging to the British nationality, heartily joined in the war and shed their blood on behalf of their "oppressors." Their wrongs, after all, cannot have been so very serious, though they may have existed to a small extent.

I see no speedy end to this war, for the Boers will never yield, until they are almost exterminated.

This is a sad close of our century. It makes one's heart bleed.
How have you been getting on since we last heard from you?
How is your health and Mrs Marshall's? And when shall we
receive your second volume? It will be a treat to read it.

Believe me, with kind regards, also from Mrs P.

Yours Sincerely,

PIERSON.

To Dr PIERSON

Balliol Croft, Cambridge

6. iv. 1900

. . . . You ask me my views as to this miserable war. I should
like to talk with you for an hour on the matter. I am not sure I
understand the Boer case. I am certain that Continental newspapers do not understand the English case. There are of course
jingoes here: and their views may tell when the time comes to
arrange the terms of peace. But, whereas the *Münchener Neueste
Nachrichten* proved in August (I was then in Süd Tirol) that
England could not send 10,000 troops to Africa, we have sent
nearly 200,000; and our barracks at home are fuller than they
have ever been; the number of cubic feet of sleeping space
allowed for each soldier has had to be temporarily reduced. And
it is certain that, if necessary, we shall send another 200,000 a
little later. This is not the work of the jingoes: they made the
war inevitable; but the determination to put through the war
is as strong among most anti-jingoes as among jingoes: and that
would be an impossible state of things if the English case were
what Continental newspapers generally suppose it to be.

I am myself an uncompromising anti-jingo: a peace-at-almost-
any-price-man. . . . . Since however I have got to know how
enormous the military preparations of the Boers were, I have
felt that, independently of the Uitlanders' grievances, England
was bound to say—"You must give material security that those
preparations will not be used against us the first time we are
in difficulties. Taking account of the strategical advantages which
your position, your revenue from the mines and other causes
give you, we cannot guarantee the security of Durban and Cape

Town against your armaments without keeping 100,000 soldiers permanently in those colonies. Therefore you *must* disarm or have the fight out at once."

I do not deny that these Boer armaments had their *main* origin in the wicked and stupid Raid.....But self-preservation is the first law of nature. If I am walking on a Quay, and my dog bites a man: if he then tries to throw me into the water and one of us has to be drowned, I shall try to push him in first and stay on the Quay myself. So, though an Anti-jingo, I say the war must go on till Natal and the Cape have security from Boer armaments. Subject to that condition and the redress of the Uitlanders' grievances, many, perhaps most Englishmen, and certainly I, would make peace tomorrow on almost any terms that the Boers might wish.

Yours protesting but very sincerely,

ALFRED MARSHALL

To Professor J. B. CLARK, *Columbia University*

Wolkenstein in Gröden, South Tyrol

2. vii. 00

My dear Professor Clark,

I write in a pine forest in the "Dolomites" to thank you for your excellent *Distribution of Wealth*. I have not been able to take more than a cursory glance at it as yet: for I am engaged in quite a different field of economics. It seems to me that our differences are largely of emphasis; but that in the main we are allies. For which I am very thankful.

I note what you say of von Thünen, the great unrecognized, with special pleasure. I cannot recollect whether I formulated the doctrine "normal wages" = "terminal" (I got "marginal" from von Thünen's *Grenze*) productivity of labour before I read von Thünen or not. I think I did so partially at least; for my acquaintance with economics commenced with reading Mill, while I was still earning my living by teaching Mathematics at Cambridge; and translating his doctrines into differential equations as far as they would go; and, as a rule, rejecting those which would not go. On that ground I rejected the wage-doctrine in Book II, which has a wage-fund flavour: and accepted that in his Book IV; in which he seemed to me to be true to the *best* traditions of Ricardo's method (I say nothing in defence of Ricardo's positive doctrine of wages) and then to have got very close to what I afterwards found to be von Thünen's position. That was chiefly in 1867–8. I fancy I read Cournot in 1868. I know I did not read von Thünen then, probably in 1869 or 70: for I did not know enough German. One side of my own theory of wages has been absolutely fixed ever since, to what by title of priority may be called the von Thünen doctrine. But I thought then, and think still, that it covers only a very small part of the real difficulties of the wages problem: I cannot yet be sure whether you agree with this or not. Perhaps I must wait for Vol. II.

Yours very truly

ALFRED MARSHALL.

Balliol Croft, Cambridge
11. xi. 02

Dear Prof. Clark,

...I have been looking a little at your *Distribution of Wealth* recently again. I am always struck by its power and freshness. But it does not lead me to yield an inch on the controverted distinction between interest and rent proper. Of course in your statical construction you are sole autocrat. But I do not follow your reasonings if they are intended to apply to the " dynamical" world in which we live; where a stationary state may result from the equilibrium of opposed forces. For in that world it seems to me that the stock of capital is not fixed as the stock of land is; that the sacrifice of waiting (marginal) is part of the cost of production of capital, and therefore of the cost of production of things made by it. And it seems to me that, as no similar proposition is true of rent proper in relation to land proper, I must continue while I live to assert that *for long periods*, THOUGH NOT FOR SHORT, interest and rent stand to value in wholly different relations.

So I am perplexed. Thus your first sentence on p. 371 seems to suggest that I deny that, if a rise of rent were caused by a diminution in the supply of land (as e.g. the subsidence under the ocean of large areas of fertile land), there would result a rise in the cost of the produce and therefore in its value. Rise of rents and cost are results of same cause. You seem to me to suggest to the reader that I have stated, or implied, that a diminution in the supply of land available for a particular crop (which may arise from an increased demand for some rival crop) will affect the value of that produce in some way other than that in which a diminution in the area of all agricultural land would affect the value of all agricultural produce.

Now if I have committed myself to any such statement or implication, will you kindly tell me *where*?

I may say that my doctrine of quasi-rent, though only gradually developed, took on substance in 1868; when I was very much exercised by McLeod's criticisms—now unjustly forgotten—on the unqualified statement that cost governs value. He said: "your economist tells you that the wages and profits of people in the iron trade govern the price of iron: but they themselves know better; they know that the price of iron governs their wages and profits." I then started out on a theory of value in which I conceded to McLeod all that he asserted *for short periods*: and in effect, though not in name and not at all clearly, I regarded wages and profits as of the nature of rents for short periods. That went with my translations of all leading economic doctrines into differential equations: and, as far as I can tell, there is no broad difference on *that* side between my position before 1870 and now. But of course in other directions I have changed much. I then believed it was possible to have a coherent though abstract doctrine of economics in which competition was the only dominant force; and I then defined "normal" as that which the undisturbed play of competition would bring about: and now I regard that position as untenable from an abstract as well as from a practical point of view.

I have written thus fully, because I do not wish to be misunderstood by you. There are only two or three people in the world by whom I am as anxious to be understood aright. For your writings and our short talk have made me

Yours ever devotedly

ALFRED MARSHALL.

Balliol Croft, Cambridge

15. xii. 02

Dear Professor Clark,

We agree so much on concrete matters that I feel sure we cannot differ much on generals.....

What difference, if any, there is between us seems to me more probably to have its roots in our attitude towards the Dynamic state.

What I take to be a Static state is—to amplify a phrase which was all too short—a position of rest due to the equivalence of opposing forces which tend to produce motion. I cannot conceive of any Static state, which resembles the real world closely enough to form a subject of profitable study, and in which the notion of change is set aside even for an instant. In my view there may be no change in fact; but only because the forces tending to make change are (or for the purposes of a particular argument or illustration are supposed to be) equal and opposite.

....I could no more write one book about my Statical state, and another about my Dynamical state, than I could write one book about a yacht moving three miles an hour through the water which was running against it, and another about a yacht moving through the still water at 5 miles an hour. If there is any *real* difference between us, I think this must be at its root. And I trust that, when you get to your dynamical state, we shall attain the desire of the two good Scotch souls, who seemed unable to agree as to the password to heaven that related to predestination; but yet each hoped that the other would get in at some other door where predestination did not enter into the password: and so they might meet after all.....

So I look eagerly for your Dynamics in the hope that that contrast between land and capital which I hold to be necessary for my Statics (which is indissolubly one with my Dynamics) will appear in your Dynamics. If so, then our difference will be apparent as mainly one of arrangement. And I shall be joyful.

Hoping soon to see you on this side of the herring pond,

I am,

Yours very sincerely,

ALFRED MARSHALL.

My dear Clark,

I thank you very heartily for your most kind and friendly letter. I had thought you selected the Austrians for mention, partly in order to show that you bore them, and especially Böhm Bawerk, no ill-will on account of his rather rough method of thumping.

I have in earlier years eaten my heart out with doubt and anxiety as to what acknowledgments I should make to others. I fear I am an awful sinner: but I have grown callous. My rule has been to refer in a footnote to anyone whom I know to have said a thing before I have said it in print, even though I may have said it in lectures for many years before I knew that it had ever occurred to him: I just refer, but say nothing about obligations either way; being quite aware that people will suppose me to imply obligations. Instances are Francis Walker and Fleeming Jenkin.

But perhaps in return for your good-natured confidence I may state the reason which has prevented me from making general acknowledgments in any Preface except the first. It is that my main position as to the theory of value and distribution was practically completed in the years 1867 to 1870; when I translated Mill's version of Ricardo's or Smith's doctrines into mathematics; and that, when Jevons' book appeared, I knew at once how far I agreed with him and how far I did not. In the next four years I worked a good deal at the mathematical theory of monopolies, and at the diagrammatic treatment of Mill's problem of international values (parts of this were printed by Pantaleoni in a kindly way in his *Principii di Economia Pura*).

By this time I had practically completed the whole of the substance of my Mathematical Appendix, the only important exception being the treatment of elasticity (Note III) and Edgeworth's contract curve Note XII bis.

Substantially my theory of capital as it exists to-day is completely outlined in Notes V and XIII–XIV; and my general theory of distribution (except in so far as relates to the element of time) is in like manner contained in Note XXI; to which the preceding notes and especially XIV–XX lead up. I worked that out for the greater part while still teaching mathematics; and while still regarding myself as a mere pupil in the hands of great masters, especially Cournot, von Thünen and Ricardo; and while still extremely ignorant of economic realities. Between 1870 and 1874 I developed the details of my theoretical position; and I am not conscious of any perceptible change since the time when Böhm Bawerk and Wieser were still lads at school or College.....

I think there is an immense deal to be done still in

(1) elaborating the influence of time;
(2) studying complex interactions with special reference to the quantities concerned;
(3) allowing for the decadence of some economic influences and the rise of others;
(4) taking account of non-economic influences, and especially such as evade quantitative measurement;
(5) applications to practical problems as to which I look for much help from "Essentials."

I see before me ten times as much work to do in these five directions as I can hope to do: and I am sure that after I am dead people will gradually discover ten times and more as much work as I see.

So I scarcely ever read controversies or criticisms. I have not read even a quarter of those which have been written about myself. The books, for instance, which I take to the Alps nearly every summer are almost exclusively concerned with matters of fact; though I try to read or skim any piece of analysis in which a man works to produce knowledge and not to controvert others. Thus I could not make acknowledgments to others properly: and I fall back on the plan already mentioned of referring in silence to any anticipation, of which I am aware, of a suggestion made by myself.

My whole life has been and will be given to presenting in realistic form as much as I can of my Note XXI. If I live to complete my scheme fairly well, people will, I think, realise that it has unity and individuality. And a man who has lost ten of the best years of his life—from 37 to 47—through illness, would, I think, be doubly foolish if he troubled himself to weigh and measure any claims to originality that he has.

One thing alone in American criticism irritates me, though it be not unkindly meant. It is the suggestion that I try to "compromise between" or "reconcile" divergent schools of thought. Such work seems to me trumpery. Truth is the only thing worth having: not peace. I have never compromised on any doctrine of any kind. As to the use of terms, that is a matter of mere opportunism and everyone should, I think, not merely compromise but positively yield against his own judgment, if he thinks that by so doing he can facilitate mutual understandings. For that reason I have shifted my use of the word capital, but I have not changed my doctrines as to capital by a hair's breadth: Irving Fisher seems to have misread me in this matter. I hope you will forgive this scrawl.

Yours very sincerely,

ALFRED MARSHALL.

To Professor JAMES WARD

Balliol Croft, Cambridge

23. ix. 1900

....I would not have you think me indifferent to mental science. About as much of my time since I came to Cambridge in 1861 has been given to it as to mathematics. My zeal for economics would never have got me out of bed at five o'clock in the morning, to make my own coffee and work for three hours before breakfast and pupils in mathematics: but philosophy did that, till I became ill and my right foot swelled to double its normal size. That was in 1867. Soon after, I drifted away from metaphysics towards psychology. When Pearson asked me to lecture on Political Economy I consented; but I should have preferred philosophy, which was his subject. Shortly after the College made me a lecturer: and I added Logic and Ethics. But I always said till about 1871 that my home was in Mental Science. Gradually, however, the increasing urgency of economic studies as a means towards human well-being grew upon me. About 1871–2, I told myself the time had come at which I must decide whether to give my life to psychology or economics. I spent a year in doubt: always preferring psychology for the pleasures of the chase; but economics grew and grew in practical urgency, not so much in relation to the growth of wealth as to the quality of life; and I settled down to it....

To Professor A. L. BOWLEY

Balliol Croft, Cambridge

21. ii. 1901

My dear Bowley,

I told you I thought there was too much mathematics in your excellent book for the ordinary economic student. Having looked again at it, I think it presents an implicit claim for the applicability of abstract reasoning in the deduction of practical precepts from economic statistics, which I hesitate to admit. So, in that hurried and imperfect way in which alone my overburdened strength will allow me to write, I venture to put my difficulty before you.

Perhaps the best way to begin is to confess that I regard the method of Least Squares as involving an assumption with regard to symmetry that vitiates all its applications to economic problems with which I am acquainted. In every case that I have considered at all carefully, I think harm has been done by treating the results as "economic." I regard them as mathematical toys. I think the economic, as distinguished from the mathematical, student is hurt by being invited to spend his time on them, before he has made a sufficiently realistic study of those statistics to know roughly, without calculation, on which side of the target the centre of the shots lies. He assumes there is no wind. I believe that a Boer marksman, who takes account of the wind, will by instinct get nearer the truth than he by mathematics. To study the wind and guess how it will deflect the bullets is, in my opinion, *the* work of the statistician. Do not you encourage men to neglect the wind? For instance, I of course accept the rule that, other things equal, it is more important to multiply items for an index number than to adjust weights: indeed, I regard the rule as almost too obvious to need proof. But I hold that in economics other things are so often not equal that greater proportionate stress ought to be laid on the necessity of examining each case to see whether the weights are important or not, than you appear to me to do. Thus one would naturally say, *prima facie*, that it is not important to weight returns of wages from branches of a trade union in order to get the true average. But I had made very little progress in the study of wage-statistics before I became convinced that it is necessary to do so, at all events for several large classes of trades.....

Again, if I had been asked to give instances of the benefit that an economic student would get from a course in statistics, none would have been more likely, to occur to me than that of being warned against the common newspaper error of regarding the statistics of unemployment among Ironfounders as a basis for broad generalizations.....Independently of its unique statistics, that trade fascinates me. I love to linger in the foundry, and I never liked mechanical invention less than when I learnt that it was bound to drive out the life-earned skill of the artizan from many of the higher, as well as the lower, branches of the trade. It was, I think, in 1885 that I was shown over the only Works in Keighley that were on full time. The Manager showed me a dozen navvies working like furies at the boxes, and each earning 10*s*. a day. It was coarse work: and I could hardly blame the founders' union for refusing it. But of course they lacked employment. He later on confirmed his statements: and told me that founders' employment statistics were utterly non-representative, even for other credit-cycle trades. On the Labour Commission I watched evidence as to Unemployment more eagerly than for any other point: and I am convinced that the common old-fashioned views as to its nature, extent and causes are very wide of the mark.

This is a fearfully long jaw. But it all leads up to one thing. You have made for yourself, in this short time and in spite of unusual difficulties, so splendid a position among students of the first rank, that you may well claim to be able to take care of yourself. But there is a tradition that an old teacher, not because he is wise but because he is affectionate, may venture something. Will you then be so very generous as to forgive me if I ask you to ask yourself whether, having now brought out this great and successful book, it is not time to make some further study of the broader relations between economic facts: to leave mathematics for a little on one side; and join more heartily in the quest for "the One in the Many, the Many in the One"?

Yours sincerely,

ALFRED MARSHALL.

Balliol Croft, Cambridge
3. iii. 01

My dear Bowley,

Thank you very heartily for your generous letter. Now that I am getting to feel the deadening hand of age press heavily on me, I am looking more and more towards a future when I shall be silent except in so far as some faint echoes of my voice may be mingled in among the sounds of progress in which some of my old pupils are leaders; and among the first of those I have for the last ten years thought of you. Others have given more time to economics than you: but no one has done as much relatively to his opportunities. So, though I grudge every hour that calls me away from my own work, I cannot bear to act on your kind hint, and leave the question as it stands.....

You say you have no memory. Memory is quite as often a curse as a blessing to the student of economics, because it tempts him to recollect particulars, and there never was a memory that could retain a hundredth part of the particulars needful for solving a very small problem. The use of the study of particulars may be controversial (and so far hateful). This use is that, when any one basing himself on particulars flatters a popular whim of the moment by instancing particulars favourable to it, the man with a memory can produce *in debate* particulars which are inconsistent with it, and so expose him.

But for the constructive student, who does not trouble himself to expose impostors, the only use of the study of particulars is to correct and enlarge his own instinct. He should, I think, read and read and read pages of statistics, not troubling to remember any, but always stopping when he comes to a figure which is not what he expected, and not leaving it without a vigorous attempt to discover whether (i) his general expectations are framed on a wrong basis, or (ii) the deviation was due to some cause which he could not have expected to anticipate: so that, though it increases the need for caution, it does not demand a shifting of his general position. You know my old "Red" curve book in which any important economic or semi-economic fact (in figure form or other) which occurred in any year, say 1867 or 1889, will be pierced through by a pin put on the proper spot and run through the book. A very great part of my work has been the study of that book, or more recently of lecture diagrams on a similar scheme. On each page or wall diagram there will be the history of from two to ten correlated movements. But I scarcely ever get any instruction worth having from a single page: I learn only by turning backwards and forwards, backwards and forwards from one correlated group to another. Thus my notion of the use of economic statistics differs widely from that which, on my second view of your book, I found implied in it; and which in your last letter you have expressed in the words: "the relation of the mathematics of the subject, which I regarded as its furthest scientific development, to actual facts."

In my view every economic fact, whether or not it is of such a nature as to be expressed in numbers, stands in relation as cause and effect to many other facts: and since it *never* happens that all of them can be expressed in numbers, the application of exact mathematical methods to those which can is nearly always waste of time, while in the large majority of cases it is positively misleading; and the world would have been further on its way forward if the work had never been done at all. It is chiefly when the mathematical method is used not for direct construction, but to train sound instinctive habits (like the practising of scales on the piano), that it seems to me generally helpful. I admit exceptions, and no doubt there are already more than I know of, and yet more will be discovered. For instance, if I were younger I would study the abstract mathematical doctrine of correlated curves, which I am ashamed to say I do not fully understand. I think it may occasionally be helpful in determining a controversy as to whether two movements have a causal connection. But at present we are not ripe for that, I think. Look at the Bimetallic controversy. (You know I am a bimetallist, but opposed to the excrescences which the League has borrowed from the U.S. silver men.) Out of a hundred things which I think are causally connected, and which —by continually passing from one page of my "red book" to another—I have got to regard as but manifestations of one broad, many-sided movement, the writers of the League select two. Without proof they assert that A is the cause of B, when it seems to me that it would be less untrue to say that B is the cause of A, and they deluge the public with these correlated curves to prove it. No doubt they can be fought with their own weapons: their own methods can be made to bring out exactly the opposite results in every particular: but that is a dreary soul-sickening waste of time. Surely *the* thing to do is to build the basis of our economic structure soundly and not to put a varnish of mathematical accuracy to many places of decimals on results the premises of which are not established within 20 or 50 per cent.: many not even so far as to put beyond dispute the question whether A is the cause of B, or B the cause of A, or A and B are the results of $a + b + c + d + \ldots$. Surely *the* thing to do is to seek the Many in the One, the One in the Many.

And who is to do it? It is a far harder task than anything that was set to candidates for the Mathematical Tripos in 1865 (I know little of what has happened since)..... It must for the greater part be done by Cambridge men, or left undone. And by which Cambridge men? There are not a score who are setting themselves to do it. There are not six who have equal faculties for doing it with the quiet and steadfast A. L. Bowley. If you do not do your best, the world will be much the poorer. If you do, you will have done something to turn the mighty forces of progress into paths that lead ever upwards, and away from alluring openings that lead to precipices, or at best are but blind alleys. To do that, even a little, is worth a life: and you can do it much. Do not refuse.

Yours in trust and hope,

ALFRED MARSHALL.

Balliol Croft, Cambridge

20. xii. 01

Dear Bowley,

It is not through negligence that I have left your letter
unanswered. For I have thought about my answer once or
twice every day since I received it. But it is most difficult to
give advice to one who has already his own position more or
less set, and yet more or less unknown to me: and it is important
I should do my best.

So far as my views on books in general go, the enclosed paper,
which I made out for my class, may interest you.

But as regards your own special work, I think the best thing
I can say is that you should select a few questions which are of
special interest to you, and in which the public is not without
interest, and set yourself to solve them. There is scarcely any
question in economics which might not be advanced by bringing
to bear on it (i) a knowledge of what statistics have to say;
combined with (ii) a knowledge of what statistics can't be made
to tell, but which has to be reckoned for in a realistic solution.

(i) without (ii) seems to me so dangerous that on the whole
it is almost more likely to do harm than good. And the best
way of working (i) usefully is, I think, to work out a few specimen
problems thoroughly, taking (ii) at least as seriously as (i).

You know I have always had this view. I have never lectured
on statistics in the abstract. But in every advanced course I
take one or two specimen problems (or problemettes—little
problems or fragments of problems), and put the statistical
aspects (in diagrammatic form, if possible) before the men, and
then go for its solution as a whole. I believe that that is the
right way to teach statistics to those who want to become not
pure mathematicians but realistic economists.

Scarcely do I write a single chapter of my wearisome book
without saying to myself—"Now, if I were a rich man, I would
have an office with one or two trained economists to rule it,
and several clerks, and I would ask them to bring out what
statistics have to say on Question A or B, etc. And when I had
got one answer as to A from English statistics, I would get

another division of the office to go over a similar problem to A with German or U.S. statistics; and look at the result. Then my chapter would be of quite a different order from what it is."

I ought perhaps to write down such questions as they arise: but I don't.

Now, would it be well that I should try to get a man of your age and position to "devil" at questions that I might have a disproportionate interest in?

But I will give you one instance, not a very important one in itself, but a good type—my purpose being mainly to try to make my meaning clear; not to urge any particular piece of work on you, but merely to indicate what is in my opinion the "real" use of statistics at the present stage of economics, i.e. the pursuit of the aim indicated by Fortry, quoted in my *Old Generation of Economists and the New*, p. 13.

The Sugar bounties.

A. Assuming that they lower the price of sugar to the British consumer by $\frac{1}{2}d$. a pound (or any other amount), what is the aggregate gain to us?

B. What would be the aggregate gain from stopping them to
(*a*) capitalists and landlords ⎫
(*b*) white labour   ⎬ in West Indian Islands and other countries?
(*c*) black labour   ⎭

C. How far is it true that the present distress in those colonies is due to physical and moral degeneration as the results of
(*a*) climate;
(*b*) self-indulgent habits engendered by the abnormal ease of making money in the old time?

How far was that ease due to circumstances which no one had a right to expect to last?

What light can be thrown on these questions by
(i) Statistics of trade and fortunes made by West Indians in the old time?
(ii) Statistics of (α) sugar obtained,
               (β) utilization of waste products,

from a ton of sugar cane in the West Indies in 1850 as compared with 1900: this ratio being compared with a similar ratio for a ton of beet in Germany?

(iii) Statistics of work done by labourers whose ancestors have lived in these islands for several generations, as compared with that done by "fresh" workers? (British Guiana capitalists said they could make a good thing of the colony if sugar bounties were abolished, and they were allowed to import an indefinite number of Asiatic etc. workers: those whom they had used for several generations were useless! Apparently that was to be supported at Imperial expense!)

(iv) Statistics of output per £1000 of capital and per x workers of (α) sugar in Queensland, (β) bananas and other miscellaneous fruit in Florida, etc.?

D. Estimate of the probable loss incurred by bolstering up unenterprising capitalists in the employment of degenerating labour, with the prospect of having later on to support that labour.

E. Pecuniary gain or loss resulting from leaving sugar bounties as they are, and giving a capital sum of £1000 as a present to each white man, woman and child in the West India Islands.

As I write this I am of course thinking a good deal about the anti-social practices which Trade Unionists sometimes sustain, though of course they did not invent them. In concocting sauce for the goose, one sometimes looks at the gander.

I am afraid the illustration has panned out rather wearisomely, however.

A similar one might be got from the question of "protection" to English agriculture: but of course the items would be much more numerous.

To take a very simple point. Only the other day I was showing a diagram in a lecture, made chiefly out of Arthur Young's Tables, which are reproduced by Tooke (*History*, vi. p. 391); and lamenting that I could not find time for the continuation by aid of your statistics.

But really they ought to be supplemented by some knowledge of the food other than wheat (or cereal) consumed by the workers at each date; with estimates of what such food would have cost at other dates; and *not omitting* (as many statisticians do inconsistently with their professed aims) those things which were not procurable at all at the earlier dates, but inserting them at rather high arbitrary figures based on those at which they first appeared; and adding that they could not be got even at those figures.

This would count to raise the purchasing power of modern wages in most things, but to lower city wages, if fresh air is counted, as it should of course be.

There: I have taken up much of your patience and I fear said very little after all. But it is difficult to say the right thing in such a case.

Yours ever,

A. M.

Balliol Croft, Cambridge

27. ii. 06

My dear Bowley,

I have not been able to lay my hands on any notes as to Mathematico-economics that would be of any use to you: and I have very indistinct memories of what I used to think on the subject. I never read mathematics now: in fact I have forgotten even how to integrate a good many things.

But I know I had a growing feeling in the later years of my work at the subject that a good mathematical theorem dealing with economic hypotheses was very unlikely to be good economics: and I went more and more on the rules—(1) Use mathematics as a shorthand language, rather than as an engine of inquiry. (2) Keep to them till you have done. (3) Translate into English. (4) Then illustrate by examples that are important in real life. (5) Burn the mathematics. (6) If you can't succeed in 4, burn 3. This last I did often.

I believe in Newton's Principia Methods, because they carry so much of the ordinary mind with them. Mathematics used in a Fellowship thesis by a man who is not a mathematician by nature—and I have come across a good deal of that—seems to me an unmixed evil. And I think you should do all you can to prevent people from using Mathematics in cases in which the English Language is as short as the Mathematical.....

I find mathematicians almost invariably follow what I regard as Jevons' one great analytical mistake, his eulogy of the Geometric mean in general: and do not see that, according to his use, erroneous weighting may do far more mischief with the Geometric Mean than with the Arithmetic Mean. I always have to spend some time in convincing them of the danger.

Yours emptyhandedly,

ALFRED MARSHALL.

Another trouble is that mathematicians insist on assuming that, if p be the price which may vary to pr or to $\frac{p}{r}$, then the two variations are *prima facie* to be assumed to be equally probable. Whereas of course, if r is a considerable quantity, that is not true: Jevons has overlooked this also, I think, as a result of not thinking in English. But of course you know far more about these things than I do: and again I say I am an unprofitable Servant.

Balliol Croft, Cambridge

7. x. 06

My dear Bowley,

I ought to have thanked you before for your excellent and interesting Section F address. I rejoiced to know that the whole meeting of the Section was eminently successful, at all events from the scientific, if not from the newspaper, point of view.....

It is however true that the longer I live the more convinced am I that—except in purely abstract problems—the statistical side must never be separated even for an instant from the non-statistical: on the ground that, if economics is to be a guide in life—individual and more especially social—people must be warned off by every possible means from considering the action of any one cause—beyond the most simple generalities—without taking account of the others whose effects are commingled with it. And, since many of the chief of these causes have either no statistical side at all, or no statistical side that is accessible practically for common use, therefore the statistical element must be kept subordinate to general considerations and included among them.....

And so you, who, in spite of your humility, are an economist by nature, should, I think, in the non-mathematical part of your work treat economic problems as a whole clearly and emphatically.

The vast services which you are rendering to economics would, I think, be doubled if you would do that: well that's too much, there's not room for it: say increased "in a considerable ratio."

Yours very sincerely,

ALFRED MARSHALL.

In the last two years I have given about a sixth of my lectures to almost purely statistical discussions of a general (non-mathematical) character. Each year I worked over rather carefully some hundred pages selected from the statistical parts of the two "Fiscal Blue Books." And now that Pigou is taking "Analytical Difficulties" I shall probably be able to do a little more in this direction. But my main aim is to help people to read *through* figures, and reach the real values, the true relative proportions represented by them.

Balliol Croft, Cambridge

15. x. 06

My dear Bowley,

.... In what I am writing I am bound to say something on the matter [of the real wages of German and English workers]: but it can only be in one or two paragraphs; and it cannot be based on thorough study. For general purposes indeed I rely more on my "field work" in the workingmen's quarters of many German towns, and on my conversations with Germans in the Tyrol, than I do on Statistics. For the Statistics seem to me specially full of traps. "Arbeitslosigkeit" for instance means something very widely removed from "Unemployment," and it is hard to find out how widely.....

A novelist has been quoted in support of the statement that German children never wear untidy shoes: they would rather go shoeless. I showed that to Dietzel and Lotz: they burst into a roar of laughter. She had obviously only observed in summer: and then most children of the working classes go barefoot; those who would have tidy shoes in winter start in the morning with clean legs: those who would wear untidy shoes start with legs covered eight inches high with indurated street muck!....

This is not Statistical. But if you could take the statistical side up, and do a little field work in Germany, you might render a great service.

Yours sincerely,

ALFRED MARSHALL.

To THEODORE LLEWELLYN DAVIES

Balliol Croft, Cambridge

30. x. 01

Dear Llewellyn Davies,

I have found a short loose end of time which I could give to the Local Taxation Report. I have dipped into the volume in several places; and have read nearly the whole of the Separate Reports on Site Values &c. I find it extremely interesting; if I were not so deeply sunk in other parts of economics, I should make a thorough study of it, and of some questions suggested by it.

The Separate Report seems to me admirably put. I agree with it on a very great number of points on which it differs from generally received opinion. And in fact I have only noticed two questions on which I do not go with it. My views on these two are indicated in my Memorandum. But they have so much interest for me that I think I will try to focus them again: partly because the answers of the signatories of that Report to the questions are implied by silence, rather than expressed.

The first is:—Given that (say) £200,000,000 have to be raised by taxation, Imperial and Local, is it possible to reduce the aggregate taxation on immoveable property without imposing other taxes which would on the whole be more burdensome and less just? I say *No*. And therefore, while I think that there is much to be said for maintaining large grants in aid of local rates for the double purpose of removing the present inequalities of the pressure of those rates which are in effect spent on matters of national concern, and of enabling the Central Authority to exercise some control over the efficiency with which those services are performed, I think that the funds for those grants should be derived from taxes on immoveable property.

I do not question that the plan of grants in aid is the easiest at starting, and that the control exerted by the central government through these grants would be beneficial in many ways. But, though the easiest, I do not think it is the best route. Westminster has already a far greater burden than it can carry; and is notoriously wanting in initiative in many directions. My own ideal is therefore the development of "Provincial" governments with duties somewhat similar to those of the Swiss Cantons, and with funds derived chiefly from taxes on immoveable property. (The Inhabited House duty might be handed over to them.) They could try experiments; inter-provincial suggestion and emulation would make for progress.

The Second question, or rather group of questions, is:—Are not the duties, which the State and private individuals have hitherto recognized with regard to the use of land, inadequate to the needs of the modern age? Is it not true that, in spite of the electrical distribution of power, of asphalt roads and motor cars, an ever-increasing portion of English children will be town bred? Is it not true that, unless our laws as regards building and open spaces are organically changed, the result must be the degeneration of the race? Is not this the most important economic issue which the present generation of Englishmen have to face? Does it not call for a large expenditure of money? Will not that expenditure, if wisely set, redound to the real value of land? Is it not therefore equitable that land values should be charged *much* more heavily towards it? Does not this case differ in nature from ordinary questions of taxation; and resemble rather the taxation of riparian *owners* for main drainage schemes, which were not contemplated by the tenants, and from which they will not reap any great benefit?

If, as I claim, this group of questions should be answered in the affirmative, then Ch. XI "Why site values should be rated" does not go far enough to be an adequate basis for a thorough solution of the problem of the taxation of land; and I would rather that no great change were made now, than that gains, made at the expense of national life, should be diverted from the restoration to the people of the sources of life, and appropriated to the needs of the moment, with the ultimate result that they are mainly spent on ephemeral comforts and luxuries....

To Professor A. C. PIGOU

Balliol Croft, Cambridge
17. vi. 02

My dear Pigou,

I don't want to be an accomplice in any way in your letter. So all I will say is that I think it very good, though rather efflorescent in its earlier part.

One word of caution. Sir R. Giffen is a sturdy combatant, helpful when on our side. But he is reckless. And if we had to defend "free trade" (in its moderate modern sense), and yet were bound to admit all the contentions by which Giffen has given away his case in recent articles, I think our position would be strategically untenable.

As to my own motives for not writing, they are not quite what you take them to be: for I have just looked at the current *Saturday Review*. My own position is that I have no time or aptitude for writing on questions of the day, as such. If I condemned aloud all the words and deeds of, say, Mr Chamberlain or Mr Webb, which I do not approve, I should have my hands full.

When I write it is always because I think some general principle, which belongs to the sphere in which I work, is being misquoted, or misunderstood.

I am a good deal tempted just now to write about the Zollverein principle, for that reason. The *Speaker's* articles count as a perceptible, but not strong, argument against my doing it. But I do not regard it as my work to attempt to make an exposition of familiar arguments such as John Morley has done with such admirable clearness and force, and with which the *Speaker* is justly delighted.....

Yours etc.

ALFRED MARSHALL.

Balliol Croft, Cambridge
19. iii. 1903

My dear Pigou,

I have just been reading your article in *E. J.* [March 1903].... Well! Am I right in supposing that your main argument is this—

Though we may pass from the utility curve of an individual to the demand curve of a nation (or other group) as regards bread or milk or any other commodity which is valued only for its direct benefit to us, yet we cannot do that for commodities which we value partly because they impart social distinction. For a large change in the supply all round of such a commodity alters the conditions which we have assumed to be practically constant when making out the curve for an individual.

So far as I can see, I concur in this: and think something of the sort ought to have been said by me. But of course I have always insisted that the demand price of a group is not any approximate measure of satisfaction, save on the assumption that people of different incomes and also of different sensibilities are evenly distributed throughout the group. And next it may be said that the continued references to the effect of changes in fashion include in their purview such changes as alter the distinction-giving power of a thing....

Next, is your second chief point that, since some moving forces are not associated with great pleasure, possibly not even with great satisfaction, therefore the consumers' surplus shown by the curve may diverge far (even in a society where all are about equally well-off) from being a measure of aggregate pleasure or even aggregate satisfaction? If so I again quite agree. I must some time consider whether I have sufficiently emphasized the fact that the schedule deals with satisfaction only in so far as that arises out of the number and excellence of the things which a man has, and not out of the quality of the man himself....

ALFRED MARSHALL.

12. iv. 1916

My dear Pigou,

I am charmed by the brilliancy and "go" of your book. But I am also a little frightened. I am certain that almost everything you say is true, with the qualifications that are latent in your mind: but some of them seem to me in danger of misleading people who do not know the ropes of economic complex interactions. For instance, what you say on p. 19 means something that is true: but I think it may be taken to be inconsistent with the *vitally* important fact that, if our soldiers and their families consume in various ways at Government expense much more than the German soldiers do, and the war last long, then Lloyd George's silver bullets in the last campaign may fail us.

Again, if A buys old lace from B, and B saves the money, the country is not weakened. But in fact B probably sells lace in order to spend—perhaps on maintaining a big establishment, dances, etc. Therefore I should be glad to hear that A had decided not to buy the lace, so long as I know nothing about B. The only thing which I have noted as apparently opposed to my own opinion is on p. 93, about railways. I have been working off and on at railways for several months; and I think I know nearly all of importance that has been said by the best authorities. I believe that they hold that it costs more to earn £100 on first class than on third class traffic; for first class insists on something like solitude, and the dead weight involved is portentous; but that, the excess of receipts over direct costs being high, they would lose net revenue by dropping first class carriages. I believe these opinions are certainly valid. My own estimate, based on no inside knowledge, is that, the direct cost to the country of A's railway journey for which £1 is paid is something like 6d.; though, especially if there is luggage, it *may* rise to a shilling. If the £10 is distributed over a dozen journeys, the cost would of course be higher. I make allowance for the time spent by ticket clerks, etc. on A's own needs: but none for the need which increasing traffic may make for increased services, and not merely tight packing of trains. (Of course that is fairly reasonable under war conditions.) If allowance is made for probable lengthening of trains, I would add half as much again: if additional trains are in view, a good deal more; and more again if A travels at times of the day at which the line is heavily worked. But I can't get beyond 4s. in any case. On the other hand I regard unnecessary motor car hiring as exceptionally unpatriotic.....

ALFRED MARSHALL.

To Professor F. Y. EDGEWORTH

Wolkenstein, South Tirol

28. viii. 02

....B. You know I never apply curves or mathematics to market values. For I don't think they help much. And market values are, I think, either absolutely abstract or terribly concrete and full of ever-varying (though individually vital) side-issues. Also *Ox* for market values measures a stock and not a "flow"; and I found that, if I once got people to use Demand and Supply curves which discussed *stocks* along the axis of *x*, they could not easily be kept from introducing the notion of stock when *flow* was essential. That is what I meant by my footnote on p. 47 of *Ec. Journal*, vol. VIII....

D. I think curves do naturally avoid the money difficulty: but I do not think they are essential for that line of argument. And I think they only get at the outer fringe of the outside of real problems of International Trade.....

F. *re* Sidgwick's theory of cost of transport, I have not decided whether to make any reference to it in my new volume. My view is that he has got quite off the rails and that it is hardly necessary to say so.

G. Trusts. I am confirmed in my opinion that Cournot's method of treatment is wholly inapplicable to the real conditions of life. His discoveries were I think—in so far as they claimed to have a bearing on real problems—rediscoveries of things that had been known in the XVII and better in the XVIII century as the result of the working of the chartered companies. In all the vast talk which I have put into writing on them I have seldom been tempted to refer to the abstract theory of monopolies, except of course in the general introduction. No instance could, I think, be better of the *mischievousness* of an academic education in *abstract* economics not continued into *real* economics [i.e. not continued for at least three years (Hm!)] than the inferences which Cournot's method suggests as to the relative efficiencies and inefficiencies, public usefulnesses and mischiefs of different forms of combination and monopoly. I have in view, e.g., what he says about a monopoly of brass versus a monopoly of zinc and a monopoly of copper (supposing zinc and copper useful only as constituents of brass). I have a notion that that is his illustration. The considerations of which he takes account seem to me to be of very slight importance relatively to those which he ignores: and the conclusion to which he points is, I believe, generally the opposite of the true one.

As to what I say in my *Aspects* about stability in relation to Trusts: that comes really under two heads. Firstly (on p. 23) I argue that they do not tend to make industry more stable (the same idea occurs in my *Principles*, p. 469 and is being developed in my vol. II); and secondly I have argued that "Trusts" in the original sense of the term, the only sense which was in vogue in 1890 (one analogous to Kartelle), were essentially unstable: that people gave far too much attention to them and ought rather to watch the *real* oncoming peril—that of consolidation. [Incidentally I may say that I am just a little swollen-headed (pride-inflated) at having predicted in 1890 what by 1900 had been effectuated, i.e. the disappearance from America (not from Germany yet) of Trusts in the 1890 sense of the word.]...

J. I am not sure that we differ about "Rent not entering into Cost." The question whether a phrase, which was from the first an indisputably bad one, can be rescued by explanation from misinterpretation, is to be solved only by experience. If I could have foreseen how many people would, in spite of my protests, persist in taking my words as I would have them *not* do, I should have from the first said what I do *now*:—It is *wisest not* to say that "Rent does not enter into cost of production": for that will confuse many people. But it is *wicked* to say that "Rent *does* enter into cost of production," because that is *sure* to be applied in such a way as to lead to the denial of subtle truths, which, in spite of their being subtle, are of the very highest importance scientifically and also in relation to the practical well-being of the world.

K. I don't recollect that I said that a tax on site values would not discourage home industry. For site value is a very complex entity, not a mere capitalisation of true economic rent; and the manufacturer is often his own landlord. But of course I hold that, if spent on fresh air, it would add so much to the industrial vigour of the population that it would go far towards arresting England's industrial (relative) decline; and might even turn the tide....

N. I think the notion of "representative firm" is capable of extension to labour; and I have had some idea of introducing that into my discussion of standard rates of wages. But I don't feel sure I shall: and I almost think I can say what I want to more simply in another way.

I had forgotten I had written (and cut out), what you quote from my Edition I, about balancing of motives. But I did so no doubt because I found it was habitually misunderstood, especially by Ethicists: they *would* take such phrases as Utilitarian manifestos. So I set myself to cut out short sentences on a big subject. What I meant however is—for the greater part—contained in the last two lines of Vol. I, p. 788. "The ground traversed in Books V and VI commands and gives access to that which lies yet before us." To that I adhere and I like it better than the old phrase "a kernel." But V and VI rest on III and IV; and VI is often concrete. In that old phrase you would perhaps take the kernel to be the essential part: I take it to be a small part; and, when taken alone, more likely to be misapplied than in the case of other sciences. In my view "Theory" is essential. No one gets any real grip of economic problems unless he will work at it. But I conceive no more calamitous notion than that abstract, or general, or "theoretical" economics was economics "proper." It seems to me an essential but a very small part of economics proper: and by itself sometimes even— well, not a very good occupation of time.

The key-note of my *Plea* is that *the* work of the economist is "to disentangle the interwoven effects of complex causes"; and that for this, general reasoning is essential, but a wide and thorough study of facts is equally essential, and that a combination of the two sides of the work is *alone* economics *proper*. Economic theory is, in my opinion, as mischievous an impostor when it claims to be economics *proper* as is mere crude unanalysed history. Six of ye one, ½ dozen of ye other!

That mere qualitative analysis, though essential, is *not* the chief work of the XXth century I have argued in "The Old Generation of Economists and the New," *Harvard Journal*, Jan. 1897 (pp. 11 and onwards of offprint). In all those pages there is no question raised for which Economic Theory by *itself* is of any use except in criticism. Nor is it of any use by itself for any one of those "Scientific inquiries" which I have suggested in Book I. ch. VII, § 3 as the *proper* work of the economist; and of course not for the practical issues which I have suggested in the following § as giving a purpose to his scientific inquiries.

Balliol Croft, Cambridge

21. iv. 09

My dear Edgeworth,

I have just noticed your review of Rae in the *Ec. J.* [Vol. XIX. p. 102]. I don't want to argue. But the hint that a rather rash and random guess has been made by those who suggest that a (moderate) rise in the price of wheat might increase its consumption in England (not generally) provokes me to say that the matter has not been taken quite at random.

When wheat was dear and men were cheap, the estimate of consumption of wheat per head in England was one quarter: now it is, I believe. between 5 and 6 bushels. And thrifty Frenchmen with all their cabbages are said to consume more than a quarter now. Ever since I saw Giffen's hint on the subject, I have set myself to compare the amounts of bread (and cake, wheaten biscuits and puddings) eaten at first class dinners in private houses and expensive hotels, with the consumption in middle class houses and second-rate hotels; and again with the consumption in cheap inns, including a low grade London hotel: and I have watched the baker's supplies to cottagers. And I am convinced that the very rich eat less than half as much bread as the poorer classes; the middle class coming midway. This proves nothing conclusively: but it is a fair basis, I think, for a surmise as to a probability.

In America the waste of cereals is said to be prodigious: I think a rise in price would check that; also all cereals, including even wheat, are sometimes fed to stock. In Germany it is known that dear wheat and rye increase the always enormous consumption of potatoes. I have never seen evidence that dear wheat has a considerable effect in that direction here.

With bad world harvests for two or three years in succession, I suggest that part of English wheat consumption would come from American and Australian waste. If not, then bread might become so dear that our consumption of wheat would diminish. I don't say I am right: but I am not random.

Yours ever,

ALFRED MARSHALL.

I forgot to speak of adulteration by bakers. When I was a boy that was done largely by potatoes. Now I think it is seldom done on a great scale: and that maize is used more than potatoes when wheat is dear. I think a great rise in the price of wheat would greatly increase the amount of maize in bread: and this of course tells on your side.

Balliol Croft, Cambridge
22. iv. 09

My dear Edgeworth,

About ten years ago I nearly completed a draft Book (No. X, I think) of my second volume "On Markets." It had an introductory general chapter, followed by others in detail. After working some time, I found the task too long to be made complete. So I decided to select two or three typical instances, and work them out carefully. Wheat was—for many reasons— my chief instance. My draft copy on it is about 40 pp. long. I read several thousand semi-technical pages, chiefly American, on the subject: and came to the conclusions which I condensed in 1903 into §§ 23–27 and 29 of my Memorandum. The substance being that, after a special analysis, it appears to be not "extremely improbable," but à priori to be expected, that the elasticity of supply of wheat in those parts of America from which most wheat has been raised in the past would obey wholly different laws from those which did prevail there a generation ago, and which now prevail in the Dakotas and Manitoba etc.: and that the evidence which could be got tended to prove à posteriori that this was the case.

Having had means of knowing that the information put before

the British public from about 1902, as to the conditions of
Northern Manitoba, Assimaboia, etc., was largely fraudulent,
and prompted by unscrupulous "Americans," who had taken
options (and in some cases bought outright) a great deal of
Canadian land, I began to read again on the same subject, and
worked through "several thousand?" pages more. Whenever
I met a high class American I asked him in effect this question,
"Is not the export of wheat from the North American Continent
in years of normal harvest highly elastic for a fall and very
inelastic for a rise?" and I understood everybody, who expressed
an opinion at all, to agree. You may perhaps recollect that
there was a dinner party here during the British Association
meeting in 1904: and that after dinner, though there were
several people to whom I wanted particularly to talk, I spent
the whole time—as it was my only chance—in getting from
Mavor, who knew much more about it than anyone else in the
world, a detailed (illustrated) account of the wheat resources
of the Canadian Northwest.

Of course I looked at the matter from the analytical point of
view also. And it seemed to me that the common opinion—
which I understand you to endorse—is based on a fundamental
misconception of the nature of wheat production in a new
country. Under some circumstances it is a complete industry;
and then it responds but slowly to changes in price. Under
others it is a mere department of general agricultural industry;
and then it responds almost instantaneously.

There is no paradox in this. Take an analogous case. If a
certain pattern of cycle, not patented, were to come into favour,
so that it could be sold for £1 more than others into which the
same amount of work was put, then its production might jump
up from five thousand to half a million instantly: because
making a particular kind of cycle merely requires minor detailed
readjustments of plant already in existence. That case resembles the case of wheat where highly capitalised *mixed*
farming predominates. For the farmer can in 1910 say "I will
have four times as much wheat a year as now," or "I will not
have any wheat at all next year." As a matter of fact however—
and on this all Americans with whom I talked seemed to agree—
the Middle West mixed farming might diminish rapidly its

supply of wheat, but is not likely to increase it rapidly; because it is not highly capitalised, such an increase would require to be preceded by a large and rather slow increase of live stock (artificial manure being impracticable unless the price of wheat rose very much).

On the other hand, when cement works are fairly busy no increase of price will bring about any considerable increase of supply for a long while; it must wait for the erection of new cement works. This corresponds to the "sole-crop" supply of wheat in the Far West; where there is very little room for mixed farming as yet. Land already in cultivation is nearly sure to be used for wheat: and in order to break up more land for wheat it is necessary to build new farmers' cabins, attract workers, perhaps get new branch railways and so on. That is to say wheat production under these conditions is a complete industry, like cement production. It is not a department of agriculture, as cycle making is of mechanical engineering. In my view true science and observation completely endorse Rae's conclusions and mine.

I am even more perplexed by what you say about elasticity of demand......I object to the phrase negative elasticity, because I think it tempts people to carry analytical mathematics beyond their proper scope. In this case, for instance, it suggests a paradox. And I submit that there is no paradox at all. Take a parallel case. I believe that people in Holland travel by canal boat instead of railway sometimes on account of its cheapness. Suppose a man was in a hurry to make a journey of 150 kilos. He had two florins for it, and no more. The fare by boat was one cent a kilo, by third class train two cents. So he decided to go 100 kilos by boat, and fifty by train: total cost two florins. On arriving at the boat he found the charge had been raised to $1\frac{1}{4}$ cents per kilo. "Oh: then I will travel $133\frac{1}{3}$ kilos (or as near as may be) by boat, I can't afford more than $16\frac{2}{3}$ kilos by train." Why not? Where is the paradox? What but needless perplexity can result from calling this negative elasticity, on the abstract ground that that name is in harmony with mathematical symbols, which are being pushed beyond their proper scope?...
I have written this prodigious scrawl because I cannot bear to think that you suppose me to have spoken of elasticity as high

for a fall and yet low for a rise, without careful thought; without having in a responsible way convinced myself that the sources of supply from which a great increase would come were not quickly responsive to stimulus, and that the sources of supply which would chiefly shrink against a fall of price would respond in that direction quickly.

Yours affectionately,

ALFRED MARSHALL.

Balliol Croft, Cambridge

27. iv. 09

My dear Edgeworth,

Many thanks for your all too kind letter. If I made any reply to your gentle criticisms I should be on the inclined plane which leads down to controversy: so my silence under rude blows might be more awkward than it is, if I once broke through my rule to leave controversy to the strong. I am trying to write out my thoughts, including of course those relating to wheat supply, without raising dust. I can't see my way through the huge difficulties of the great issue, even when there is no dust: I work ever slowly. But yet I have a notion that I really have something to say; partly on subtle points, for which my mind is now of little use, only I have a good many notes made before I became a dotard; but more on the One in the Many and the Many in the One, i.e. the relations of details to fundamentals, a matter on which the experience of age is some atonement for its stupidity.....

But I wish that some one who has the strength would hit such fallacies.....It wants steady persistent hammering; and it can't well be done except by a trained thinker. Even the generally excellent *Westminster Gazette* gave itself away by saying that the true reason why a German sending goods to the English market need not be charged with the equivalent of English domestic taxes was that the German paid heavy domestic German taxes—an answer fit to make Ricardo's bones rattle in their grave.....

Yours most ever,

ALFRED MARSHALL.

To Mrs BOSANQUET

Balliol Croft, Cambridge

28. ix. 02

Dear Mrs Bosanquet,

Thank you much for *The Strength of the People*. What I have already been able to read of it makes me sure that I shall find it very suggestive when I can find time to read more.

But I am moved to a mild remonstrance as to a criticism on p. 70. Had it not come from an economist I should have taken it as a matter of course. As it is I am rather puzzled. I admit that it is not only the rich who consume wastefully. Most people earn enough to be able to lead a fairly high life if they spend wisely. Wisdom also might diminish the wastes of war. But as human nature is, the high consumption of the rich seems to me excessive and to necessitate in effect a meagre life on the part of others.

To that argument you raise what I confess seems to me to be an invalid objection that those particular people who are in the worst conditions do not work directly for the rich.

No doubt it is true that labour which is scarce and performs important services is highly paid as a rule. But the issue here (I mean in the passage quoted from mê) is a different one; viz.:—Is the share of the total price of products which goes to manual labour as large as is compatible with a wholesome and "free" state of society? Could we by taking thought get the work of our great captains of industry and financiers done with rather less of their present huge gains?

Again, costly professional services are generally paid for by the rich, and not by the poor. But surely to speak of this as covering a great part of the field is inaccurate—independently of the question whether it is relevant to the main argument. Surely it is the characteristic of those developments of manufacture which are specially American that the highest wages, salaries and profits are got by making things, and engines for making things, which appeal to the demand of the working and lower middle classes.

But these are minutiae. I think I agree with you in the main. I have always held that poverty and pain, disease and death are evils of much less importance than they appear, except in so far as they lead to weakness of life and character; and that true philanthropy aims at increasing strength more than at diminishing poverty.

And now that democratic economics are so much more popular than they were a generation ago; now that the benefits of socialistic and semi-socialistic action are so much more widely advertised, and its dangers so much underrated by the masses of the people, I think it is more important to dwell on the truths in Mill's *Liberty* than on those in his *Essays on Socialism*.

A powerful plea for *Strength*, written, as this is, with insight and sympathy, cannot fail to contribute largely to true progress. Thank you again for it.

Yours very sincerely,

ALFRED MARSHALL.

Balliol Croft
2. x. 02

Dear Mrs Bosanquet,

Of course I accept your premises. I have insisted on them in season and out of season. But I cannot get from them your conclusions.

The matter is too long for argument, especially in writing. But one opinion of mine may be submitted as illustrative of what seems to me, alas! the gap between us. I hope it is not really big!

I start by assuming that it is possible to levy taxes and rates, which would not fall mainly on the well-to-do, in such ways as not to impair individual effort and responsibility. I think everyone should pay rates and know that he pays them. But I regard rates as elastic.

I assume also that the well-to-do spend largely on things that do not make life really more worth living; and the loss of which would involve no serious detriment to the progress of art and knowledge, or to general refinement. [I believe there are no statistics available as a basis for estimating the amount of this. But I am sure it is over *one* hundred million in England; and I think it is very much larger.]

I admit that Municipal Socialism has many dangers, economic and moral. I think municipalities should not speculate or employ "direct" labour nearly as much as they already do.

I think also that public authority cannot meddle with the inside of a man's house very much without risking injury to self-reliance and wholesome independence. Municipal housing seems to me scarcely ever right and generally very wrong. Municipal free baths seem to me nearly always right.

But the outside of a man's house is not his affair: it is the affair of the State or Municipality. The darkness and the polluted air of his surroundings narrow the life and undermine the springs of strength and independence of character for him and his wife and above all for his children, who lack play.

I should *like* an expenditure comparable with that required for the South African war to be devoted to the removal of this source of degradation for a good many years to come. When the evil of the past had been undone, the future might be prevented from engendering evil without much expenditure of money, but not without much expenditure of thought. I should *like* this: though as a practical politician I should not dare to ask for many millions a year....I hold that such action is righteous, that it makes for strength, and that the economist has no higher duty than to examine the principles and the limits appropriate to it....

I know you will be so kind as to forgive my frankness.

Yours very sincerely,

ALFRED MARSHALL.

Balliol Croft

28. x. 03

Dear Mrs Bosanquet,

    ...I contend that it would be possible to provide opportunities of healthy play for all children, and to bring fresh air and light more generously into all urban homes, and in other ways to lessen the *real* evils of the poorer classes, without touching on that expenditure of the rich which is necessary for their *true* well-being. I think this is *possible*. But I think also that the attempt to do it in a hurry would be dangerous; for, carelessly done, it might sap the springs of freedom and energy. And in that danger I see the most urgent of all the calls on the efforts of students such as you and me.

Yours very sincerely,

ALFRED MARSHALL.

To PERCY ALDEN

Balliol Croft, Cambridge

28. i. 03

Dear Mr Alden,

.... I think that unemployment is a symptom of several distinct social maladies, which require different treatment.

For instance, the occasional unemployment of capable energetic workers of all grades is, I think, a wholly different disease from systematic unemployment. It seems due to the inability of beings of finite intelligence to forecast coming economic needs and opportunities with perfect precision: I believe that this form of unemployment is not increasing, but rather diminishing: and that it can be further diminished by a better understanding of the causes of trade fluctuations and changes; and by the widening of world markets: while something may be gained through the diffusion of the notion, that to spend the whole of one's income in prosperous times and to be without resource when the tide turns, is inconsistent with the respect that every one owes to himself.

On the other hand, systematic unemployment is, I believe, caused by the existence of large numbers of people, who will not or can not work steadily or strongly enough to make it possible that they should be employed regularly. They are hunters for odd jobs, which are generally "soft" jobs. A large part of the present unemployment seems to me to be this kind: that is, it is a symptom of disease rather than a cause. And remedies addressed to the symptoms of it are likely, I fear, to increase the disease.

No doubt we ourselves, society at large, are responsible for the existence of this disease, more than the victims of it are. And we ought not to be afraid of very large expenditure of public and private funds in removing or lessening the causes of the disease; on methods of which you and our common friend Lawrence are high authorities. I refer especially to methods for de-urbanizing life, in the sense in which urbanized life is enfeebled life. This should, I think, be supplemented by kindly but severe discipline of those who are bringing up children under physical and moral conditions which will make them recruits to the great army of the habitually unemployed.....

Yours very truly,

ALFRED MARSHALL.

To Sir H. H. CUNYNGHAME

Balliol Croft, Cambridge

14. vi. 03

FOOD SUPPLY IN TIME OF WAR

My dear Cunynghame,

I am no authority on either agricultural or military questions; and I am very far from wishing to offer myself as a witness before the Commission on Food Supply in Time of War: indeed I could not do it. But the matter has been much in my mind during many years; and I think I should like to be sure that certain questions which have occurred to me have been considered, if only to be put aside as unpractical. Will you kindly look through the following?

A. *The question of storing*

1. Is it not worth while to induce the growers of wheat which is ultimately to be consumed here to store it here rather than at a distance, if that can be done cheaply?

2. Can it not be done cheaply by enacting that (say) 1s. per ton shall be paid to everyone who on (say) the first Monday night in every month posts a sworn statement that he has on that night a certain number of tons of wheat in store at a certain

place? (His statement need not be checked save by occasional surprise visits, with penalties for fraudulent declarations. I reckon that this amount would not only make it amply worth while to store grain here rather than abroad, but might even make it worth while to carry over grain from one year to another.)

3. Would not the English farmer obtain by this route some reward for the service which he renders in keeping a stock of wheat on hand? Is not such a reward just?

4. Might the plan possibly be extended at a lower scale to other grains, which on emergency could be used as bread-stuffs?

B. *Military questions*

5. Could we not in time of war with continental nations obtain grain from U.S. more easily than from Canada? Even if grain for us were made contraband of war, would it not suffice to convoy ships containing U.S. grain from the nearest friendly or neutral European port, to which they could run safely; while Canadian grain would be prize of war in all its course across the Atlantic?

6. If we were at war with U.S., would Canadian wheat reach us? If they kept their own grain at home, would they not certainly cross the border and seize or destroy Canadian grain which they thought was coming to us?

7. If U.S. government forbad the exportation of grain to any part of Europe, would not it speedily cause such ruin among their own farmers as to cause the evasion or abrogation of the rule? And if they allowed its exportation to, say, France or Germany, should we not be able to buy most of what we wanted from markets to which that wheat came, directly or indirectly?

Balliol Croft, Cambridge

7. iv. 04

My dear Cunynghame,

I am glad indeed that you are writing a book on curves.....
I do not know on what lines you are writing, nor whether the history of those MSS. would be in any way relevant. But I would like you to have its outline in your hand, in case you should wish to use any part thereof.

In 1874–7 I nearly completed the MSS. of a book on Foreign Trade. What I then regarded—though I do not do so now—as a fairly realistic treatment of the problem, adapted for the use of business men and other non-academics, was the text. Then followed appendices, consisting of the foreign trade curves; and also the other class of curves in order to get at consumers' surplus (*a*) in open market, (*b*) in monopoly sales: where I wanted to get in some hyperbolas drawn by a certain machine you know of. I wanted these, because I found all methods of representing the "total benefit" of foreign trade by their special curves very troublesome. Also I wanted to get out in print those hyperbolas, etc. And lastly, in the appendices, I developed or tried to develop the abstract notion of international trade between employers' associations and trade unions.

Consequently the Appendix had no realism about it: all that seemed in any way real was put into the first part, which was to be in bigger print.

The first chapter was "philosophical," on the abstract idea of an economic nation. Then came the chapters on foreign trade which Sidgwick printed (you know I was very ill and consented to his printing some chapters for private circulation, but left the selection to him); then came a chapter applying those curves to the incidence of import and export duties and bounties. He did not print that: I wish he had. It was quite finished. Some of the others were not.

But my case II, that of increasing returns, never seemed to me of much practical use; and in later years I warned people off it, on the ground that, if time was allowed for the development of economies of production on a large scale, time ought also to be allowed for the general increase of demand.

And now, in recent years, I have gradually gone away from the fundamental hypothesis on which the curves are based. They lead to the result that a great part of an import duty will probably fall on the export nation: and I have become convinced that, though the reasons which the old free-traders gave for the opinion that import duties are paid almost entirely by the consumer are wrong, yet their result is pretty well true. And on inquiry I found I had fallen into a trap. I had followed Mill in taking a yard of cloth as *representative* of England's exports and Germany's imports: which I still think is right. But then I had glided, as he had done, unconsciously into regarding the demand for imports in general as having a similar character to that for a single commodity. And I now think that is illegitimate, and vitiates a great part of my curves. My old chapter on the incidence of import duties is at least as slashing as Edgeworth's articles. But I do not believe his conclusions, nor those of Seligman, whom the Birmingham League and Ashley quote with such reverence. I have never said anything about the subject of this page in print as yet. But I hope soon to explain what are, in my opinion, the conditions which govern the incidence of import duties. My Volume II could not be got ready in tolerable time. So I have decided to bring out an intermediate book.....

This is long. But I do not apologise. For it takes us back to those queer rooms with the little windows close to the floor, from which I used to look out on noble elms, and in which I used to see some faces that I still love very much: and to one of these this is sent by a worn-out old pedagogue

ALFRED MARSHALL.

Balliol Croft, Cambridge

28. vi. 04

My dear Cunynghame,

Your kind and generous letter makes me all the more regret that I have not been able as yet to read your article in the September number of the *Econ. Journal*. Just now I am inquiring how much of the progress of U.S. industries, which is popularly attributed to the Law of Increasing Returns, is really due to it. I can't answer the question: but I am sure there is a large error in the common estimate.....

I believe that we differ a little as to the function of curves. I like to keep them as simple as possible, and to fill in qualifications and limitations *in the text*. I recollect that this was the reason of my not following you in the use of successive cost curves. Human nature varies: and I know some people find your method simpler than mine. (I may be wrong, but I think the majority do not.) And it is a very great gain that things should be treated from two points of view.

If there could be imagined an improvement in your discussion, it would perhaps be that you should indicate that such qualifications as you put into your diagrams are only samples of a great many others which might be introduced. If they were all introduced, the diagrams would be a mass of curves; and I prefer to keep all that I can out of the diagrams. I have hinted this in my note on them in my *Principles*, p. 524.....

As to International Trade curves:—Mine were set to a definite tune, that called by Mill. It is improbable that I shall ever publish them: but I am not certain. I am rather tired of them.

I find that it takes a long time to get men to understand the theory: though, when they do, they are proud of it, and are rather contemptuous of any one who undertakes to teach them without understanding it. There is no subject on which I lecture so many times to the same men from different points of view. One of these is that which I understand you are following. I set a question as to the immediate and ultimate effects of an import duty on some thing (named in the question); and, in answering it myself, I often follow what I call "the practical man's route." I talk of prices throughout, and work up to generalities; and thus get a good *part* of the science of International Trade as a side issue to a special problem. I say "a *part*": for much that is most interesting from my point of view cannot, I think, be conveniently reached by this route.

But I always find that the best men are relieved when I go over the ground again, starting with aggregates and subordinating details. My experiences on this matter are so numerous that I think it is impossible I can ever be convinced that your method is *the* method.

But I am sure it is *a* method: and I am *most heartily* glad that a man of your very high constructive force is tackling it: it will be a great boon to all students, here and elsewhere. For indeed there is no subject, I think, on which English thought has led the way so consistently as this.

I have promised Macmillan to keep the text of the book I am writing (not the *appendices*) in a form as attractive as I can to the practical man: and I shall probably go *much* more nearly on the price-of-particular-commodities line than in lecturing to an advanced class: but I do not yet know *how* much more.

Of course I shall not touch a curve of any kind in the text. . . . .

I doubt whether I should be able to add usefully to the long letter I have now inflicted on you, if I saw your MSS. For I *do* want my time. But I will try if you wish it.

Yours affectionately,

ALFRED MARSHALL.

To Professor F. W. MAITLAND

(This letter is concerned with the place to be assigned to law in the proposed Cambridge Economics Tripos.)

Balliol Croft, Cambridge

8. xi. 04

My dear Maitland,

Probably "Company Law" is technically more serious than I know. But I thought I had avoided the term. I want phrases to be as broad as possible. The Law relating to Joint Stock Cos., which I am most interested in just now, is proposed by J. B. Clark of Columbia. Its main purpose is to *defeat* practices such as those from which the Mogul Co. suffered, and one of its main means is to *allow* railway poolings, federations and similar "Northern Securities" practices. I am not sure that I agree with this. I rather think I do not. But I am sure that economists of the next generation will have to consider questions of this sort very carefully: and that, if they do not know more law than I do, though I have read a good many law books and a great many appeal cases, they will be in a weak position. That is why, as I have so often said, I want them, while still plastic, to be taught how to read law books; though I do not want them to become lawyers in any sense of the term.

I knew of course that the Mogul case had nothing to do with Company Law. But I think that the XXth century will need much Company legislation which pivots around the same fiduciary relations of directors of Joint Stock Cos. (and especially of such of them as would be called Trusts in America, on the ground that they exercise a predominating—not necessarily monopolistic—influence in certain branches of trade) towards the public. The economists' complaint against the law generally is that it cares too exclusively for the shareholders, customers and creditors of the Joint Stock Cos.; and neglects the quasi-fiduciary obligations of the company and its directors to other classes.

I don't want you to pay attention to any detail, right or wrong, in this suggestion; but simply to go for as broad phrases as you can. In particular it would be a good thing if monopolies could be included—partly because the question of national, and even more of international, patent rights is growing rapidly in urgency. But even now I should like, if it were possible, though I fear it may not be, to include the general question of the basis and limitations of the right of a private business to the privilege of secrecy, when its dimensions become so large as to give it a semi-public character. That is the kernel of most of the legal questions which interest myself—and I believe other economists —to-day. What will be the kernel twenty years hence, I have not the smallest notion.

Yours very sincerely,

ALFRED MARSHALL.

To F. W. PETHICK LAWRENCE

(Referring to a proposal to tax British investments
in foreign countries)

12. i. 04

My dear Lawrence,

I thought your article extremely interesting: and in every way an improvement on Chamberlain's scheme. But I could not follow all your arguments completely.

New elements are introduced by the Colonial exemption. I think the result would be vast arbitrage operations by which nearly all British dependency securities in the hands of foreigners (especially French and Dutch) would be transferred to England in exchange for Argentine, U.S.A. and others. In so far as this was done we should not get much of the tax: the commercial interests of the empire would be knit together: but it might weaken our position in time of political friction. For at such a time it is specially convenient to us to be able to bring capital home by selling international securities. Colonials do not serve well. And further the chauvinism of certain factions of foreign nations, especially the French, is sometimes mitigated by the commercial interests of other factions; who in consequence speak out when they might otherwise have kept silent. The effect of French holdings of Kaffirs was, I believe, very important in this respect. Of course if the Colonies would really bear their share of imperial military burdens, that would not matter. But in fact they only make believe.

The difference between the yield on good U.S.A. and U.K. securities is nearly £1 per £100: I do not feel sure that changing the £1 into 19s. 6d. would have a very great effect on the course of investment. I think that is governed mainly by (a) rate of average yield, and (b) confidence that the investor knows what he is about. The average Englishman is much more sure of his ground when comparing two English railways than two U.S.A. or two Canadian railways. I do not deny that sentiment influences a large number of small investors: but I do not think it influences much the great bulk of large investments.

For these reasons I should put items 3, 5 and 6 at the end of your article lower than you do. [I quite go with 4.]

Coming to your letter. I do not object to taxing foreigners if we do it by a simple plan, i.e. one that is really simple, not one that merely looks so, like Charles Booth's. But who are foreigners? In this whole controversy, nothing has angered me more than the action of Chamberlainites, and especially his Canadian bodyguard, in reviling the U.S.A. as "foreigners." The last page of the inclosed typed speech of mine indicates my views on that. I am not sure that the tax would *immediately* increase employment at home, except in so far as the price of English securities is kept high by sentiment. Nothing seems to cause a sharper *temporary* bout of unemployment than the buying back by foreigners of their own securities held in England. It causes dumping, or at least semi-forced sales of foreign goods; and so temporarily disturbs the English employment market.

And I do not see how the investor in foreign securities evades English taxes: other than those which have been imposed since the goods were made, by the exportation of which he—or his predecessors in title—obtained control of the means of purchasing foreign securities. Also I fear that a firm, which sold largely in U.S.A. and was thinking of starting a branch there, might be decided by the tax to send one of the partners over there to start an independent factory. What I mean is that, if Smith and Brown decide that this foreign branch shall stand wholly in Brown's name, he obtaining a foreign domicile, the plan is defeated.

I have said all I can against your scheme: for I think you put its merits too high. And I am not prepared, as at present advised, to look with favour on *any* scheme which differentiates against our greatest colony.

I admit however that U.S.A. are no longer in great need of external capital: and that your scheme would be much less offensive and friction-making from their point of view than Chamberlain's.

Yours very sincerely,

ALFRED MARSHALL.

To Sir SYDNEY CHAPMAN

Balliol Croft, Cambridge
29. x. 04

My dear Chapman,

I am proud of your two books. So far as I can see, your *Cotton Industry* is the best monograph of the kind that has ever been published. It is both a realistic-impressionist study of human life, and an economic treatise.

Work and Wages I have not yet seen much of. But I shall use it a great deal during the next few months. It fits in with my own work. I think the combination of Lord Brassey's knowledge of the inside of big affairs—a knowledge the lack of which at first hand has hampered me always and hampers me still—and his strong solid judgment combined with the faculties and mental elasticity which you have developed make a splendid team.

I have bought duplicates of them and taken them to the bookcase in L.L.R. 5: and at the same time Cunynghame's *Geometrical Political Economy*.

I am awfully proud of the three Cambridge products.

I bragged indeed and said I thought that there were few Universities which could show as good a series as our Adam Smith Prize lot. First Bowley's which got him the Silver Medal of the Statistical Society at (I believe) an unprecedently early age, next Lawrence's *Local Variations of Wages*, next yours; and there is one good one still to come, that of Pigou on Arbitration and Conciliation, nearly ready for the Press.

So I *am* proud of the "Cambridge Stables"; and I think the quantity and quality of the work you have got through is wonderful. Our best regards to you and Mrs Chapman.

Yours affectionately,

ALFRED MARSHALL

You may be amused by this photograph of our house party (Edgeworth had gone), Sarah working the bulb.

To MANOHAR LÀL

Balliol Croft, Cambridge
28. i. 09

.... Thanks for the cutting you sent me. But the writer has not caught my drift. It is true that I think that the reasons, which make Protection specially unsuitable to Britain now, do not apply to India. But neither do I think that simple Protection to Indian industries would work well: and the particular proposals made by the Tariff Reform League, in regard to India, seem to me fraught with the maximum of evil and the minimum of benefit to both India and Britain. I was disgusted at the neglect of India's interests by the Colonials at the recent Conference and I do not like the way in which the Tariff Reformers are arguing now that their scheme is necessary for India's safety. I hold, on the contrary, that any *serious* Preferential Scheme for the Empire would be likely to call into being a formal or informal Middle-Europe-Customs-Union directed against the Empire. Tariff Reformers say that the Continent "must" have Indian products. That seems to me true only as to jute. A Tariff war would, I think, exclude Indian tea, silk, cotton, hides, etc. in a great measure from the Continent. (I expect the United States would not join in the war unless specially attacked: but would remain neutral.) The Tariff Reformers say that round-about trade is always bad, and that India would do better to sell direct to Britain than to sell to the Continent and pay Britain with the proceeds. But I hold that roundabout trade never exists without good cause. The Continent spins chiefly low count yarns, and therefore is glad to buy short stapled Indian cotton. Who would gain by forcing us to buy short staple yarns at relatively lower prices than the Germans can pay, and causing rather more of the American cotton to go to Germany?

I do not see my way clear as to India's policy. I have never advocated the excise duty on Indian cotton manufactures. But yet I do not like to preach a crusade against it without knowing more of the facts than I do. I hold that, before any such action is taken, the plan should be considered of devoting the excise duties on cotton to subsidizing pioneer works in industries which are still in an infant stage; an industry that employs a quarter of a million people cannot be described as "an infant."

But I do not believe that any device will make India a prosperous nation, until educated Indians are willing to take part in handling *things*, as educated people in the West do. The notion that it is more dignified to hold a *pen* and keep accounts than to work in a high grade engineering shop seems to me the root of India's difficulties....A high authority in an Indian Railway is now in my house. He says—"a native who has discretion is above working in our engine shops." That is my point. Until the judgment necessary for high grade industry can be developed in native workers, no expenditure on the importation of white foremen will make India a progressive country....

Balliol Croft, Cambridge

22. ii. 11

Dear Manohar Làl,

I am very glad to receive your kind and interesting letter. But I must adhere to my resolve not to publish anything about India, till I can incorporate my opinion about Protection to her industries in a more general discussion. I think I have already indicated my reasons: they are too long to be written out; but I think they are strong, and for me at least they are decisive. I never speak of a "Free Trade Principle." But I go rather near to one when I say that in my judgment no tax should be levied in such a way as to raise the price of things which are consumed by the people, but yet do not contribute to the revenue, unless it is what the Germans call an "educative" tax: and I think that a Protective tax on cottons would not now be educative. I think Government should incur economic loss for the sake of industrial education: but I am not in a position to say *confidently* in what ways; I can only speak tentatively.

I do not think that manufactures are more conducive to prosperity than agriculture is, unless they evoke initiative. A score of Tatas might do more for India than any Government, British or Indigenous, can accomplish. The dark spots of western Europe are not agricultural. They are the homes of those manufactures which are divorced from initiative. To try for manufactures as in themselves a remedy for India's ills seems to me a fatal error.

I have understood that the handloom, adapted to the use of the automatic shuttle, is breaking the factory weaving sheds in India. That seems to me a strong reason against laying exceptional stress on the cotton industry.

I am very glad to know of the excellent work you are doing.

Yours very sincerely,

ALFRED MARSHALL.

To LOUIS DUMUR

Stern im Abtei, Süd Tirol

2. vii. 09

Dear Sir,

The questions, which the Alliance for promoting the increase of population in France is discussing, are of deep interest. I do not know France well enough to answer them; but I will venture to make a few remarks bearing on them.

From the military point of view a check to the growth of numbers may of course be a source of danger, mitigated by the automatic tendency, which the predominance of any great military nation has, to stimulate alliances or understandings for cooperative self-defence among its neighbours. But such matters do not lie within my scope.

I do not regard a moderate retardation of the growth of population as a great social and industrial evil in itself. And, though I think it often does go together with national decadence, I doubt its being the cause of that decadence. But I think it may often be a consequence of the same causes which bring about that decadence. These are, I think, often associated with the growth of wealth and the cessation of the need for incessant energy and self-devotion in the overcoming of difficulties. In so far as the retardation of the growth of population may be caused by a consequent weakening of individual, and therefore of national character, the remedy seems to me to lie chiefly in combating its evil causes. In so far as it has no such evil origin, I should regard it without grave anxiety.

The rather violent checks to population, which have recently appeared in some strata of some Anglo-Saxon peoples, seem to be partly caused by a selfish devotion to "sports" and other amusements on the part of men: and partly to a selfish desire among women to resemble men; with the effect that, without rendering any high service to the State in masculine work, they destroy that balance and mutual supplementary adaptation of masculine and feminine character, which enabled a man to secure rest and repose by marriage; though he might probably have been worried beyond endurance by the lifelong incessant companionship of another man. This cause does not seem to diminish the number of marriages much; but it tends to make men delay marriage till their best strength has gone. I believe that these two evil tendencies exist in France, though less than elsewhere.

The evils of town life are being combated by the drift of population from the central districts to suburbs where most families can have separate houses, many can have gardens, and nearly all children can play freely in the open air. The movement of France in this direction has perhaps been rather slow. More energy seems urgently needed to check the drift towards living in small apartments in crowded cities, where children are not easily accommodated; and where placid recreations, which build up strength of body and character, are supplanted by nervous excitements, which consume strength, and consume also a large part of the family income unprofitably. It is of course true that but a small part of the population of France suffers much from this evil.

But there remains one from which I fear that France may suffer much. It is very likely that I am mistaken; and I speak with the utmost diffidence. But is it not true that a preference for a secure income, free from anxiety, and unlikely to be forfeited without grievous fault is specially strong in France? Is not this preference associated, partly as cause and partly as effect, with the law of equal inheritance, and with the large part which dowries play in marriages? Does not a small income derived from land, or from Government employment where promotion goes mainly by seniority, tend to concentrate attention on small cares, and petty savings? No doubt this has its good side; and the masterly, unrivalled economy of many French households is admired and envied throughout the world. But does it not also disincline people for bold creative enterprises? Does it not make the expense of rearing and providing a dowry for an additional child too serious a burden? Does it not make the dowry too important; and thus diminish the chance of marriage for those who come from fertile stocks, and give a fatal premium to infertile stocks?

No doubt it is well to insure people against calamities which are beyond their own control. But is it not a condition of vigorous individual and national life that men should seek, rather than avoid, those risks which are inherent in bold action, and which can be overcome by their own courage and energy? Does not this matter need the careful attention of France, and other old countries? Would not some gain be derived from a little infusion of American audacity, to supplement the splendid industrial qualities of the French people? I am perhaps rash in making this suggestion: but I am encouraged to it by noticing that some of the suggestions under the consideration of the Alliance point in the same direction.

Taxes on childless people, combined with special privileges to parents of many children, would, I think, have but little direct influence in England: I cannot speak as to France. But in such matters legislation is an expression of the public conscience; and a national protest against the restriction of births from selfish motives might perhaps exert a good deal of influence indirectly.

Yours very faithfully,

ALFRED MARSHALL.

To LORD REAY

Balliol Croft, Cambridge

12. xi. 09

Dear Lord Reay,

I wish it were in my power to give an adequate answer to the questions you have put to me. But my only confident dogma in economics is that every short statement on a broad issue is inherently false. It was in 1903 that the Chancellor of the Exchequer set me two questions. I have done nothing else that I could help except write out my answers to those questions, with their kith and kin. It is now 1909: and the answers are not yet nearly ready. Partly for that reason I have paid very little attention to Budget controversies; and I have remained silent even when my published opinions were misquoted or misinterpreted.

You will therefore kindly understand that the few remarks which I make in answer to your questions do not claim to be true: the most I can hope for is that they are on the whole on the side of truth.

I do not know what "socialistic" means. The *Times* has just said that it means taking away *property* from individuals and giving it to the State. But the Budget proposes to take *money*: and if, say, £M150 have to be levied by taxation, the Budget, *whatever its form*, must be accordingly Socialistic to the extent of £M150, neither more nor less.

My own notion of Socialism is that it is a movement for taking the responsibility for a man's life and work, as far as possible, off his shoulders and putting it on to the State. In my opinion Germany is beneficially "socialistic" in its regimentation of those who are incapable of caring for themselves: and we ought to copy Germany's methods in regard to our Residuum.

But in relation to other classes, I regard the Socialistic movement as not merely a danger, but by far the greatest present danger to human well-being. It seems to me to have two sides, the administrative and the financial. Its chief sting seems to lie on the administrative side.

I do not deny that semi-socialistic or Governmental methods are almost inevitable in ordinary railways etc.: though a vigorous despot in America breaks through them occasionally. But the sting of socialism seems to lie in its desire to extend these rather than to check their expansion. I believe that they weaken character by limiting initiative and dulling aspiration; and that they lower character by diverting energy from creation to wirepulling. I therefore regard Protection as socialistic, in that, especially in a democratic country, it gives a first place to those business men who are "expert" in hoodwinking officials, the legislature and the public as to the ability of their branch of industry to take care of itself.

On the financial side, Socialism may be rapacious, predatory, blind to the importance of security in business and contemptuous of public good faith. But these tendencies lie on the surface: they provoke powerful opposition and reaction; and personally I fear them less than those which are more insidious. In moderation they are even beneficial in my opinion. For poverty crushes character: and though the earning of great wealth generally strengthens character, the spending of it by those who have not earned it, whether men or women, is not nearly an unmixed good. A cautious movement towards enriching the poor at the expense of the rich seems to me not to cease to be beneficial, merely because Socialists say it is a step in their direction.

But it may be urged that, though much of the *expenditure* of the very rich tends to lower rather than to raise human character, yet their *capital* is needed for the expensive methods of modern industry. Britain's capital however grows fast relatively to her area, and a small check to its growth would but postpone a little the day when most of her new accumulations are exported. I admit however that the interest on her foreign investments is a mighty bulwark against the blows of foreign tariffs.

For about fifteen years I taught somewhat eagerly that "Death Duties" were a grievous evil because they checked the growth of capital. For the next few years I hesitated. Now I think they are on the whole a good method of raising a rather large part of the national revenue; because they do not check accumulation as much as had been expected, and a small check does not seem to me now as great an evil as it did then.

As regards the influence of taxation on employment, I hold it to be indirect only. All income is spent on the purchase of services including that of postponing consumption, or "saving": excepting in so far as it goes to the owner of land and other forms of wealth that have not been created by individual effort. I have repeatedly stated my opinion that the owners of such land have not truly paid income tax. It is true that they have not "evaded" it. But the law has hitherto been a sustained social injustice in this respect: what they have been required to return as income is only a part of it. This injustice I regard as "predatory"; its redress I regard as anti-socialistic.

The case of stock exchange securities which have appreciated is similar in some respects. But (1) to require individuals to make return of all increments got in 1907, and of the decrements in 1908, would be impracticable. (2) Few forms of intellectual effort are more important socially than forecasting the future and contriving so that the future may turn out well. The shareholder who directly or indirectly takes part in the management of a company is generally doing good service; and his rewards, like those of the able and courageous fisherman, come largely in the form of big hauls or "windfalls." I do not see how to tax the passive stockholder, without taxing the active one. And I do not want to tax "increments" except in cases in which *either* it is possible to compensate for "decrements," *or* the decrements are relatively rare and small.

Lastly. The term land*owner* does not exist in English law: and English public opinion has never admitted that the land*holder* has the same rights of usance, without reference to the public interest, in regard to his land, as he has in regard to his carriage or his yacht. Morally everyone is a trustee to the public—to the All—for his use of all that he has: but the trusteeship under which he "holds" land is of a specially binding nature.

At the same time I have always scouted the notion that there is a monopoly of land: or that the State can quietly resume the full ownership of land: I am as great a heretic in the eyes of Mr Wedgwood or Mr Fillebrown, as in the eyes of Mr Chaplin.

To return to the relation of taxation to employment. The State by taxes takes part of the national income and spends it almost exclusively on services; just as the individual would have done, if it had been left to him. The small share that goes to those who have rendered no services, in the form of pure rent, may be neglected in either case. Hence I conclude that, if taxes are so levied as to impair enterprise, they *pro tanto* lessen employment at good wages: but if they are so spent as to increase vitality, they increase employment at good wages; because they increase earning power. I am certain that Tariff Reform would, and that the present Budget would not, lessen employment at good wages.

The notion that the investment of funds in the education of the workers, in sanitation, in providing open air play for all children etc. tends to diminish "capital" is abhorrent to me. Dead capital exists for man: and live capital that adds to his efficiency is every way as good as dead capital. It is not more important to have cheap maize than cheap wheat, merely because maize is the raw material of pigs, and wheat of men.

Foolish ostentatious expenditure by the State, like the similar expenditure of private persons, is, no doubt, an enemy to good employment: because the funds used up in it do not create, as they pass away, fresh sources of future production, and therefore future income; as they would if they were spent on building up improved iron works or human beings.

I think it would be difficult to frame a budget which got so much revenue, with so little burden to the working classes, as the present one does: though I do not entirely approve of all the details of it that I know, and I do not know all.

But if the budget is not to be used as a means of diminishing the existing inequalities of income, then I think it is quite possible to get a total of £M200 a year by the addition of taxes on articles of general consumption, independently of their source; and therefore without taking, as Tariff Reform taxes would do, much more from the people, directly or indirectly, than would be received by the State.

This is I fear a very poor answer, very slovenly and meagre. But my power of work is waning: and it has taken all that I can do in a morning.

Yours sincerely,

ALFRED MARSHALL.

Carolside, Earlston, Berwickshire, N.B.
14. xi. 1909

Dear Professor Marshall,

I am indeed greatly obliged for your illuminating letter and the trouble you have taken to answer all my questions.

On the whole I was very glad to see that your opinion of the budget is favorable as regards increment and death duties.

Do I understand that you hold that the interest of capital invested abroad pays for imports to England and *pro tanto* neutralises the evil effects of high tariffs in penalising our exports which otherwise would have to pay for the imports?

I suppose that you regret the excessive outlay in armaments as representing unproductive expenditure, but that you do not object to old age pensions, which may be considered as deferred or supplementary wages.

I take it that your opinion that the landholder has not paid his proper share of income tax only applies to building land, not to agricultural land, and that you approve the concession made to the latter with regard to deductions for repairs and management. I also suppose that you admit that the effect of reducing the spending power of individuals and increasing the spending power of the State is to create a disturbance in the labor market.

I hope I am right in thinking that you do not advocate an addition of taxes on articles of general consumption *independently of their source* except as an alternative of tariff reform.

Again apologising for my inquisitiveness and with very sincere thanks.

Your obliged,

REAY.

Balliol Croft, Cambridge
15. xi. 1909

Dear Lord Reay,

You have interpreted my short answers as I meant them. But perhaps I should add a few words on two points.

My view is that foreign import duties on British imports must be paid almost entirely by the consumer (setting aside a few small exceptional cases), unless British exports are thereby reduced to so low an aggregate that Britain is compelled to give up some imports which she urgently needs. If she were, her need would force her to export even at the cost of paying a part or the whole of the duties herself. Such conditions would be unlikely in the present state of world commerce anyhow: and they are rendered impossible in my opinion by the fact that the very few cases in which a foreign country has any approach to a monopoly of an import which we need very urgently are more than covered by our power of drawing about £100,000,000 worth of those things which we most need even if all our exports were barricaded out. This is a complex, but I think important fact; and I am giving a considerable space to it in the book on *National Industries and International Trade* at which I am slowly toiling.

Next as to armaments. I am not a good judge of the question how far we might safely reduce our armaments or even abstain from increasing them now. But I think that, if half a dozen of the noisiest speakers and writers who exulted over the insult inflicted on Germany, when one of her mail ships was taken into a South African harbour, though her captain had given his word of honour that he had no contraband of war, could have been suppressed, and similar conditions stopped, we should have had no call to build ships very fast.

Yours sincerely,

ALFRED MARSHALL.

To Sir HORACE PLUNKETT

Balliol Croft, Cambridge

17. v. 10

Dear Sir Horace,

I have read through your instructive and impressive plea for a Country Life Institute twice. I have learnt much from it and profited much by it. But I am not in a position to form an opinion on nearly the whole of its subject matter: and I ought not to sign it. I am very unwilling to say "no" to an invitation urged in such kind and pleasant words by you, and this morning in a letter by Mr Butcher. But I must not stray so far from my last.

Of course there are some topics raised in your plea which I have considered. But on those I have formed rather definite opinions, which do not march entirely with yours.....

There would be no use in my urging my views on you, for you could not be expected to adopt them. And, indeed, many of them are not in accordance with common opinion, and could hardly be expressed in a paper of this kind, without lengthy explanation.

Some of these relate to the history of the relations between classes—landlords, farmers, agricultural labourers, and industrialists in the first half of last century: some to the increase in the purchasing power of the produce of land during the greater part of the second half of the century: some to the opposition between the movements of rural and agricultural population: some to the influence for good of agencies in England and Scotland that are not to be found to any large extent in Ireland and so on.

Perhaps I should add a little on the last two of these groups. I know a good deal of the habits of life of the rural population within an old man's cycle ride of Cambridge, say an area of about 600 square miles. I doubt if there is any rural population on the Continent of Europe, unless it be in Scandinavia, which is so prosperous, so happy, or so much given to thoughts and emotions larger and higher than those of merely local life. I attribute this chiefly to the influence of non-conformist chapels, with whose theological views I have nothing in common; but which I believe give an individuality and a holy sanction to the inner life of even the 14s. a week labourer that is very rare elsewhere. No doubt the farmer's education is generally very bad in the neighbourhood; and a great many Scots are brought in for that reason. But we take in, for the benefit of our servant, a weekly paper—*The Cambridge Independent Press*. It almost ignores the existence of the University, and pays little attention to Cambridge town affairs: and I think it is ignored by gentle-folk generally in the town and elsewhere. But I often look at it, as a zoologist might look at a kangaroo: and I am astonished at the width of range, the clearness, and—so far as I can judge—the scientific thoroughness of its long weekly articles on things which the agriculturist ought to know, and did not know a little while ago. (These articles are I presume supplied to it by a Press Agency of some sort.) The continued growth of factories in villages; of the free use of cycles by unskilled labourers; of motor omnibuses running out ten miles into the country; of warehouses where there used to be slums and of cottages with gardens where there used to be solitude etc. make me cheerful. An optimistic tone, in nearly all matters except the relations of family life under the influence of aggressive womanhood, fills my voice more and more as I grow old. And though I feel it is a good thing that the weak spots in our social system should be pourtrayed so as to strike into the attention of the negligent, I don't feel that I ought to sign a paper which implies that the conditions of rural life in England are going backwards. I expect what you say as to Ireland is true: there is perhaps no one who knows as well as you do what Ireland needs and how to help her. And no doubt what you say of America is based on knowledge much better than mine: but I could not speak on America from this point of view, without probing some doubts and dreads in my mind as to the dangers of American industrial life (rather than rural) which arise from the aversion of the new strains of immigrants for agriculture.

I have two or three times in my life signed documents with many propositions drafted by others: and every time I have deeply regretted it. My notion is that a document should be the work of an individual, or at most of two or three people working intimately together. If pruned down to please many it really satisfies none, and generally loses all vitality. Then others may express a general approval of its aims, without committing themselves to its details or to the arguments by which it is supported.

I agree with you that even in England and Scotland, a strong Institute might do good work by coordinating all the large movements for the amelioration of rural life, and the dissemination of agricultural knowledge now at work. And I am always glad when anyone takes a hopeful view of any new departure.

I was even enthusiastic when the Institute of Social Service was founded: it seemed to have a definite work to do, and the will to do it. But it has lacked a strong hand at the helm; and its recent history has rather saddened me.

It may prepare the way indeed for a larger semi-official Institute or Bureau. And when one considers the vast number of specialists and business men and others who are working for the increase and dissemination of knowledge in regard to agricultural economy in the country—when one thinks of the literary Department of the Board of Agriculture, the numerous Agricultural Societies, the Agricultural Departments at many of our Universities and so on, may not one incline to urge the Government to summon a meeting of representatives from them to consider how a central Institute might best focus their work? The matter lies beyond my knowledge I can get no further than asking a question.

The work of the Country Life Institute which you suggest for Ireland seems to me a large undertaking; but if your strong hand were in it, I feel sure it would do a glorious work. Little as I am justified in speaking specially of Irish affairs, I would gladly express this confidence in such work in such hands, if you should wish it.

I grieve much not to be able to say more. But I am not in a position to do it.

Yours sincerely,

ALFRED MARSHALL.

To Professor FINDLAY SHIRRAS

(In answer to questions arising out of a Government of India enquiry into the causes of the rising prices.)

Weybourne, Norfolk

6. vii. 10

....I will say briefly one or two things which may possibly be of interest to you.

(1) I made, in preparation for a conversation with Mr Morison and Mr Abrahams, some little study of prices in India in recent years, and compared them with other histories of prices, especially American. I laid stress on America because the lowering of the direct and indirect costs of transport, which has been a chief cause of recent changes in prices, has of course tended to bring up prices of agricultural produce in Indian and American ports relatively to the prices of the same things in western Europe; and to bring up their prices in Upland districts of India and America relatively to their prices at the ports of the same countries. And I concluded that there was a strong *prima facie* case in favour of the opinion that similar causes had produced similar results in the two countries. Cheaper transport and more abundant gold had lowered the value of gold relatively to agricultural produce in about the same degree in the two.

(2) I do not doubt that the facilities for getting currency, in all its forms, back from inland districts where it has done special work in moving harvests or relieving famine, are sadly deficient

in India: but it is better that I should not attempt to write about conceivable remedies. I have on the other hand some conviction that *adaerations* are setting in nearly all over India in various directions and in different degrees: and that consequently a great deal of currency stops up-country, not because it cannot easily get down, but because it is needed where it is. I trust that the important set of local inquiries, which you are organising, will throw light on this subject. American literature, official and unofficial, affords the best means that I know of for studying (1) the influences of cheap transport on prices of imports versus exports; and on upland prices versus prices at the ports; and (2) the varying powers of absorbing a large amount of currency per head under the influences of varying degrees of (*a*) self-contained life of individual "farmers" and groups of farmers, (*b*) payment of wages and in some cases rent in kind, rather than in money, and (*c*) the use of farm carts etc. rather than railways, carriers' carts, etc., all of which I include under the general term *adaerations*....There is a rather old report, published I think as a "bookseller" book, on The Purchasing Power of Gold...which shows how the price of wheat was rising in some American uplands at the very time when the rapidity of its fall in Liverpool was greatest....

To B. MUKHERJEE, *Lucknow University*

Balliol Croft, Cambridge

22. x. 10

Dear Sir,

My excuse for not answering your question as to my opinions about India is suggested by yourself. If I were to answer all the questions which are sent me, my book would never appear. As it is I shall not live to serve up to table one half of the dishes which I have partly cooked.

I had an hour's talk a little while ago with an Indian on such questions as you ask. By question and answer we got on quickly, each guiding the other. To reach similar results in writing would be a long week's work.

I will however indicate the general trend of my opinion.

I have no objections on principle to the "Protection" of Nascent Indian Industries. But a customs tariff is an expensive method to this end: and under existing circumstances it would— as you partly hint—enrich European capitalists rather than Indian.

Therefore I think it should not be applied until other methods have been tried, nor until those industries which already receive a *very high* protection from cost of carriage (in some cases double cost of carriage) have succeeded in evoking Indian enterprise: strong cases in point I understand to be the leather, paper and oil seed industries.

If India had a score or two of men like Mr Tata, and some thousands of men with Japanese interest in realities, with virile contempt of mere speech-making in politics and law courts; and with no scorn for work on *things* while the mind was full of *thought*, India would soon be a great nation. Nothing could stop her: no tariff system could hinder her: she would enter into her heritage.

But so long as an Indian who has received a high education generally spends his time in cultured ease; or seeks money in Indian law suits—which are as barren of good to the country as is the sand of the sea shore—nothing can do her much good. So long as, with the exception of Bombay cotton—which after all is of Parsee origin—and a few works, of which Mr Tata's are at the head, all enterprise seems to be in European hands: in spite of the fact that the unhealthiness of India for the young children of Europeans is in effect a Protective duty of perhaps 50–100 per cent. in favour of Indian enterprise in India as against European.

For twenty years I have been urging on Indians in Cambridge to say to others: "How few of us, when we go to the West, think of any other aim, save that of our *individual culture*? Does not the Japanese nearly always ask himself in what way he can strengthen himself to do *good service to his country* on his return? Does he not seek real studies? Does not he watch the sources of Western power? Is not that the chief reason for Japan's quick progress? Can not we imitate her? Do we need any other change than, like the Japanese, to think of our country in the first place and ourselves a long-way behind?"

You will complain that I have not indicated what I would do if I were responsible for India. My silence is due to two causes. I have not been able to learn enough about India to speak confidently: and I do not venture, in writing to a stranger, to indicate the vague, crude, tentative suggestions which I shall perhaps ultimately publish. I have occasionally discussed them in confidence with Indian friends.

I have said nothing about Preference. The more closely schemes for Preference are examined, whether in relation to India or to Self-Governing Colonies, the more futile and dangerous do they seem to me. Their advocates do not win my confidence.

Yours very truly,

ALFRED MARSHALL.

P.S. Perhaps you have already seen the "White Paper" which I am sending you. I thought a good deal about India when writing it, but my only reference to her is in its last lines.

You will of course understand that I know that some of the Indians who come to the West do really care to make themselves strong in action: I am very fortunate in counting several such men among my friends. But many more are needed.

Balliol Croft, Cambridge

12. iv. 11

Dear Sir,

I am very much obliged for the papers you have sent me: they are most interesting.

I cannot say "yes" or "no" to the question whether I am in favour of Protection to Indian industries. Either answer would be as misleading as it would be if given to the celebrated question "Have you stopped beating your wife?" I have not authorised anyone to say anything on my behalf: but I have suggested to several persons, Indian and English, that the Excise duties should be earmarked for purposes such as were indicated by Sir Sassoon David at the end of his speech.

I do not think the Indian cotton industry has a right to Protection on the exceptional ground that it is "nascent." And I am not hopeful that Government can do much for India so long as the best Indian minds seek self-culture, or the barren work of pleading in the Courts, rather than those creative enterprises which might make their country strong. But I hold it bound to do its utmost, in spite of difficulties, to aid new enterprises which are educative, and especially when they are being worked by brave Indians, who care little for either comfort or dignity, provided only they can help India to be great. Would that there were more such men! I am not prepared to say that a Protective duty on imports can *never* be justified when a nascent industry needs help, and no other help is possible. But I think it is a clumsy, wasteful, demoralizing method; and that India can help her young industries much better by other means. I think, for instance, that the Sugar industry needs help; and that a Protective duty would be poison to it. It wants to be waked: and a Protective duty would be a mere sleeping draught.

Yours very truly,

ALFRED MARSHALL.

To Professor IRVING FISHER

Balliol Croft, Cambridge

16. ix. 11

Dear Professor Fisher,

I desire to associate myself heartily with your appeal for national, and if possible international, inquiries into changes in the purchasing power of money, with special reference to the costs of living of various sections of the community in various countries. I go with the spirit of your aspirations heartily: but I am inclined to doubt whether a thorough scientific treatment of the whole problem can be achieved quickly; and to suggest that for the present attention should be concentrated on those parts of it which can be treated broadly and quickly.

In particular I doubt whether a study of wages and budgets should be pressed very far at this stage. I do not think we have yet reached satisfactory methods for dealing with those problems. The work that has been done at them is worthy of all honour: but those who have made the chief advances are those who are the least satisfied with what has already been achieved.

Standardisation is as yet in so early a stage that we can get no trustworthy price lists, which range over a fairly long period, and which are applicable to many things which are not either raw or in the first stage of manufacture. No doubt technical progress has been conspicuous in the arts of transport: and in this one direction the commodities that are entered in the artisan's budget do represent fairly well the forces of economic progress. They bring out the fact that his food is still earned at a low cost of effort, although the soil around him may yield small supplies of it. But they seldom represent the economies of modern manufacture which are embodied even in simple clothing: for such things are not yet reduced to any common standard. And scarcely any lists take account of the vast amounts of light, water, reading matter, personal transport and other amenities of life which he does buy cheaply but which would have cost much more than all his wages not long ago. I submit that our main purpose—that of mitigating the evils caused by broad changes in the real cost of production of gold— ought not to wait for further calculations by methods as crude as the best which are within our reach to-day.

Thus for the present I would limit international inquiries to a selection of the best representative commodities for the whole consumption of the world. It must be rather a short list; and each commodity must have a large consumption and a fairly standardised marketing. It cannot therefore be other than crude: it must probably be cruder than our best national index numbers. But it will be simple and definite: and its purpose will be intelligible to the working classes in advanced countries and to the ruling classes in others.

I think the time is not ripe for an official international inquiry into the causes of these variations. The excellent work that has been done recently, for instance, in estimates of the rapidity of circulation of money would perplex the ordinary man, even if it were really complete: and in my opinion it has not yet made a very great advance towards that end.

Only on such a simple definite basis does it seem to me that it could be hoped—if the hope can be entertained at all—to reach an international convention for the establishment of an artificial inconvertible paper currency in which each nation should have its due share; and of which it could truly be said that, though very far from ideal perfection, it was only about half as bad as a gold currency. But I am myself not very hopeful: partly because I do not see how it would work out in a war as intense as that in which Pitt was charged with issuing forged French paper money.

You inquire as to my early scheme for remedying the chief evils that arise out of the ever-changing relations of the supply of gold to the work to be done by it. My proposed "Remedies for fluctuations of general prices" are set out in the *Contemporary Review* for March 1887. They were on familiar lines already suggested by Lowe, Scrope, Jevons, Walras and others: but they had some little peculiarities. I thought then that any plan for regulating the supply of currency, so that its value shall be stable, must be national and not international. But I thought that each nation might possibly have a paper currency the value of which was in effect tied to that of certain fixed quantities of gold, silver and other commodities which "have great value in small bulk, and are in universal demand, and which are thus suitable for paying the balances of foreign trade." I no longer think that such a currency is on the whole at all likely to answer.

But a quarter of a century has made me ever more desirous that every country should have an official "unit" of general purchasing power, made up from tables of price percentages like those of Sauerbeck and others: and that it should authorise long period obligations for the payment of rent and interest on loans of all kinds to be made at the option of the contracting parties, in terms either of this general unit, or of a selection of price percentages appropriate to the special purpose in hand. Public authority should make out such lists as appeared suitable to particular classes of transactions: but the parties concerned should have perfect freedom to make special selections. Any wages contract, such as a sliding scale in the iron trade, might "take account not only of the price of the finished iron, but also on the one hand, of the prices of iron ore, coal, and other expenses of the employer; and on the other, of the prices of the things chiefly consumed by the workmen."

I think that could be done at once. If it succeeded, the world would I think be prepared in say twenty years for an international "fixed standard" paper currency: provided it can be helped on the way by a vigorous movement such as that in which you are active.

Yours very truly,

Alfred Marshall.

Balliol Croft, Cambridge

14. x. 12

Dear Professor Fisher,

....The scheme for a national stable-value currency which you send me has very great attractions. But as you know I now, though not in 1887, think that international trade would be too much troubled by a set of national currencies; and that a national value-unit (or groups of such units) should be kept for long period domestic contracts and customary rates (wages etc.) only. I admit heartily that, if national currencies on your plan were generally set up, the limits of fluctuation of the Foreign Exchanges would be less than on any other plan for artificial national currencies which I know. But I can get no further than that.

And I would ask you to consider whether your regulations would supply a sufficiently powerful force to keep the volume of the U.S. currency at the level required for your purpose, unless the other chief countries had nearly the same regulations. When $100 purchased *more* than a hundred dollar units of general commodities, gold might indeed be brought to the mint in spite of the seignorage which was still being charged (though charged at a lower rate of course than when prices were higher). But even in this case the adjustment might not be very rapid: the speculative strain involved in deciding whether the seignorage was likely to go lower or not would be considerable: and the new dollars might for a long while be insufficient for their work; might they not?

And on the other hand if, when the gold dollar, *i.e.* the unit of value, was much above its gold value, a development of banking or other cause reduced the total purchasing power needed to be held in coin, might not there be a great rise in prices in U.S. while prices elsewhere were at rest? Would not the gold dollars need to stay until their value had been caught up by that of gold bullion?

These are only hasty half-thoughts. But even so they throw me out of my feeble stride. I *must* adhere to my rule of not going into any complex matter that does not arise out of the particular writing which I have in hand at the time. May I therefore ask you to be so very good as to let these few weak words be my last on the subject?

I am yours very sincerely,

ALFRED MARSHALL.

Balliol Croft, Cambridge

15. x. 12

Dear Professor Fisher,

On further consideration it occurred to me that I could not have advocated an artificial national currency in 1887. I have just looked up my article in the *Contemporary Review*, and I find that my goal was an artificial *unit* for long standing contracts and arrangements, and the restriction of currency to passing bargains. When Giffen uttered his vehement trumpet blast against "Fancy Monetary Standards" (No. XIX of his collected *Inquiries and Studies*), I chaffed him about his energy; and I recollect that he said that his argument was not opposed to my scheme. Recollecting that just now, I further remembered that my doubt about the practicability of my original scheme was connected with International Stock Exchange securities bearing a fixed rate of interest (among other things).

Yours very sincerely,

ALFRED MARSHALL.

To J. M. KEYNES

Balliol Croft, Cambridge
9. iii. 1914

Dear Keynes,

The Indian Currency Report came in at lunch time. I am behindhand with copy for the Press; so I thought I could not do more than get to know its general drift just at present.

But I dipped in here and there, and then read the conclusions: and finally turned negligently to the Annexe. But that held me. I had had no idea you had written it. Much of it, as of the Report itself, deals with matters beyond my knowledge and judgment. But there is quite enough of it within my understanding for me to have been entranced by it as a prodigy of constructive work. Verily we old men will have to hang ourselves, if young people can cut their way so straight and with such apparent ease through such great difficulties.

I thought of several objections as I read: but on going further, I found all of them met except one. Probably there is an answer to that also; but I did not see it. The objection is that in being generous to the shareholders in the Presidency Banks, you may possibly have been a little less than just to other credit institutions (I purposely use a broad vague term), English and Native; and also perhaps to the Indian State. I have always felt a little jealous of those Presidency Banks: they seem to me to have none of the obligations of a State Bank, and yet some of its sources of profit; and the new Bank would be able to override competitors who might have held their own against the Presidency Banks.

Again I have always thought the Bank of England Parlour, as it was described by Bagehot, contained elements which a State Bank should consider; and try to get something of them if possible. I admit that the fortunate accidents, which made it so strong say 40 years ago, are not as prominent now as then: and that State Banks are for many reasons in a stronger position than then. But yet, I think, I should like to enquire—if I ever went into the matter, which of course I shall not do—whether some Assessors might not be nominated (subject perhaps to conditions, including a veto in exceptional cases) by other financial authorities. Also some of them might perhaps have the right to subscribe for a few shares of the Bank at par.

I found in talking to the Indian experts in 1898 that the work of the native financiers (Banyans I fancy they were called) was not fully understood: and I doubted even whether Englishmen in India understand it. Several natives of India have talked to me confidentially about the relations of Indians and English: and they were unanimous in their opinion that Anglo-Indians, even the best-informed, have no conception how much there is to be known about India which is beyond the knowledge of Englishmen. The extent of native hoarding was one of the subjects to which these conversations referred.

But I have made a sufficient display of matters on which I certainly know much less than you: so I will end.

Yours enthusiastically,

ALFRED MARSHALL.

Balliol Croft, Cambridge
8. x. 1914

Dear Keynes,

I have just read with great admiration and profit your splendid article on war finance. I think I agree with you on all points on which I can form an independent opinion. But there is a good deal of ground beyond my ken. I have never seen my way to form an opinion on the controverted questions as to the relative advantages of the English and Continental methods of dealing with (1) specialized bills, or (2) the financing of businesses. My general notion is that system counts for less than men; and that the British system suited British conditions in Bagehot's time. But the consolidation of banks since his time opens out new problems, which I cannot grasp.

As to the ill conduct of particular banks in recent times, I know nothing: I am not inclined to suppose them all to be raised above sin. But, on the other hand, my little experience inclines me to think that those, whose stories of the wickedness of banks are the most incisive, are often those of whom the banks (if free to speak) could tell wicked stories.

Yours very sincerely,

ALFRED MARSHALL.

Balliol Croft, Cambridge
12. x. 1914

Dear Keynes,

Many thanks for your letter, which interested and informed me greatly.

Your experience goes on similar lines to that which I had on the Labour Commission: the preponderance of heavy minds in the management of businesses that can be reduced to routine is a great evil. The minds of leading working men seemed often more elastic and strong.

I had this danger partly in mind when I thought of the need of some financial agencies outside of the banks, whose chief concern is with routine: much of which could, theoretically at least, be discharged by automatic machinery.

I had mistaken the nature of the fault which you found with the bankers.

But I must stop.

Yours very sincerely,

ALFRED MARSHALL.

Balliol Croft, Cambridge
14. xii. 1914

Dear Keynes,

I have to thank you for what seems a most important article once more. I am too far away from all monetary questions, and too imbecile, to be able to read it through properly. But I seem to find myself agreeing with all I read. I think your concluding paragraph clears up your position well.

I don't think you have said anything about invasion in regard to the B. of E.'s stock of gold. I have always regarded the two as intimately connected. We have been warned that the Germans did intend, though *perhaps* they do not now, to risk the loss of many ships and lives in the endeavour to put 150,000 or 200,000 men at least on our shores: weather, *new model* submarines (capable of firing torpedoes without turning), etc. may conceivably favour them. If so, many people will go mad with terror; and demand gold to bury in their gardens, etc.

Until the danger of such mad, senseless terror is over past (perhaps it nearly is now) I do not want the Old Lady's stocking to be thinned out.

My reasons are partly political: partly a fear that such a panic would put a premium on gold, if the Old Lady did not oblige. And in this matter also I look at the sentimental side more than the material: but our national credit seems to have a larger sentimental element in it than that of any other country; and to have a very large gold value.

Yours very sincerely,

ALFRED MARSHALL.

Don't trouble to answer.

Balliol Croft, Cambridge

21. ii. 1915

Dear Keynes,

I know so little about either war or politics that I am afraid of speaking publicly, lest I do mischief. But some time you—with your full access to knowledge—will perhaps tell me whether I am right in fearing that our attitude to food supplies may cost us dearly in the future; though of course France and Russia can see no danger in the new precedent.

I shall not live to see our next war with Germany; but you will, I expect. For I am convinced that Germany is resolute in saying that her quarrels with Russia and France are capable of adjustment: but that she will not accept our superiority at sea, unless we allow her unhampered expansion—which of course includes unlimited fortified coaling stations. So I think of the next war almost as much as of the present; and the two together oppress me.

The more severely we use our power of starving Germany, the more eagerly do I think that she will set herself to prepare during a generation for a war with England, turning nominally on questions in which France and Russia have little concern: that she will at last spring it suddenly, and have several score of fast cruisers already out to sea.

The "Alabama," always evading battle, did immense mischief to North American trade: and though aerial telegraphs have helped our cruisers more than the "Emden," a great number of "Emdens" might stop most of our food supplies, except such as were convoyed by powerful fleets.

Further, submarines, some swift, but most broad and able to fire torpedoes in all directions, would be ready by the hundred; with light engines and large displacement, so as to be independent of fresh air for a day and of fresh supplies for a month.

Such a war would cost her but little; for we could not hurt her, while we should need to keep incessant guard during perhaps several years against invasion and hunger; unless Russia vetoed German ambitions.

So I say to myself anxiously, is the present gain to be got by bringing hunger to the people of Germany, against the judgment of many neutrals, worth what it may cost to England a generation hence? You must be busy, so don't answer till we meet.

Yours ever,

A. M.

Of course I do not think that peace ought to be concluded on terms which fail to make Germany regret that she engineered the War.

Don't bother about this if you are busy. It is merely an old man's nervousness.

Balliol Croft, Cambridge
22. ii. 15

My dear Keynes,

So far as I can judge, the Government declaration as to Germany's trade is required and wise. I am glad that no precedent is to be made for declaring food unconditional contraband.

Take care of yourself in this heavy strain.

Yours ever,

ALFRED MARSHALL.

To the Right Hon. LOUIS FRY

Balliol Croft, Cambridge

7. xi. 14

Dear Mr Fry,

My favourite *dictum* is:—Every statement in regard to economic affairs which is short is a misleading fragment, a fallacy or a truism. I think this dictum of mine is an exception to the general rule: but I am not bold enough to say that it *certainly* is.

Also I am able to work only for a very short time without a break: and my long promised book goes very slowly. I am quite well: but feeble. So I generally avoid letters and conversation. But I do not like to leave your letter without some poor attempt at an answer.

My patron Saint is Abbe, who, in control of the "Zeiss" works, has done more than anyone else, I believe, to revolutionise the higher glass industry, and attain results which a little while ago were thought impossible. His maxim was—keep financial control, but allow yourself for personal expenditure only as much as will enable you to keep your (and your family's) physical and mental energies at their highest. That is, my attitude towards "luxuries," in the distinctive sense of the term, does not get beyond toleration. Nevertheless I was not altogether sorry when, at the outbreak of the war, some cold-blooded and perhaps not altogether disinterested people cried out:—"Don't alter your mode of expenditure more than you can help. By refusing to buy accustomed luxuries you throw out of employment highly specialised workers, who cannot turn to anything else. Presently they will be wanting charitable relief. Pay for work would have been better for them, and would have avoided disorganisation of labour, with its attendant financial nervousness: and that is a thing specially to be dreaded from the point of military efficiency at the present time."

But I also think that everyone ought to begin to turn his expenditure into channels, which tend to the general good. A panic movement, which caused a wholesale discharge of elderly butlers would have been an evil: but a steadfast diminution in the demand for unnecessary domestic servants would turn people, who were not too old to change their vocation, into work that would make for the public good. Just at present of course the best of that work is at the front in the North of France and in Belgium.

Meanwhile chauffeurs, who are not able or willing to render direct public service, should, I think, be employed, as many of those belonging to my neighbours' establishments are, in taking convalescent soldiers for drives in the country. Other neighbours are retrenching in small ways, and either taking refugee Belgians into their own houses, or subscribing for their relief otherwise: and so on.

So now I think the time has come for the general principle:— Make towards a more steadfast suppression of personal luxuries and a larger devotion of resources to public ends. When the war is over, let the new seriousness, which it has brought into life, endure. Let more of the resources of the nation go to keeping children longer at school, and at better schools; to clearing out all unwholesome dwellings; and to levelling up the incomes of the poorer classes by an extension of the general principle that all may use freely roads, bridges etc. which are made at public expense.

By this means the employments that are subservient to luxury will be depleted gradually, without shock, and with no considerable hurt to any one: and the nation as a whole will grow in physical, moral and mental strength and joyousness.

On the question whether, when such a thing as sugar threatens to become scarce, well-to-do people should stint their consumption of it, I should be inclined to advocate moderate stinting: but I do not think the matter is practically important. If grain supplies ran short, I think educated people should eat oats etc. to which those with less elastic minds cannot accommodate themselves easily. Horses might put up with other food. The conversion of barley etc. into beer and spirits should be almost stopped. And, if milk runs short, healthy adults should leave it for children and invalids as much as possible.

As to the expenditure by Public Bodies on undertakings, other than relief works, I hesitate: because I cannot forecast the needs of the country after the war. Of course any unnecessary borrowing is a grave injury to the general business of this country. We ought to be financing our weaker allies, perhaps more than we are. It is said that we have lent fifteen millions to Australia. Our power in this direction is less than our will: and any one who still further lessens it without cause, is not acting rightly.

I have maintained from the first that, so long as the sea was open, there was no reason to expect much unemployment in the country *during* the war. Some persons would of course have to shift their occupations a little: but the whole trend of modern industry is towards the removal of impassable barriers to migration from one occupation to another of *the same kind*. The number of subdivisions is increasing: and when work becomes slack in any one, those in it say truly that they cannot get work in any other. But that only means that they cannot get it easily. If pressure lasts in their special work, they can, with a good-will, gradually get fairly good employment in other work. This was nearly certain *à priori*: and the experiences of the last three months have shown it to be true. See e.g. Board of Trade Labour Statistics for October; and Prof. Ashley's recent investigation into the conditions of work in Birmingham.

The building trades are, I admit, likely to become slack when the work arranged before the war is done: and though I think it would be most unwise and even wrong for any Public Body to commit themselves to large expenditure without most urgent need, there may be cause for getting plans ready for building and navvy work *after the war is over*. The unemployment, which is to be expected in many trades then, will be specially heavy in building trades: partly because they are so large, and those in them have no wide alternative openings; and partly also, I think, because ordinary people will then first realise how much the resources of the country have been depleted by the war and how much incomes generally must shrink; and will be on the look out for cheaper houses rather than larger. Of course, if we are invaded, the building trades will be busy after the war in some places: and have no employment at all in those which have not been devastated. But our present concern is not to keep at home young strong men—such as affect the building trades—but to help them to the front.

Such alone are the poor and fragmentary remarks which I can offer you as an expression of my particular views on large questions.

Yours very sincerely,

ALFRED MARSHALL.

P.S. On reading this over, I see that it ought to be re-written: but I trust you will kindly pardon its slovenliness.

In forecasting, as best I may, conditions after the war, I have made no allowance for an indemnity from Germany. Though I think she should be forced to pay for the havoc she has wrought in Belgium and France, I think also that the world does partially endorse Germany's charge that we alone among her enemies are influenced by sordid commercial considerations; and partly for this reason I hope that all *our* demands will be concentrated on lasting security against her military pretensions.

To Professor Sir WILLIAM RAMSAY

Balliol Croft, Cambridge

9. xii. 14

Dear Sir William Ramsay,

In my chapter on Germany's contribution to "Industrial Leadership" I talk about Lorraine and Luxemburg ores and Gilchrist in few words: but I did not know that the Germans were held up for a time by patents. That is an important fact. I will put it on to the proofs.

§§ 78, 79 of the inclosed [Fiscal Policy of International Trade] indicate that I have no objection on principle to "combative" taxes on dumped goods. But though I have read carefully everything that throws light on the practical working of such taxes, I have found nothing to show that they can be worked efficiently.

What is said about ether leaves me cold. If the Excise people are pigheaded, the scientific world is able to bring pressure on them. Possibly however the Excise may have a stronger case than appears at first sight. During the last thirty years I have come across scores of instances in which there is more to be said for the regulation than is admitted by those to whom it is objectionable.

But generally I agree that the Government in general and most especially the legal members of the House of Lords need to be bullied into common sense and some knowledge of business. Of course Moulton does not belong to the old gang..... But Halsbury went out of his way to preach an economic sermon in favour of unlimited freedom to grant rebates: and had no idea that American economists—who are the highest authority on this particular subject—are convinced that those rebates strengthen the destructive and antisocial effects of unscrupulous trade combinations more than almost anything else: and, as far as I know, English economists agree.....

Yours very sincerely,

ALFRED MARSHALL.

Balliol Croft, Cambridge

1914

Dear Sir William Ramsay,

I was told by a youth, who had been taught chemistry for two years at a leading University, that his teacher dictated a sort of text-book of his own; and that the lesson was chiefly one in writing from dictation facts useful to be remembered. Allowing for some exaggeration I thought this a bad sign; and there were others of the same kind on a smaller scale elsewhere.

Impressed by the personality of Sir David Dale (whom I met at the Labour Commission) I invested some of my small means in the Dundesland Iron Ore Co. I was *disgusted* when I found that they had recourse to Edison for a method of dealing with the ore, and spent enormous sums on setting up plant on his method; when a small experimental station at home might have indicated that the plan was not suitable for the ore. I was *terrified* when the directors, with millions of money at their back, went (as it seemed to me on their knees) to Krupp; and asked him to let one of his chemists make some experiments for them. Dale had died meanwhile. Krupp's chemist made them successfully: but I was chagrined by his success.

In consequence I have scarcely ventured to touch on industrial chemistry in revising my old proofs; though I have felt able to speak with confidence on a good many matters connected with industrial mechanics.

Your letter heartens me very much; but I am not yet in good spirits. Ought not you, and the few men who, like you, are raising the reputation of British chemistry throughout the world, to set yourselves to see whether the rank and file of British teachers of chemistry work up at all near to your own high ideals?—This is the question which occurs to me: it may probably show nothing but impertinent ignorance. And in any case do not trouble to answer. We ought both of us to be at our own hard work.

Yours very sincerely,

ALFRED MARSHALL.

I would rather have your testimonial as to a pupil than that of any body of examiners: but I would not give a halfpenny for one by the man who dictated a text-book.

To Professor C. R. FAY

Balliol Croft, Cambridge
23. ii. 15

BRAVO!

M. le Professeur

Capitaine Fay!

I am glad every way. I shall be delighted with analogies between economics and militarics. I don't guess what they are, except that the relations between long- and short-period policies and causations are—I suppose—rather similar in the two cases.

Life and Labour, 1800–1850 is a fascinating study. But a thousand years hence 1920–1970 will, I expect, be *the* time for historians.

It drives me wild to think of it. I believe it will make my poor *Principles*, with a lot of poor comrades, into waste paper. The more I think of it, the less I can guess what the world will be like fifty years hence.

Yours affectionately,

ALFRED MARSHALL.

To Professor F. W. TAUSSIG

Balliol Croft, Cambridge

37. iii. 1915

Dear Professor Taussig,

....I am in excellent health: wholly free from illness of any sort. But the smallest excitement sets up blood-pressure and cripples me for the rest of the half day. And I may not even write quietly for much more than an hour on end; and, still less, talk. I tell you this because one of its chief hardships is that it prevents me from seeing visitors; among whom no place has been higher in my esteem than that of Americans, and especially American economists. And next to them come German economists. Alack the day! But I love them still.

I think with you that the outlook is evil. I think more about the next war, in some moods, than even about the present. For if Germany were to declare war on England alone, we could do nothing against her, except to push her Commerce into indirect channels, and harry her Colonies: and that would strengthen Germany's opinion that our attitude to her is one of mere commercial jealousy. That may be true of the Germanesque tendencies of the "Tariff Reformers": but it is not true in the least of the people at large. Our dread, which latterly has become envenomed, is that, in such a war, we should need to spend perhaps two hundred millions a year on defences by land and sea against invasions, which might reduce a part at least of the land to the condition of Belgium. They would then have ready beforehand perhaps two hundred submarines, some swift, others with immense power of life without return to a base; and we might be brought to misery during many years, even if we evaded perdition. That is why many of us, who would be glad to see private property at sea immune, if it might be, feel that the right of capture at sea is our only bulwark, other than our alliances, against the monster-army of Germany.

And yet, I love the Germans through it all. They are not what they were in the 60's; because they have all passed under the schooling of German officers; and these are, it seems to me, far more selfish, as well as arrogant, than Germans in general. That is I think shown by the particular form which they have given to Agrarian Protection. The broad lines, which Wagner advocates for it, may be wise or foolish: but they are not lines of class-selfishness in any narrow sense. But protection, nearly the whole of the pecuniary gains of which come to the class from which the officers are almost exclusively drawn, while many of the smaller cultivators gain nothing net by them, seems to me to indicate a narrower class-selfishness.

I fear *that*: and I fear the sayings of the Bismarckians that the use of German colonies is not to draw the population away from the Fatherland: *i.e.* it is not economic. It is to supply bases for naval stations, from which military operations may be worked.

If we thought that Germany would use her colonies merely for commercial purposes, many of us would most heartily welcome the extension of her colonies far and wide; even though we know that her present colonies afford immense opportunities, which she has no real inclination to develop with her full energy.

Yours in prolixity, but most heartily,

ALFRED MARSHALL.

To JOHN HILTON

Balliol Croft, Cambridge

3. x. 1918

Dear Mr Hilton,

I am delighted to find that you are Secretary to the Committee on Trusts: it is a most important post; and, I think, admirably filled.....

I began the study about twenty years ago; and have given most of my time to it during recent years. I began with a bias against American developments, and in favour of German. But the American situation has greatly improved; and—except for the good mingled with the ill in the Stahlwerks-Verband—I do not think the German situation gets better. The Americans are absolutely frank, I think; and the pictures of German cartels which seem to have been supplied to some of the Board of Trade's Committees on particular trades after the war differ widely from those which I have formed as years went on. It is very unfortunate that they have not published the evidence on which they have based opinions, which are not, I think, in accordance with the evidence on the subject furnished by the Kartell-Enquête and the discussions at the Social Verein on the subject.

As to the relation of law to monopoly I have learnt very little from English sources: it seems never to have been thoroughly studied here. But American analysis and experience seem to show that in almost every difficult case there comes a stage at which the right of appeal to a "Supreme Court," or its equivalent, becomes necessary. But I do not think that a Court of Law is at all likely to find out what are the really significant points in such a problem, unless guided by highly trained specialists: and I think that some of the *obiter dicta*, even of many able judges, as to matters of economic policy might have very disastrous results if any authority came to be attached to them.

In short, I think the Federal Trade Act (somewhat modifying the duties of the old Bureau of Corporations and preserving in the main its personnel, though changing its name to Federal Trade Commission) is a master stroke of genius. It has been repeatedly argued, both here and in America, that the Common Law in regard to monopolies etc. has done admirable service, because its traditions are so vague as to be incapable of exact interpretation: it merely suggests a general tendency; and each generation has interpreted its vagueness with more or less success, in accordance with the needs and the administrative resources of the time. If that great heritage is to be swept away in the troubled waters of war time, I trust that nothing will be done of a far-reaching character without a careful study of the toilsome steps by which American expedients have been developed. I presume you have full access to the official literature relating to the work of the Federal Trade Commission. I have learnt from it, and that of the Bureau of Corporations, more perhaps than from any other source relating to the functions of a democratic government in regard to complex economic issues. On the other hand I have learnt nothing from *official* German pronouncements on such matters, unless it be in the art of saying what one does not mean. I am still a great admirer of Germany, in some connections, but those sides of her character, which the war has made prominent, seem to have misguided the policy of her cartels, and of her Government in relation to them.

I concur in the suggestion made by the Engineering Committee [Cd. 9078], p. 26, that secrecy is at the root of many of the evils of cartel policy: but not in their proposal that the constitution of a cartel should be registered *privately* with the Board of Trade. Bureaucratic rule has been necessary during the war: but if it became permanent, grave evils might arise from it, I fear, in this country, which is rapidly becoming a true democracy.

At such a time as this I think everyone who has studied a matter that is becoming urgent should submit his conclusions without reserve to those who are responsible, and, though I do not suppose that mine will be found very helpful, I have ventured to burden you with a long letter.

Yours faithfully,

ALFRED MARSHALL.

LETTERS TO NEPHEWS

To HAROLD E. GUILLEBAUD, *a schoolboy at Marlborough*

Balliol Croft, Cambridge

3. x. 04

My dear Harold,

I am glad you are in the Sixth. Just for the present you must I suppose be content to live as a parasite of Greeks and Romans. But do not overdo it.

Do not overstrain your health; and do not shut your mind to broader and harder matters of thought than Classics suggest.

Recollect that two boys out of three, who show exceptional ability at public schools in England, are pushed into classical studies on narrower lines than prevail in Germany, or indeed anywhere save in England. And recollect that in after life the large majority of these boys are passed by numbers of others, who probably had less natural ability and certainly had less careful education. Recollect that, even in literature, the best strength is generally shown by people who at school did not narrow their thoughts mainly to classics.

I speak with deep feeling. From six to seventeen years of age I studied practically nothing but classics. I then obtained a place in the school which entitled me to a "close" probationary classical fellowship at Oxford. (These things are abolished now.) I spent the next five years mainly on mathematics and the next three mainly on philosophy. I have forgotten my mathematics and philosophy as well as my classics: but I am intensely grateful to them. And I am not very grateful to my classics.

For of course the *Knowledge* gained by them is of no great use to anybody. They are the most invigorating studies of which boys are capable up to the age of (say) fourteen: and there are some, though not many *ideas and ideals*, which older boys and men more easily assimilate, perhaps, if presented in Greek surroundings than if associated with modern problems. But, on the whole, the mental vigour of the chief adult men of the world has been trained chiefly in work that uses bigger muscles of the mind than those which are chiefly exercised by classics.

Do then your classics, but recollect that by a mere study of them your faculties—be they great or small—are much less likely to be made as strong, and as serviceable to your generation, as they would be if you passed on from them to work in which you would be standing on your own feet, and not merely carried by men who were great, *because they studied the problems of* THEIR OWN AGE. The Alexandrines were classical scholars: the great Greek genius was educated in direct work at real difficulties.

Your very affectionate

ALFRED MARSHALL.

Give my love to Claude when you see him.

To Captain ARTHUR RAYMOND MARSHALL, R.G.A., who was wounded on Dec. 8, 1917, and died in hospital at Rouen on Feb. 2, 1918.

Balliol Croft, Cambridge

18. i. 18

My dear brave Arthur,

How good and strong you are under your grievous pains! The latest news of you is always *the* news of the day, rivalled only by the inch high headings—if there are any—over the war news in the "Times." Poor dear lad! It is sad that you are thus struck, and in parts of the body that are specially sensitive and self-willed. But all brave soldiers, when hit, have the consolation of being able to say, "it was for my country": and in this war there is even more to be said. The whole world—other than Germany—is in a sense "the country" of those who are fighting for a future of peace: you suffer on behalf of the world; and the world will be grateful to you in coming times. Even should the worst befall and the world seem to darken before you, you can say "*Dulce et decorum est pro patria mori*": and then you can say it over again, and put *pro orbe* instead of *pro patria*. But that is only for moods when you are cast down. In other moods you will be looking forward to a noble life in quiet hero garb. First you will be looking after recruits, and then you will be settling down to engineering work, in which your mind will be all the keener, and have all the qualities of true leadership, because you have seen so much, and done so much, and felt so much. And this is the mood that you should foster. Among the happiest of men, are those who have gone through great tribulation, and have worked through it all to a noble life, ever nearer their Ideal, ever nearer to God.

Your loving, anxious, hopeful

ALFRED MARSHALL.

ALFRED MARSHALL, *in his garden shelter at Cambridge*, 1920

MARSHALL'S EIGHTIETH BIRTHDAY

On the occasion of Alfred Marshall's eightieth birthday (July 26, 1922), the following Address was presented to him by members of the Royal Economic Society:

On the occasion of your eightieth birthday we—many of us formerly your pupils, all of us admiring students of your writings —make bold to send you a brief message of congratulation. You have held up through a long life, with single aim and steady purpose, a high scientific ideal; to look through the sign to the thing signified, to shun the superficial and the plausible, and never to be content with the good when the better may still be attained. You have given inspiration to youth and counsel and enlightenment to age. The School of Economics at Cambridge is your child; on the Labour Commission and in your evidence before the Gold and Silver and other Commissions you have rendered important direct service to the State and have advanced Economic Science. But it is as a master of method and a path-breaker in difficult regions that we, the signatories of this letter, desire especially to greet you. Through you, British economists may boast among their foreign colleagues that they have a leader in the great tradition of Adam Smith and Ricardo and Mill, and of like stature. In gratitude and affectionate esteem we wish you continuing power and happy days and the sense of work well done.

HALDANE OF CLOAN, President of the Royal Economic Society.
BALFOUR, Vice-President of the Royal Economic Society.

A. ANDRÉADÈS . . .	Professor in the University of Athens.
WILLIAM ASHLEY, KT. .	,, ,, ,, Birmingham.
C. F. BASTABLE . . .	,, ,, ,, Dublin.
STEPHAN BAUER . . .	,, ,, ,, Basle.
W. H. BEVERIDGE, K.C.B. .	Director of the London School of Economics.
ARTHUR L. BOWLEY, SC.D. .	Professor in the University of London.
L. BRENTANO . . .	,, ,, ,, Munich.
EDWIN CANNAN . . .	,, ,, ,, London.
T. N. CARVER, PH.D. . .	Professor in Harvard University.
GUSTAV CASSEL . . .	Professor in the University of Stockholm.
S. J. CHAPMAN, K.C.B. .	Formerly Professor in the University of Manchester.

J. H. CLAPHAM, LITT.D., C.B.E.	Formerly Professor in the University of Leeds.
F. Y. EDGEWORTH	Professor Emeritus in the University of Oxford.
IRVING FISHER	Professor in the University of Yale.
A. W. FLUX, C.B.	Formerly Professor in the University of Montreal.
CHARLES GIDE	Professor in the University of Paris.
A. T. HADLEY	Formerly President of Yale.
H. M. HALLSWORTH	Professor in the University of Newcastle.
H. STANLEY JEVONS	„ „ „ Allahabad.
A. W. KIRKALDY	„ „ „ Nottingham.
DOUGLAS KNOOP	„ „ „ Sheffield.
R. A. LEHFELDT	„ „ „ Johannesburg.
D. H. MACGREGOR	„ „ „ Oxford.
E. MAHAIM	„ „ „ Liège.
H. O. MEREDITH	„ „ „ Belfast.
J. S. NICHOLSON	„ „ „ Edinburgh.
C. H. OLDHAM	„ „ „ Dublin.
A. C. PIGOU	„ „ „ Cambridge.
J. A. SCHUMPETER	„ „ „ Vienna.
W. R. SCOTT, LITT.D., LL.D.	„ „ „ Glasgow.
EDWIN R. A. SELIGMAN, PH.D.	„ in Columbia University, New York.
T. A. SMIDDY	„ in the University of Cork.
W. R. SORLEY, LITT.D.	„ „ „ Cambridge.
F. W. TAUSSIG	„ in Harvard University.

R. MARY ABBOT.

W. M. ACWORTH, K.C.S.I., KT.

C. S. ADDIS, K.C.M.G.

LEONARD ALSTON.

G. ARMITAGE-SMITH, LITT.D.

PERCY ASHLEY, C.B.

D. BARBOUR, K.C.M.G., K.C.S.I.

A. E. BATEMAN, K.C.M.G.

HUGH BELL, BART.

JAMES BONAR, LL.D.

R. H. BRAND, C.M.G.

LESLIE D. CLARK.

CLARA E. COLLET, M.A.

LEONARD DARWIN.

WILLIAM H. DAWSON.

THOMAS H. ELLIOTT, BART, K.C.B.

M. EPSTEIN, PH.D.

OSWALD T. FALK, C.B.E.

C. R. FAY.

H. FOUNTAIN, C.B.

H. SANDERSON FURNISS.

GEORGE S. GIBB, KT.

LYNDA GRIER, Principal of Lady Margaret Hall, Oxford

C. W. GUILLEBAUD.

F. C. HARRISON, C.S.I.

R. G. HAWTREY.

H. D. HENDERSON.

HENRY HIGGS, C.B.

ALFRED HOARE.

C. K. HOBSON.

B. L. HUTCHINS.

J. M. KEYNES, C.B.

J. N. KEYNES, SC.D.

F. LAVINGTON.

H. B. LEES-SMITH.

E. LIPSON.

H. LLEWELLYN-SMITH, G.C.B.

HENRY W. MACROSTY.

THEODORE MORISON, K.C.I.E.

MARIAN F. PEASE.

J. HENRY PENSON, K.B.E.

F. W. PETHICK LAWRENCE.

L. R. PHELPS, Provost of Oriel.

L. L. PRICE.

HELÈNE REYNARD.

D. H. ROBERTSON.

CHARLES P. SANGER.

G. F. SHOVE.

J. C. STAMP, Sc.D., K.B.E

MARY STOCKS, B.Sc.

R. H. TAWNEY.

BARBARA WOOTTON.

G. UDNY YULE, C.B.E.

Dr Marshall replied to the Secretary of the Society as follows:

SEA VALE, EAST LULWORTH,

DORSET,

July 27, 1922.

MY DEAR KEYNES,

The address, which you have sent to me on my eightieth birthday, fills me with gratitude and joy. It is all too kind: but I am so avaricious that I would not give up a jot of it.

It is true of almost every science that, the longer one studies it, the larger its scope seems to be: though in fact its scope may have remained almost unchanged. But the subject-matter of economics grows apace; so that the coming generation will have a much larger field to study, as well as more exacting notions as to the way in which it needs to be studied, than fell to the lot of their predecessors. The Chinese worship their ancestors: an old student of economics may look with reverential awe on the work which he sees young students preparing themselves to do.

If I have helped in putting some young students on the way to grapple with the economic problems of the coming age, that is far more important than anything which I have been able to do myself: and, resting on the hope that I have done a little in this direction, I can depart in peace.

Yours happily,

ALFRED MARSHALL.

BIBLIOGRAPHICAL LIST OF THE WRITINGS
OF ALFRED MARSHALL[1]
by J. M. KEYNES

THE following is an attempt to record those of Alfred Marshall's occasional writings and lectures, as well as his published books, which are extant in print, and have some permanent interest. Those which are printed in this volume are marked with an asterisk.

*(1) 1872. Review of Jevons's *Theory of Political Economy*. (*Academy*, April 1, 1872.)

 (2) 1873. Graphic representation by aid of a series of Hyperbolas of some Economic Problems having reference to Monopolies. (*Proceedings of the Cambridge Philosophical Society*, Oct. 1873.)

*(3) 1874. The Future of the Working Classes: a Paper read at a conversazione of the Cambridge "Reform Club," Nov. 25, 1873. (Published in the *Eagle*, the St John's College, Cambridge, magazine, and afterwards printed separately for private circulation.)

*(4) 1876. On Mr Mill's Theory of Value. (*Fortnightly Review*, April 1876.) A defence of Mill against criticisms in Cairnes' "Leading Principles."

 (5) 1878. The Economic Condition of America. A lecture delivered at Bristol. (*Bristol Mercury and Daily Post*, Dec. 1878.)

*(6) 1879. Water as an Element of National Wealth. A Gilchrist lecture delivered at Bristol. (*Bristol Mercury and Daily Post*, March 6, 1879.)

 (7) 1879. *The Economics of Industry*. By Alfred Marshall and Mary Paley Marshall. (Macmillan and Co.).

       1879: First Edition, pp. viii + 230.
       1881: Second Revised Edition, pp. xvi + 230.
       Reprinted 10 times, making 15,000 copies in all.

 (8) 1879. Pure Theory of Foreign Trade.
       Pure Theory of Domestic Values.
       These were non-consecutive chapters of the second Part of "The Theory of Foreign Trade" at which A. M. was working from 1869 to 1877. After they had been circulating in manuscript, Henry Sidgwick printed them for private circulation in 1879.

 (9) 1881. Review of Edgeworth's *Mathematical Psychics*. (*Academy*, April 1881.)

(10) 1881. Address on leaving Bristol. (*Western Daily Press*, Sept. 30, 1881.)

(11) 1881. Evidence before the Committee on Intermediate and Higher Education in Wales.

(12) 1883. Progress and Poverty. Three lectures delivered at Bristol. (*Western Daily Press*, March 1881.)

---

[1] The dates given are those of publication in each case, not of composition.

*(13) 1884. Where to House the London Poor. (*Contemporary Review*, March 1884. Reprinted separately by W. Metcalfe and Son, Cambridge, in 1887.)

*(14) 1885. *The Present Position of Economics.* An Inaugural Lecture. Pp. 57. (Macmillan and Co.)

(15) 1885. The Present Position of Political Economy. (A letter to *The Times*, June 2, 1885.)
Referring to a lengthy review of *The Present Position of Economics*, published in *The Times* of May 30, 1885.

(16) 1885. Theories and Facts about Wages. (*Co-operative Annual*, 1885.)
An account of former Wage Theories and the first published outline of the Theory of Distribution developed in *The Principles*.

(17) 1885. How far do Remediable Causes influence prejudicially (A) the Continuity of Employment, (B) the Rates of Wages? (A Paper read at the Industrial Remuneration Conference, Jan. 1885.)
This address was printed in the Report of the Conference together with the four following appendices: (A) *Overcrowding of Towns* (on the same lines as the *Contemporary Review* article of 1884, above); (B) *The Interdependence of Industries* (a short quotation from Bagehot's "Lombard Street"); (C) *A Standard of Purchasing Power* (the first appearance of the proposal for an Optional Tabular Standard); (D) *Theories and Facts about Wages* (a reprint of the contribution to the *Co-operative Annual*, 1885, above). This publication (22 pp. altogether) is the most important indication of the progress of his ideas between 1879 and 1885. Extracts from it were reprinted in *Money Credit and Commerce*, pp. 260–263.

*(18) 1885. On the Graphic Method of Statistics. (Jubilee volume of the Royal Statistical Society, pp. 251–260.)
This paper contains three important novelties:
(1) The proposal for the construction of *historical curves, i.e.* the grouping together of allied historical curves so as to suggest possible correlations to the eye.
(2) A device for making it easy to see the *proportional rates of increase* on historical curves.
(3) The definition of *elasticity of demand*, which appears here for the first time.

(19) 1885. The Pressure of Population on the Means of Subsistence. (A lecture delivered at Toynbee Hall, Sept. 10, 1885.)
No report of this lecture exists, but a brief summary is given in *The Malthusian*, Oct. 1885. The lecturer strongly supported Malthusian doctrines, but disappointed orthodox Malthusians by saying nothing in favour of limitation of births. "I understood him to say," the reporter records, "that it would be a calamity if we English, by limiting our numbers, allowed foreigners to have a larger share than ourselves in peopling the world; and there was no need to fear the effects of our prospective increase at home."

(20) 1885. Preface to Bagehot's *Postulates of English Political Economy*, pp. v–vii. (Longmans.)

(21) 1886. Answers to Questions on the Subject of Currency and Prices, circulated by the Royal Commission on the Depression of Trade and Industry. (Third Report, Appendix C, pp. 31–34.)
His proposal for an optional tabular standard is developed and that for Symmetallism is also put forward.

(22) 1886. Political Economy and Outdoor Relief. (A letter to *The Times*, Feb. 15, 1886.)

Against undue severity in the administration of outdoor relief and in favour of relief works to meet unemployment. "The pay should be enough to afford the necessaries of life, but so far below the ordinary wages of unskilled labour in ordinary trades that people will not be contented to take it for long, but will always be on the look-out for work elsewhere. I for one can see no economic objection to letting public money flow freely for relief works on this plan." The letter provoked a protest "on moral grounds" from the Rev. J. Llewellyn Davies, who stood up for the straitlaced school.

(23) 1887. The Royal Commission on Trade Depression. (A letter to *The Times*, Jan. 18, 1887.)

Expressing general agreement with the Report of the Commission and commenting on some details.

*(24) 1887. Remedies for Fluctuations of General Prices. (*Contemporary Review*, March 1887.)

This is, perhaps, the most important of A. M.'s occasional writings. It includes his proposals (1) for a Tabular Standard of Value, independent of gold and silver, called "The Unit," to be established officially for optional use in contracts; (2) for a "Symmetallic" system of currency, the unit being made of twenty parts silver and one part gold; (3) for the "chain" method in the compilation of Index Numbers of Purchasing Power. He points out (*a*) that the evils of a fluctuating standard for deferred payments are chiefly of modern origin, but that now they are of overwhelming importance; and (*b*) that bi-metallism, even if successful, aims only at curing long-period fluctuations in the value of money, whereas the harm was done by the short-period fluctuations, corresponding to the Trade Cycle, which no metallic system could cure.

(25) 1887. A Tabular Standard of Value. (A letter to *The Economist*, March 12, 1887.)

The Economist of March 5, 1887, had been seriously shocked by the *Contemporary Review* article, and concluded: "The Standard which Professor Marshall proposes is, it seems to us, impossible and impracticable, and to say more of it would be superfluous." In this letter A. M. defends himself, particularly against the misrepresentation that he proposed "The Unit" for use as actual cash currency.

*(26) 1887. Preface to *Industrial Peace*, by L. L. F. R. Price.

Deals mainly with the rationale of Arbitration and Conciliation. Mr Price's book was "A Report of an Inquiry made for the Toynbee Trustees." A. M.'s Preface begins with a tribute to Toynbee.

(27) 1887. Evidence before the Gold and Silver Commission.

A. M.'s written answers were submitted on Nov. 9, 1887, and occupy six and a half columns. His oral cross-examination took place on Dec. 19, 1887, Jan. 16 and 23, 1888, and the reports occupy eighty-three folio columns; after which he put in a "Memorandum as to the effects which differences between the currencies of different nations have on international trade" (twelve columns). This Memorandum is a fuller version of "an abstract of my opinions on the complex question of the relation between a fall of the exchange and our trade with countries which have not a gold currency," which he submitted to the Commissioners, in print, between his evidence of Dec. 1887 and that of Jan. 1888. The importance of this Memorandum lies in the fact that it contains a clear enunciation of the "purchasing-power parity" theory of the exchanges between countries having mutually inconvertible currencies.

(28) 1887. On the Theory of Value. (*Quarterly Journal of Economics*, Vol. I. p. 359.)

A short letter answering a criticism by Prof. Laughlin of a passage in the *Economics of Industry*.

(29) 1887. The Theory of Business Profits. (*Quarterly Journal of Economics*, Vol. I. p. 477.)

A Memorandum answering a criticism by General Walker of a passage in the *Economics of Industry*.

(30) 1888. Wages and Profits. (*Quarterly Journal of Economics*, Vol. II. p. 218.)

A Memorandum answering a criticism by Mr Macvane of a passage in the *Economics of Industry*. See also a short letter published in the *Q.J.E.*, Vol. III. p. 109, disclaiming the accuracy of a paraphrase of his views set forth in the same Journal by Mr Macvane.

(31) 1889. Bimetallism. (Letters to *The Times*, Jan. 25 and 31, 1889.)

The first letter repudiates a statement that A. M. was one of those who have "substantially approved the Bimetallic theory"; the second enters into controversy with Mr Henry Chaplin.

*(32) 1889. Presidential Address before the Co-operative Congress, Ipswich, June 10, 1889. (Reported in *The Times*, June 11, 1889; reprinted as a pamphlet by the Central Co-operative Board, Manchester, pp. 32.)

The Address was a great popular success, but *The Economist* commented that "Professor Marshall's Address seems to us obscured, instead of brightened, by its sentimental tone....We are entirely friendly to co-operation as a most sensible plan for enabling the public, which buys, to share in the profits of those who sell, and to compel the latter to be honest, but we believe in it because it is based on intelligent self-interest, and not because it will extinguish that powerful motive force." The Address contains the following characteristic, and double-edged, passage: "It was common to hear it said that England was divided into two nations, the rich and the poor. He was not sure that it would not be better for the poor if that statement were strictly true....But, unfortunately for the poor, they had to make room among their ranks for a large accession every year of the most stupid and profligate of the descendants of the rich (*loud cheers*), and in return they every year gave over to the ranks of the rich a great number of the strongest and ablest, the most enterprising and far-seeing, the bravest and best of those who were born among themselves."

(33) 1890. *Principles of Economics*. Vol. I. The successive editions of this book were as follows:

1890.	1st edition,	pp. xxviii +754.	2000 copies, 12s. 6d. net.		
1891.	2nd ,,	pp. xxx +770.	3000 ,,	,,	,,
1895.	3rd ,,	pp. xxxi +823.	2000 ,,	,,	,,
1898.	4th ,,	pp. xxix. +820.	5000 ,,	,,	,,

1907. 5th edition, pp. xxxvi + 870. 5000 copies, 12s 6d. net.
1910. 6th   „   pp. xxxii + 871. 5000   „   „   „
1916. 7th   „   5000   „   „   „
1920. 8th   „   pp. xxxiv + 871. 5000   „   18s.   „
(This edition (1920) has been stereotyped.)
1922. Reprint   5000   „   „   „
The most important changes were introduced into the third
and fifth editions. The sixth edition is the first in which the
Suffix Vol. I. is dropped.

*(34) 1890. Some Aspects of Competition. (Presidential Address to the
Economic Science and Statistics Section of the British Association, Leeds, 1890, pp. 35.)

(35) 1890. Proposal to form an English Economic Association. (A circular
letter.)

(36) 1890. Speech at the Meeting for the Foundation of the British Economic
Association. (*Economic Journal*, Vol. I.)

(37) 1891. The Post Office and Private Enterprise. (Letters to *The Times*,
March 24 and April 6, 1891.)
Criticising the legal monopoly of the Post Office.

(38) 1892. *Elements of Economics of Industry:* being the first volume of
Elements of Economics.

1892. 1st edition, pp. xiii + 416. Reprinted 1893, 1894.
1896. 2nd   „   pp. xiv + 432. Reprinted 1898, 1899.
1899. 3rd   „   pp. xvi + 421. Reprinted 8 times.
1913. 4th   „   pp. xvi + 440. Reprinted 7 times.

The above editions and reprints represent 81,000 copies in all.
"An attempt to adapt the first volume of my *Principles of
Economics* to the needs of junior students....A chapter on *trade-
unions* has been added....A few sentences have been incorporated
from the *Economics of Industry,* published by my wife and myself
in 1879."

(39) 1892. The Poor Law in Relation to State-Aided Pensions. (*Economic
Journal*, Vol. II. pp. 186–191.)
A plea for a Commission of Inquiry into the problems of
State Relief generally before committing ourselves to old-age
pensions.

(40) 1892. Poor Law Reform. (*Economic Journal*, Vol. II. pp. 371–379.)
A rejoinder to criticisms of the preceding article by Mr
Bosanquet.

(41) 1892. A Reply to "The Perversion of Economic History" by Dr
Cunningham. (*Economic Journal*, Vol. II. pp. 507–519.)
Dr Cunningham's article, which was printed immediately in
front of the above, was an attack on the Economic History in
The Principles.

(42) 1892. Discussion on Mr Booth's "Enumeration and Classification of
Paupers." (*Statistical Journal*, Vol. LV. pp. 60–63.)

(43) 1893. On Rent. (*Economic Journal*, Vol. III. pp. 74–90.)
With special reference to the Duke of Argyll's "Unseen
Foundations of Society."

(44) 1893. Speech at the Meeting of the British Economic Association,
June 19, 1893. (*Economic Journal*, Vol. III. pp. 387–390.)
On economic motive and the independence of Economics from
utilitarian ethics—following an address by Mr Goschen.

*(45) 1893. Obituary: Professor Benjamin Jowett. (*Economic Journal*, Vol. III. pp. 745–746.)

(46) 1893. Consumers' Surplus. (*Annals of the American Academy*, Vol. III. pp. 618–621.)
A reply to misconceptions about Consumers' Surplus in a paper by Prof. Patten. "In every case," A. M. here emphasises, "all other things are supposed to remain unchanged; and particular stress is laid on the fact that there is no change in the conditions of supply of any other commodity (say meat), which is a 'rival' to it (the bread), and can partially satisfy the same needs."

(47) 1893. Discussion on Mr Higgs' "Workmen's Budgets." (*Statistical Journal*, Vol. LVI. pp. 286–288.)

(48) 1893. The Aged Poor. (A Preliminary Statement prepared for the Royal Commission.)

(49) 1895. Evidence before the Royal Commission on the Aged Poor. (Report of the Commission, Vol. III. pp. 529–550.)
The examination was held on June 5, 1893, and occupies forty-three columns.

(50) 1895. Discussion on Mr Bowley's "Changes in Average Wages (nominal and real), 1860–1891." (*Statistical Journal*, Vol. LVIII. p. 279.)

(51) 1895. The Venezuela Question. (Letter to *The Times*, Dec. 22, 1895.)
A plea for appreciation of the American point of view.

(52) 1896. On Cambridge Degrees for Women, 8 pp. 4to. (A Fly-sheet issued to Members of the Senate of the University of Cambridge.)

*(53) 1897. The Old Generation of Economists and the New. (*Quarterly Journal of Economics*, Vol. XI. pp. 23.)
An Address delivered at the first meeting of the Cambridge Economic Club, Oct. 29, 1896.
"Speaking generally, the nineteenth century has in great measure achieved *qualitative* analysis in economics; but it has not gone farther. It has felt the necessity for *quantitative* analysis, and has made some rough preliminary surveys of the ways in which it is to be achieved; but the achievement itself stands over for you."

*(54) 1898. Distribution and Exchange[1]. (*Economic Journal*, Vol. VIII. pp. 37–59.)
A reply to Prof. Hadley's "Some Fallacies in the Theory of Distribution."
Mainly an essay in method. As regards Prof. Hadley: "I venture to adhere to the opinion that distribution and exchange are fundamentally the same problem, looked at from different points of view."

(55) 1898. The Slow Progress of our Exports. (Letters to *The Times*, Nov. 10 and Dec. 2, 1898.)
He suggests "that we already import from abroad nearly as much tropical and other produce, which we cannot raise ourselves, as we want; and that, as our real income increases, we prefer to spend its growing surplus largely on such personal services as conduce to domestic comfort, recreation, education, etc."

---

[1] Part of this is here reprinted with the title "Mechanical and biological analogies in Economics."

(56) 1899. Evidence before the Indian Currency Committee. (Minutes of Evidence taken before the Committee, Part II. [c. 9222], pp. 167–185, and Appendix [c. 9376]. Diagrams 64–69.) The examination was held on Jan. 11 and Feb. 16, 1899, and occupies thirty-four columns.

(57) 1899. Memoranda on Classification and Incidence of Imperial and Local Taxes. (Written replies to a Questionnaire circulated by the Royal Commission on Local Taxation. Report of the Commission, [c. 9528], pp. 112–126.)

*(58) 1900. Speech at a Meeting held at the Lodge of Trinity College, Cambridge, Nov. 26, 1900, to consider what steps should be taken to perpetuate the memory of Professor Sidgwick. (*Cambridge University Reporter*, Dec. 7, 1900.)

*(59) 1901. An Export Duty on Coal. (Letters to *The Times*, April 22 and May 9, 1901.)
"The Chancellor of the Exchequer's proposal to put an export duty on coal...is not, as some have asserted, to be condemned on general economic principles....On the other hand, a tax on the export of coal appears to present many technical difficulties; and to be not worth the disturbance it must cause unless it is to be permanent. And, what is more important, it is, to a certain extent, a breach of international comity....My doubts have never been resolved; but I admire the courage of the Chancellor." These letters were reprinted in the *Economic Journal*, Vol. XI. pp. 265–268.

(60) 1902. A Plea for the Creation of a Curriculum in Economics and Associated Branches of Political Science. Pp. 18. (A pamphlet printed for circulation to the Cambridge Senate.)

(61) 1902. Economic Teaching at the Universities in relation to Public Well-being. (A Paper read at a Conference of Members of the Committee on Social Education, Oct. 24, 1902.)

(62) 1903. The Proposed New Tripos. (A Fly-sheet to the Cambridge Senate.)

(63) 1903. Discussion in the Cambridge Senate on the proposal to establish a Tripos in Economics and Associated Branches of Political Science. (*Cambridge University Reporter*, May 14, 1903, pp. 772–774.)

(64) 1903. Fiscal Policy: a letter to the secretary of the Unionist Free Trade League. (*The Times*, Nov. 23, 1903.)
"About thirty years ago I became convinced that a protective system, if it could be worked honestly as well as wisely, might on the whole benefit countries in a certain stage of industrial development, and that set me on the inquiry whether a free-trade policy was wholly right for England. I have pursued that inquiry ever since, and have gradually settled down to the conclusion that the changes of the last two generations have much increased the harm which would be done to England by even a moderate protective policy, and that free trade is of more vital necessity to England now than when it was first adopted."

(65) 1904. Discussion on Mr Schuster's "Foreign Trade and the Money Market." (*Journal of the Institute of Bankers*, Vol. XXV. pp. 94–98.) On the theme that the maintenance of Free Trade is essential to the position of Great Britain.

(66) 1904. On a National Memorial to Herbert Spencer. (*Daily Chronicle*, Nov. 23, 1904.)

"There is probably no one who gave as strong a stimulus to the thoughts of the younger Cambridge graduates thirty years or forty years ago as he. He opened out a new world of promise; he set men on high enterprise in many diverse directions; and though he may have regulated English intellectual work less than Mill did, I believe he did much more towards increasing its utility. He has, perhaps, been more largely read and exercised a greater influence on the Continent than any other recent English thinker except Darwin."

(67) 1905. Education and the Classics. (A letter to *The Times*, March 3, 1905.)

In favour of the reformers in the compulsory Greek controversy. Nevertheless he holds that "for several years the child's most educative study is that of words, for he is still too young to make a scientific study of things....Experience shows that he has more to gain from handling words than from any other exercise, perhaps more than from all others put together. The materials for his work come to him gratis and in abundance; and in building with them, he is called on to exert the highest spontaneity of which he is capable. Demands are made on his general intelligence, his judgment, his perceptive sensibility and his taste; and in a greater or less degree he can rise to these demands. He is architect, engineer, and skilled artisan all at once."

(68) 1905. University Education for Business Men. (Letters to *The Times*, Dec. 18 and 29, 1905.)

(69) 1906. Introduction to the Tripos in Economics and Associated Branches of Political Science. Pp. 16.

*(70) 1907. The Social Possibilities of Economic Chivalry. (*Economic Journal*, Vol. XVII. pp. 7–29.)

An Address delivered before the Royal Economic Society on Jan. 9, 1907.

One of the best of A. M.'s occasional utterances on social questions: on the two themes, "We have more reason to be proud of our ways of making wealth than of our ways of using it," and "Social disaster would probably result from the full development of the collectivist programme, unless the nature of man has first been saturated with economic chivalry."

(71) 1908. Memorandum on the Fiscal Policy of International Trade. Pp. 29. (House of Commons Paper, No. 321 of 1908.)

This Memorandum was written in August 1903, but was pigeon-holed in the Foreign Office unprinted (with the acquiescence of the author), in circumstances described in the *Memoir*, until 1908. See also A. M.'s letter to *The Times*, Nov. 23, 1908.

(72) 1909. Rates and Taxes on Land Values. (Letter to *The Times*, Nov. 16, 1909.)

Blessing, on the whole, the proposals of the "Social Welfare Budget" of that year.

(73) 1910. Alcoholism and Efficiency. (Letters to *The Times*, July 7, Aug. 4, and Aug. 19, 1910.)

In controversy with Professor Karl Pearson.

(74) 1914. A Fight to a Finish. (Letters to *The Times*, Aug. 20 and Aug. 25, 1914.)

An appeal for the moderation of national hatred.

(75) 1914. Civilians in Warfare. (A letter to *The Times*, Oct. 28, 1914.)

A "plea for the dissemination of accurate information as to the conditions under which the civil population of a country may oppose the violence of an invading army."

(76) 1915. Milk in Germany: the Oversea Supply of Fats. (Letters to *The Times*, Dec. 29 and Dec. 31, 1915.)

(77) 1916. The Need for more Taxation. (A letter to *The Economist*, Dec. 30, 1916.)

In support of Prof. Pigou's plea for increased taxation to defray the expenses of the war.

(78) 1917. The Uses of Hatred. (Letter to *The Times*, Dec. 28, 1917.)

A protest against Sir Conan Doyle's proposal for the systematic development of hatred against Germany as a political weapon. "To foster hatred as an end would strengthen the position of pacifists, whose noble sentiments seem to me to make for a premature peace which would inflict a disaster almost unparalleled in history on the coming generation."

*(79) 1917. National Taxation after the War: I. The Appropriate Distribution of its Burden; II. Taxes on Imports—the New International Situation[1]. (An Essay contributed (pp. 313–345) to *After-War Problems*, a volume "by the Earl of Cromer and others," under the editorship of Mr W. H. Dawson.)

A re-endorsement of Free Trade in post-war conditions. "A broad system of Protective duties would deprive Britain of the strength which has enabled her to carry the chief financial burdens of the war, would confer some benefits on particular industries at the cost of much greater injury to the people at large; and would lessen the funds available for paying pensions to wounded men and to widows; and for lowering the present mountain of debt, which may threaten to turn some peril of a later generation into disaster." He favours an income-tax which would exempt savings, would take account of the number of people dependent on each income, and would be steeply graduated.

(80) 1919. *Industry and Trade*. Pp. xxiv + 875. (Macmillan and Co.)

1st edition, 1919. 18*s*. net, 2000 copies.
2nd   „   1919. 2000 copies.
3rd   „   (stereotyped), 1920. 2000 copies.
4th   „   1921. 2000 copies.
5th   „   1923. 3000 copies.

(81) 1920. Premium Bonds. (A letter to *The Times*, Nov. 17, 1919.)

A protest against "a form of State Lottery."

(82) 1923. *Money Credit and Commerce*. Pp. xv + 369. (Macmillan and Co.)

1st edition, 1923, 10*s*. net, 5000 copies.

---

[1] Part of this is here reprinted with the title "The Equitable Distribution of Taxation."

INDEX

Abbe and the "Zeiss" works, 484

Acland, A. H. D., *see* LETTERS

Adam Smith, 35, 36, 78, 100, 121; new point of view, 126, 157; relation to Physiocrats, 157 n., 379; originality, 379; on trade combinations, 267, 272; Government in his time, 334–5; Prize, 59, 456

Aged Poor Commission, 52–3, 70

Airey, 3, 5 n.

Alden, Percy, *see* LETTERS

American visit and its lessons, 14, 27, 67, 262–3; wealth compared with U.K., 134; protection, 258–64; early difficulties of manufacturers, 260–1; and English business compared, 266–7; railways, 267; Trusts, 268–72, 274, 492–3; combination law, 273; doctors and lawyers, 388; new strains of immigrants, 469; economists on rebates, 488; Federal Trade Commission, 492–3

Arbitration, 222–5; broad principle of, 224

Ashley, Prof., 486

"At Homes" with pupils, 48–9, 57–9, 60 n., 87–8, 381

Avon, estimate of its value, 138

Bagehot, and Ricardo, 292; and English banking system, 480

Baker's *Monopolies and the People*, 276 n.

Balliol College, influence of Jowett on, 294

Balliol Croft, 48–50, 74–7

Bank of England, in relation to a bimetallic currency scheme, 204–7 n.; Parlour, 479; stock of gold in case of invasion, 481–2

Barbour, 194

Bateson, Dr, Master of St John's, 4 n., 11 n.

Benians, E. A., Reminiscences of lectures, 78–80

Bentham, 11, 22 n., 23, 71

Bimetallism, 18 n., 28 n., 39, 67–8; and stability of prices, 193, 196–7; is strictly speaking Fixed-Ratio-Mintage, 188, 199–203; proposal for stable, 31–2, 204–6, 423

Biological sciences, their influence on Economics, 154, 317–18

Birmingham Bedstead Association, 385 n.

Blandford, 374

"Board of Trade Unit" of electricity, 364

Böhm Bawerk, Prof., 416, 417

Bonar, James, *see* LETTERS

Boole, 20

Booth, Charles, London statistics, 328

Bosanquet, Mrs, *see* LETTERS

Bowley, Prof., 26 n., 456. *See* LETTER

Brentano, Prof., on German Iron Combination, 271 n.

Brick makers, 1866 Parliamentary Commission on, 107

Bristol, 15–16; University College, 16, 293; lectures at, 16; farewell address at, 16–17; medical charge at, 388

British Economic Association (now the Royal Economic Society), foundation of, 54

Browne, Sir Benjamin, 399

Budget of 1909, 465

Burke's dictum, 66

Burt, Thomas, 50; letter from, 378

Business, analysis of motives in, 281–2, 331–2; Socialists underrate its difficulties, 283–4; increasing size of, 308; chivalry in, 329–32

Cæteris Paribus, economic method of, 314–15

Caird, Edward, Master of Balliol, 398; letters from, 401. *See* LETTERS

Cairnes, *Some Leading Principles of Political Economy*, 19; criticism of its attitude toward J. S. Mill, 119–33, 160 n.

Cambridge, and falling away of Christian dogma, 7–9; first age of married society, 49; and economics, 171–4, 380; compared with Oxford, 382–3; "Stables," 456; *Independent Press*, 468; Economics Tripos, 54, 55–7, 171–2; rural population, 468

Cannan, Prof., *see* LETTERS

Capital, from individual and social point of view, 404–6; Death Duties and growth of, 463; dead and live, 464

Carey and cost of *reproduction*, 128 n.; *Social Science*, 167 n.; and protection, 259

Cartels, 492, 493

Cassel, Prof., 30

"Chain" method of compiling Index-numbers, 31

Chapman, Sir Sidney, *see* LETTERS

Chemistry, teaching of, 488–9